WHAT YOU CAN LEARN IN 35 DAYS WITH THIS PRACTICAL HOME-STUDY COURSE

23 Keeping the dangerous opponent off lead
24 When to draw trumps
25 How the experts count
26 Planning your play
27 Watch your entries
28 Expert plays (safety and throw-in plays, the trump coup, and squeezes)
29 What to lead
30 Defensive rules—and when to break them
31 Deceptive play
32 Third review and self-testing quizzes
33 Modern bidding conventions (including the Italian systems)
34 Manners, morals, and laws
35 Final review

When your course is over, you still may not be able to win a world championship—but if you do your part faithfully, you can expect to play a better game consistently, confidently, and often quite victoriously.

5
WEEKS
TO
WINNING
BRIDGE

Alfred Sheinwold

POCKET BOOKS

New York   London   Toronto   Sydney   Tokyo

Born in London, Alfred Sheinwold came to the United States at the age of nine, settling in New York City. During his undergraduate days at City College he became interested in bridge and after his graduation in 1933 he joined the legendary Ely Culbertson as a technical editor.

He returned to bridge after serving as Chief Code and Cipher Expert for the O.S.S. during World War II. In four years of tournament play, he amassed the amazing total of 2,000 Master Points and won, among other trophies, the U.S. Master's Team Championship.

He has written six previous books on bridge, is editor of **The Bridge World** magazine and **American Bridge Digest** and is Cards Editor for **Argosy** magazine.

Player, writer and teacher, Sheinwold is one of the leading figures in international bridge. An active member of the National Laws and Rules Commission, the high court of bridge, his syndicated column appears in some two hundred newspapers daily.

Another *Original* publication of POCKET BOOKS

POCKET BOOKS, a division of Simon & Schuster, Inc.
1230 Avenue of the Americas, New York, N.Y. 10020

ISBN: 0-671-47214-3

First Pocket Books printing January 1960

42 41 40 39 38 37 36 35 34

POCKET and colophon are trademarks of
Simon & Schuster, Inc.

Printed in the U.S.A.

CONTENTS

II. Competitive Bidding 111

20th DAY:

21st DAY:

22nd DAY:

23rd DAY:

24th DAY:

30th DAY:

31st DAY:

32nd DAY:

IV. Final Touches and Review 421

33rd DAY:

34th DAY:

Manners, Morals and Laws 441

Bridge Etiquette 442
Kibitzing 443
Table Talk 443
Bridge Language 444
Intonation 445
Reading the Opponents 446
Bridge Laws 447
Simplified Digest of New Official Bridge Laws— Revised 1963 448
Losing and Winning 450

35th DAY:

Final Review 468

Review Questions 468   Answers to Review Questions.485

V. Duplicate Bridge—Winning Techniques 504

Mechanics of Tournament Play 505
Pair Contests 506
Match-Point Scoring 507
Small Differences 510
Notrump Pays Off 511
Minor Suit—Last Resort ...513
Sacrifice Bidding 516
Your True Opponents 517
Going Against the Field ...518
Overcalls in Duplicate 519
Competitive Bidding 520
Playing for an Overtrick ...522
Abnormal Contracts 524
What Others are Doing ...524
Safety Plays 526
Defending Against Overtricks.527
Cashing Out 528
Taking Desperate Chances .530
Total-Point Team Play ...531
I.M.P. Team Play 532
Board-a-Match Team Play ..533
Tournament Etiquette 533

VI. For Your Reference 535

Meaning of Bids 536

Home and Party Bridge 540

Scoring Table 547

Bidding Guide 548

HOW TO USE THIS BOOK

Anybody who follows the advice and instruction in this book can become a winning bridge player in only five weeks. If you already have a good knowledge of the game, you can progress much faster than this, but we urge you to start at the very beginning and do at least one lesson a day.

(If you have never played bridge before, it will take a few extra days to familiarize yourself with the *mechanics* of the game, as explained on the fourteen pages that follow. Anyone who has previously played bridge may skip this section unless he wishes to brush up a bit before getting to the heart of the matter—winning bridge.)

This book will do you no good if you just put it on the shelf. The road to you-know-where is paved with good intentions, but there's no need for you to join the millions of bridge players who are already there.

The book is laid out in the following course for home study:

You will find hundreds of illustrative hands as well as quiz questions in the chapters that follow. In addition there is a set of review questions to be answered when you reach the end of each section. These will test how well you have mastered the material. Both kinds of questions will be a good guide to your progress. Try not to leave any section until you have scored at least a passing grade on the review test.

Even if you are already an excellent bridge player, be sure to skim through the early chapters. You will find some new material in each chapter—tips to winning bridge, plus advanced and expert points on bidding and play—and a practical point of view at all times.

Keep this book handy, so that you can make a habit of reading your daily chapter. The bedside table is a good spot.

Start your first chapter now—and set your feet on the road to winning bridge!

IF YOU HAVE NEVER PLAYED BRIDGE BEFORE . . .

you need this chapter to get you started.

Bridge is played by four people, two playing as partners against the other two. Partners sit opposite each other at a square table.

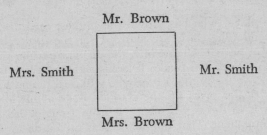

The diagram shows how the players might take seats if Mr. and Mrs. Brown are pitted against Mr. and Mrs. Smith.

THE PACK

The deck (or pack) of cards consists of 52 cards. There are four suits:

♠ Spades
♡ Hearts
♦ Diamonds
♣ Clubs

In each suit there are thirteen cards, ranking as follows: Ace (highest), king, queen, jack, 10, 9, 8, 7, 6, 5, 4, 3, 2 (lowest).

CHOOSING PARTNERS

When the partnerships are not arranged beforehand, the traditional method of establishing them is to cut the cards. Spread out a deck, face down, and ask each player to select a card. Those who draw the two higher cards play as partners against those who draw the two lower cards.

THE SHUFFLE, CUT AND DEAL

The player who has drawn the highest card deals the first hand. The cards are shuffled for the dealer by the player at his left. Meanwhile, the dealer's partner shuffles the other deck and places it at his right, where it is conveniently close to the player who will deal the next hand.

The dealer picks up the shuffled deck at his left and moves it to the right, where it is in front of his right-hand opponent. That opponent cuts the cards by lifting a portion from the top of the deck and placing that portion nearer to the dealer.

The dealer completes the cut by placing the farther portion on top of the nearer portion.

The dealer then distributes the cards one at a time face down to the four players. He begins with the player at his left and continues in a clockwise rotation until all 52 cards have been distributed. The last card comes to the dealer, and each player should at that time have 13 cards face down in front of him.

It is part of the etiquette of bridge to wait until the deal has been completed before you pick up any of your cards. This does not waste time, because you have to wait for the dealer to assort his hand and start the auction before any other player can act.

Your first step, on picking up your 13 cards (called

your *hand*) is to assort them into suits. Most players also put the cards in order of rank, with the higher cards at the left. If you alternate black and red suits you stand a better chance of recognizing your cards without error.

THE BEGINNING OF PLAY

After the bidding has ended, one of the players takes a card out of his hand and puts it face up in the middle of the table. This card is called the *opening lead*.

The next player puts his cards face up on the table as the *dummy*. This player is also called the dummy.

The player opposite dummy is the *declarer*. He plays the dummy's cards as well as his own.

Declarer selects a card from dummy and places it in the middle of the table on or near the opening lead. The leader's partner next places a card face up in the middle of the table. Finally, declarer takes a card from his own hand and puts it face up in the middle of the table.

We now have four cards face up in the middle of the table, one card from each player's hand. These four cards are called a *trick*.

One of the four cards wins the trick, as we shall soon see. The player who wins the trick leads to the next trick, and so it goes until all thirteen tricks have been played. In each trick the turn to play goes clockwise, beginning with the leader.

WINNING A TRICK

Each player must play a card of the suit that is led, if he has such a card in his hand. This is called *following suit*.

If a player has more than one card of the suit led, he may follow suit as he pleases—with either a high, a low, or a middling card. If a player has no card of the suit led, he may play any card from his hand.

In some hands there is a trump suit, determined by the bidding. Any card of the trump suit outranks any card of the other three suits. The deuce of trumps, for example, outranks any ace of the other three suits.

When a player cannot follow suit, he may play a trump. If so, his trump will win the trick unless somebody else plays a higher trump. A player who cannot follow suit need not play a trump; if he prefers, he may *discard* a card of another suit.

A trick that does not contain a trump is won by the highest card of the suit led. A trick that contains a trump is won by the highest trump in the trick.

THE BIDDING

Now that we have discussed tricks and trumps, we can go back to the bidding, which precedes the beginning of play.

The dealer speaks first. He may pass or bid. Then the player at dealer's left speaks. The turn goes in rotation to the left, just like the deal and the turn to play.

A bid consists of a *number* and a *trump* (or notrump). The number indicates the *number* of tricks to be won beyond *book* (six tricks). The *trump* names the trump suit. The word "notrump" means that there will be no trump suit.

If all four players pass, the hand is thrown in and the next player deals a new hand.

If any player makes a bid at his turn, an *auction* begins—to be won by the side that bids higher. The side that bids higher names the trump suit or notrump and specifies the number of tricks to be won in the play. There are rewards for *fulfilling the contract* (winning at least the number of tricks promised by the bid); there are penalties for *going down* (failing to make the contract).

After the *opening bid*, any player at his turn may make a higher bid. A bid is higher if it promises either a larger number of tricks than the previous bid or the same number of tricks in a higher denomination (suit or notrump).

Denominations rank as follows:

Notrump (highest)
Spades
Hearts
Diamonds
Clubs (lowest)

Thus a bid of one spade is higher than a bid of one heart. A bid of two clubs is higher than a bid of one notrump.

DOUBLES AND REDOUBLES

At your turn to bid you may say "Double" if the previous bid was made by an opponent.

For example:

SOUTH	WEST	NORTH	EAST
1 ♠	Double		

or

SOUTH	WEST	NORTH	EAST
1 ♠	Pass	Pass	Double

The general meaning of the double is that you want to increase the penalties if the opponent fails to make his contract. However, the opponent will earn a bigger reward if he makes his contract in the teeth of your double.

When an opponent doubles, you may redouble:

SOUTH	WEST	NORTH	EAST
1 ♠	Double	Redouble	

or

SOUTH	WEST	NORTH	EAST
1 ♠	Double	Pass	Pass
Redouble			

The general meaning of the redouble is that you want to increase the reward for making the contract. However, if you go down, the penalties will be larger.

Any double or redouble is canceled by a bid:

SOUTH	WEST	NORTH	EAST
1 ♠	Double	Redouble	2 ◇

The bid of two diamonds canceled both the double and the redouble. If South now bids *two* spades, the opponents may pass if they wish to do so. The double of *one* spade does not carry over to *two* spades.

When a bid is followed by three passes in succession, the auction ends. The highest bid becomes the *contract*.

Sometimes only one member of a partnership has bid the denomination of the contract. He is the declarer.

SOUTH	WEST	NORTH	EAST
1 ♠	Pass	Pass	Pass

South is the declarer.

When both members of a partnership have bid the denomination of the contract, the declarer is the one who named it first.

SOUTH	WEST	NORTH	EAST
Pass	Pass	1 ♠	Pass
4 ♠			

North is the declarer; he named spades first.

SCORING

At the end of play each side counts its tricks and compares the result with the promise of the final bid.

The score keeper then enters the score for the hand on the score pad. The typical score pad looks something like this:

WE	THEY

All scores made by the score keeper's side are entered under WE in the left column. All scores made by the other side are entered under THEY in the right column.

Very often a member of each side keeps score. The WE of one scorekeeper is the THEY of the other scorekeeper.

The heavy left-to-right line on the score pad serves a very important purpose of separation. Scores for tricks bid and made go *below the line*. All other scores go *above the line*.

A player scores for tricks bid and made only if his side was the declaring side and made its contract.

You normally score:

20 points per trick bid and made in diamonds or clubs
30 points per trick bid and made in spades or hearts
40 points for the first trick bid and made in notrump
30 points for each additional trick bid and made in
   notrump.

For example, you would score 60 points below the line
for bidding three diamonds and winning nine tricks; 120
points below the line for bidding four hearts and winning
ten tricks; 190 points below the line for bidding six notrump and winning twelve tricks.

GAME AND PART SCORES

A score of 100 points or more below the line is *game*.
You may score game in one hand or by adding two or
more hands together. To score game in one hand you
must bid and make

3NT (nine tricks at notrump)	=100 points
or 4 ♡ or 4 ♠ (ten tricks at a *major suit*)	=120 points
or 5 ♣ or 5 ◇ (eleven tricks at a *minor suit*)	=100 points

A lower contract, called a *part score* or a *partial*, may
be added to one or more other part scores, provided that
the opponents don't complete a game in the meantime.
After either side scores game, a fresh start must be made
toward the next game. In a sense, the game *wipes out*
previous part scores, but they will still be counted when
the scores are eventually added up.

WE	THEY
(a) 60	120 (c)
(b) 20	

(*a*) WE bid and made two hearts, scoring 60 points below the line.
(*b*) WE bid and made one diamond,
scoring an additional 20 points below
the line.
(*c*) THEY bid and made four spades,
scoring 120 points below the line. This
is a game, and a line is drawn to signify
that a fresh start must be made by both
sides toward the next game.

RUBBER

A side wins the rubber by winning two games out of three. You may win the rubber two games to none, or two games to one.

If you win two to none, you score a bonus of 700 points. If you win two to one, the bonus is only 500 points. The rubber bonus is scored above the line.

The rubber is the customary unit of a session of bridge. You sit down to play a rubber of bridge; change partners after each rubber; agree to stop play at the end of the rubber; and so on.

A rubber may last only two hands (about ten minutes) or it may go on for dozens of hands (more than an hour).

VULNERABILITY

A side that has scored a game toward rubber is said to be *vulnerable*. This means that the vulnerable side is exposed to higher penalties for failing to fulfill its contract. By way of compensation, however, a vulnerable side scores higher bonuses in most cases than a nonvulnerable side.

DOUBLED AND REDOUBLED TRICK POINTS

When you make a doubled contract, you score the trick points at double their normal value:

60 points per trick bid and made in spades or hearts
40 points per trick bid and made in diamonds or clubs
80 points for the first trick bid and made at notrump
60 points for any other trick bid and made at notrump

This means that you can score a game by bidding and making two hearts doubled or any higher contract. Two diamonds doubled would be only 80 points, not quite enough for game.

When you make a redoubled contract you score the trick points at twice the doubled value, or four times the normal value. A contract of one heart redoubled (or any higher redoubled contract) is a *game-going* contract.

OVERTRICKS

You score below the line only for tricks bid and made. If you win more tricks than called for by the contract, called *overtricks*, you score them above the line.

The normal score for overtricks is the same as the trick value. The only difference is that you write the score above the line instead of below the line.

Each overtrick (regardless of the denomination of the contract) is worth more if the contract is doubled or redoubled:

Doubled, not vulnerable	100 points per overtrick
Redoubled, not vulnerable	200 points per overtrick
Doubled, vulnerable	200 points per overtrick
Redoubled, vulnerable	400 points per overtrick

There is a 50-point bonus for making a doubled or redoubled contract. This bonus is not increased by the redouble or by vulnerability.

UNDERTRICK PENALTIES

There is always a penalty for failing to make your contract:

Undoubled, not vulnerable	50 points per trick
Undoubled, vulnerable	100 points per trick
Doubled, not vulnerable	100 points for the first trick
	200 points for each additional trick
Doubled, vulnerable	200 points for the first trick
	300 points for each additional trick
Redoubled	Twice the doubled value

HONORS

You score certain bonuses just for being dealt certain high-ranking cards, called *honors,* in one hand. At a trump suit the five highest trumps are the honors; at no-trump, the four aces are the honors.

All honors (A, K, Q, J, 10 at a trump suit, or the four aces at notrump)	150 points
Four trump honors	100 points

Any player may score for honors—whether he is declarer, dummy or even one of the defenders.

It is customary to announce the honors at the end of the hand, as by saying, "I had a hundred honors," or "Give me a hundred and fifty honors."

The bonus for honors is scored whether or not the contract is made, and regardless of doubles, redoubles, and vulnerability.

SLAMS

There are special bonuses for bidding and making twelve tricks (*small slam*) or all thirteen tricks (*grand slam*):

Small slam not vulnerable	500 points
Small slam vulnerable	750 points
Grand slam not vulnerable	1,000 points
Grand slam vulnerable	1,500 points

You get nothing for making twelve tricks if you have bid a grand slam. (You are down one and lose points.)

UNFINISHED GAME OR RUBBER

If the players cannot finish a rubber, score 300 points for a game and 50 points for a part score in an unfinished game.

BIDDING
WITHOUT
OPPOSITION

HOW TO VALUE YOUR HAND

√ The Point Count	√ Dummy's Points
√ How Points Are Used	√ Defensive "Points"
√ Whose Hand Is It?	√ Quick Tricks
√ Good and Bad Points	√ Playing Tricks
√ Declarer's Points	√ The Effect of the Bidding

IN ORDER TO BID PROPERLY you must know the value of your hand. This is easier said than done.

The true value of your hand depends on:

- Your high cards
- Your long and short suits
- How well your hand *fits* your partner's hand
- The location of high cards held by the opponents
- How well you and your partner play
- How well the opponents play

This is just a beginning! It might also be important to keep track of which players are in a good mood, which are discouraged, which pairs get along well as partners, who has had more iced coffee (or whatever) than was good for him, who is looking for a chance to show up one of the other players, and so on.

In short, you never really *know* what your hand is worth. The best you can do is to come pretty close most of the time.

This uncertainty is one of the charms of the game. If anybody ever succeeds in making bridge really cut and dried, so that you can bid or play automatically, people will desert the game and take up something more adventurous.

For this reason, please don't expect a cut-and-dried discussion of valuation (or of anything else, for that matter). If you're new to the game, this chapter will give you an effective guide in a few minutes; if you're an experienced player, you may get food for thought and an idea or two that will improve your game and add to your enjoyment of it.

√ THE POINT COUNT

Most players use the 4-3-2-1 point count to work out the value of a hand. It's all a beginner needs, and it's a good basis for an experienced player.

HIGH CARDS

Each ace	4 points
Each king	3 points
Each queen	2 points
Each jack	1 point

SHORT SUITS

Each void suit	3 points
(no cards in a suit)	
Each singleton	2 points
(one card in a suit)	
Each doubleton	1 point
(two cards in a suit)	

Do not count short-suit points in valuing a hand for notrump.

For example:

	HIGH CARDS	DISTRIBUTION
♠ K J 8 3	4	—
♡ A Q 9 4	6	—
◇ 8	—	2
♣ Q J 7 6	3	—
	13	2

The full value of the hand is 15 points at a suit contract, but only 13 points at notrump.

∨ HOW POINTS ARE USED

Whenever you bid you say something about the number of points your hand is worth. Your partner does the same when *he* bids. If you use a good bidding system, this exchange of information helps you pick out a good contract for most hands.

Remember these *key* numbers:

> 26 points—game in major suits and notrump
> 29 points—game in minor suits
> 33 points—small slam
> 37 points—grand slam

This does *not* mean that you can *always* make a game at a major suit or at notrump when the partnership count comes to 26 points. It does mean that you almost always have a reasonable play for game. If there is no fit at a major suit and if notrump is out of the question, you probably cannot make a game with your 26 points.

Much the same is true of the figures for small and grand

slams. Nobody gives you a guarantee. With the right partnership total you should have a reasonable play for your slam.

The key numbers are slightly elastic. You need 26 points for game, but you can often get by with 25 points —perhaps even 24. Stretch them too far, and they may snap back at you.

√ WHOSE HAND IS IT?

There are only 40 *high-card* points in the entire deck. If your side has 26 points, the opponents can have only 14 points. You should be able to make a game; they should be able to make nothing very much. The hand *belongs* to your side.

Naturally, this is even clearer when your side has enough points for a slam. Very little is left for the opponents.

Some allowance should be made for *distributional* points. Both sides may be counting heavily on short suits, which means that they have long suits elsewhere.

On most hands, however, you can tell *whose hand it is* by counting points. If your side has about 20 points, the opponents must likewise have about 20 points. It's *anybody's* hand. If your side gets up to about 24 points, the opponents can have only about 16 points. And *that* is *your* hand.

When the hand belongs to *your* side, don't let the opponents get away with a foolish bid. Punish them by doubling for penalties.

If the hand belongs to the opponents, let them have it. You should expect to be doubled if you wander out beyond your depth. (However, see Chapter 13, Shutout Bids, for more advice on bidding a lot on very little.)

✓ GOOD AND BAD POINTS

Not all points are equally valuable. After all, nobody ever won a trick with a point. You win tricks with high cards, long suits, and trumps; the point count is just a good (but not perfect) attempt to translate these three types of values into a single simple scale.

For example, let's take the singleton king. Should you count this as 3 points for a king and also as 2 points for a singleton? That's counting a lot of points for a card that may well have no value at all. I ordinarily count it at 4 points and hope.

Consider, also, the value of Q-x or J-x. Should you add the high-card value to the 1 point for a doubleton? In most cases I'd say no. As you know, Q-x in an opponent's bid suit may be not a bit better than x-x. But Q-x in your *partner's* suit may be as valuable as an ace.

These are fairly obvious cases. Somewhat less obvious is the fact that the 4-3-2-1 point count gives slightly too much value to queens and jacks. It would be possible for you to devise a more accurate scale of points, but you might not be able to keep it simple.

The fact remains that a hand such as:

    ♠ Q J 7 4   ♡ Q J 5   ◇ Q J 6   ♣ Q J 3

counts up to 12 points, the same as:

    ♠ A 7 4 2   ♡ A 6 5   ◇ A 6 5   ♣ 7 3 2

But the two hands are not really equal in value. Aces are almost always worth more.

Aces and kings are very valuable for slams and for trump contracts. Queens and jacks, even tens and nines, are valuable for notrump contracts below the slam level.

What should you do about all this in counting up the

value of your hand? If you are a beginner, do nothing at all; use the point count without any worries. If you are an experienced player, make a mental note of it if your hand is really worth more (or less) than the point count; use this mental note as a guide in borderline decisions.

Take the following items into consideration:

- An aceless hand is worth less than its point count.
- A hand with three or four aces is worth more.
- A queen or jack deserves its full value only when accompanied by the king or ace of the same suit.
- Singleton kings or singleton or doubleton queens and jacks are not worth full value.

✓ DECLARER'S POINTS

When you are the declarer (the person who is playing the hand) your long suits are useful. Each extra trump is usually worth an extra trick. So is each extra card in a strong side suit.

How do you count values of this kind?

For suit contracts you can get a reasonable total by adding the short-suit values of the point-count table—3 points for a void, 2 points for a singleton, and 1 point for a doubleton. If you have length in one suit, you are bound to have shortness somewhere else—and it usually makes no difference whether you count the length or the shortness.

This is not enough, however, for the hands with really good distribution. You can get a more accurate total if you add extra points for suit length in a *solid* suit or in a suit that has been raised by your partner. Use the following scale:

Fifth card in a long suit ....1 point

Each card over five ....2 points

For example, after your partner has raised your spades:

♠ A 9 6 3 2   ♡ A K Q J 5   ◇ 8 3   ♣ 4

add 1 point for the fifth card in the supported spade suit and 1 point for the fifth card in the solid heart suit. The full count of the hand is 14 points for high cards, 2 points for the singleton, 1 point for the doubleton, and 2 points for length in spades and hearts—a total of 19 points. Note that you still include your short-suit points.

♠ A J 9 7 6 3 2   ♠ A K 5   ◇ 8 3   ♣ 4

Add 5 points for length in spades after partner has raised the suit (1 point for the fifth spade, 2 points each for the sixth and seventh spades). The full value of the hand is 12 points for high cards, 2 points for the singleton, 1 point for the doubleton, and 5 points for length in spades—a total of 20 points.

✓ DUMMY'S POINTS

When you have four or more trumps in support of your partner, your short suits are worth more than the ordinary count. For a dummy with such strong trump support, count:

5 points for a void suit
3 points for a singleton
1 point for a doubleton
(no change here)

Deduct one point from the above scale if you have raised with only *three* trumps. Do not count anything for short suits on the side if you are obliged to raise your partner with fewer than three trumps.

A queen or jack in your partner's suit is worth about 1 point more than its normal value. Add 1 point if your trumps are headed by the jack, queen, or both. Add 1 point for the queen or queen-jack in your partner's side suit (if he has bid one). Do not add anything for stronger holdings in your partner's suit; there's a limit to what can be counted in any suit.

✓ DEFENSIVE "POINTS"

Do *not* count points for defense (any hand in which the opponents do most of the bidding).

Count your *Quick* Tricks (see below) and your probable trump tricks for defense against suit contracts. You can use points as a rough guide if the contract is notrump, but don't rely on them very much.

✓ QUICK TRICKS

When you make a strong bid you should always guarantee a reasonable number of aces and kings. These cards, unlike queens and jacks, will be useful at almost *any* contract—even for defense.

A convenient way to count your value in aces and kings is the Quick-Trick Table:

A-K	—	2 Quick Tricks
A-Q	—	1½ ″ ″
A or K-Q	—	1 ″ ″
K-x	—	½ ″ ″

A normal opening bid, as you will see in the next chapter, promises at least 2 Quick Tricks. Other uses of Quick Tricks are found in the discussions of two-bids and of other strong bids.

In counting your Quick Tricks, pay no attention to queens and jacks that are not found in the table. For example, A-K-Q is only 2 Quick Tricks; K-Q-J is only 1 Quick Trick; Q-J-x does not count at all. These queens and jacks are worth more than treys and deuces—but they are not *Quick* Tricks.

✓ PLAYING TRICKS

When your suits are fairly solid, you can often count the value of your hand in *actual* tricks rather than according to any scale of *Quick* Tricks or points.

For example:

♠ Q J 10 9 7 6 2   ♡ K Q J 10 5   ◇ 4   ♣ ―――――

Count five playing tricks in spades and four playing tricks in hearts. In spades, you can use the queen to force out the king, and the jack to force out the ace. You can draw any other spades with the ten and nine, after which the rest of your suit will be good. In hearts, you use the king to force out the ace and can draw the rest of the hearts with the queen, jack, and ten. The last heart will then be good.

You count playing tricks chiefly for defensive bids and for two-bids.

✓ THE EFFECT OF THE BIDDING

As we have seen, the value of your hand in points is often affected by the bidding. You count something extra for length in a suit after your partner has raised the suit. You count singletons and voids one way as declarer and a different way when you expect to be the dummy.

The bidding of the *opponents* is likewise taken into consideration. If the player at your right bids spades, for example, you feel confident of winning a trick with K-x of spades. If the same suit is bid by the player at your left, however, you feel very doubtful of the value of K-x.

In general, you tend to rate your cards a trifle higher when the right-hand opponent bids, a trifle lower when the left-hand opponent bids. However, avoid counting the high-card value for such combinations as Q-x or J-x in a suit bid by an opponent.

2nd DAY

THE VERSATILE ONE-BID

√ When to Bid	√ Two 3-Card Suits
√ Fourth-Hand Bids	√ A 5-Card Suit and a 4-Card
√ Which Suit to Bid	Suit
√ When Is a Suit Biddable?	√ Two 4-Card Suits
√ Two 6-Card Suits	√ Three 4-Card Suits
√ A 6-Card Suit and a 5-Card Suit	√ In Short

THE OPENING BID of one in a suit is the most versatile of all bids. You sometimes make it on a hand so light that the cards threaten to float up to the ceiling. At other times the hand is as full of bone and muscle as a physical-culture ad. More often you have something between these extremes.

For example, a light opening bid may consist of:

♠ A Q J 8 4   ♥ K 10 9 7 4   ♦ 4 3   ♣ 6

Or, at the other extreme, you may have:

♠ 3   ♥ A Q 5   ♦ A K J 4   ♣ A K J 6 2

The first hand should be opened with one spade; the second, with one club.

✔ WHEN TO BID

You should open the bidding whenever you have a good excuse to do so. Consider the various possibilities:

- If the strength is equally divided between the two partnerships, the side that lands the first punch usually plays the hand.
- If the hand clearly belongs to your side, an opening bid gets you started in a way that is familiar to you and your partner.
- If the hand clearly belongs to the opponents, your opening bid indicates a favorable opening lead and forces the opponents to bid their cards in an unfamiliar way.

Think about that for a moment. Your opening bid, your partner's response, your rebid, and his rebid—these are like a road that you have traveled many times. Start the very same hand with an opponent's bid, and you must now bid the hand differently; and so must your partner. You're on a strange road, and you may well get lost.

This doesn't mean that you must make your opening bids weaker and weaker each day. Just don't fall into the habit of passing when your hand is really worth an opening bid.

We can set up a few easy rules to tell you which minimum hands are worth a bid and which should be passed:

A. Open *any* hand that counts to 14 points in *high cards*.

(1) ♠ K J 3   ♡ K J 4   ◇ Q J 3   ♣ Q J 6 4

Bid one club. This is the worst possible 14-point hand because it includes too many queens and jacks and not enough aces and kings. Nevertheless it is worth an opening bid.

(2) ♠ K J 3   ♡ K J 4   ◇ A 3   ♣ Q 6 4 3 2

Bid one club. This is a normal 14-point hand (15 points counting the doubleton, but now we are interested only in high-card points). You *enjoy* opening this hand with its ace, 5-card suit, and doubleton. You *tolerate* an opening bid with Example 1.

B. Open a hand that counts to 12 or 13 points in high cards only if you have at least 2 Quick Tricks and a comfortable rebid.

(1) ♠ K Q 10 8 5   ♡ K Q 2   ◇ Q 7 6   ♣ 4 3

Bid one spade. You have 12 points in high cards, 2 Quick Tricks (the two K-Q combinations), and a comfortable rebid in your strong 5-card spade suit.

(2) ♠ K Q 10 8   ♡ K Q 2   ◇ Q 7 6 5   ♣ 4 3

Pass. The high-card structure is the same, but you have lost the comfortable rebid.

(3) ♠ Q J 8 5 2   ♡ Q J 7   ◇ Q J 6   ♣ K J

Pass. You have 13 points in high cards but not even 1

Quick Trick. If your partner doubles an opponent, your queens and jacks will not come up to his expectation.

C. Open a hand that counts to 10 or 11 points in high cards when you have not only your 2 Quick Tricks and your comfortable rebid but also good length in the major suits.

(1) ♠ A Q J 8 5   ♡ A 9 7 4   ◊ 4 3   ♣ 6 2

Bid one spade. You have 11 points in high cards, with 2½ Quick Tricks, a comfortable rebid, and very good length in the major suits. A fine minimum opening bid.

(2) ♠ A Q J 8 5   ♡ K 10 9 7 4   ◊ 4 3   ♣ 6

Bid one spade. You have only 10 points in high cards, but the hand contains two strong 5-card major suits and 2 Quick Tricks.

(3) ♠ 4 3   ♡ 6   ◊ A Q J 8 5   ♣ K 10 9 7 4

Pass. Don't open a 10-point hand without good length in the major suits.

D. After two passes, open in third position with 10 or 11 points even without the usual requirements of 2 Quick Tricks and length in the majors—provided that your bid indicates a good opening lead to partner.

(1) ♠ 4 3   ♡ 6   ◊ A Q J 8 5   ♣ K 10 9 7 4

Bid one diamond in third position. If your partner must eventually make the opening lead, a diamond lead will be most welcome. In fact, with such a good diamond suit and such good distribution, you would bid in third position even if the clubs were headed by the queen instead of the king.

(2) ♠ K 7 5 3 2   ♡ K J 5   ◇ K 4   ♣ 9 5 2

Pass in any position. There is no reason to encourage a spade opening lead, and there is no other reason for bidding with so weak a hand.

✓ FOURTH-HAND BIDS

After three players have passed, you may open the bidding or pass the hand out. Which should you do?

You will feel very foolish if you open the hand and wind up with a substantial minus score. You will then remember—or perhaps your partner will remind you— that you could have broken even by passing the hand out.

It is just as foolish, however, to pass out a hand that should give your side a substantial plus score. Even a part score is not to be sniffed at.

Open any hand that you would surely bid in first or second position. Pass a borderline hand that lacks strength in the majors. Strain to open a hand with a strong rebiddable spade suit.

The emphasis on the major suits is not just a matter of looking for game. You are wondering whether the hand "belongs" to your side or to the opponents. If there is a doubt, the side that can bid major suits, especially spades, can outbid the opponents without getting too high.

If you know the players very well, you can sometimes settle a difficult bidding problem by relying on their habits. For example, suppose your partner consistently opens very light hands. Don't strain to open a light hand in fourth position after he has passed. He probably has a poor hand, and you won't miss much if you pass the hand out.

If both opponents are notorious light bidders, their failure to bid is evidence that the hand belongs to *your* side. But if both opponents are timid bidders, avoid opening a light hand in fourth position. Let sleeping dogs lie.

(1) ♠ A 7 4   ♡ K J 8   ◇ Q J 9 6 5   ♣ K 3

Bid one diamond after three passes (or in any other position). Never pass a hand that counts 14 points (or more) in high cards.

(2) ♠ Q 4   ♡ K 3   ◇ Q J 9 6 5   ♣ K J 5 2

Pass in fourth position. You have 12 points in high cards but only 1 Quick Trick. The fatal flaw is the shortness in both major suits.

(3) ♠ A K 10 9 6 5   ♡ Q 7 4   ◇ 8 6 5   ♣ 3

Bid one spade. Always strain to open the bidding when you have a really powerful spade suit.

✓ WHICH SUIT TO BID

Your first bid is usually no problem. If the hand is not worth a bid, you pass. If it is worth a bid, you bid one in your longest suit.

What if you have more than one long suit?

The general rule is:

• If your suits are *unequal* in length, bid the *longer* one.
• If your suits are *equal* in length, bid the higher-ranking one.

You have to disregard this general rule on some hands in order to prepare for a convenient second bid. You want to keep the bidding low when you have a minimum opening bid.

You never have a problem when you have just one long suit of five cards or more, particularly if it's a strong suit. If you must speak a second time, you rebid your long suit.

Likewise, you have no problem when you have real strength—say 18 points or more in high cards. If you push yourself up to a high level, you are strong enough to stand it.

The hands that call for thought are those with 12 to 17 points in high cards and more than one biddable suit.

✓ WHEN IS A SUIT BIDDABLE?

- Any 5-card or longer suit is biddable.
- A 4-card suit is biddable if it is headed by Q-J or better.

A warning goes with these rules. When you bid spades or hearts, your partner thinks of raising your suit. When you bid diamonds or clubs, he thinks of shifting to a major suit or to notrump.

For these reasons it doesn't pay to open a weak 4-card *major* suit. There is no harm, however, in opening a weak 4-card *minor* suit.

What do you bid if your only long suit is a weak 4-card major? For example:

    ♠ J852   ♡ AQ2   ◇ 762   ♣ AK8

You cannot afford to pass 14 points in high cards, yet you do not relish the idea of bidding those weak spades.

The solution is to bid one *club*. Your partner is not likely to take a minor suit seriously. (If he does raise, you pass and make the best of it.) If your partner responds in spades, you raise. If he bids another suit, you may bid one notrump or may even bid the spades belatedly.

Don't go out of your way to bid a 3-card club suit. Always bid a 5-card suit when the hand is worth a bid, and bid a "real" suit when you have two 4-card suits. Use the "short club" bid when your only long suit is a weak 4-card major.

In this situation it is sometimes proper to bid diamonds instead of clubs:

♠ J 8 5 2   ♡ A Q 2   ◇ A K 8   ♣ 7 6 2

Bid one diamond. When you decide to bid a 3-card minor suit, choose the suit in which you have reasonable strength. You will be more comfortable if your partner decides to raise your minor suit or if he must make the opening lead in your bid suit.

If both of your minor suits are strong 3-carders, bid clubs. That gives your partner more room for a convenient response.

Now we can return to the question of which suit to bid first when you have more than one biddable suit.

✓ TWO 6-CARD SUITS

Bid the higher suit first, even if the lower suit is much stronger. You expect to bid both suits (unless the first suit is raised by your partner), and you can afford to follow the normal rule.

♠ J 8 6 5 3 2   ♡ A   ◇ K Q 9 6 4 3   ♣ ———

Bid one spade. If necessary, you will bid and rebid the diamonds at your later turns. This sequence always shows that *both* suits are rebiddable. If your partner must express a preference for spades with only two small spades in his hand, you can await the outcome without fear.

√ A 6-CARD SUIT AND A 5-CARD SUIT

The normal procedure is to bid the 6-card suit first, intending to bid and rebid the other suit later.

However, when the hand is a minimum opening bid, start with the higher-ranking suit (regardless of which suit is longer). This helps you keep the bidding low, which is always desirable when you have minimum values.

(1) ♠ K Q 8 7 4   ♡ Q J 8 6 5 3   ◇ A   ♣ 3

Bid one spade with this minimum hand. If partner bids one notrump or two of a minor suit, you will make a rebid of two hearts. This leaves your partner in position to pass or bid two spades. He can choose between your two suits without getting uncomfortably high.

(2) ♠ K Q 8 7 4   ♡ K Q J 6 5 3   ◇ A   ♣ 3

Bid one heart. You can afford to bid spades at your next turn. This may force your partner to bid three hearts just to show which of your two suits he prefers. Since your hand is very strong, you can afford to push yourself up to this high level.

√ TWO 5-CARD SUITS

When you have two 5-card suits, the normal rule is to bid the higher-ranking suit first. Later, if necessary, you will bid the lower suit. Still later you may even rebid the lower suit.

This may get you rather high. You don't mind bidding up to a high level when you have a really good hand, but you must avoid it when your hand is of minimum strength.

Sometimes you can avoid trouble by bidding only one suit.

(1) ♠ K Q J 7 5   ♡ 5   ◇ A J 9 6 3   ♣ 6 2

Bid one spade. If partner responds one notrump or two clubs, you can comfortably make a rebid of two diamonds. If partner's response is, however, two hearts, you will not bid *three* diamonds. That would get you too high. You will simply bid two spades.

When your suits are spades and clubs, you can keep the bidding low by starting with the lower suit:

(2) ♠ K Q J 7 5   ♡ 5   ◇ 6 2   ♣ A J 9 6 3

Bid one club. If partner responds with one of a red suit (as he probably will), you can then bid one spade. At your next turn you can, if necessary, bid two spades, thus telling your story. In this sort of auction, partner should not credit you with six clubs and five spades; he should figure on five of each and a hand of mediocre strength.

It is both unnecessary and undesirable to start with the lower suit when you have a *strong* hand:

(3) ♠ K Q J 7 5   ♡ 5   ◇ A 2   ♣ A K 9 6 3

Bid one spade, not one club. If partner raises to two spades, you will jump to game in spades. If partner, instead, bids two of a red suit, you are quite willing to proceed to three clubs.

√ A 5-CARD SUIT AND A 4-CARD SUIT

With a 5-4 two-suiter you can show both suits if you have a strong hand or if the bidding takes a convenient turn. Otherwise you must either show only the longer suit or begin with the shorter suit to avoid trouble. A few examples will clarify this:

(1) ♠ K Q 6 3   ♡ 5 2   ◊ 8 4   ♣ A K 8 6 3

Bid one club. If partner responds in a red suit, you can conveniently bid one spade. If partner's first response is one notrump, however, you will pass and let him struggle.

(2) ♠ K Q 6 3   ♡ 5 2   ◊ A K 8 6 3   ♣ 8 4

Bid one diamond. If partner bids one heart, you will gladly show the spades. If partner bids one notrump, you will pass. If his first response is two clubs, you will just rebid the diamonds.

(3) ♠ A K 6 3   ♡ K Q 5 3 2   ◊ 5 2   ♣ 8 4

Bid one spade, not one heart. If partner bids one notrump or if he goes to two of a minor, you can conveniently bid two hearts. It is possible, thus, for the bidding to stop at the level of two. If you start with one heart and next bid two spades, however, your partner may have to bid *three* hearts with a poor hand.

(4) ♠ K J 6 3   ♡ A K J 6 3   ◊ 5 2   ♣ 8 4

Bid one heart. If partner bids spades, you will raise; otherwise you will simply rebid your hearts. Don't bid a weak 4-card suit before a strong 5-card suit. Start with the longer suit and, if necessary, ignore the 4-card suit altogether.

(5) ♠ K J 6 3   ♡ A K J 6 3   ◇ A K 2   ♣ 4

Bid one heart, intending to bid the spades later. With a really strong hand you can well afford to push the auction up to a high level, and you therefore bid the hand naturally (longer suit first).

✓ TWO 4-CARD SUITS

The trouble with a hand distributed 4-4-3-2 is that it's not really a two-suiter. It may play comfortably at no-trump.

If you bid your two suits, partner may credit you with nine or ten cards in your suits and may therefore shy away from a good notrump contract. However, if you make no effort to show the suits, you may go down at notrump instead of making a comfortable suit contract.

How can you steer between these two dangers?

- If the two suits are touching, bid the higher-ranking one. (Touching suits are spades-hearts, hearts-diamonds, and diamonds-clubs, but not clubs-spades.)
- If the two suits are not touching, bid the lower one.

If the bidding goes conveniently, you will show the other suit next. Otherwise you can forget about the second suit and think about notrump or about partner's suit.

(1) ♠ K Q 8 7   ♡ A 2   ◇ 9 7 5   ♣ A J 9 4

Bid one club. With four cards in each of the black suits, it is always convenient to show the clubs first. If partner responds in a red suit, you can then bid one spade.

(2) ♠ A 2   ♡ K Q 8 7   ◇ 9 7 5   ♣ A J 9 4

Bid one club. If partner responds one diamond, it will

be convenient for you to bid your hearts. If partner's response is one spade, however, you will just
bid one notrump.

(3) ♠ A 2   ♡ K Q 8 7   ◇ A J 9 4   ♣ 9 7 5

Bid one heart. When your two suits are touching, begin with the higher-ranking suit. You probably won't
be able to show the other suit, since that would
make your hand sound like a real two-suiter.

(4) ♠ A K 8 7   ♡ A Q J 9   ◇ 6 2   ♣ 9 7 5

Bid one spade. Bid hearts at your next chance. When
your strength is concentrated in the majors, it is reasonable enough to bid both suits.

✓ THREE 4-CARD SUITS

When you have three 4-card suits, you want to find a
fit with partner's length in one of those suits. The most
convenient way to do so, as a rule, is to start with the
middle suit or the lowest suit.

Your object is to let partner respond at a low level. If
he bids one of your suits, you have found the fit. If he
bids your singleton, you can conveniently bid notrump
or another suit.

Most of the older textbooks advise you to bid the suit
"below the singleton," but this does not always lead
to a comfortable auction. This rule makes you open with
one spade when you have a singleton club, eliminating
all suit responses at the level of one.

The examples show how easy it is to keep the bidding
low.

(1) ♠ K Q 7 3   ♡ K J 7 5   ◇ A J 8 4   ♣ 6

Bid one heart. If partner bids spades or diamonds, you
can raise. If he bids one notrump or two clubs, you

can bid two diamonds. (You may, instead, pass a response of one notrump.) If the partnership has a fit in either spades or hearts, you discover it without getting uncomfortably high.

(2)   ♠ K Q 7 3   ♡ K J 7 5   ◇ 6   ♣ A J 8 4

Bid one club. If partner responds in either major, you can raise. If he responds one diamond, you can bid one heart. This allows partner to raise hearts or show a spade suit if he has one.

(3)   ♠ K Q 7 3   ♡ 6   ◇ K J 7 5   ♣ A J 8 4

Bid one club or one diamond. Either way, you are ready if partner bids hearts or spades.

(4)   ♠ 6   ♡ K Q 7 3   ◇ K J 7 5   ♣ A J 8 4

Bid one club or one diamond. If partner bids hearts, you can raise. If he bids spades, you will bid one notrump. If his response is one notrump, you will pass.

✓ IN SHORT

If you have the values, land the first punch by opening with a bid of one in a suit. You need:

- 14 points in high cards, or
- 12 or 13 points in high cards, with 2 Quick Tricks and a comfortable rebid, or
- 10 or 11 points in high cards, with 2 Quick Tricks, a comfortable rebid, and length in the majors, or
- In third position, just 10 or 11 points if your bid suggests a favorable opening lead to partner, or
- In fourth position, any borderline hand with strength in the majors, particularly spades.

HOW TO HANDLE YOUR NOTRUMPS

√ The Basic Rules
√ Distribution
√ Stoppers
√ The Right Count
√ Opening with Two or Three Notrump
√ What to Do with In-Between Hands

√ Responding to One Notrump
√ The Stayman Convention
√ Stayman at Higher Levels
√ Responding to High Notrump Bids
√ Rebids by the Opener
√ In Short

√ THE BASIC RULES

BID NOTRUMP with balanced distribution and all suits stopped. Count only high-card points for notrump valuation:

1 NT—16 to 18 points

2 NT—22 to 24 points

3 NT—25 to 27 points

With 19 to 21 points, open with one of a suit and make a jump bid in notrump at your next turn.

A contract of three notrump is the shortest road to game. Perhaps this is why many players get into the habit of bidding three notrump sooner or later on almost any hand that has a chance for game.

This practice has the same appeal as roulette: you don't have to think while you're losing your shirt.

If you have better uses for your shirt, you can find a time to bid notrump, a time to shy violently away from notrump, and a time to fence about in the hope of choosing wisely between notrump and some suit contract.

> *The time to bid notrump is when you have balanced distribution and all suits stopped.*
>
> *The time to shy away from notrump is when you have lopsided distribution, with weakness in one or more suits.*
>
> *The time to fence about is when you have the right distribution without the stoppers, or vice versa.*

✓ DISTRIBUTION

Distribution is mostly a matter of shortages: void suits, singletons, and doubletons.

A short suit is usually worth a trick or two if some other suit is trump. For this reason, a hand with short suits usually plays better at a suit contract than at notrump.

At notrump, moreover, a short suit may be a liability. Your short suit is usually the enemy's long suit. Your biggest danger is that an opponent will establish and cash a long suit against you. Hence the short suit may be the weak spot at notrump but may provide a trick or two at a suit contract.

A hand without any short suit must contain four cards in one suit and three cards in each other suit, which we abbreviate thus: 4-3-3-3 distribution.

The next most balanced distribution is 4-4-3-2: two 4-card suits, a tripleton, and a doubleton. Another distribution with just one short suit is 5-3-3-2.

These are the balanced distributions, useful for notrump. Other distributions, called either semibalanced or unbalanced, usually play better at a trump than at notrump.

Avoid bidding notrump when you have a void suit or a singleton, or even if you have more than one doubleton.

Look for a chance to bid notrump when your distribution is 4-3-3-3, 4-4-3-2, or 5-3-3-2—one doubleton at most.

✓ STOPPERS

A card that will win a trick is called a *stopper* because it stops the opponents from running the suit.

The ace is a sure stopper. The king-queen of a suit is a sure stopper, and so is Q-J-10 or J-10-9-8.

If you waited for *sure* stoppers, you might never be able to bid notrump. You must be satisfied most of the time with probable stoppers and even possible stoppers.

For example, K-x is a probable stopper. Your king will be good for a trick if the suit is led by your left-hand opponent no matter which opponent has the ace. If the suit is led by your right-hand opponent, your king will still win the trick if the ace is at your right.

You will probably win a trick with Q-J-x if the opponents go after that suit. You can even feel fairly hopeful about Q-10-x or Q-x-x.

Certain weaker holdings may be considered partial stoppers. For example, J-x-x is not a stopper by itself, but it becomes a stopper if partner has Q-x. Similarly, a singleton king is not a stopper, but it promotes partner's Q-x to a sure stopper.

Mere length will not stop a suit, but it may discourage the opponents from leading the suit. For example, during the play of a hand, an opponent may be reluctant to shift to a suit when he sees that dummy has four small cards in that suit. He will look for something more promising, and you may survive even though the suit is unstopped.

The opponents usually defeat your notrump contract if they can run a long suit. For this reason you need stoppers in all suits. In a pinch you can get along with one suit unstopped; perhaps the opponents will fail to take their tricks or perhaps they cannot get enough tricks in the suit to beat you.

Avoid bidding notrump when a suit is unstopped. Don't even consider it when two suits are unstopped.

Look for a chance to bid notrump when all suits are stopped.

✔ THE RIGHT COUNT

When you open the bidding with one notrump, your partner should be able to judge whether the combined strength is enough for part score, game, or slam. He does this by adding his points to those shown by your bid.

When the partnership strength is less than 26 points he thinks of a part-score contract. When the total is 26 to 32 points he thinks of a game. When the total is 33 to 36 points he aims at a small slam. And when the total is 37 points or more he thinks of a grand slam.

It is easy for your partner to choose the right goal if he knows your strength to within one point or so. Not so, however, if he has to guess at your strength.

For example, suppose you have the amiable habit of bidding one notrump whenever you like the look of your hand. Sometimes you have only 14 points, and at other times you have 19 or 20 points. "It's a free country," you say to yourself, "and what use is the Bill of Rights if a man can't bid notrump when he feels like it?"

Just put yourself in your partner's place. He has a couple of kings and perhaps one jack, a total of just 7 points. This is enough for *game* if your opening bid indicates the 19-point hand. It may not be enough for even *seven tricks* if you have the 14-point hand. What is he to do?

Whatever he does, guesswork takes the place of skill.

Your partner doesn't have to guess if your opening bid of one notrump always shows a hand of 16 to 18 points. He can assume that you have 17 points, and never be more than a point away from the truth. He can add his own points to your assumed 17 points, and easily see which goal to head for.

This doesn't mean that it's a criminal offense to get a hand of 19 or 20 points. Greet each extra point with a joyful spirit—but don't bid one notrump.

And now for a few examples:

(1) ♠ K J 8   ♡ Q J 7 4   ◊ A 6 2   ♣ K Q 5
Bid one notrump. You have 16 points, balanced distribution, and all suits stopped.

(2) ♠ K J 8 2   ♡ Q J 7 4   ◊ A Q   ♣ K Q 5
Bid one notrump. Don't avoid the natural bid just because you have two biddable major suits.

(3) ♠ A Q 6   ♡ K 6 2   ◊ K 5   ♣ K Q 10 4 2
Bid one notrump. The good 5-card suit will be useful at a notrump contract.

(4) ♠ K Q 8   ♡ A Q 7 4   ◊ K Q 2   ♣ 9 5 4
Bid one notrump. You should have a stopper in each suit, but in a pinch it is reasonable to bid one notrump with three or more small cards in one suit, provided that the hand is otherwise ideal for the bid.

(5)   ♠ K Q 8   ♡ A Q 7 4   ◇ K Q 9 2   ♣ 5 4

Bid one heart. Avoid an opening bid of one notrump when you have a doubleton worse than Q-x in any suit. The opponents will probably lead your short suit, and your shortness and your weakness will be a handicap.

(6)   ♠ Q J 8   ♡ A J 9 3   ◇ K 9 2   ♣ K J 5

Bid one club. Do not open with one notrump when you have only 15 points. The opening bid of one club in a 3-card suit is often made when the hand is just a point or two short of an opening bid of one notrump.

(7)   ♠ A J 8   ♡ A J 9 3   ◇ K J 2   ♣ A J 5

Bid one heart or one club. Do not open with one notrump when you have 19 points (or more). Your partner will pass if he has 7 points, and you will be left in one notrump even though the combined strength of 26 points should give you a reasonable play for game. Open this kind of hand with one of a suit, intending to make a jump rebid in notrump at your next turn. We will have more to say about this later, including a discussion of which suit to bid.

(8)   ♠ A J 8   ♡ K 4   ◇ A J 9 3 2   ♣ A J 5

Bid one diamond. Your hand is too strong for an opening bid of one notrump when you have 18 points *and* a good 5-card suit. As in the 19-point hand in Example 7, bid your suit first and make a jump rebid in notrump later.

(9)   ♠ K 7   ♡ K Q 8 7 3   ◇ A J 9 4   ♣ A 5

Bid one heart. Avoid an opening bid of one notrump when you have two doubletons. In this case you can afford to bid hearts and diamonds first. You may eventually get around to notrump, but by then you will have a foundation of knowledge rather than of guesswork.

✓ OPENING WITH TWO OR THREE NOTRUMP

The opening bid of two notrump shows 22 to 24 points, and the opening bid of three notrump shows 25 to 27 points. In each case the distribution should be balanced, and the hand *must* include a stopper in each of the four suits.

(1) ♠ K J 5 ♡ A Q 9 ◇ A K J 4 ♣ A J 6

Bid two notrump. The distribution is balanced, all suits are well stopped, and the count is 23 points. This is an ideal hand for the opening bid of two notrump.

(2) ♠ K Q 5 ♡ A Q 9 ◇ A K J 4 ♣ A Q 6

Bid three notrump. It is the same as the last example except that the count is now 25 points.

(3) ♠ J 5 2 ♡ A K J ◇ A K J ♣ A Q 8 2

Bid one club. Do not open with two notrump with one suit unstopped even if the hand is otherwise ideal.

(4) ♠ A Q 9 6 5 ♡ K 10 4 ◇ A Q 8 ♣ A K

Bid two notrump. The hand is not strong enough for a forcing opening bid of two spades. (See Chapter 6 for a discussion of Strong Two-Bids.) You are happy to forgo the bid in the strong 5-card major in favor of the more descriptive two-notrump bid.

(5)   ♠ A Q 9 6 5   ♡ A K J   ◇ A Q 8   ♣ A K

> *Bid two spades.* A count of 27 points is maximum for an opening bid of three notrump, and the good 5-card suit makes the hand too strong for this bid. Your problem is to make sure of game without missing an obvious slam. Your best solution is to show the spades first and then bid game in notrump if partner makes a negative response. This allows you to tell about the spades as well as about the great general strength.

The opening bid of two notrump is not forcing to game. Your partner needs about 4 points for a response. He will pass with less, and you will be in a reasonably safe contract instead of in a hopeless game.

✔ WHAT TO DO WITH IN-BETWEEN HANDS

You can open the bidding in notrump with hands of 16 to 18 points or with hands of 22 points or more. What should you do with the in-between hands of from 19 to 21 points?

Open such hands with one of a suit. At your next turn, if the bidding goes normally, jump in notrump.

One such auction:

OPENER	RESPONDER
1 ◇	1 ♡
2 NT	

Another:

OPENER	RESPONDER
1 ◇	2 ♣
3 NT	

A third possibility is the double jump:

OPENER	RESPONDER
1 ◇	1 ♡
3 NT	

There are two pitfalls to avoid in this bidding situation: opening with the wrong suit, and jumping to the wrong number of notrump.

Make a normal bid if you have a 5-card (or longer) suit. There may be a slam in the long suit.

Bid a *low* suit if you have only a 4-card suit. If partner happens to respond in your true suit, you will raise; otherwise, you will go ahead with your plan of jumping in notrump. The trouble with opening in your best suit, if it is a major, is that partner may have to respond one notrump. Such hands usually play about a trick better if the strong hand is concealed and the weak hand is the dummy. That is why you make an effort to prevent the opposite situation.

(1) ♠ A Q 8 5 2   ♡ K J 5   ◇ A J   ♣ K 7 4
   Bid one spade. If partner bids a new suit, you will jump to three notrump; if he bids one notrump, you will raise to two notrump.

(2) ♠ A Q 8 5   ♡ K J 5   ◇ A Q 3   ♣ K 7 4
   Bid one club. If partner responds in hearts or diamonds, you will jump to two notrump. If partner bids one spade, however, you will raise to three spades.

The problem of how high to jump is easily solved. When you have only 19 points a single jump is enough to show your strength, even if it means bidding only two notrump. When you have 21 points or a very strong suit, however, make sure of getting to game; bid three notrump yourself—no matter whether it is a single or double jump. With a hand of 20 points you may go either way, depending on whether the hand is skimpy or well-bolstered.

YOU	PARTNER
1 ◊	1 ♡
?	

(1) ♠ K 8 3   ♡ K Q 4   ◊ A Q 8 6 3   ♣ A J

Bid two notrump. The typical 19-point hand.

(2) ♠ K Q 3   ♡ K Q 4   ◊ A Q 8 6 3   ♣ A J

Bid three notrump. A jump to two notrump would be only invitational, and you want to get your partner to game even if you have to drag him there by the scruff of the neck.

(3) ♠ A Q J   ♡ 10 4   ◊ A K J 6 3   ♣ A Q J

Bid three notrump. You would have opened with two notrump except for the weakness in hearts. Now that your partner has bid that suit you can afford to jump to game.

(4) ♠ A J 4   ♡ 10 5   ◊ A K Q 6 3 2   ♣ A J

Bid three notrump. You expect to win eight tricks in your own hand—six diamonds and two black aces. There should be a sound play for game if partner can provide as little as one trick. With such a wealth of playing tricks you can shade the point-count requirements down a point or so.

(5) ♠ A K Q   ♡ J 6 4   ◊ A J 4 2   ♣ K Q 5

Bid two notrump. Your 20 points are skimpy. Bolster the hand with some tens and nines, and you jump to three notrump.

V RESPONDING TO ONE NOTRUMP

It's easy to respond to one notrump because you know almost everything about your partner's hand. Add your own points to those shown by partner's bid.

Your Points	Goal
0 to 8	Part score
9 to 14	Game
15 or 16	Possible slam
17 or more	Slam

It isn't necessary to memorize these figures. You already know that the partnership needs about 26 points for game and about 33 points for a small slam. You also know that your partner's bid shows 16 to 18 points. Add your own points and see where you should be heading.

Most of the responses are very simple and natural.

With 0 to 8 Points: Pass a balanced hand. Bid with a long suit, particularly if you have a singleton or void suit (The opener passes your bid of two in a suit about nine times out of ten, so don't worry about getting too high.)

9 to 14 Points: Raise to two notrump (9 points)* or to three notrump (10 points or more) with balanced distribution. Jump to three of a long major suit (forcing to game) to suggest an alternative game contract.

More than 14 Points: Jump to three of a long suit and then make a slam try by bidding past game. With balanced distribution, raise to four notrump (a good 15 or 16 points) or all the way to slam (17 or 18 points).

---

* If your partner is a very good player, you may raise to two notrump with 8 points, particularly if the hand contains a 5-card suit or a sprinkling of tens and nines.

With 19 points or more, think about a *grand* slam. (See Chapter 7 on How to Bid Your Slams.)

✓ THE STAYMAN CONVENTION

When responder has 4-card (or better) support for one or both majors, he may have a bidding problem: how can he find out about major suits without giving a false picture of his hand?

For example, responder may have:

    ♠ A J 3 2   ♡ A J 3 2   ♢ 4 3 2   ♣ 3 2

There should be a reasonable play for game, since responder has 10 points in high cards. The combined count must be 26 to 28 points.

If the opener has a 4-card major, responder wants to play in game in that suit. Otherwise, responder wants to bid three notrump.

If responder bids only two spades, the opener will probably pass. If responder jumps to *three* spades, he gives an impression of a much longer suit and does not find out about the hearts.

The problem is solved by a response of *two clubs*, widely known as the Stayman Convention. This bid says nothing about clubs. It merely asks the opener: Do you have a major suit?

If the opener has one 4-card (or better) major, he bids it. If he has biddable holdings in *both* major suits, he bids the spades and waits for a chance to bid the hearts later. If he has no biddable major suit, he bids two diamonds and awaits developments.

This makes it very easy for the responder. If a major suit is bid for which responder has 4-card support, he raises. Otherwise he goes back to notrump. Occasionally responder may bid a 5-card major to indicate that he will be satisfied with even 3-card support.

SOUTH	WEST	NORTH	EAST
1 NT	Pass	2 ♣	Pass
2 ◇	Pass	?	

(1)   ♠ K864   ♡ AQ963   ◇ 62   ♣ 87

  Bid two hearts. This bid shows at least five hearts, since the opener has denied four cards of either major. If partner had bid a major suit, you were ready to raise to game. You are still willing to play at hearts if partner has fair 3-card support. Otherwise partner will probably bid two notrump. (Some partnerships allow the opener to pass in this situation; others don't. When you are strong enough, jump to *three* hearts to make sure of reaching game.)

(2)   ♠ K864   ♡ AQ96   ◇ 62   ♣ 875

  Bid two notrump. If partner had bid a major suit, you would be ready to raise to game. (But if your queen of hearts were only the jack, you would raise a major-suit bid to only *three* instead of four.) Since partner has no major suit, you scramble back to notrump. A retreat to *two* notrump shows about 8 or 9 points; with 10 points or more in high cards you would jump to *three* notrump. Notice that you would bid *game* in a major suit but can afford to bid only *two* notrump when no suit fit is found. The doubleton in diamonds is a liability at notrump but is an asset if some other suit is trump.

✓ STAYMAN AT HIGHER LEVELS

You can use the Stayman Convention over an opening bid of two notrump or three notrump. Just bid a mini-

mum number of clubs. This asks partner to bid a major
suit if he can.

To use the Stayman Convention over such a strong
opening bid, you don't need a good hand—just the major-
suit support. You expect to get to game anyway with a
very weak supporting hand, so there is no harm in finding out about the major suits on the way to game.

For example, in response to partner's opening bid of
two notrump:

(1) ♠ J 8 6 4   ♡ Q 7 5 3   ◇ Q 6 5   ♣ 8 2
   Bid three clubs. If partner shows a major, you will
   raise to game. If he bids three diamonds, denying a
   major, you will bid three notrump.

(2) ♠ K 8 6 4   ♡ Q J 5 3   ◇ A 6 5   ♣ 8 2
   Bid three clubs. If partner shows a major, you will
   raise to six! If partner bids three diamonds, you will
   jump to five notrump, inviting a notrump slam. You
   have 10 points and therefore know that the combined count is 32 to 34 points.

A Note of Caution: If you haven't previously agreed
with your partner to use the Stayman Convention, avoid
bidding two (or three) clubs with major suits in mind.
Stick to the "natural" bids.

✓ RESPONDING TO HIGH NOTRUMP BIDS

The opening bid of two notrump shows 22 to 24 points.
Responder passes with 0 to 3 points, gets to game (any
bid is forcing to game) with 4 to 8 points, and thinks
of a slam with more than 8 points.

The opening bid of three notrump shows 25 to 27

points. Responder needs very little for a slam. Almost any response stirs up the bidding to the level of five, so responder should keep quiet unless he has 3 or 4 points or a very long suit.

✓ REBIDS BY THE OPENER

If you have opened with one notrump, you have told practically your whole story. Avoid repeating yourself.

If partner bids two of a suit (other than clubs), you are expected to pass. Raise partner's suit to three only if you have fine support for his suit and an 18-point notrump. If you have only 16 or 17 points or if you lack the fine support, just pass and accept a part score.

If partner raises to two notrump, you may pass with a bare 16 points, particularly if you have one very weak suit. If you have any excuse to do so (and there is almost always *some* excuse), go on to game.

If partner tries for a slam, accept all invitations with 18 points; decline them with 16 points. Use your judgment with the middle value of 17 points.

✓ IN SHORT

All opening bids in notrump show balanced distribution, stoppers, and a definite number of points.

In responding, add your own points to those shown by partner's bid. Head for game if the total is 26 points, for slam if the total is 33 points.

Use the Stayman Convention to discover if there is a good fit in a major suit.

If your first bid has told your whole story, stick to it. Let your partner make most of the decisions from then on.

RESPONDING TO THE OPENING BID

√ Which Type of Response?   √ Two-over-One Responses
√ Raising a Major Suit   √ Notrump Responses
√ Single Raises   √ The Jump Response in a New
√ Double Raises   Suit
√ Triple Raises   √ Raising a Minor Suit
√ The Forcing Principle   √ Responses by a Passed Hand
√ One-over-One Responses   √ In Short

EVEN IF YOUR HAND is very weak, you should make an effort to find some response to your partner's opening bid of one in a suit. If your partner has a very strong hand, your meager strength may be enough for game. If he has a two-suited hand, he may be much better off in his second suit than in the suit he bid first. A further point is that almost any response tends to make it more difficult for the opponents to enter the auction.

For these reasons the opener's partner should respond on any hand that comes to 6 points in high cards. In some cases the responder may have even less in high cards— say only 4 or 5 points.

With less than this the responder should pass. With more, the responder tries to describe his hand so that one member of the partnership can eventually pick a reasonable contract.

⩔ WHICH TYPE OF RESPONSE?

If we dismiss the pass from consideration, there are three main types of response:

A *raise*
A *new suit*
A *notrump bid*

In general, a raise shows trump support for partner's suit and a fairly definite number of points. A notrump bid shows balanced distribution and again a fairly definite number of points. A bid in a new suit shows length in that suit but a wide range of points.

Sometimes your hand clearly calls for one type of bid rather than any other. At other times you have a choice. In general, you raise partner's *major* suit in preference to bidding either a new suit or notrump. If partner's suit is a *minor*, however, you show a suit of your own or bid the appropriate number of notrump.

∨ RAISING A MAJOR SUIT

When partner opens with one of a major suit, you look first for the chance to raise. For this you need adequate trump support and the right amount of strength.

Both requirements vary according to how high you raise:

Raise from 1 to:	Points You Need (high cards plus short suits)	Minimum Trump Strength
2	6 to 10 points	x-x-x-x or Q-x-x
3	13 to 16 points	Q-x-x-x
4	less than 10 high-card points	x-x-x-x-x

The higher you raise, the more trumps you promise.

You also promise more points—except for the jump to four, which is a sort of shutout bid.

Note the gap between the single raise (6 to 10 points) and the double raise (13 to 16 points). What do you bid with a hand of 11 or 12 points?

With such a hand you bid a new suit first and raise partner's suit later. This is a raise to "2½" of partner's suit.

You must sometimes adopt this method if you have 13 or more points but insufficient trump support for a double raise. You bid a new suit and then raise partner to three or even to four.

√ SINGLE RAISES

A single raise in a *major* suit shows:

> *trump support*
> *6 to 10 points*

Ideally, the trump support consists of four or more cards. Next best is 3-card support, headed by at least the queen. In rare cases you raise with three small cards. You *never* raise partner's opening bid of one in a suit with less than 3-card trump support.

The strength requirement is also slightly elastic. You prefer to have at least 7 points (high-card plus short-suit) for a raise. If you get the right kind of hand with only 6 points, you still have to raise. Some experts even shade this down to 5 points.

Let's see some examples:

SOUTH	WEST	NORTH	EAST
1 ♡	Pass	?	

(1)   ♠ 6 3   ♡ K 8 4 2   ◇ 9 7 5 4   ♣ Q 7 4

Bid two hearts. You have fine trump support and 6

points—5 in high cards and 1 point for the double-ton. Change the queen of clubs to the jack, and the hand becomes a doubtful case. I would still recommend the raise, but some players would prefer a pass.

(2) ♠ 6 3   ♡ K 8 4 2   ◇ A 7 5 4   ♣ Q 7 4

Bid two hearts. Maximum value for the single raise. Add a jack somewhere, and you would bid two diamonds first and raise hearts at your next turn.

(3) ♠ 6   ♡ K 8 4 2   ◇ 9 7 5 4   ♣ J 7 4 3

Bid two hearts. Fine trump support and 7 points—4 in high cards and 3 points for the singleton.°

(4) ♠ 6   ♡ K 8 4 2   ◇ K 7 5 4   ♣ J 7 4 3

Bid two hearts. Maximum value for the single raise. Add a jack somewhere, and you would bid two diamonds first and raise hearts later.

(5) ♠ 6 3   ♡ Q 8 4   ◇ A 7 5 4   ♣ 8 7 4 3

Bid two hearts. A minimum raise with 3-card trump support. You have 6 points in high cards and 1 point for the doubleton. You can add 1 point for the queen of partner's suit, but you would have to deduct it for a raise with only three trumps. No matter how you count it, this is still a minimum raise.

(6) ♠ 6 3   ♡ Q 8 4   ◇ A 7 5 4   ♣ K 7 4 3

Bid two hearts. A maximum raise with 3-card trump support.

(7) ♠ 6   ♡ 9 8 4   ◇ K Q 5 4   ♣ Q J 4 3 2

Bid two hearts. Your hand is not quite worth a bid in

° Just a reminder: a singleton is worth only 2 points when you value your hand as declarer, but the singleton becomes worth 3 points when you are considering a raise. See page 8 in Chapter 1.

a new suit followed by a show of support for hearts. Just raise the hearts and leave the rest to partner. Your trump support is substandard, but the side strength makes up for it. The singleton makes a response of one notrump unattractive.

√ DOUBLE RAISES

A double raise in a *major* suit shows:

> *Strong trump support (Q-x-x-x or better)*
> *13 to 16 points*

The double raise in a major suit often paves the way to a fine slam contract. For this reason you avoid a double raise when you have a doubtful trump holding, such as x-x-x-x.

The strength requirement is slightly elastic. In rare cases you may decide to treat a 12-point hand as though it were a 13-pointer; conversely, you may treat a 17-point hand as though it were a 16-pointer.

In general, however, a hand of only 12 points is not worth a double raise; you bid a new suit and then raise partner's suit. A hand of 17 points is too strong for a double raise; you fence about by bidding *two* new suits and then showing the trump support. *A double raise in a major suit is forcing to game.*

SOUTH	WEST	NORTH	EAST
1 ♡	Pass	?	

(1) ♠ 6 3   ♡ K 8 4 2   ◇ A J 5 4   ♣ A 4 3

Bid three hearts. You have strong 4-card trump support and 13 points—12 in high cards and 1 point for the doubleton.

(2) ♠ 6   ♡ K 8 4 2   ◇ A J 5 4   ♣ Q 7 4 3

Bid three hearts. Strong trump support and 13 points —10 in high cards and 3 points for the singleton.

(3) ♠ 6   ♡ K 8 4 2   ◇ A J 5 4   ♣ A J 4 3

Bid three hearts. The maximum value of 16 points.

(4) ♠ 6   ♡ K 8 4 2   ◇ A Q 5 4   ♣ A J 4 3

Bid two diamonds. At your next turn, show the clubs. Only then should you raise the hearts. The hand is too strong for an immediate raise to three hearts, but not quite good enough for a jump to three diamonds or three clubs.

✓ TRIPLE RAISES

A triple raise (from one to four) in a *major* suit shows:

> *Five or more trumps*
> *Good distribution, but not more than 9 points in high cards*

The raise to game is a shutout bid. The opening bidder is warned that slam is unlikely. The hand should be rich in distribution (containing a singleton or void suit) but not in high cards.

SOUTH	WEST	NORTH	EAST
1 ♡	Pass	?	

(1) ♠ 6   ♡ J 8 6 4 3   ◇ K Q 8 5 2   ♣ 7 4

Bid four hearts. You have the prescribed five trumps, good distribution, and only 7 points in high cards (counting 1 point extra for the jack of partner's suit). This is a model raise to game.

(2)   ♠ 6 2   ♡ J 8 6 4 3   ◇ K Q 8 5   ♣ 7 4

Bid only two hearts. Do not raise to game just because
you have five trumps. You also need very good distribution—either a singleton or a void suit.

(3)   ♠ 6   ♡ J 8 6 4 3   ◇ A K Q 5 2   ♣ 7 4

Bid two diamonds. At your next turn you will jump to
four hearts. This shows concentrated strength in
these two suits. Partner may try for a slam if he has
the right sort of hand. There is no real objection to
an immediate jump to three hearts, but you describe
your hand better to him when you bid diamonds en
route. The hand is too strong for a raise to *four* hearts.

✓ THE FORCING PRINCIPLE

Can you afford to bid a suit of your own when you
have strong support for your partner's suit? If your partner passes, you will never get the chance to show your
support.

You don't have to worry about this danger if your
partner is an experienced player. Your response in a new
suit is *forcing for one round* of bidding.

SOUTH	WEST	NORTH	EAST
1 ♡	Pass	1 ♠	Pass
?		or 2 ♣	
		or 2 ◇	

South must bid. North's response in a new suit is forcing for one round.

This is a different situation:

SOUTH	WEST	NORTH	EAST
1 ♡	Pass	1 ♠	2 ♣
?			

South may pass. East's bid gives North another chance to bid, so there is no need for South to act.

SOUTH	WEST	NORTH	EAST
1 ♡	Pass	1 ♠	Pass
2 ♡	Pass		

North may pass. His response in a new suit requested another chance to speak, but North did not promise to say anything. In other words, the response in a new suit forces the *opener* to bid again but does not force the responder.

Certain other bids are forcing *to game:*

> A *double raise in a major suit*
> A *jump response in a new suit*
> A *jump to two notrump*

When any of these responses is made, both partners are supposed to keep the bidding open until game is reached—or until the opponents have been doubled for penalties. However, if the partner making the bid had passed at his first turn, the response is merely invitational —not forcing.

V ONE-OVER-ONE RESPONSES

The one-over-one response is a non-jump bid in a higher-ranking suit:

SOUTH	WEST	NORTH	EAST
1 ◇	Pass	1 ♡	
		or 1 ♠	

The one-over-one response is, as we have seen, forcing for one round. It promises:

> *Four or more cards in the suit*
> *6 to 18 points (high-card plus short-suit)*

Almost any 4-card (or longer) suit is acceptable. This is particularly true when the opening bid is in a minor suit.

SOUTH	WEST	NORTH	EAST
1 ◇	Pass	?	

(1) ♠ K 3   ♡ 9 8 5 2   ◇ A J 5   ♣ 8 7 6 2

Bid one heart. Almost any 4-card suit is good enough for a response at the level of one. Respond in a major if you can, rather than raise a minor suit.

(2) ♠ K 8 5 3   ♡ 9 8 5 2   ◇ A J 5   ♣ K 8

Bid one heart. When you have a choice of 4-card suits, bid the cheapest of them. This is sometimes called *stepwise* bidding. If partner likes hearts, he will raise; if not, he may be able to bid spades. In this way you can find out about a fit in *both* major suits. If you made your first response in spades, your partner might find it awkward to show a 4-card heart suit and the partnership would miss a good 4-4 fit in a major suit.

(3) ♠ K 9 8 5 3   ♡ J 8 5 2   ◇ A J 5   ♣ 8

Bid one spade. When the choice is between a 5-card and a 4-card suit, show the 5-card suit.

(4)   ♠ 9 8 5 3   ♡ 8 5 2   ◇ A J 5 4   ♣ K 3

Raise to two diamonds. With very good support for a
minor suit and a very poor 4-card major suit, raise
the minor. This is, however, exceptional. Bid the
major if it is headed by the queen or better; and bid
any 5-card or longer major suit.

∨ TWO-OVER-ONE RESPONSES

The two-over-one response is a nonjump bid in a low-
er-ranking suit:

SOUTH	WEST	NORTH	EAST
1 ♠	Pass	2 ♡	
		or 2 ◇	
		or 2 ♣	

Such a response is forcing for one round. It promises:

A good suit, usually of five or more cards
Usually 10 high-card points
10 to 18 points, including short suits

Note that the two-over-one response promises greater
general strength *and* a better suit than the one-over-one
response. The two-over-one response is treated by most
experts as a decisive step in the direction of game. The
one-over-one response may be quite tentative.

In general, you make a two-over-one response only if
you have the strength for at least two responses. You
show your long suit, intending to do something else later
—for example, raise the opener's suit, bid a new suit, or
bid notrump.

When the hand is not worth two bids, you are usually better off if you make a response of one notrump rather than two of your suit. However, if you have a good suit and very poor distribution for notrump, you may bid two and later three of your suit. This shows just a good suit with no real interest in game. You do not need 10 high-card points in such cases.

SOUTH	WEST	NORTH	EAST
1 ♠	Pass	?	

(1)   ♠ 8 7 5   ♡ A 5   ◇ A Q J 8 4   ♣ 9 6 3
Bid two diamonds. You have 11 points in high cards, more than enough for a two-over-one response. If partner rebids the spades, you raise. Otherwise you probably bid notrump at your next turn.

(2)   ♠ 7 5   ♡ A 5   ◇ K Q J 8 4   ♣ Q 9 6 3
Bid two diamonds. You expect to bid notrump at your next turn.

(3)   ♠ J 8 7 5   ♡ K 5 2   ◇ K J 9 8 4   ♣ 5
Bid two diamonds. You intend to raise spades next, showing a hand that was too good for a single raise but not good enough for a double raise. You don't have the promised minimum of 10 high-card points, but your fine spade support and good distribution make up for what is missing.

(4)   ♠ 7   ♡ 8 5 3 2   ◇ A Q J 9 8 3   ♣ 4 2
Bid two diamonds. You expect to bid three diamonds at your next turn, thus showing a hand that is good for diamonds but for nothing much else. However, if partner makes his rebid in *hearts,* you raise that suit.

√ NOTRUMP RESPONSES

A response of one notrump is made with almost any weak hand (6 to 10 points) that does not qualify for a raise or for a one-over-one response.

A response of *two* notrump shows:

> 13 to 15 points in high cards
> strength in each of the unbid suits
> balanced distribution (no singleton, no more than one doubleton)

A response of *three* notrump shows:

> 16 or 17 points in high cards
> strength in each of the unbid suits
> 4-3-3-3 distribution

Note that short-suit points are not counted for notrump. If your partner is a good player, avoid the response of three notrump. It's far too easy to miss a laydown slam by using this bulky, awkward bid.

SOUTH	WEST	NORTH	EAST
1 ♡	Pass	?	

(1) ♠ K J 8   ♡ 6 2   ◇ A Q 9 4   ♣ K J 9 5

Bid two notrump. You have 14 points in high cards, balanced distribution, and strength in each of the unbid suits.

(2) ♠ Q 10 7   ♡ 6 2   ◇ A K Q 9 4   ♣ Q 10 8

Bid two diamonds with a good partner, but jump to two notrump if you play the hands better than your partner. (In short, bid two notrump.)

(3)   ♠ K Q 8   ♡ J 6 2   ◇ K Q 9 4   ♣ K Q 8

Bid three notrump. You have 16 points, flat distribution, and strength in each of the unbid suits.

(4)   ♠ K 10 7   ♡ 6 2   ◇ Q J 9 4   ♣ 9 8 6 3

Bid one notrump. You have 6 points in high cards and no other convenient response. If your spades and diamonds were exchanged, you could make a one-over-one response in the 4-card spade suit.

(5)   ♠ 10 7 3   ♡ 6 2   ◇ K Q J 9 4   ♣ K 6 3

Bid one notrump. You have 9 points in high cards and a fairly good diamond suit, but the hand is not quite worth a response at the level of two. Save such a response for hands that are pretty clearly worth two responses; this hand is worth just one bid.

✓ THE JUMP RESPONSE IN A NEW SUIT

A jump response in a new suit is forcing to game and hints very strongly that the partnership may be able to make a slam even if the opening bidder has a minimum opening bid.

The jump response promises:

> *A good suit (or very good support for the opener's suit)*
> *19 points or more, counting high cards and distribution*

SOUTH	WEST	NORTH	EAST
1 ♡	Pass	?	

(1)   ♠ A K Q J 7 5   ♡ 8 3   ◇ A Q 4   ♣ K 3

Bid two spades. You will rebid the spades at your next

turn, thus indicating that that backbone of your jump is a very powerful suit of your own.

(2)   ♠ A Q J 7 5   ♡ K Q 8 3   ◇ K J 4   ♣ 3

Bid two spades. You will bid hearts at your next turn, indicating that you have strong support for hearts as well as a good spade suit and at least 19 points.

(3)   ♠ A Q J 7 5   ♡ K 10 8 3   ◇ A Q 4   ♣ 3

Bid two spades. You expect to make a cue-bid in diamonds at your next turn, after which you will show the heart support. (Bidding three suits in this fashion with a jump included shows a singleton in the fourth suit.) There should be a slam in this hand unless partner has a minimum opening bid with too much wasted strength in clubs.

(4)   ♠ A Q J 7 5   ♡ Q 8 3   ◇ K J 4   ♣ A 10

Bid two spades. You have 17 points in high cards and should count 1 point for the doubleton and 1 point extra for the queen in partner's bid suit (hearts). At your next turn you will bid notrump, thus indicating that your jump bid is based on general strength.

(5)   ♠ A J 5   ♡ K Q J 8 3   ◇ A K 4   ♣ 8 3

Bid three diamonds. For lack of a real suit of your own you must "invent" one. You have 18 points in high cards and 1 point for the doubleton—far too much for a mere double raise. Only a jump takeout will show your full strength.

▼ RAISING A MINOR SUIT

You raise a minor suit from one to two when you don't know what else to do. You raise from one to three when you *really* don't know what to do. In other words, you respond in a major suit, in the other minor, or in notrump if you possibly can. The minor-suit raise is a last resort.

A single raise of partner's *minor* suit shows:

> *good trump support*
> *6 to 10 points*
> *no biddable major suit*

A double raise of partner's *minor* suit shows:

> *very strong trump support*
> *about 12 to 14 points, including distribution*
> *no convenient bid of any other kind*

The double raise of a minor suit is treated by some experts as not quite forcing to game. If in doubt, the opening bidder should grit his teeth and bid again.

The raise of a minor suit causes such confusion that some experts have looked for unusual solutions. Some believe in responding, when necessary, in a 3-card major suit; but this is a dangerous practice. Others use the response of one notrump to a minor suit, particularly to one club, to show about 9 to 11 points.

The best solution, in my opinion, is the Inverted Raise, devised a couple of years ago by Edgar Kaplan.° The single raise (one club-two clubs) is strong, forcing for one round; the double raise (one club-three clubs) is a weak shutout bid. Don't try this without first discussing it with your partner; it's embarrassing to make a weak jump to three and then discover that your partner is trying for a slam because he thinks you have a good hand!

° Fully described in *How to Play Winning Bridge*, by Edgar Kaplan and Alfred Sheinwold (New York: Fleet Publishing Corporation, 1958).

✔ RESPONSES BY A PASSED HAND

When you have passed in first or second position your partner knows that your hand was not worth an opening bid. If his own hand is a doubtful or minimum opening bid, he should have serious doubts about game. For this reason your partner may pass your response even though your bid would ordinarily be forcing.

SOUTH	WEST	NORTH	EAST
Pass	Pass	1 ♡	Pass
2 ♣	Pass	?	

North may pass. If he were the dealer, he would treat your response of two clubs as forcing for one round.

Even a double raise is not forcing when made by a passed hand:

SOUTH	WEST	NORTH	EAST
Pass	Pass	1 ♠	Pass
3 ♠	Pass	?	

North is allowed to pass if he has a sketchy opening bid.

The opener should not take pleasure in passing any such response. If he has a sound opening bid, he should make a normal rebid. He should pass only when his own opening bid is slightly suspect.

The responder can afford to make certain jump responses a little lighter than normally. He needn't worry about overstating his strength since he is known to have a hand that wasn't worth an opening bid.

When made by a passed hand:

> A *double raise shows about 11 to 13 points, counting distribution.*

A raise to game (normally a weak shutout bid) shows 14 or 15 points, counting distribution.

A jump to two notrump shows about 11 to 12 points, with balanced distribution and strength in the unbid suits.

A jump in a new suit shows a good suit, a fit with partner's suit, and about 14 points (counting distribution). This bid should be treated as forcing for one round.

SOUTH	WEST	NORTH	EAST
Pass	Pass	1 ♡	Pass
?			

(1)   ♠ 8 5 3 2   ♡ K Q J 4   ◇ 9   ♣ A 6 4 3

Bid three hearts. This raise may be dropped by your partner if he has a very doubtful opening bid.

(2)   ♠ 8 5 3 2   ♡ K J 9 4   ◇ ————   ♣ A Q 6 4 3

Bid four hearts. Your partner probably has a reasonable play for game even if he has a very sketchy opening bid. Don't *invite* a game when you can *bid* it.

(3)   ♠ K J 3   ♡ 9 6 2   ◇ Q J 9 4   ♣ A J 8

Bid two notrump. This is about a point or two lighter than the normal jump to two notrump. Your partner may pass if he has a very sketchy hand.

(4)   ♠ K Q 10 5 3   ♡ K Q 9 4   ◇ 9   ♣ 6 4 3

Bid two spades. You want to reach game and could jump to four hearts if you so chose. You will show your heart support next. The idea is to show the location of your strength in case partner has the sort of hand that may be good for a slam.

✓ IN SHORT

Respond to partner's opening bid with 6 points or more.

With a *weak* hand, 6 to 10 points, raise partner's suit from one to two, bid one of a higher suit, or bid one no-trump as a last resort.

With a *fair* hand, 10 to 13 points, make two responses—first in your own suit and then either in partner's suit or in notrump.

With a *strong* hand, 13 to 16 points, look for a game. Make a forcing bid, such as a double raise or a jump to two notrump. If these bids do not describe your hand, bid a new suit and follow with a second suit or a jump in partner's suit or notrump.

With a *very* strong hand, 19 points or more, make a jump bid in a new suit and then explore slam possibilities.

Certain bids are forcing:

> *For one round*
> • One over-one response
> • Two-over-one response
>
> *To game*
> • Double raise in a major suit
> • Jump takeout in a new suit
> • Jump to two notrump

If you have previously passed, only the jump takeout in a new suit is forcing, and then for one round only.

5th DAY

REBIDS—WHERE JUDGMENT BEGINS

√ After a Single Raise
√ After a Double Raise in a Major Suit
√ After a Triple Raise in a Major Suit
√ After a Response of One Notrump
√ After a Response of Two Notrump

√ After a One-over-One Response
√ After a Two-over-One Response
√ Reverse and Skip-Level Bids
√ Rebids by the Responder
√ Accepting an Invitation
√ Tips on Rebidding

It isn't very hard to pick your first bid or your first response. However, your rebid may take some judgment.

Your rebid depends on the nature of your hand and on how the bidding has started. However, you can follow a few general principles in most cases:

- Work out the number of points shown by partner's response.
- Add your own points.
- Steer toward part score, game, or slam, according to the combined total of points.

If your hand calls for some further bid, you can indicate the nature of your hand in the following ways:

- Rebid in notrump—balanced distribution, stoppers in unbid suits
- Rebid in own suit—good suit
- Rebid in new suit—unbalanced distribution
- Raise of partner's suit—trump support and unbalanced distribution

- Jump in bid suit (own or partner's)—substantial extra strength
- Jump bid in new suit—enough strength to force to game

✓ AFTER A SINGLE RAISE

Remember partner's single raise shows 6 to 10 points.

- With 12 to 15 points: Pass
- With 16 to 18 points: Bid three of your suit, two notrump, or a new suit. (Only the new suit is a forcing bid.)
- With 19 points or more: Jump to game or bid a new suit.

SOUTH	WEST	NORTH	EAST
1 ♡	Pass	2 ♡	Pass
?			

(1)   ♠ 8 7 3   ♡ A K J 9 4   ◇ A 8 5   ♣ 9 4

Pass. You have only 14 points (12 in high cards, 1 for the doubleton, and 1 for the fifth card in a raised suit). Even if partner has the maximum value of 10 points, the total is not enough for game.

(2)   ♠ K 7 3   ♡ A K J 9 4   ◇ A 8 5   ♣ 9 4

Bid three hearts or, as second choice, two notrump. You have 15 points in high cards, 1 point for the fifth heart, and 1 point for the doubleton. There should be a reasonable play for game if partner has 9 or 10 points.

(3)   ♠ A 3   ♡ A K J 9 4   ◇ Q J 8 5   ♣ 9 4

Bid three diamonds. You have enough to invite game

but not enough to insist on it. You want partner to
lend special weight to high cards in your new suit
(diamonds) to help him decide a close point.

(4)   ♠ A 3   ♡ A K J 9 4   ◇ K Q J 8 5   ♣ 4

Bid four hearts. You want to be in a game no matter
how weak partner's raise may be. With a good partner you might bid three diamonds with the intention
of trying for a slam if partner can then jump to four
hearts.

✓ AFTER A DOUBLE RAISE IN A MAJOR SUIT

Partner's raise has shown 13 to 16 points. This response
is forcing to game.

- With 12 to 16 points, bid three notrump or four of
  your major suit. Slam is unlikely.
- With 17 points or more, make some move in the direction of slam. (See Chapter 7, How to Bid Your
  Slams.)

SOUTH	WEST	NORTH	EAST
1 ♡	Pass	3 ♡	Pass
?			

(1)   ♠ A 9 6   ♡ K Q 8 7 4   ◇ A 8 5   ♣ 9 4

Bid four hearts. Game in a good 5-card major suit is
usually safer than game at notrump.

(2)   ♠ A 9   ♡ K Q J 7   ◇ A 8 6 5   ♣ J 10 4

Bid three notrump. Your clubs are a bit weak, but the
hand is otherwise ideal for notrump and only fair
for suit play. Your partner can still bid four hearts
if he has an unbalanced hand.

∨ AFTER A TRIPLE RAISE IN A MAJOR SUIT

Partner's raise shows good distribution but at most 9 points in high cards.

- Pass unless you have at least 20 points, including three aces.

∨ AFTER A RESPONSE OF ONE NOTRUMP

Partner's response has shown 6 to 10 points.

- Pass a balanced hand of 12 to 15 points, but with unbalanced distribution rebid your suit or show a new suit.
- With 16 to 18 points and balanced distribution you should have opened with one notrump yourself. With unbalanced distribution, rebid your own suit or show a new suit.
- With a strong 18 or 19 points, raise to two notrump or jump to three of a suit (either your original suit or a new one).
- With 20 points or more, raise to three notrump or bid three of a *new* suit.

SOUTH	WEST	NORTH	EAST
1 ♡	Pass	1 NT	Pass
?			

(1)   ♠ J 8 5   ♡ A K 9 6 2   ◇ K Q 4   ♣ 8 3

Pass. Do not rebid a minimum balanced hand just because you have a 5-card suit. One notrump is as good a spot as any.

(2) ♠ J 8 5   ♡ A K 9 6 2   ◇ K Q 9 4   ♣ 3

Bid two diamonds. The hand is a minimum, but the unbalanced distribution steers you away from no-trump.

(3) ♠ K J 8   ♡ K Q J 9 6 2   ◇ A 4   ♣ K 3

Bid two notrump. (With a weak partner, jump to three hearts.) You have 17 points in high cards and should count something extra for the length in hearts. (Do not count anything for short suits if you are considering a bid in notrump.) The partnership total should be enough for game if partner has fairly good values for his response of one notrump.

(4) ♠ K J 8   ♡ K Q J 9 6 2   ◇ A Q 4   ♣ 3

Bid three hearts. You have 16 points in high cards, 2 points for the singleton, and at least a point or two for the long and almost solid heart suit. This jump bid is invitational but not forcing. Your partner is expected to pass with 6 or 7 points, to bid game with 9 or 10 points, and to use his judgment with the middle value of 8 points.

(5) ♠ A 8   ♡ K Q J 9 6 2   ◇ A Q J 4   ♣ 3

Bid three diamonds. You have 17 points in high cards, 3 points for the two short suits, and at least a point or two for length in hearts. You want to reach game even if partner has only the minimum value of 6 or 7 points for his response of one notrump.

(6) ♠ A J 8   ♡ K Q J 6 2   ◇ A Q J   ♣ Q 3

Bid three notrump. You have 20 points in high cards and therefore want to reach game even if partner has only 6 points for his response of one notrump. It is true that the clubs are weak, but it isn't always possible to get your bank manager to guarantee your bids.

¥ AFTER A RESPONSE OF TWO NOTRUMP

Partner's bid has shown 13 to 15 points, with strength in each of the unbid suits. This response is forcing to game.

- With 12 to 17 points, raise to three notrump to show balanced distribution; rebid a suit with unbalanced distribution. Even if your distribution is balanced, you may rebid a good 5-card major suit.
- With 18 points or more, try for a slam. With 20 points or more, make sure of a slam.

SOUTH	WEST	NORTH	EAST
1 ♡	Pass	2 NT	Pass
?			

(1)   ♠ 8 3   ♡ K Q J 5   ◊ A Q J 4   ♣ J 10 4

Bid three notrump. You have 14 points in high cards, and partner has only 15 points at most. The total is not enough for a slam. Since your distribution is balanced you have no reason to be dissatisfied with game at notrump.

(2)   ♠ 8 3   ♡ K Q J 5 4   ◊ A Q J   ♣ J 10 4

Bid three hearts. You are not really dissatisfied with three notrump, but you can afford to suggest game at hearts as an alternative. If partner has 3-card heart support, he will bid the game in hearts; otherwise he will bid three notrump.

(3)   ♠ 8   ♡ K J 9 5 4   ◊ A Q J 5   ♣ K 10 4

Bid three diamonds. This bid indicates unbalanced distribution. If partner has three hearts, he will show a preference by bidding three hearts. Otherwise he will probably bid three notrump, particularly if he has good values in the unbid suits. If he has doubts about the unbid suits and only two hearts, he may raise diamonds and you will try five diamonds.

✔ AFTER A ONE-OVER-ONE RESPONSE

Partner's response has shown length in the suit he has bid and a count of 6 to 18 points. The response is forcing for one round.

- With 12 to 16 points, make a *minimum* rebid: one notrump, a rebid of your own suit, a raise of partner's suit, or a bid in a new suit.

- With 17 to 19 points, make an *invitational* bid: two notrump, a jump in your own or partner's suit, or a non-jump bid in a new suit. (The non-jump bid in a new suit may be either weak or invitational. When possible, choose a bid that more clearly describes the nature of your hand.)

- With 20 points or more, make a *forcing* bid or jump to game: three notrump, game in partner's suit, a jump bid in a new suit. A jump to game in your own suit promises excellent distribution but does not guarantee a large number of high-card points.

SOUTH	WEST	NORTH	EAST
1 ♡	Pass	1 ♠	Pass
?			

(1)   ♠ 6 3   ♡ K Q J 7   ◇ A J 8 4   ♣ Q J 5

Bid one notrump. This shows a balanced minimum opening bid, which is exactly what you have.

(2) ♠ 6 3   ♡ K Q J 7 6   ◊ A J 8   ♣ Q J 5

Bid two hearts. A minimum opening bid with a rebiddable suit.

(3) ♠ K J 5   ♡ K Q J 7 6   ◊ A J 8   ♣ 6 3

Bid two spades. A minimum opening bid with support for partner's suit. Note that a raise in partner's suit is more encouraging than a rebid in your own.

(4) ♠ 6 3   ♡ A Q J 7 6   ◊ A J 8 4 3   ♣ 3

Bid two diamonds. Unbalanced distribution. The hand may be minimum or in the 17-to-19-point range. Partner tends to bid again if he can find an excuse to do so, but he is at liberty to pass if he has a weak hand with more diamonds than hearts.

(5) ♠ 6 3   ♡ K Q J 7   ◊ A K J 4   ♣ K Q 5

Bid two notrump. This shows about 19 or 20 points, with balanced distribution and strength in the unbid suits. It is often the best bid even when you have only 18 points.

(6) ♠ K 3   ♡ A Q J 9 7 6   ◊ A Q 4   ♣ 6 3

Bid three hearts. This bid, invitational but not forcing, shows a strong rebiddable suit (six cards or more) in a hand of 17 to 19 points.

(7) ♠ K 8 5 3   ♡ A Q J 7 6   ◊ K Q 5   ♣ 3

Bid three spades. This raise, highly invitational but not forcing, promises strong 4-card trump support and about 18 or 19 points in support of partner's suit. The count is 15 points in high cards and 3 points for the singleton (valuing your hand as *responder*, since you plan to play at partner's suit).

(8)   ♠ Q 5   ♡ A Q J 7   ◇ A K J 5   ♣ 7 3 2

Bid two diamonds. Partner may pass, but he will tend to bid if he has some excuse to do so. If he bids two notrump, you will be delighted to raise to game. Note that you didn't open one notrump in the first place because the strength was too concentrated in only two suits.

(9)   ♠ Q 5   ♡ K Q J 7   ◇ A K J 4   ♣ K Q 5

Bid three notrump. This shows about 21 or 22 points, with balanced distribution and strength in the unbid suits. It is often the best bid with a good 20-point hand.

(10)   ♠ A 5   ♡ K Q J 7 6   ◇ A K J 4 3   ♣ 3

Bid three diamonds. This jump rebid is forcing to game. You may have a good two-suiter, as in the example; you may be planning to raise partner's suit later; or you may hope that partner can try game in notrump.

(11)   ♠ A J 5 3   ♡ K Q J 7 6   ◇ A K 4   ♣ 3

Bid three diamonds. You plan to show the spade support later, hinting at a slam and promising a singleton in your unbid suit. (See Chapter 7, How to Bid Your Slams.)

(12)   ♠ A 5   ♡ K Q J 7 6   ◇ A K Q 4   ♣ 6 3

Bid three diamonds. You are ready for almost anything. If partner rebids in either major, you will raise that major to game. If partner bids three notrump, you will accept the contract. If he raises diamonds, you will go on to game in that suit.

(13)   ♠ K Q 5 3   ♡ A Q J 7 6   ◇ A Q   ♣ 7 4

> *Bid four spades.* This raise promises strong 4-card
> trump support and about 20 or 21 points in support
> of partner's suit. You have 18 points in high cards
> and 2 points for the two doubletons. You tend to
> deny a singleton because with such great strength
> and a singleton you would usually jump in a third
> suit in order to show the singleton, as in Hand 11.

(14)   ♠ Q 5 3   ♡ K Q J 10 7 6 4   ◇ A K   ♣ 3

> *Bid four hearts.* This promises a very good suit and
> a reasonable play for game, but does not guarantee
> great high-card strength. You have only 15 points
> in high cards. You should make a game if partner
> has as little as some spades headed by K-J, since
> you will then lose only one spade, one heart, and
> one club.

√ AFTER A TWO-OVER-ONE RESPONSE

Partner's response has shown a good suit and 10 to
18 points. He will almost always bid again.

- With 12 to 16 points, make a minimum rebid of some
  kind: bid two of your own suit, two notrump, three
  of partner's suit, or two of a new suit. A rebid of two
  of your own suit is the most discouraging and should
  be made when you have only 12 to 14 points.
- With 17 to 19 points, make a strong rebid: a jump in
  your own suit, partner's suit, or notrump; or a bid
  in a new suit.
- With 20 points or more, bid game or make a forcing
  bid.

SOUTH	WEST	NORTH	EAST
1 ♡	Pass	2 ♣	Pass
?			

(1)   ♠ A 9 4   ♡ A Q J 7 5   ◊ 8 3 2   ♣ J 4
Bid two hearts. A minimum bid; a rebiddable suit.

(2)   ♠ 9 4   ♡ A Q J 7 5   ◊ A Q J 4   ♣ 8 5
Bid two diamonds. Promises a biddable suit and awaits partner's next move. Occasionally, it is true, partner will pass; but in such a case there is no game in the hand.

(3)   ♠ K 9 4   ♡ A Q J 7 5   ◊ K J 4   ♣ 8 5
Bid two notrump. You have 14 points in high cards and should count something for length in hearts. Your rebid in notrump promises balanced distribution, strength in at least one of the unbid suits, and somewhat more than the barest minimum opening bid.

(4)   ♠ 8 5   ♡ A Q J 7 5   ◊ A 4   ♣ K 9 4 2
Bid three clubs. This promises good trumps and about 15 to 17 points in support. You would avoid getting up to the level of three with only 12 to 14 points.

(5)   ♠ A 9   ♡ A Q J 7 5 4   ◊ A 3 2   ♣ J 4
Bid three hearts. This shows a strong 6-card or longer suit in a hand of 17 to 19 points. Partner is allowed to pass if he has a "club bust" and was planning to bid two clubs and then three clubs. Partner is expected to accept the invitation to game with any 10-point or better hand.

(6) ♠ 8 5   ♡ A Q J 7 5   ◊ A K Q 4   ♣ 8 5

Bid two diamonds. This bid may be made on a good hand when the strength is concentrated in the two suits. You cannot quite make a jump bid.

(7) ♠ K 9 5   ♡ A Q J 4   ◊ A K J 6   ♣ 8 5

Bid three notrump. According to the textbook this bid shows 19 to 21 points, but practical players jump to three notrump with a good 18 points (and sometimes with an especially good 17 points). A jump to three notrump with 20 points is a shameful underbid; with 21 points, an outright abomination.

(8) ♠ 8 5   ♡ A Q J 5   ◊ A Q 5   ♣ K 9 3 2

Bid three clubs. This excursion to the level of three shows about 15 to 17 points in support of partner's suit.

(9) ♠ 8   ♡ A Q J 5 4   ◊ A Q 5   ♣ K 9 3 2

Bid four clubs. This jump raise promises good trumps, a singleton or void suit, and about 18 or 19 points in support of partner's suit. (When you jump past three notrump, be sure you have a good reason—such as a singleton or a void suit.)

(10) ♠ A K J 8   ♡ A Q J 5 4   ◊ K 9 3   ♣ 2

Bid two spades. This *reverse* bid (in a higher suit than your first bid) guarantees at least 18 points and is virtually forcing in expert games. (See next page.)

(11) ♠ 8   ♡ A Q J 5 4   ◊ K Q J 8 5   ♣ A 3

Bid three diamonds. You are willing to insist on game no matter what partner has for his two-over-one response.

(12)   ♠ 8   ♡ K Q J 10 7 6 3   ◇ A K   ♣ 8 3 2

     Bid four hearts. The jump to game does not promise great high-card strength. You are willing to be in game if partner has a good club suit and nothing else.

√ REVERSE AND SKIP-LEVEL BIDS

     As we have seen, you don't need tremendous strength to bid at the level of one. You must have fairly good values, however, to get up to the level of two. You need a very decent hand to drive the bidding up to the level of three.

     The following is strong bidding even though no jump bid has been made:

SOUTH	WEST	NORTH	EAST
1 ♡	Pass	2 ◇	Pass
3 ♣			

     South should have some such hand as:

     ♠ 8   ♡ A K J 9 4   ◇ K 5   ♣ A Q J 8 3

     It is hard to imagine any hand that North should pass with, even though technically no forcing bid has been made.

     What should South do with weaker hands? For example:

     ♠ 8   ♡ A Q J 9 4   ◇ 6 5   ♣ A J 8 3 2

     South's rebid should be two hearts, not three clubs. He cannot afford to indicate substantial strength when he has only a near-minimum opening bid.

     The same principle applies when the opening bidder asks his partner to show a preference at the level of three:

SOUTH	WEST	NORTH	EAST
1 ♡	Pass	1 NT	Pass
2 ♠			

South shows more hearts than spades. He wants North to go back to hearts (at the level of *three*) unless he has a decided preference for spades. Since South has bid his suits in the *reverse* of the normal order (the higher suit is normally bid first), his spade bid is called a *reverse*.

The *reverse* shows strength only when it compels partner to go to the level of three. A reverse at the level of one may be made with a minimum opening bid:

SOUTH	WEST	NORTH	EAST
1 ◇	Pass	1 ♡	Pass
1 ♠			

South may have a 13-point hand. However:

SOUTH	WEST	NORTH	EAST
1 ◇	Pass	2 ♣	Pass
2 ♠			

South must have a *good* hand.

Is a reverse forcing? In an expert game a reverse is practically never passed. It doesn't matter whether or not the players admit that the reverse is forcing; in effect, they treat it as a forcing bid.

This is somewhat extreme. In a good partnership you can distinguish between the reverse that is surely *honest* and the reverse that may well be *artificial*.

An expert often makes a reverse bid in an "unbiddable" suit when he likes his partner's response. The idea is to delay the raise and thus indicate extreme shortness in the unbid suit. For example:

SOUTH	WEST	NORTH	EAST
1 ◇	Pass	1 ♠	Pass
2 ♡			

South may have some such hand as:

♠ A J 9 3   ♡ A 7 4   ◇ A Q J 9 3   ♣ 4

South plans to raise to four spades at his next turn. The reverse in hearts is artificial, enabling South to indicate his shortness in the unbid clubs. If North passes two hearts, South will probably make a short sharp speech.

The reverse in this case is honest:

SOUTH	WEST	NORTH	EAST
1 ◇	Pass	1 NT	Pass
2 ♡			

South cannot be planning some spectacular bid for a later turn since North has not bid a suit. If South is passed at two hearts in *this* situation he will be disappointed, but his language will be quite moderate.

✔ REBIDS BY THE RESPONDER

By the time your second turn comes as responder, you usually have a fair idea of the opening bidder's strength. You can therefore tell whether your objective for the hand should be part score, game, or slam.

In many situations your partner's bidding asks you to indicate whether you have minimum or maximum values for the response you have already made. In some, your partner describes his own hand and leaves the next move up to you.

When you have not been forced, guide yourself by this schedule:

Your Points	*How Often to Respond*
0 to 5	Not even once
6 to 10	Once
11 or 12	Twice, without forcing to game
13 to 17	Make sure of getting to game
18 or more	Think about a slam

When your partner has made a strong bid, add his points to yours. If the total is about 26, head toward game even though you have a weak hand.

If you have made a two-over-one response, you should have had a rebid in mind. Carry through with that or some other reasonable bid. Don't blow hot and then cold on the same hand.

✓ ACCEPTING AN INVITATION

In some situations, as we have seen, the opening bidder makes an invitational bid at his second turn. Responder may accept or decline the invitation. The choice does not depend on whether the responder has a good or bad hand as hands in *general* go; it depends only on whether he has more or less than his partner has a right to expect.

For example:

SOUTH	WEST	NORTH	EAST
1 ♡	Pass	2 ♡	Pass
3 ♡	Pass	?	

North is *invited* but not forced to bid game. He may have:

♠ 8   ♡ K 9 6 3   ◇ K 7 5 4 2   ♣ 8 5 3

This is a very weak hand by itself, but North should

cheerfully bid four hearts. He has 6 points in high cards
and 3 points for the singleton—an excellent 9 points.
Since North would have raised with only 6 points, he has
substantially more than South has a right to expect. That
is the test.

Similarly:

SOUTH	WEST	NORTH	EAST
1 ♡	Pass	1 ♠	Pass
3 ♠	Pass	?	

North is invited, but not forced, to bid a game. He may
have:

♠ A 9 7 6 4   ♡ 8 3 2   ◇ A 6 4   ♣ 5 2

He should bid four spades like a shot. He has only 8
points in high cards and 1 point for the doubleton, but
he would have made his response with only 6 points. His
3 *extra* points enable him to accept the invitation. Another
way of looking at it is that South's jump raise shows
about 18 or 19 points in support of spades. North adds
his own points and sees that the partnership total should
be 27 or 28 points—which should be enough for game.

✓ TIPS ON REBIDDING

- If your hand calls for a bid of some kind, make the
  bid that gives the best description of your hand.
- With trump support, raise a major suit.
- With a good suit, bid it.
- With balanced distribution and no fine suit, bid no-
  trump.
- With unbalanced distribution, bid a suit, not no-
  trump.
- The best way to show weakness is to pass—provided
  you are not forced to bid.

TWO-BIDS—STRONG AND WEAK

√ Requirements for a Strong Two-   √ The Weak Two-Bid
Bid   √ Responding to a Weak Two-Bid
√ Responding to a Two-Bid   √ The Opening Bid of Two Clubs
√ Rebids After a Two-Bid   √ In Short
√ Limited Two-Bids

MOST PLAYERS USE the opening bid of two in a suit to show a tremendously powerful hand—enough for game opposite almost any kind of weak hand. Partner is therefore instructed to keep the bidding open until game is reached (or until the opponents have been doubled for penalties).

V REQUIREMENTS FOR A STRONG TWO-BID

Most bridge books give you a schedule to tell you when to make a two-bid. You need so many points with a 5-card suit, somewhat less with a 6-card suit, something else with a 7-card suit or a two-suiter—and so on.

Don't you believe it! In the first place, you should not be counting points for a two-bid. In the second place, who on earth bothers to remember such a complicated schedule?

There *is* a way to know when your hand is good enough for a strong two-bid, but it has nothing to do with points. It is based on *both* playing tricks *and* Quick Tricks (see Chapter 1, How to Value Your Hand).

An opening bid of two in a suit says that you expect to

75

have a reasonable play for *game* even if partner has no high cards at all. You expect to have a reasonable play for *slam* if partner has moderate values.

What kind of hand measures up to both of these requirements?

You need a very long suit or a good, solid two-suiter. You should be able to look at the suits and say, "I have one loser here and one loser there; otherwise these suits are solid."

For example:

♠ K Q J 9 4   ♡ A K Q 10 6   ◇ A 2   ♣ 2

Bid two spades. If partner has no high cards, you will lose one spade, one diamond, and one club. You may also lose another trick in either spades or hearts. It's reasonable to expect your partner to have three or more small cards in either spades or hearts. If so, you should be able to hold the loss to three tricks at a contract of four in *his* better major suit.

However, there is a different story to tell with:

♠ K 9 6 4 2   ♡ K Q 6 3 2   ◇ A K   ♣ A

Your points and distribution are the same, but the suits are too weak for a two-bid. You can't add up enough *tricks,* and *tricks* are what count.

To make a two-bid in spades or hearts you should expect to win at least nine tricks even if your partner has a terrible hand. In a minor suit you need at least *ten* tricks (somewhat less if your hand is balanced enough to play at three notrump).

If your suits are so broken that you can't clearly tell how many tricks you can win, don't make a two-bid. Start out modestly with a one-bid (or with two notrump if the hand qualifies) and see if your partner can give you the slight encouragement you need.

So much for the playing tricks. What about the Quick Tricks?

You need at least 4 Quick Tricks, usually in three suits.

Why do you need Quick Tricks? What's wrong with making a bid of two spades with such a hand as:

♠ A K Q J 10 9 8 7 6 5   ♡ 4   ◊ 3   ♣ 2

This hand will surely produce ten tricks at spades. The only thing that can beat you is a revoke.

The trouble is that your partner will put you in a *slam* if he has a few scattered kings and queens. And *that* will beat you just as surely as a revoke.

You can handle this kind of one-suit monster with an opening bid of *one* spade. You will not be passed out. The *two*-bid should be reserved for hands of great *general* strength as well as great playing strength.

Test yourself on the following hands:

(1) ♠ A K J 10 5   ♡ A K J 7   ◊ A K 3   ♣ 4

Bid two spades. You should win four spades, two diamonds, and two hearts—eight tricks in all, and you have a chance for another trick or so in hearts. The fine Quick Trick count should persuade you to be slightly optimistic in counting the playing tricks.

(2) ♠ A Q 10 7 4   ♡ A Q 8 6 3   ◊ A K   ♣ 4

Bid one spade. You have the Quick Tricks, but your suits are so broken that you cannot gauge the playing tricks. Change one of the small hearts to the jack, and you would open with two spades.

(3) ♠ A Q J 7 4   ♡ A Q 8   ◊ A Q 3   ♣ A 5

Bid two notrump, not two spades. You have the Quick Tricks for a two-bid, but not the playing tricks. A hand with strength in all *four* suits often qualifies for an opening bid of two or three notrump if it is not quite good enough for two of a suit.

(4) ♠ 3   ♡ A K Q 10 7 3 2   ◇ A K 5   ♣ 8 4

Bid two hearts. You prefer slightly greater strength in Quick Tricks, but settle for 4 Quick Tricks when the playing-trick requirement is well met. You should win the seven hearts and the two top diamonds even if partner has nothing. Game is assured if he turns up with as little as the queen of diamonds, perhaps even less.

(5) ♠ 3   ♡ A K 5   ◇ A K Q 10 7 3 2   ♣ A 4

Bid two diamonds. The two-bid in a minor suit is usually stronger than a two-bid in a major suit, because a minor-suit game requires one trick more.

V RESPONDING TO A TWO-BID

In responding to your partner's two-bid, your first duty is to say whether or not you have slam values. If you have such values, you make a positive response; otherwise you make a *negative* response.

You don't need to count points; you are not interested in stray queens or jacks. You should count primarily aces and kings; secondarily, trump support and ruffing tricks.

- Make a *positive* response to a strong two-bid when you have better than 1 Quick Trick.
- Otherwise make the *negative* response of two notrump.

Any response other than two notrump is positive.

A positive response should be descriptive. With good support for partner's suit, raise; otherwise bid a suit of your own or jump to *three* notrump.

SOUTH	WEST	NORTH	EAST
2 ♡	Pass	?	

(1) ♠ J 4   ♡ 9 7 4 3 2   ◇ Q J 5   ♣ Q J 6

Bid two notrump. You will have a chance later to show your fine heart support. You first duty is to deny slam values.

(2) ♠ 8 5 4   ♡ Q 4 3 2   ◇ K 5 2   ♣ K 5 2

Bid three hearts. You have good trump support and better than 1 Quick Trick.

(3) ♠ K J 8 5 4   ♡ 4 3   ◇ A 5 2   ♣ 9 6 3

Bid two spades. With better than 1½ Quick Tricks you have ample values for a positive response. The suit bid is the best description of your values. If your partner is interested in aces, he can make a cue bid or use the Blackwood Convention (see Chapter 7, How to Bid Your Slams).

(4) ♠ K J 8   ♡ 4 3   ◇ A 5 4 2   ♣ Q 9 6 3

Bid three notrump. You have the values for a positive response, and a bid in notrump best describes your hand. The jump is necessary to make it clear that your bid is positive rather than the negative two notrump.

All the foregoing are *natural* responses to opening two-bids. Some players prefer ace-showing responses, but these are less flexible (see Chapter 33, Modern Bidding Conventions).

✔ REBIDS AFTER A TWO-BID

When the first response has been two notrump, the opener makes a descriptive rebid. He may show a second suit, rebid the original suit, or raise notrump.

SOUTH	WEST	NORTH	EAST
2 ♠	Pass	2 NT	Pass
?			

(1)   ♠ A K Q J 9 4   ♡ A K Q 10 6   ◇ 2   ♣ 3

Bid three hearts. You intend to end in four spades or four hearts, whichever partner prefers. If partner bids three notrump or four of a minor at his second turn (showing no real preference for either major), you will bid four spades. Partner may have no preference, but *you* do.

(2)   ♠ A K J 10 8 5 3   ♡ A K 6   ◇ A 4   ♣ 2

Bid three spades. Partner must still keep bidding until game is reached. There is no advantage in jumping to four spades, and there is a great *dis*advantage. You are perfectly willing to give partner the chance to show a long suit belatedly. If he bids four hearts, you will raise to *six* hearts; if he bids anything else, you will stop at four spades.

(3)   ♠ A Q J 10 4   ♡ A Q J   ◇ A K 3   ♣ A 5

Bid three notrump. This shows strength in all four suits as well as a very strong spade suit.

When partner immediately raises your two-bid, you should make some move in the direction of slam. If you have barely enough for the two-bid, make a cautious move; if you have substantial extra strength, you can afford to bid more vigorously. You should follow this general principle: *A two-bid plus a positive response equals a slam.*

If the first response is a bid in a new suit, you can go ahead in the usual way. That is, you may raise to show support, rebid your own suit, show a new suit, or bid notrump.

SOUTH	WEST	NORTH	EAST
2 ♡	Pass	3 ♡	Pass
?			

(1)   ♠ A 5   ♡ A K Q 10 6 3   ◇ A K 8 5   ♣ 3

Bid four diamonds. You are interested in a slam if partner has help for the diamonds.

(2)   ♠ A K   ♡ A K Q 10 6 3   ◇ K Q J 5   ♣ 3

Bid four notrump (Blackwood Convention). You are interested only in the number of aces held by partner. (See Chapter 7, How to Bid Your Slams.)

SOUTH	WEST	NORTH	EAST
2 ♡	Pass	2 ♠	Pass
?			

(1)   ♠ A Q 7 3   ♡ A K J 10 6 3   ◇ A K   ♣ 3

Bid three spades or four notrump. You will not settle for less than six spades. The only problem is whether or not to bid *seven.*

(2)   ♠ 3   ♡ A K J 10 6 3   ◇ A K   ♣ A Q 7 3

Bid three hearts. You plan to bid clubs at your next turn. The delay in showing the clubs should indicate the hearts are *much* longer and stronger.

(3)   ♠ A 3   ♡ A K J 10 6   ◇ A K J 8 5   ♣ 3

Bid three diamonds. If partner rebids the spades, you can then afford to raise his suit.

Strangely enough, most of the ambition and energy should be displayed by the responder. The opening bidder has shown so much strength by his opening bid that he can afford to coast and leave it up to his partner. If the responder makes unmistakable moves toward a slam, the opening bidder will usually meet him halfway.

✓ LIMITED TWO-BIDS

A few experts advocate an opening bid of two on hands
slightly weaker than those described thus far in this chapter. If partner makes a negative response, the partnership may stop short of game.

SOUTH	WEST	NORTH	EAST
2 ♡	Pass	2 NT	Pass
3 ♡	Pass	?	

North is allowed to pass—provided that he and his partner have definitely agreed to use "limited" two-bids. (It
is also necessary for them to describe their understanding
to the opponents—preferably at the beginning of the
rubber.)

However:

SOUTH	WEST	NORTH	EAST
2 ♡	Pass	2 NT	Pass
3 ♢	Pass	?	

The auction is now forcing to game. South indicates
this by showing a new suit.

If the first response is positive, the auction is forcing to
game even though the opener merely rebids his suit.

Very few players have adopted limited two-bids, and
therefore very little is known about their value in actual
competition. There are good arguments pro and con—in
theory.

In the absence of a very clear discussion, always assume
that your partner's two-bid is meant to be forcing all the
way to game. Most bridge crimes go unnoticed and many
others are quickly and tolerantly dismissed, but few players are amiable enough to forgive a partner who passes a
forcing bid.

✓ THE WEAK TWO-BID

Many of the leading American players use the opening
bid of two as a shutout bid. It shows a good suit in a
hand that is not quite worth a normal opening bid. (The
opening bid of two *clubs* is, however, reserved for all tremendously powerful hands—regardless of which suit is
longest and strongest.)

Used wisely, the weak two-bid can be very helpful.
Most players overuse it.

A weak two-bid should promise:

- A good 6-card suit, worth five playing tricks
- 1½ to 2 Quick Tricks, mostly in the bid suit
- Less than the requirements for a one-bid

It is the sort of hand that is worth an overcall at the
level of two, but not quite worth an opening bid of one.

(1)   ♠ K Q J 7 6 3   ♡ 8 2   ◇ K 9 4   ♣ 6 3
   Bid two spades. The spades are likely to produce five
   tricks; the hand has 1½ Quick Tricks, mostly in
   spades.

(2)   ♠ Q 10 7 6 3 2   ♡ 8 2   ◇ A Q J   ♣ 6 3
   Pass. Not enough strength in the long suit; too much
   strength outside.

(3)   ♠ K Q J 7 6 3   ♡ 8   ◇ A 9 4 2   ♣ 6 3
   Bid one spade. Just a little too strong for a two-bid.
   Beware of making a weak two-bid with 6-4-2-1 (or
   stronger) distribution or with a 7-card suit. Your
   partner will have too much trouble deciding when
   to try for game and when to pass.

√ RESPONDING TO A WEAK TWO-BID

A response in a new suit or of two notrump is forcing for one round. A raise to three of the bid suit is usually treated as weak, adding to the shutout.

The responder needs somewhat more than the value of an opening bid to consider a game. If each partner has an opening bid, the partnership can usually make a game. If one partner has slightly less than an opening bid, therefore, the other needs slightly more to make up the difference.

The responder may likewise bid game when he has distributional values instead of high cards. He may bid game out of fright when he has good distributional help but very little in high cards.

SOUTH	WEST	NORTH	EAST
2 ♡	Pass	?	

(1)   ♠ A K J 8 5   ♡ 6 2   ◊ A Q 3 2   ♣ 8 2

Bid two spades. Game is likely if partner has a spade fit, but not otherwise.

(2)   ♠ A K J 8   ♡ 6 2   ◊ A Q 3 2   ♣ Q 8 2

Bid two notrump. You want to get to three notrump or four hearts. The opener is invited to bid the suit in which he has side strength. If that happens to be clubs, you will bid three notrump. Otherwise you will get to four hearts.

(3)   ♠ A K J 8   ♡ A 7 6   ◊ A 6 3 2   ♣ 8 2

Bid four hearts. Don't consider a slam. Remember that your partner has less than a normal opening bid.

(4) ♠ 8 2   ♥ 1 0 7 6 2   ♦ K J 7 6 3 2   ♣ 8

> *Bid four hearts.* Of course your partner cannot make
> four hearts. However, the opponents can probably
> make 11 or 12 tricks at one of the black suits. Your
> bid may crowd them so that they must guess which
> their best suit is. If they guess wrong, your partner
> may have enough to beat them. Or they may not bid
> enough; they may play a cold slam hand at a mere
> game. You may even buy the hand, amazingly
> enough, since each opponent may credit you with
> all of the missing strength (actually held by his part-
> ner).

✔ THE OPENING BID OF TWO CLUBS

If you use weak two-bids, the opening bid of two clubs
is used for all very powerful hands. These fall into two
classes:

- Game going hands in a suit
- Notrump hands of 23 points or more

The game-going suit hand is our old friend the *strong*
two-bid. The opener starts with two clubs but bids his
real suit at his next turn. (The opener does not promise
a good club suit; if he has club length, it is purely co-
incidental.)

The negative response to two clubs is two diamonds.
Any other response (even two notrump) is positive.

SOUTH	WEST	NORTH	EAST
2 ♣	Pass	2 ♦	Pass
2 ♠			

South has a strong two-bid in spades. North lacks the values for a positive response.

The rest of the auction proceeds in much the same way as though *strong* two-bids were being used. But note that very often a round of bidding is saved by the economical bid of two clubs.

The opening bid of two clubs gains most when the opener has a very strong notrump hand. He shows 23 or 24 points by bidding a *minimum* in notrump at his second turn; 25 or 26 points by making a *jump* bid in notrump.

SOUTH	WEST	NORTH	EAST
2 ♣	Pass	2 ◇	Pass
2 NT			

South should have 23 or 24 points, with balanced distribution and all suits stopped. For example:

♠ K J 8   ♡ A Q 9   ◇ A K J 5   ♣ A Q 4

North may pass with 0 to 2 points. He should proceed to game with 3 points or more.

What about the *opening* bid of two notrump? That can be used for a hand of 21 or 22 points. Responder may pass with 0 to 4 points but should proceed to game with 5 points or more.

Another possible auction:

SOUTH	WEST	NORTH	EAST
2 ♣	Pass	2 ◇	Pass
3 NT			

South should have 25 or 26 points, with balanced distribution and all suits stopped. For example:

♠ A K   ♡ K J 10 8   ◇ A K Q 4   ♣ K Q 9

South would make the same bids over a positive response. For example:

SOUTH	WEST	NORTH	EAST
2 ♣	Pass	2 ♠	Pass
3 NT			

South has the 25-26-point hand. The partnership can surely make a slam. North will, of course, make further bids.

One of the advantages of this method is that the standard opening bid of two notrump is now broken down into two levels—the 21-22-point hand and the 23-24-point hand.

This enables the responder to gauge the power of the hand more accurately.

Sometimes the responder starts out with a negative response and then comes to life with a slam try. This indicates that he has points but not aces and kings. For example:

SOUTH	WEST	NORTH	EAST
2 ♣	Pass	2 ◇	Pass
2 NT	Pass	6 NT	

North should have some such hand as:

♠ 3 2   ♡ Q J 6 2   ◇ Q J 4   ♣ K J 8 4

He should make the negative response first. His hand may be worth very little if South has a two-bid in spades. When South shows the 23-24-point notrump hand, however, North can revalue his hand. Now his 10 points are enough to give the partnership a total of 33 or 34 points, enough for a slam.

✓ IN SHORT

A strong two-bid is forcing to game. It promises:

- A solid or nearly solid suit
- Within one or two playing tricks of game
- 4 or more Quick Tricks in three suits

The negative response is two notrump.
Any other response is positive, promising better than 1 Quick Trick.

.   .   .

A weak two-bid shows a good suit but less than a normal opening bid.
A response of two notrump or a new suit is forcing for one round.

.   .   .

An opening bid of two clubs (when the partners use weak two-bids) shows either:

- A strong two-bid in *any* suit, *or*
- A notrump hand of 23 points or more

The negative response is two diamonds.
The opener rebids in a suit if he has the ordinary game-going hand in a suit.
A minimum rebid in notrump shows 23-24 points.
A jump rebid in notrump shows 25-26 points.

HOW TO BID YOUR SLAMS

√ Normal Slam Requirements
√ Controls
√ The Blackwood Convention
√ When Are You Conventional?
√ Stopping at Five Notrump
√ Showing a Void Suit
√ The Gerber Convention

√ Cue Bidding
√ Fake Cue Bids
√ Help from the Enemy
√ Showing a Singleton
√ Direct Slam Bidding
√ Declarer's Skill

THE AVERAGE RUBBER is worth about 800 points; the bonus for a slam runs from 500 to 1500 points—or somewhat more than the value of the average rubber. That's why good slam bidding can be the difference between winning and losing bridge.

One way to get to a slam is to bid it first and think about it later. Another way is to be as timid as a high-school girl out on her first date.

As you might expect, neither attitude makes good sense. To get the best results you must be both bold and thoughtful.

The boldness will come by itself if you know what to be thoughtful about.

√ NORMAL SLAM REQUIREMENTS

Think about slam when you have:

- High cards or good suits
- Controls

High cards: There are 40 high-card points in the complete deck. If the opponents have 8 points or more, they may well have enough material to win two tricks—either immediately, as with two aces, or eventually. If they have only 7 points or less, you have a reasonable chance to limit them to one trick. *Hence, if you intend to bid a slam on sheer power, you need about 33 of the 40 points in the deck.*

You can get by with fewer points if you have strong suits or unusually good distribution. Conversely, when the partnership hands fit very poorly, you may need 34 or 35 points for the slam.

Good suits: The low cards of a powerful suit eventually take tricks just as though they were aces or kings. To take the most extreme example, you can make a grand slam with only 10 points in high cards—if you have all thirteen cards of a suit.

Many slams can be made with a strong trump suit and a strong side suit to furnish the bulk of the tricks. The normal bidding usually indicates if you have two powerful suits.

✓ CONTROLS

You can't make a small slam if the opponents take the first two tricks. To prevent this from happening you must *control* the first trick in all four suits, or at least the first trick in three suits and the second trick in the fourth suit.

Normally your control of a suit is the ace. Less often the control is a void suit when some other suit is trump.

In one suit the partnership may be satisfied with a second-round control. Usually this is the king. Occasionally it is a singleton with trumps on the side.

When you have all the controls in your own hand, you can decide all by yourself whether or not to bid a slam. If you are missing a control or two, you must try to find out if your partner has them. If you are missing more than two controls, the burden of trying for a slam is usually not on *your* shoulders.

✓ THE BLACKWOOD CONVENTION

The easiest way to find out about controls is to use the Blackwood Convention. This asks your partner how many aces he has.

A *bid of four notrump*, especially after the partnership has agreed on a suit, *asks partner to show how many aces he holds:*

Number of Aces	Response
None or all four	5 ♣
One	5 ♦
Two	5 ♥
Three	5 ♠

After getting partner's response, you can count your own aces to see if any are missing. If two are missing, you must stop at five. Your partner must accept your decision because you know—and he doesn't—how many aces are missing.

If only one ace is missing, you can bid six of the agreed suit, or possibly six notrump. Your partner must not bid a grand slam because an ace must be missing. Here again, you know and he doesn't.

If no aces are missing, you may bid five notrump to find out how many kings your partner has. He answers in much the same way:

Number of Kings	Response
None	6 ♣
One	6 ◇
Two	6 ♡
Three	6 ♠
Four	6 NT

Perhaps you noticed that the response is five clubs with either no aces or all four. If your partner can't tell whether you have all four aces or none at all, you can probably get a court order to keep him out of your games. The purpose of this little wrinkle is to give the partnership the chance to bid four notrump to ask for aces and then five notrump to ask for kings. (If the responder had to bid five notrump to show all four aces, there would be no way to ask about kings.)

The most important thing to know about the Blackwood Convention is when to use it and when to use some other method of trying for a slam. Most players overuse Blackwood.

Take a situation like this:

SOUTH	NORTH
1 ♠	3 ♠
4 NT	

You are South, and your bid of four notrump is the beginning of the Blackwood sequence. When you get your partner's response, *you should know what to do next.* This is true if you have such a hand as:

♠ A K J 8 5   ♡ K Q J 4 2   ◇ A 3   ♣ 5

If partner has no aces at all, he will bid five clubs. You will see that two aces are missing, and will sign off at five spades. Partner will pass, and you will be safe.

If partner has one ace, he will bid five diamonds. You will see that one ace is missing, but you will be confident that a small slam is very safe. You will jump to six spades, and partner will pass.

If partner has two aces, he will bid five hearts. You will thereupon jump to *seven* spades. Your partner should have two aces and either five small trumps or four to the queen. The odds are overwhelming that you need nothing else for the grand slam.

Now take the same bidding situation and change your hand:

♠ A Q 10 8 5   ♡ K Q J   ◇ A Q 3   ♣ 5 2

What can you find out by bidding four notrump? If your partner bids five diamonds, showing one ace, where are you?

Partner may have:

♠ K J 7 3   ♡ A 10 5 4   ◇ K J 10   ♣ Q 4

and the opponents can take the first two club tricks.

But partner may have:

♠ K 9 7 3   ♡ A 10 5 4 3   ◇ 4 2   ♣ K Q

and a small slam is laydown.

These are types, not just particular hands. The trouble is that you don't know how (or whether) to proceed without knowing which type of hand your partner has.

You're no better off if your partner shows *two* aces by bidding five hearts. He may have this type of hand:

♠ K 9 7 3   ♡ A 10 5 4   ◇ K 4 2   ♣ A 4

and a grand slam is laydown.

But he may have *this* type:

♠ K J 7 3   ♡ A 10   ◇ 7 5 4 2   ♣ A J 4

and you may be unable to make even *five* spades!

What have we learned from this discussion? That you

must not ask a question when the answer will do you no good.

Use Blackwood when you have good suits, with aces, kings, or singletons in the shorter suits. Don't use Blackwood when you have a worthless doubleton or a void in an unbid suit.

✓ WHEN ARE YOU CONVENTIONAL?

Not all bids of four notrump should be interpreted as part of the Blackwood Convention. However, if you want to use four notrump in certain situations as a *natural* bid, make sure that your partner has the same ideas.

For example, take this case:

SOUTH	NORTH
1 NT	4 NT

Most experts treat this as a natural, invitational bid, not part of Blackwood. North knows that the opening bid shows 16 to 18 points. He should have 15 or 16 points of his own. He wants the opener to pass with 16 points, to bid slam with 18 points, and to use his judgment with 17 points.

A similar situation:

SOUTH	NORTH
2 NT	4 NT

A natural, invitational bid. South has shown 22 to 24 points. North should have about 9 or 10 points. He wants the opener to pass with 22 points, to bid slam with 24 points, to use his judgment with the middle value of 23 points.

Not all experts agree on the raise of notrump that occurs after a suit has been bid:

SOUTH	NORTH
1 ♣	1 ♡
2 NT	4 NT

Is this Blackwood or natural?

This is something you should agree on with your favorite partner. With everybody else you'd better treat it as Blackwood, because the bid is almost surely meant that way. This may not be scientific, but you may as well recognize the fact that you live in an imperfect world.

∨ STOPPING AT FIVE NOTRUMP

In tournament bridge you sometimes stop at five notrump when it becomes obvious that slam is out of the question. For example:

SOUTH	NORTH
1 ♡	3 ♡
4 NT	5 ◇
?	

South has only one ace and therefore knows that the opponents have two aces. He bids five *spades*—a suit other than the "agreed" suit—to ask his partner to bid five notrump. When North bids five notrump, South will pass.

South cannot bid five notrump himself, since that would ask for kings.

Do not use this bidding maneuver in rubber bridge. Just play the hand at five of the agreed suit. Do not use it even in tournament bridge unless you are sure that your partner knows all about it. All experts *should* know it, but some of them *don't*.

✓ SHOWING A VOID SUIT

You would not dream of using the Blackwood Convention if you had a void suit. You would not then be interested in the *number* of aces held by your partner; you would want to know *which* aces he held.

There is, however, nothing to prevent your *partner* from bidding four notrump (Blackwood) when you have a void suit. Life and partners are like that.

For example:

SOUTH	NORTH
1 ♡	3 ♡
4 NT	?

You, North, hold:

♠ 8763   ♡ A1094   ◊ AQ962   ♣ ————

What response do you make to four notrump?

If you bid five hearts, showing just two aces, partner may make the wrong decision because he doesn't know about the void suit. For example, he may bid six hearts— and you would wonder about a grand slam.

In this situation, my own solution, with highly trusted partners only, is to jump to *six in the void suit!* In the example, North would jump to *six clubs*.

South would know that North has full value for his previous bids, with a void in clubs. South can decide whether to bid six or seven hearts, and North has no further problem.

There are two exceptions to this rule:

- If the void suit is higher than the agreed suit, jump to six in the *agreed* suit. In the example, if North were void in spades, he would jump from four no-trump to six hearts. South is expected to work out which suit is the void suit.
- If you have the slightest doubt about your partner, just make the normal Blackwood response. You'll look very foolish if a less reliable partner misunderstands you and lets you play the hand at six of your void suit!

/ THE GERBER CONVENTION

The Gerber Convention is much the same as Blackwood except that you ask for aces by jumping to four *clubs,* and you ask for kings by bidding five *clubs.* This keeps the bidding lower than Blackwood, but it interferes with normal club bids.

A few experts use Gerber instead of Blackwood, but most use Gerber only directly over an opening bid of one or two notrump. In these two cases only, a jump to four clubs asks the opening bidder to state how many aces he holds.

Number of Aces	*Response*
None or all four	4 ◇
One	4 ♡
Two	4 ♠
Three	4 NT

As in the Blackwood Convention, it is then possible to check on kings if no aces are missing. The player who has bid four clubs would bid five clubs to ask about kings.* The response is made in much the same way:

---

* Some players use a different bid to ask about kings, but the method described here is simpler and better.

Number of Kings	*Response*
None	5 ♦
One	5 ♡
Two	5 ♠
Three	5 NT
Four	6 ♣

The chief trouble with the Gerber Convention is that you use it about once every two or three years. By that time either you or your partner has forgotten about it. You wind up playing the hand at four clubs when you were trying to find out about a grand slam in spades!

Forget all about it in the average rubber bridge game. You can afford to miss a slam now and then, but it's too demoralizing to be dropped in some silly contract of four clubs or the like.

✓ CUE BIDDING

What about slam tries with hands that are not suitable for Blackwood? Sometimes you use *cue bids* and other times you use direct methods.

A cue bid is a show of strength intended as a slam try. You show some value (usually an ace) and give partner the chance to encourage or discourage your slam ambitions.

This is the most typical situation:

SOUTH	NORTH
1 ♠	3 ♠
4 ♦	

North's double raise in spades is forcing to game. If South is interested only in game, he bids four spades or three notrump. Only when South is interested in a slam does he bid a new suit in this situation.

For example, take the hand we were discussing before:

♠ A Q 10 8 5   ♡ K Q J   ◇ A Q 3   ♣ 5 2

You	Partner
1 ♠	3 ♠

After partner's double raise, you bid four diamonds. This "promises" the ace of diamonds and asks partner to indicate whether he is for or against a slam. It also denies the ace of clubs, because it is standard practice to show the cheapest ace when cue-bidding.

If partner has no aces, he returns to the agreed suit. In this case he would bid four spades.

If he can show an ace without getting past game, he almost invariably does so. If his ace cannot be shown below the game level, he has a choice. He may sign off in the agreed suit, or he may bid his ace even though this takes him past game. The sign-off is discouraging; a response at the level of five, very encouraging.

OPENER	RESPONDER
♠ A Q 10 8 5	♠ K 9 7 3
♡ K Q J	♡ 6 2
◇ A Q 3	◇ K 8 5
♣ 5 2	♣ A K 7 2

OPENER	RESPONDER
1 ♠	3 ♠
4 ◇ (1)	5 ♣ (2)
6 ♠ (3)	Pass (4)

(1) A cue bid, showing the bidder's cheapest ace. The failure to bid four clubs warns partner that the ace of clubs is missing.

(2) Responder takes the bidding past game to show

his ace. The *cheapest* ace here would be four hearts, so Responder *denies* the ace of hearts and shows the ace of clubs by this bid. If Responder had more of his strength in queens and jacks and less in aces and kings, he would sign off at four spades instead of bidding five clubs. Cue bidding is not automatic; it calls for judgment.

(3) Satisfied to be in a slam contract as long as partner promises a good hand that includes the ace of clubs.

(4) Has told his full story.

Compare the previous auction with one that stops short of a slam:

OPENER	RESPONDER
♠ A Q 10 8 5	♠ K 9 7 3
♡ K Q J	♡ A 2
◊ A Q 3	◊ K 8 5
♣ 5 2	♣ Q J 7 2

OPENER	RESPONDER
1 ♠	3 ♠
4 ◊ (1)	4 ♡ (2)
4 ♠ (3)	Pass (4)

(1) The same cue bid as before.

(2) Showing the cheapest ace. Responder may have more than one ace; if so, he will bid more later.

(3) Still worried about the clubs. Opener has suggested a slam but can do no more at this moment. The next move, if any, is up to Responder.

(4) The club danger stands out like the proverbial sore thumb. Opener's failure to bid four clubs means that the ace of clubs must be missing. Opener cannot have the king or singleton in clubs, since he has failed to use the Blackwood Convention. Opener cannot be void in clubs, or he would have bid something more vigorous than four spades at this stage. Responder would make another move

if he had the king or a singleton in clubs. Since Responder lacks a club control he must pass and be satisfied with a mere game. It is both dramatic and satisfactory to bid slams that can be made; it is just as profitable to stay out of slams that cannot be made.

Cue bids are better than Blackwood in three ways:

1. You can try for a slam without getting past game.

2. You can find out about a *particular* suit instead of getting only general information about aces and kings.

3. *Both* partners can use their judgment. With the Blackwood Convention one partner is the boss and the other is just a stooge.

For these reasons, experts use cue bids far oftener than Blackwood. The average player, however, acts as though it were immoral to bid a slam without first going through the mumbo-jumbo of four notrump.

✓ FAKE CUE BIDS

A player may sometimes "promise" an ace that he doesn't actually hold. For example, with the last hand:

♠ A Q 10 8 5   ♡ K Q J   ◇ A Q 3   ♣ 5 2

OPENER	RESPONDER
1 ♠	3 ♠
?	

If, as the Opener, you now want to bid four clubs with the two small clubs, the District Attorney's office will refuse to prosecute. The bid will probably get you some information, and may also discourage a club opening lead. Even if you stop short of a slam, you may profit by confusion in the ranks of the enemy.

If the idea of making a larcenous cue bid has never

occurred to you, give it some thought. There is room in contract bridge for much low cunning as well as logic and science. Amiable larceny of this kind is perfectly sporting and provides some of the biggest thrills in the game.

A highly respected clergyman of my acquaintance makes it a point to throw a fake cue bid at his opponents now and then. He practically always gets away with it; how can anybody doubt a clergyman? But sometimes a suspicious opponent will lead up to the cue bid, and then it may turn out that the Reverend has a perfectly normal ace-queen and is delighted to get such a friendly opening lead.

This is, of course, the chief reason for making fake cue bids. They correspond to the bluff in poker. If you never bluff, you are easy to play against. *The true art of bidding consists of keeping your partner trustful and the opponents mistrustful.*

✓ HELP FROM THE ENEMY

Sometimes an opponent unwittingly helps you during a slam auction, either by giving you valuable information or by enabling you to transmit valuable information to your partner.

Help from the enemy usually comes in the form of a penalty double of a cue bid:

SOUTH	WEST	NORTH	EAST
1 ♠	Pass	3 ♠	Pass
4 ♣	Double		

West's double shows that he has length and strength in clubs. Since West is scheduled to make the opening lead against a spade contract, his double is not lead-directing. (See Chapter 16.) Conceivably it may persuade East to sacrifice at six or seven clubs against a spade contract. The chances are, however, that West has simply done something foolish under the impression that he was acting like an expert.

If North has two or three small clubs, he will slow down, knowing that the slam will probably fail. If North has a singleton in clubs, he will know that the partnership hands fit very well.

Sometimes an opponent doubles a Blackwood response, usually to indicate a favorable lead. Here again, the double may boomerang.

OPENER	RESPONDER
♠ A K Q 8 5	♠ J 10 6 3
♡ 6	♡ A 5 4
◇ A J 2	◇ K 6 5 3
♣ K Q J 2	♣ A 3

OPENER	RESPONDER
1 ♠	3 ♠
4 NT	5 ♡

Normally, Opener will bid five notrump and discover that his partner has only one king. If this is the king of hearts, Opener still has to worry about a losing diamond. He will probably have to stop at six spades, missing the grand slam.

Now suppose that the Blackwood response of five hearts is doubled. Opener is entitled to assume that the doubler has the king of hearts.

He goes ahead with his Blackwood bid of five notrump anyway, discovering that his partner has one king. He assumes that this is the king of diamonds and jumps to *seven* spades. This contract will be virtually laydown if Responder has king-queen of diamonds or a holding of not more than six cards in clubs and diamonds combined.

At worst, Opener may have to finesse the jack of diamonds in the hope of finding the queen in favorable position.

In the actual example no finesse is necessary. Trumps are drawn and Responder's losing diamonds are discarded on the extra high clubs in Opener's hand.

Sometimes the opponents help by *bidding* rather than doubling. Consider this sort of hand:

OPENER	RESPONDER
♠ A K J 8 5 2	♠ Q 7 6 3
♡ 8 5 4	♡ 6
◇ A 2	◇ K 8 5 4
♣ K 6	♣ A J 7 3

OPENER	RESPONDER
1 ♠	3 ♠
4 ◇	4 ♠
Pass	

The slam is muffed. Opener doesn't know about his partner's singleton heart, and Responder has no way of knowing that he has exactly the right cards for his partner.

Leave the cards as they are, and change the auction:

OPENER	OPPONENT	RESPONDER	OPPONENT
1 ♠	2 ♡	3 ♠	4 ♡
5 ◇	Pass	6 ♠	

When both opponents bid hearts, Opener assumes that they have eight or nine hearts between them. Hence he knows that Responder is very short. Opener can afford to show his ace of diamonds, for he should be safe at five spades even if his partner has *two* losing hearts.

Responder has likewise drawn correct inferences from the bidding. He knows that Opener has his side values in diamonds and clubs rather than in hearts. The king of diamonds and the ace-jack of clubs must be of great value, and the singleton heart prevents the opponents from defeating the slam with two immediate tricks in their strong suit.

Clearly, defensive bidding is a two-edged sword. It may tell the other side just what they need to know.

✓ SHOWING A SINGLETON

You can sometimes show a singleton without relying on the opponents for help. The standard method is to bid the other three suits very strongly. The general idea is that length in three suits must mean decided shortness in the fourth suit.

OPENER	RESPONDER
♠ K Q 7 3	♠ A J 9 5
♡ A K J 6 4	♡ 8 5
◊ A 6 2	◊ K Q 3
♣ 5	♣ J 9 4 3

OPENER	RESPONDER
1 ♡	1 ♠
3 ◊ (1)	3 NT (2)
4 ♠ (3)	6 ♠ (4)

(1) A deliberate falsehood. Opener does not really have length in diamonds. Opener is not worried about deceiving his partner, for he is ready to bid spades later on. The jump is forcing to game.

(2) The normal bid. Responder assumes that his partner has good diamonds and hearts.

(3) This lets the cat out of the bag. Opener has raised a spade suit that his partner has bid only once. Hence Opener must have strong 4-card support for spades. He

also has length in hearts and (presumably) in diamonds.
In this manner Opener guarantees a singleton in the unbid suit. Opener bid the diamonds with exactly this
purpose in mind: to guarantee a singleton club by the
time he had shown the spade support.

(4) Relies on the guarantee. There should be an excellent play for this slam contract.

Responder would not be so enthusiastic if he had a
substantial part of his strength in his partner's singleton
suit. For example, he might have:

♠ A J 9 5   ♡ 8 5   ◇ J 9 4 3   ♣ K Q 3

Responder would meekly pass at four spades.

When you have only low cards opposite your partner's
singleton or void suit, you have a good fit. When you
have high cards opposite partner's short suits, you have
a *duplication* of values. You can often make a slam with
28 or 29 points when you have a good fit; you need the
full 33 points (perhaps even more) when there is a
duplication.

Part of the reason for bidding in such a way as to show
a singleton is to let partner make a decision. If he can
see the good fit, he will bid a slam; if he can see duplication, he will stop short.

✓ DIRECT SLAM BIDDING

In your enthusiasm for scientific slam bidding, don't
despise the crude jump to slam. Direct methods have
their value.

One reason for jumping right to slam may be that you
have nothing else of value to say. For example, suppose
your partner opens with one notrump, showing 16 to 18
points in high cards. You hold:

♠ K 10 2   ♡ A 10 3   ◇ A Q J 4   ♣ K 9 5

You have a count of 17 points in high cards and therefore know that the combined count is 33 to 35 points. This should be enough for a small slam, but not enough for a grand slam. Hence you jump right to six notrump. Do not conduct a complicated auction when you know just where you are heading.

The same sort of direct jump is available after many other notrump bids. For example, you open a 20-point hand with one of a 4-card suit, and partner jumps to two notrump. His bid shows 13 to 15 points, and simple addition tells you that the partnership count is 33 to 35 points. A jump to six notrump is your best course.

The direct jump to slam is easy after a notrump bid because most notrump bids limit the hand very sharply. Most other bids have a wider range. If your partner has minimum values for his bid, the small slam may be doubtful; and if he has maximum, the *grand* slam may be a good risk.

Another *limited-range* situation exists when your partner has failed to open the bidding. For example:

PARTNER	YOU
Pass	1 ♠
3 ♠	?

You hold:

♠ A Q J 9 4   ♡ A Q J 6   ◇ A 7   ♣ K 3

It's hard to imagine a responding hand that won't give you a reasonable play for six spades. Your best course is to bid six spades without further ado.

What about a grand slam? This is a poor gamble unless your partner has the missing ace and the missing three kings. But how can he have all of those cards in view of his original pass?

The best time to jump directly to a slam is when you

have something to hide from the enemy. For example, suppose you are North in the following bidding situation:

EAST	SOUTH	WEST	NORTH
1 ♡	1 ♠	Pass	?

You hold:

♠ A 10 8 5 3   ♡ ——————   ◇ A K Q 9 3 2   ♣ 7 6

What should you bid?

A jump to six spades is probably the best action. This contract should be easy against the expected heart opening lead. Even if West becomes suspicious and decides not to lead a heart, he may hit upon a diamond opening lead. Thus your partner will probably make his small slam not only when he has clubs controlled, but also, very often, when the clubs are wide open.

What are you giving up by making this gambling bid? Even if partner has the ace of clubs, you probably won't bid the grand slam. Scientific bidding simply tells the opponents how to defend but does not really help your side very much—except to keep you out of an "unmakable" slam that your partner would actually make.

√ DECLARER'S SKILL

One last thought about slam bidding: Don't put too much strain on the declarer. If your partner is a very fine card player, it's quite all right to put him into difficult slam contracts. If he's a beginner or a worry wart, you can spare his nerves and your pocketbook by stopping at game whenever the going looks rough.

The same idea applies to you. If you're a comparative beginner, don't stretch too hard to get to slam. Wait until you've finished this book.

8th DAY

~~~~~~~~~~~~~~~~

FIRST REVIEW AND SELF-TESTING QUIZZES

1st Through 7th Days

You HAVE NOW COMPLETED the first week's study of BID-DING WITHOUT OPPOSITION. Before you go on to the next section you should test yourself on how well you have mastered this material. Turn to page 468 and answers, which begin on page 485. Rate yourself accord-down on a separate piece of paper. Then turn to the answer questions 1 through 90, jotting your answers ing to this scale:

> 85 or more right ....excellent
> 76–84 right ....good
> 70–75 right ....fair
> Below 75 right ....you need to reread the
> chapters

No matter how good your score is, it will pay you to go over those questions you missed and refer back to the chapters on which they were based. This is the way to spot your weak points and bone up on them. If you did not do well on the quiz, this kind of check-up is all the more important.

Taking the quiz and checking up on the incorrect answers will insure your mastering this material while it is fresh in your mind, so that it will always be on tap thereafter.

COMPETITIVE

BIDDING

BIDDING WITH A PART SCORE

Your Part Score	√ Mild Slam Tries
√ The Expanded Notrump	√ Trapping the Enemy
√ Playable Suits	Opponents' Part Score
√ Semi-Forcing Bids	√ Light Overcalls and Takeout
√ Opening Two-Bids	Doubles
√ Suit Raises	√ In Short
√ Jump Takeouts	

A PART SCORE usually has a big effect on the bidding of both sides. It changes the meaning of some bids and may affect your tactics and strategy.

If your side has the part score, you can try to reach game with a lower contract than usual. If the opponents have the part score, you must compete a little more fiercely than usual in the effort to stop them from scoring a cheap game.

We shall deal with these two situations separately.

Your Part Score

If your opponents are timid, it pays to open a trifle lighter than usual in the hope of stealing a cheap game. If you do this, get out of the auction as quickly as you can. It's all right to persuade the opponents that you have a good hand, but don't fool *yourself*.

If your opponents are full of fight, avoid a light opening bid in first or second position. If the opponents have any cards, they will compete. Your partner, relying on the strength of your opening bid, may get you overboard or may double the opponents at a bid that they can make.

A slight shading is permissible in third or fourth position. By that time, at least one opponent has announced that he cannot make even a shaded opening bid.

Aside from the values needed for an opening bid, there are three important principles to follow when your side has the part score:

- Bid notrump with balanced hands, even if your strength is above or below the normal range.
- Bid only *playable* suits.
- Respect your partner's forcing bids, even if you have already reached game.

⩔ THE EXPANDED NOTRUMP

The most useful opening bid with a part score is one notrump. This shows support in advance for partner's long suit, if he has one, and defense against the opponents. Your partner can then bid in comfort; the opponents, in fear.

You can afford to stretch a point or two in order to make an opening bid of one notrump for two reasons:

1. The bid is valuable offensively and as a mild shutout.

2. When you have balanced distribution you want to avoid bidding a suit, particularly a weak 4-card suit.

Normally, an opening bid of one notrump shows 16 to 18 points. When you have a part score, however, you can shade this down to a good 14 points. You might also extend the range upward to include a skimpy 19 points.

The full range of the opening bid of one notrump when your side has the part score is therefore 14 to 19 points.

How will your partner know your actual strength? He won't, but he doesn't need to know. You're going to stop at a fairly low contract, usually in partner's best suit. There is no need for precision bidding.

Your partner must be cautious about doubling the opponents. He should rely on you only for the 14-point or 15-point hand, not the 18-pointer or 19-pointer. If in doubt, he can afford to let the enemy play undoubled at a part-score contract. He who fights and runs away will live to fight another day.

✓ PLAYABLE SUITS

Don't open the bidding or respond in a shabby suit, particularly a weak 4-card suit. If you don't have a good suit of your own, raise the suit partner has bid if you have support, or bid notrump.

For example, as dealer with 30 points on score:

(1)　♠ J 9 4 2　　♡ A Q 9　　◇ 9 4 2　　♣ A K J

   Bid one notrump. Without the part score you would open with one club. The "prepared" bid is no longer necessary. When you *bid* clubs with a part score, you should *have* clubs.

(2)　♠ K Q 8 2　　♡ A Q 9 3　　◇ A 4 2　　♣ 7 3

   Bid one notrump. Without the part score you would bid one spade.

Similarly, as responder, you avoid bidding a bad suit and go out of your way to bid a good suit.

SOUTH	WEST	NORTH	EAST
1 ♡	Pass	?	

North-South have a part score of 60 points. What should North bid with each of the following hands?

(1)   ♠ 8 3   ♡ 9 4   ◇ 6 3 2   ♣ K Q 8 7 5 3

Bid two clubs. In this situation a bid at the level of two promises a good suit but does not promise the usual 10 points in high cards. Partner is allowed to pass if he has a tolerance for clubs.

(2)   ♠ 8 3   ♡ A 9 4   ◇ 6 3 2   ♣ A Q 7 5 3

Bid two hearts. You would bid two clubs without the part score, expecting to show the heart support later. With the part score, there may not be a later turn; you must show the heart support rather than bid a mangy club suit.

(3)   ♠ K J 8 5   ♡ 6 2   ◇ A J 6   ♣ 7 5 3 2

Bid one spade. You can just barely afford to bid this weak 4-card suit. If it were weaker, you would bid one notrump instead.

♥ SEMI-FORCING BIDS

With a part score of 40 points or more, an opening bid of one in a suit should be considered semi-forcing (unless it is already enough for game).

For example, suppose your partner opens with one heart when your side has a part score of 60 points.

(1)   ♠ 8 3   ♡ J 7 5 4   ◇ Q 9 4   ♣ 8 7 5 3

Bid two hearts. You would pass without the part score, since you could hardly hope to gain anything by bidding. Now, however, you hope to gain a game.

(2)   ♠ Q 9 4   ♡ 8 3   ◇ J 7 5 4   ♣ 8 7 5 3

Bid one notrump. If partner can bid clubs or diamonds next, you may be able to score a cheap game. If he lets you play the hand at one notrump, you will be in a game contract. Be sure to keep the quaver out of your voice. Bridge opponents, like wild beasts, are most dangerous when they smell the odor of fear.

✔ OPENING TWO-BIDS

An opening bid of two in a suit should be treated as forcing even when it is enough for game. If the opener has a very powerful hand, he will welcome a second chance to bid; there may be a laydown slam in his second suit even if his first suit doesn't appeal to the responder.

If the opener has only a medium-size two-bid (he may shade the values slightly when his side has a part score), he may pass a negative response of two notrump. But if the response is positive (even a simple raise), the opener must bid at least once more.

In subsequent bidding, the general theory is that any new suit is forcing for one round. The way to sign off is to bid notrump or to go back to some suit that has been mentioned before.

There is no need to shade the opening bid of two notrump. If your partner is unwilling to respond to a bid of one in a suit (which is semi-forcing, as we have seen), you don't want to be in two notrump with only 20 or 21 points. Moreover, you don't want to frighten the opponents off when you have such great general strength. Open with one of a suit and get the ax ready.

For much the same reason you avoid a response of two notrump when partner opens with one of a suit. Give the opponents a chance to enter the auction and get themselves clobbered.

✓ SUIT RAISES

A double raise in partner's suit is forcing to game, just as if you had no part score. But usually a contract of three is enough for game with the part score, so partner can pass. There is no need to shade the values for the double raise; it should, as always, provide a firm base for exploration of slam chances. A simple raise will coax partner to continue on to game if two of his suit is not already a game contract.

However, a *single* raise must have more flexibility, because of the semi-forcing nature of partner's opening one bid. A range of 5 to 12 points is ideal (instead of the usual 6-10) because it allows you to raise on modest values and also trap the opponents into action on real muscle.

✓ JUMP TAKEOUTS

A jump takeout in a new suit, like the opening bid of two in a suit, must be treated as forcing for one round even though it is enough for game. The partnership must not abandon all slam-bidding methods just because it has a part score.

Responder may shade the requirements slightly if he has a solid suit of his own or very good support for the opener's suit. It is poor policy to shade the values with broken suits and general strength. With such a hand, make a minimum response in a new suit. If partner makes a strong rebid, you can then try for a slam. If the opponents yield to the temptation to enter the auction, you can give them a real surprise.

✓ MILD SLAM TRIES

When your side has a part score it is possible to make a mild slam suggestion by bidding beyond game. For example, with a part score of 40:

OPENER	RESPONDER
1 ♠	2 ♠
?	

Opener can suggest a slam by bidding two notrump, three of a new suit, or even three spades. Responder may drop two notrump or three of the original suit, but he cannot drop three of a *new* suit.

As previously noted, responder may have a range of 5 to 12 points for his single raise. After opener's slam try, responder may show a sign of life if he has 11 or 12 points, should wait for further slam tries by the opener with only 9 or 10 points, and should sign off resolutely with 8 points or less.

When it is quite clear that the opponents are not to be enticed into the auction, you may be able to make a slam try with a jump bid in notrump. For example, with a part score of 60 for North-South:

WEST	NORTH	EAST	SOUTH
Pass	1 ♡	Pass	?

South may jump to two notrump with:

♠ K 8 2   ♡ Q 6 3   ♦ A Q 7 4   ♣ A J 5

Or, with the same part score:

WEST	NORTH	EAST	SOUTH
Pass	1 ♡	Pass	1 ♠
Pass	?		

North may jump to two notrump with:

    ♠ K 8   ♡ A Q 9 6 3   ◇ A K J   ♣ K J 9

In each case it is clear that the opponents are not going to enter the auction. The only question is whether or not North and South have a slam.

The jump to two notrump when one notrump would be enough for game should invite a slam if partner has a good hand but should be safe if partner is broke. Requirements: 1 or 2 points more than the normal *maximum* value for your bid. The response of two notrump usually shows 13 to 15 points; with a part score of 60 or more, it should show 16 or 17. Opener's jump rebid of two notrump usually shows 19 or 20 points; with the part score it should show 21 or 22 points.

Following the same principle, as we have observed, an opening bid of two notrump may be made with 25 or 26 points. The opponents probably won't be able to get into the auction, so you might just as well make your mild slam suggestion at a safe level.

The Blackwood Convention has the same meaning whether or not there is a part score. Similarly, cue bids at a high level mean just what they do without the part score.

Not all bids past game are slam tries. An opening bid of three or four in a suit is pre-emptive, even if it is more than game. A simple raise is a mild shutout bid, particularly if the bid of one was enough for game.

For example, with a part score of 70 for North-South:

SOUTH	WEST	NORTH	EAST
1 ♠	Pass	2 ♠	

North could jump to *three* spades if he had 13 points or more. The raise to two spades is still 5 to 12 points even though it goes past game. The chances are that

North wants to make it difficult for the opponents to enter the auction.

It would be false economy for North to pass with a light hand that includes spade support. The opponents would probably compete, and North might then have to raise to *three* spades when he was doubtful about bidding *two* spades.

✓ TRAPPING THE ENEMY

You should encourage the opponents to get into the auction when you are ready to murder them. It isn't necessary for your side to bid very high to reach game, and your failure to bid high may be interpreted by an opponent as a sign of weakness.

For example, with a part score of 60 for North-South:

SOUTH	WEST	NORTH	EAST
1 ♠	Pass	1 NT	Pass
Pass	?		

North may have 14 or 15 points for his response of one notrump! If West decides to enter the auction, the reception committee will be ready for him.

With a part score of 40, a response of one notrump should be considered forcing:

SOUTH	WEST	NORTH	EAST
1 ♡	Pass	1 NT	Pass
?			

North may again have a very good hand, and South must not pass at this unlikely moment. If South merely rebids two hearts, North will pass even though he has a good hand. If the opponents can be lured into the auction, they may acquire some scars to show their grandchildren.

Opponents' Part Score

When the opponents have a part score you expect to get into the auction in the attempt to push them too high. If an opponent opens the bidding, your side will compete with a bid or a double.

It is even safer to open the bidding yourself and thus strike the first blow. The next player, perhaps having been ready to open the bidding himself, may be reluctant to overcall, particularly if he has no very strong suit.

It is sound tactics to open a slightly substandard hand in first or second position. Your tendency in third position should depend on the nature of the other players. Pass if the last player is conservative about fourth-hand bids; get the first punch in if the last player hates to pass a hand out.

In fourth position, pass out any doubtful hand. Don't open an auction in which you will be at a disadvantage.

If your partner also understands these tactics, you will be even more reluctant to open a doubtful hand in third or fourth position. The fact that your partner has passed tells you that he doesn't have even a shaded opening bid. If you also have doubtful values, the hand probably belongs to the enemy. Against conservative opponents, your best chance is to go quietly.

✓ LIGHT OVERCALLS AND TAKEOUT DOUBLES

When an opponent who has a part score opens the bidding, you must often get into the auction with doubtful values. If you don't, it may be much more difficult for your partner to bid when his turn comes or for you to get in at your next turn.

This is, of course, dangerous, but what are your alternatives? Are you willing to sit by passively whenever the opponents have a part score? Or do you wish to pass at your first turn and guess whether or not to enter the auction—at a higher level—at your next turn?

In this situation it pays to overcall with a long suit and a rather poor hand. For example, against an opening bid of one spade you would bid two clubs with:

♠ 6   ♡ 7 2   ◇ K J 4   ♣ Q J 8 7 4 3 2

Without the part score, such an overcall is sheer folly. You can't hope to become declarer unless your partner has strength enough to bid independently. The chances are that an opponent will become declarer, and then your bid will give him information about distribution; or perhaps your partner will double a makable contract because of your bid; or maybe your partner will lead a club from A-x and thus hand the opponents an undeserved trick.

However, this kind of overcall becomes useful when the opponents have a part score. If partner has club support, he may be able to push the opponents one trick too high. If he has a good suit of his own, he will be encouraged to compete instead of passing. Moreover, he will make allowance for the fact that you have bid under pressure.

The takeout double may likewise be shaded when the opponents have a part score. Your partner should assume that the double is about 2 points weaker than usual. With the right distribution, in fact, the double may be shaded down almost to the vanishing point:

♠ Q J 6 3   ♡ 6   ◇ K 9 7 4   ♣ K 8 6 3

Double an opening bid of one heart if the opponents have a part score. You don't expect to rebid, but your double should enable partner to compete if he has any long suit with very modest values.

✓ IN SHORT

When *your* side has a part score: Don't worry about showing your exact strength; just get to game. Bid no-trump if you lack a good suit. Respond to a forcing bid even if game has been reached.

When the *opponents* have a part score: It is important, although risky, to get into the auction quickly with an opening bid, an overcall, or a takeout double. When necessary, shade the requirements for such action by a point or two. Bid normally when the opponents stay out of the auction: your *opponents* can stop as soon as they have found a good suit, but *you* must find not only the right suit (or notrump) but also how high to bid in it.

10th DAY

OVERCALLS

WHAT DO YOU NEED to bid your own suit when an opponent has opened the bidding?

The answer depends on three factors:

- How high you must bid
- What sort of opponents you have
- The state of your bank balance

To take the last point first, you can laugh at bidding requirements if you have more money than brains. This would not, of course, be true of any of *my* readers, but I am constantly amazed to discover how many players bid as though the points mean nothing at all.

Perhaps the people who amaze me have got that way by playing against timid opponents. After all, if your opponents don't know how to double, you don't need to be cautious. Conversely, if your opponents double at the drop of a trick, you must be especially cautious. Clearly, your requirements for a defensive overcall should vary with the nature of your opponents.

If other factors are normal, the requirements for your overcall depend on how high you must bid. The higher the bid the more you need.

So much for generalities. Now let's get down to tricks.

✓ POINTS OR TRICKS?

Unlike an opening bid, an overcall does not depend on *points*. It depends on playing tricks.

For example, suppose your right-hand opponent has bid one spade. You should *not* bid two hearts with:

   ♠ Q 5 3   ♡ A 8 7 4 2   ♢ A Q 5   ♣ Q 6

but you *should* bid two hearts with:

   ♠ 5 3   ♡ K Q J 10 4 2   ♢ K Q 5   ♣ 6 4

The first hand counts to 14 points in high cards but is not worth an overcall. The second hand counts to only 11 points in high cards but is a fine overcall.

The difference is in the playing trick values of the two hands. The first hand may take only the two aces if the breaks are fantastically bad. Down six doubled comes to 1100 points even if not vulnerable. That's more than the whole rubber is worth.

With *average* breaks, that first hand may take a total of four tricks. That still costs you a penalty of 700 points. Hardly worth it, considering that your opponents may be unable to make a game. (It would be a bad bargain even if they had a cold game, but then it would be just bad rather than outrageous.)

With the *second* hand you should be able to win five heart tricks and a diamond even against horrible breaks. Forgetting about the 100 honors for the moment, down two costs you only 300 points not vulnerable, or 500 points vulnerable. If those are the only tricks you can get, the opponents probably have a game, and you have lost nothing by your bid.

✓ RISK VERSUS GAIN

Before we set up requirements for overcalls, let's see what you stand to gain and what you stand to lose by overcalling.

When an opponent opens the bidding you will practically never make a slam, and you will only occasionally bid and make a game. Most of your overcalls will succeed only in settling which side plays at a part-score contract.

If this were all, there would be little to gain from overcalling, compared to what you might lose. There are three additional main benefits from the overcall:

- Your partner may make a favorable opening lead (your suit) instead of a poor lead. This is particularly true if the player at your left is likely to try for game in notrump if you pass.
- Your partner may have a fine fit for your suit and may make a paying sacrifice against the opponents (see Chapter 14) or better yet, may push them one trick too high.
- Your bid, together with your partner's raise, may deprive the opponents of bidding room and thus prevent them from reaching their best contract. (This is especially true if your overcall is a *jump* bid.)

This is quite a bit to gain. What do you stand to lose? Usually, just your shirt. If you have a husky partner, you may lose part of your skin as well.

In rubber bridge you don't mind losing 100 or 200 points to prevent the opponents from making a part score. You don't cry your eyes out at losing 500 points to prevent them from making a game—provided it was a game that they were actually going to bid and make rather than just a possible game that imaginary opponents might conceivably bid.

Other penalties are greeted with less enthusiasm. To give up 300 points when the opponents have only a part score is to raise their morale and lower your partner's. To give up 700 points against a game is a very poor bargain. Any bigger penalty ranks as some kind of disaster.

√ THE RULE OF 500 POINTS

When you are tempted to make a doubtful overcall, ask yourself this question: Will this bid cost me more than 500 points if the next player doubles me with gusto?

To answer this question, count up the tricks called for by your bid and consider the vulnerability. Suppose, for example, that you are considering a bid of two diamonds: You are bargaining for eight of the thirteen tricks. If you take only six tricks, vulnerable, a penalty double will net the opponents 500 points. If you take only five tricks, not vulnerable, a penalty double will, again, net the opponents 500 points.

To put it another way, you want to be within two tricks of your contract when you are vulnerable, within three tricks when you are not vulnerable.

This rule is only a rough, general guide. You don't mind losing 500 points if the opponents take all their tricks *with aces and kings*. If they hadn't doubled you, they would surely have used those aces and kings to bid and make a game. But you don't enjoy going down 500 points if the opponents take their tricks with some stray queens and jacks and low trumps. They weren't going to bid a game; and if they had, they wouldn't have made it.

The second flaw in the Rule of 500 Points is that a single hand proves nothing. A bid is not unsound just because it costs you 700 points on a single occasion. The question is whether that type of bid gains or loses points for you in the long run. If you make the bid ten times and gain 100 points on nine occasions, you can afford to lose 700 points the tenth time.

For the moment let's note that we don't mind losing tricks to aces and kings. We just don't want to lose tricks to low trumps and stray queens and jacks.

This leads us to a fundamental principle: *All sound overcalls are based on very strong trump suits.*

✓ REQUIREMENTS FOR OVERCALLING

To overcall at the level of one you need a trump suit that will take at least four tricks even against a bad break. The hand as a whole should be not far below the strength of an opening bid.

To overcall at the level of two you need a trump suit that should take five tricks. (A 6-card suit is normal, and a 7-card suit is not unusual.) The strength of the hand should be about the same as for an opening bid. If you are vulnerable, you should certainly have the high-card strength of an opening bid.

This means that you don't overcall with one spade when you have such garbage as:

♠ J 8 7 5 3 2   ♡ 7 4   ◇ K Q 4   ♣ 6 2

The suit is too weak, and the hand as a whole is too worthless, regardless of the vulnerability.

Beef up the suit:

♠ K Q J 5 3 2   ♡ 7 4   ◇ K 8 4   ♣ 6 2

and you have a reasonable overcall, vulnerable or not.

Take away the side strength:

♠ K Q J 5 3 2   ♡ 7 4   ◇ 8 4 2   ♣ 6 2

and your overcall is safe but pointless. How can your partner tell what you are doing and what his hand is worth if you allow yourself the luxury of a bid on cheese of this kind?

✓ RESPONDING TO AN OVERCALL

When your partner overcalls he should have a strong suit and roughly the same kind of high-card strength that he would need for an opening bid. He may have a trifle less in high cards if his overcall is at the level of one. Conversely, he may have a good suit and as much as 17 points in high cards, particularly if he has made a vulnerable overcall at the level of two.

You should think about game if you likewise have close to opening-bid strength. You can raise partner's suit with a good fit and as little as 7 points in high cards. You can safely pass, however, with a mediocre hand and a poor fit for partner's suit.

There's no point in bidding some mediocre suit of your own; partner would have made a takeout double if he was interested in such a suit.

The nature of your responses and what you need for them can be seen from the following:

EAST	SOUTH	WEST	NORTH
1 ◇	1 ♡	Pass	?

(1)   ♠ 5 2   ♡ K 7 6 3   ◇ 8 4   ♣ A 9 7 5 4

Bid two hearts. Game is very unlikely but not impossible. Your chief purpose is to make it impossible for the opening bidder to make a cheap rebid. This kind of "jockeying" raise often allows you to steal a part score when the strength is evenly divided between the two partnerships.

(2)   ♠ A 5 2   ♡ 7 6 3   ◇ 8 4   ♣ A Q 7 5 4

Bid two hearts. Game is possible if partner has a really juicy overcall. Don't hesitate to raise with three small trumps; partner needs a strong suit of at least five cards for his overcall.

(3)   ♠ A 5   ♡ K 7 6 3   ◇ 8 4   ♣ A 9 7 5 4

Bid three hearts. Game is very likely, but it is wise to give partner a little leeway just in case he has overcalled with a "dog." He will accept the invitation to bid game whenever he has a sound hand.

(4)   ♠ 5   ♡ Q 7 6 3 2   ◇ 8 4   ♣ A K J 5 4

Bid four hearts. Game should be a laydown even if partner has a horrible overcall. Don't ask your partner to do what you can do by yourself.

(5)   ♠ Q J 5   ♡ 7 6   ◇ K J 8 4   ♣ K Q 9 7

Bid one notrump. This is not a rescue or a courtesy bid, since you would simply pass with a bad hand. You are suggesting game in notrump if partner has maximum strength for his overcall.

(6)   ♠ K Q 5   ♡ 7 6   ◇ K J 8 4   ♣ A Q 9 7

Bid two notrump. This is a strong invitation rather than a mild suggestion. Partner may pass if he has a bad overcall.

(7)   ♠ K 5   ♡ 7 6   ◇ K 8 4   ♣ A K Q 9 7 4

Bid three notrump. This type of jump is usually based on a solid minor suit rather than on exceptionally great strength in high cards. You expect to take six club tricks and three fast tricks elsewhere.

(8)   ♠ 5 2   ♡ 7 6   ◇ 8 4 3   ♣ A K J 9 8 4

Bid two clubs. Not a rescue but a denial of support for hearts. You expect partner to pass, and you think that you will be better off in your suit. Conceivably your bid may enable partner to try for game in no-trump.

(9)   ♠ 5 3 2   ♡ 7   ◇ 8 4 3   ♣ A Q 8 7 4 2

Pass. You don't like hearts, but you cannot be sure that your side will be better off in clubs. When the hand is a possible misfit, the best rescue is a prompt pass. Don't holler before you're caught in the wringer.

(10)   ♠ 5   ♡ A 7 6 3   ◇ 8 4 2   ♣ A K Q 9 7

Bid three clubs. This jump takeout is forcing for one round. You expect to bid four hearts at your next turn, thus showing great strength in clubs and hearts. If partner has the right sort of hand, he may try for a slam.

(11)   ♠ 5   ♡ A 7 6 3   ◇ A 8 4   ♣ K Q J 9 7

Bid two diamonds. This cue bid in the opponent's suit is forcing to game. You hope to show the clubs and then raise hearts. You want to suggest a slam without getting past game.

✔ JUMP OVERCALLS

For many years the jump overcall was used to show a strong hand. There's no doubt that this works very well on some hands.

Meanwhile younger, more venturesome experts were using the jump overcall with weak hands, to interfere with the bidding of the opponents. They got even better results.

How should you use the jump overcall in *your* game?

The one thing you can't do is mix 'em up. The strong jump overcall invites partner to raise with a light hand— a hand having as little as one or two playing tricks. The weak jump overcall warns partner to stay out of the auction. If you have to guess which type of hand your partner has for his jump overcall, you'd better wire ahead for a room in the poorhouse.

If most of the players in your game use strong jump overcalls, stick with them on this point. Don't try the weak variety except with a partner of your own choosing, and then only after a careful discussion.

✔ STRONG JUMP OVERCALLS

The best hand for a *strong* jump overcall is a powerful one-suited hand. All you need from partner for a game is an ace or a couple of kings.

For example, after an opponent's bid of one diamond, you would jump to two spades with:

♠ A K Q 9 4 2   ♡ K Q 8   ◇ 4   ♣ K 5 2

If your partner has a terrible hand, he can pass. The jump overcall is highly invitational, but not forcing.

If your partner has moderate strength without trump

support, he can bid two notrump or show a suit of his
own.

𝒱 WEAK JUMP OVERCALLS

I have been using the *weak* variety of jump overcall
with considerable success for many years. (This means
that I have to rely on a *non*-jump overcall when I have
a strong two-suiter. It has been my experience that *somebody* always makes another bid—partner or one of the
opponents. My overcall is practically never dropped. I
get the chance to bid my other suit.)

The weak jump overcall is used to show a fairly decent
suit with no side strength to speak of. For example:

♠ K Q J 5 3 2   ♡ 7 4   ♢ 8 4 2   ♣ 6 2

Bid two spades over an opponent's opening bid of
one in hearts, diamonds, or clubs.

The opponents know, of course, that your jump overcall
is weak. (If they don't know about it, you're supposed
to tell them at the beginning of the rubber. See Chapter
34, Manners, Morals and Laws.) You don't expect to
frighten them out of the auction. You just hope to rob
them of bidding room and thus make it difficult for them
to find their best contract.

Don't make the weak jump overcall with substantial
side strength. If the hand is good enough, make a *non*-
jump overcall; otherwise pass. Your partner is entitled to
assume that you have *no defense* when you make your
jump overcall. This knowledge will help him decide
whether or not to sacrifice against the opponents.

If your partner is reliable, you may shade the jump
overcall down almost to the vanishing point. Instead of
six to the K-Q-J you may have only six to the Q-J—of
course without the vestige of side strength!

This type of impudence is recommended chiefly against non-expert opponents and for times when you are not vulnerable and the opponents are. You don't stand to gain as much when neither side is vulnerable, and you may lose too much if you are vulnerable.

✓ RESPONDING TO THE WEAK JUMP OVERCALL

When your partner has made a weak jump overcall you will not go far wrong if you pass without even looking at your hand!

It practically never pays to raise to three of your partner's suit. This seldom helps you but often helps the opponents.

EAST	SOUTH	WEST	NORTH
1 ◇	2 ♡	Pass	Pass
?			

If East has a minimum opening bid, he will probably pass with misgivings. If he has just slightly more than a minimum, he will reopen with a bid or a takeout double. East makes the same reopening bid or double even if he has a really good hand. There is no way for West to know how good his partner's hand is. This may lead to trouble.

The situation is clarified if North raises to three hearts instead of passing. East can then afford to pass if he has a doubtful hand, and this will make it clear that he has only a minimum opening bid. If East does bid or double after a raise to three hearts, it will be clear that he has a really good hand; and West can then safely consider aggressive action on a light hand.

You raise your partner's jump overcall to game with either of two very different types of hand: a *very strong*

hand with a good fit, and a *very weak* hand with a good
fit. You *always* need the fit.

EAST	SOUTH	WEST	NORTH
1 ◇	2 ♡	Pass	?

(East-West vulnerable)

(1) ♠ A 5   ♡ A J 8 3   ◇ 4   ♣ K Q J 9 7 4

Bid four hearts. Even if partner merely solidifies the
trump suit, the combined hands should lose only
one spade, one diamond, and one club. Don't bid
less; the opponents can probably make four spades.

(2) ♠ 5 2   ♡ J 8 3 2   ◇ 4   ♣ Q J 9 7 4 2

Bid four hearts. You'll probably make at least seven
tricks, minus 500 points if you're doubled, but minus
only 150 points if the opponents believe your bid is
honest and don't double. Either way it is a profitable
sacrifice. (See Chapter 14, When to Sacrifice.) The
opponents probably can make a slam against you.
If they bid game, let them have it. Don't push them
into a slam that you expect them to make.

(3) ♠ 5   ♡ Q J 8 3 2   ◇ 4   ♣ Q J 9 7 4 2

Bid something grotesque—like six hearts, or four notrump, or perhaps even two spades! The opponents
can surely make a slam, but you may be able to
talk them out of the hand if you are audacious
enough.

▼ WHEN SILENCE IS GOLDEN

When an opponent has opened the bidding it isn't
necessary for you to bid. Life will go on even if you pass.
If both opponents have bid by the time your turn

comes, beware of stepping into the middle of the auction. If you don't have either a very powerful suit or very fine distribution, just pass and hope that the opponents get beyond their depth.

It is especially important to pass when your right-hand opponent opens the bidding in one of your strong suits. For example, after an opening bid of one spade you hold:

♠ Q J 9 4   ♡ 4   ◇ A K 8 6 3 2   ♣ K 3

This is no time to bid two diamonds. The next player is likely to be short in spades and will be itching to double any suit in which he has length. Pass and let the opponents struggle.

✔ OVERCALLS IN NOTRUMP

An overcall of one notrump guarantees at least one stopper in the opponent's suit and shows the same sort of hand as the normal opening bid of one notrump: 16 to 18 points, with balanced distribution and stoppers in at least three suits.

A jump to *three* notrump is a sort of gambling bid, based on a long, solid minor suit and some scattered stoppers.

A jump to *two* notrump used to mean much the same thing, but some experts now use it to ask partner to bid a minor suit. (See The Unusual Notrump, in Chapter 17.)

✔ FREE BIDS

In most hands the side that opens the bidding has things all its own way; the opponents stay out of the auction. When both sides get into the auction fairly promptly the responses and rebids of the opening bidder and his partner are usually slightly weightier.

For example:

SOUTH	WEST	NORTH	EAST
1 ◇	Pass	1 ♠	

North may have a weak 4-card spade suit with a total count of about 6 points. As we have observed, he must respond with a very weak hand to make sure that South has a second chance to speak. North's slight show of strength may be enough to lead South to a sound game contract.

The situation is altered if West overcalls:

SOUTH	WEST	NORTH	EAST
1 ◇	1 ♡	?	

There is no need for North to speak if he has a weak suit and a 6-point hand. Even if North passes, South will have another chance to speak.

If North does bid, his response is *free*—not forced. A free bid should show substantial values:

- One of a suit—strong suit and 10 points or more
- One notrump—a stopper, balanced distribution, and 10 points
- Two of a suit—a good suit and usually more than 10 points
- A raise in a minor suit—at least 9 points with support
- A raise in a major suit—good trumps but no more strength than usual

A few comments are in order. If responder bids one of a suit or one notrump with only 9 points, nobody will

point an accusing finger at him. A good 9-point hand may
be better than a mangy 10-point hand.

A free response at the level of *two* shows real values.
You surely expect to bid again, and you have no qualms
about making this bid. (If there had been no intervening
overcall, you might have had to respond at the level of
two with a good 6-card suit and no side strength or
with some other doubtful hand.)

A free raise in a minor suit likewise follows the general
principle that a free bid shows more value than the very
same bid minus the overcall. The sequence   1◊—Pass
—2◊ shows diamond support with about 6 to 10 points.
The sequence 1◊—1♡—2◊ shows diamond support
with at least 9 points.

The free raise in a major suit is just the same as an
unforced raise. That is, the sequence 1♡—1♠—2♡
promises no more than 1♡—Pass—2♡.

This may scandalize the textbook players, but it won't
surprise the *practical* bridge players. When a practical
player opens with one of a major suit he has either a
very strong 4-card suit or a 5-card suit. He will not be
in serious trouble if his partner raises with a light hand.

On the contrary, the responder will be in trouble if he
fails to raise. He will never get a cheaper chance to
speak up with his light hand. If he passes, the opponents
may steal the hand; if he raises, he may steal the hand
himself.

SOUTH	WEST	NORTH	EAST
1 ♡	1 ♠	?	

You are North. What do you say?

(1)   ♠ 7 3   ♡ 8 2   ◊ A 10 7 4   ♣ A K J 9 7

Bid two clubs. With 12 points in high cards, including
  3 Quick Tricks, you want to reach game if you can

find a fit. There is no question about your willingness to make a free response on such a hand.

(2) ♠ 7 3   ♡ 8 2   ◇ Q 7 4 2   ♣ A K J 5 3

Pass. You have 10 points in high cards but cannot see any reasonable hope for game unless your partner can rebid without being forced to do so. There is no need to make a free response when you have minimum values and no fit for partner's suit.

(3) ♠ A J 7   ♡ 8 2   ◇ K 10 7 4   ♣ Q 9 7 4

Bid one notrump. This shows balanced distribution, at least one stopper in the opponent's suit, and about 10 to 12 points in high cards.

(4) ♠ 7 3   ♡ 10 8 6 3   ◇ K J 4 2   ♣ Q 9 7

Bid two hearts. Now or never with this hand.

(5) ♠ 7 3   ♡ Q 8 6 3   ◇ K J 4 2   ♣ A Q 7

Bid three hearts. The overcall has no effect on really strong responses.

(6) ♠ 3   ♡ Q 10 8 6 3   ◇ K Q 7 4 2   ♣ 9 7

Bid four hearts. It's harder to shut the opponents out after one of them has overcalled, but there's no harm in trying.

√ FREE REBIDS

The same principles apply when the overcall is made by the *other* defender:

SOUTH	WEST	NORTH	EAST
1 ◇	Pass	1 ♡	1 ♠
?			

North's one-over-one response of one heart is forcing for one round, but there is no need for South to bid. Even if South passes, North will have another chance to speak.

If South does bid, nevertheless, he shows extra values of some kind. The exception, as before, is the raise of the major suit. In the example, South should raise hearts if he has 4-card or strong 3-card support and even if he has pretty close to a bare minimum opening bid. For example, with

♠ 7 3   ♡ A Q 6   ◇ A K 8 5 4   ♣ 9 7 4

Bid two hearts. You have only 13 points in high cards and only mediocre distribution, but it would be foolish to pass.

A rebid of one notrump is not just a courtesy rebid. It shows at least one stopper in the opponent's suit, with balanced distribution and about 15 to 17 points in high cards.

When the opener freely rebids his own suit, he shows a 6-card suit or a very strong 5-card suit in a hand of more than minimum strength—say 15 points or more.

✔ IN SHORT

An overcall shows a strong suit and usually about the same high-card strength as an opening bid. The higher you bid the better your hand must be.

A weak jump overcall shows a long topless suit and no defensive strength.

If partner overcalls (non-jump), consider a game with roughly the strength of an opening bid.

If partner makes a weak jump overcall, get ready to pass. Bid only if you have a good fit for partner's suit and either great strength (for a serious game bid) or great weakness (for a sacrifice bid).

Above all, don't overcall on a weak suit. Forget about *points;* your overcall should be based on *tricks.*

When an opponent overcalls:

- Make a free bid to show strength
- Pass with minimum values

11th DAY

DOUBLING FOR TAKEOUT

√ Takeout or Penalty Double?	√ When Not to Double
√ Requirements for a Takeout Double	√ In Short

How DO YOU show a hand with support for two or three unbid suits? For example:

SOUTH	WEST	NORTH	EAST
1 ◇	?		

West holds:

♠ K Q 7 3   ♡ A Q 8 6   ◇ 4   ♣ K Q 5 2

What should he do?

If West *passes,* the final contract may become one diamond. Yet West and his partner may have a juicy partial or even a game in spades or hearts.

If West bids one of his suits, he may pick his partner's worst suit. Then West will wind up playing the hand at one spade or one heart and may go down at that contract, when he could have fared far better in a different suit.

For example, suppose East has:

♠ J 8 5 4 2   ♥ 7 5   ♦ 8 3 2   ♣ A 6 4

The partnership can make ten tricks at spades without even breathing hard. At hearts, four or five tricks is probably the limit.

A nasty problem if West has to guess which suit to bid. No problem at all, however, if *East* is allowed to pick the suit. East doesn't have to guess; he just looks at his hand and bids his longest suit.

The problem is solved if West *doubles* the opening bid of one diamond and thus persuades his partner to choose a suit. This double is called a *takeout double* because it asks the partner to take out into his best suit.

✓ TAKEOUT OR PENALTY DOUBLE?

When your partner doubles, your first question is: What kind of double is this—takeout or penalty? Only when you have answered this question can you begin to think about your proper action.

The basic rule is that your partner's double is meant for takeout only when he has no clue to your distribution.

If you have bid, doubled, or redoubled, he has a clue to your distribution; then if he doubles something later in the auction, his double is meant for penalties. But if you have done nothing but pass, or if the bidding hasn't got around to you yet, then partner's double is probably meant for takeout.

There are two other rules:

- A double is meant for takeout only if made at the *first* chance to double that suit.

- A double of one or two of a suit is meant for takeout (provided it meets the other tests); a double of any other bid may be partly or entirely for penalties.

Let's get the first rule out of the way. Take this case:

SOUTH	WEST	NORTH	EAST
1 ♡	Pass	1 NT	Pass
2 ♣	Double		

The double of two clubs is meant for takeout. This is West's first chance to double clubs. He should have some such hand as:

♠ Q J 5 3   ♡ A Q 7   ◇ K Q 7 6 2   ♣ 4

West's bidding is logical. Over the opening bid of one heart, West was reluctant to bid a 4-card spade suit or to go to the level of two in diamonds. He could not double for takeout with only a singleton in one of the unbid suits. Hence West passed. He is happy to double two clubs for takeout, however, since there should be a safe spot at spades or diamonds (the two unbid suits) if he can only get his partner to make the choice.

This case is different:

SOUTH	WEST	NORTH	EAST
1 ♡	Pass	1 NT	Pass
2 ♡	Double		

West had a chance to double one heart for takeout, but he didn't double. His hand didn't become more suitable for a takeout double when South bid two hearts. Therefore West's double must be meant for penalties. Presumably West was playing a waiting game with some such hand as:

♠ 7 3   ♡ A Q J 9   ◇ K Q J   ♣ K J 4 2

Some players like to use the double for *takeout* (rather

than for penalty) in this situation. This is poor tactics.

If the hand is any good, the takeout double should be made at the *first* opportunity. If the hand is doubtful, this is no time to put your nose into the auction.

You can afford to pass your doubtful hand a second time, just as you did the first time. The responder may bid again, in which case you'll be happy you kept quiet. If the responder passes, your partner will have his chance to reopen the bidding. (See Chapter 17, Reopening the Bidding.)

Now let's go on to the rule about *one or two of a suit.* A double of such a bid is for takeout. A double of any other bid may be partly or entirely for penalties.

At low levels, takeout doubles are both necessary and safe. You have reason to hope that the hand "belongs" to your side and that nothing too horrible will happen if your partner has the equivalent of thirteen deuces.

There is less need for takeout doubles at very high levels. Moreover, it is very dangerous to barge into the auction with a bid of four or more. Mistakes at this level are very expensive.

A double of a bid of *five* is meant for penalties, not for takeout. A double of *four* spades is treated in the same way. A double of *four hearts* is perhaps three fifths for penalties and two fifths for takeout. When you double four hearts, that is, you fully expect your partner to pass; but you are not thunderstruck if he decides to bid with a long spade suit and a fairly strong hand.

If you really want to *force* your partner to bid when an opponent has opened with four spades, you can bid *four notrump.* This is a sort of gigantic takeout double, promising safety at the level of five even if partner has a miserable hand.

For example, suppose the dealer bids four spades. You are next, holding:

♠ ——   ♡ A K Q 5 3   ◇ K Q J 9   ♣ K Q J 6

You bid four notrump, asking your partner to choose one of the unbid suits.

At any rate, that is the theory. However, before you bid four notrump in this situation, be sure that you know all about your partner.

A couple of years ago one of the best players in the world bid four notrump over an opening bid of four spades. The next player doubled, and there were two passes. Not a bit daunted, our hero *re*doubled, confident that this would force his partner to bid.

The redouble was followed by three passes. This little adventure cost the tidy total of four thousand points!

Our unlucky expert had the melancholy pleasure of pointing out that his side could have made a small slam in anything except spades or notrump. The pleasure of the opponents was untinged with melancholy.

Another danger is that your partner may misinterpret the four notrump bid as a query about his aces (see the discussion of the Blackwood Convention in Chapter 7). In short, don't use the four-notrump bid as a gigantic takeout double in this position with an unreliable partner.

To return to our theme, a double of an opening bid of *three* means different things to different people. Some experts use it as a takeout double, pure and simple. Most experts mean it about four fifths for takeout and one fifth for penalties. Some reverse these proportions.

It isn't important for you to know how many experts belong to each school of thought. You do need to know what the players in your game mean; and you want your partner to understand what you mean. If you're playing with a new group, avoid doubling a bid of three unless you're strong enough to stand either a pass or a bid by your partner. Just pass a doubtful hand and accept a small loss.

With your favorite partner I suggest you use the double of a bid of three as primarily for takeout. Just be sure to have a sound hand when you double so that it will be no tragedy if your partner passes.

A double of an opening bid of *one notrump* is supposed to be primarily for penalties. However, the textbooks say, your partner is allowed to take the double out if he has a bad hand with a long suit.

This "rule" is about four fifths nonsense.

The opening bid of one notrump shows about 16 to 18 points. Let's suppose that you double in the next seat with a hand of equal strength. This leaves from 4 to 8 points to be divided between the other two players.

It is therefore perfectly normal for the doubler's partner to have a "bad" hand. If he follows the "rule," he will usually bid when he shouldn't. Only when the doubler's partner has neither length nor strength will he pass the double; and then, as often as not, the doubled contract is made.

To avoid this kind of nonsense, don't double an opening bid of one notrump just because you have some set number of points. Double when you expect to defeat one notrump *by running a long suit.*

You need a long suit that you can confidently expect to cash fairly quickly. You also need a couple of high cards on the side. If you have *only the long suit,* bid it instead of doubling; if you have *only the high cards* without the strong suit, pass and accept a small profit. (The profit may go the other way if you warn the declarer that all the strength is behind him.)

You need the high cards in the side suits partly to help you defeat one notrump and partly to punish the opponents if they run to the wrong escape suit. Your partner is expected to double any rescue suit in which he has J-10-x-x or better, particularly if he has a high card or two on the side.

What if the opponents run to a suit that cannot be doubled? No damage has been done. Almost surely they would have reached the same contract no matter what you did. Your double just increases your chance to punish the opponents when they *don't* have a good escape suit.

For example, over an opening bid of one notrump:

(1) ♠ K Q J 9 7 4   ♡ A 5 4   ◇ K 9   ♣ 8 2

   Double. You will lead the king of spades and establish your long suit. You hope to win five spades, the ace of hearts, and quite possibly the king of diamonds, all in your own hand. Anything your partner shows up with is pure gravy. This double is a bare minimum, and the contract will sometimes be made against you—but declarer will then score only 80 points below the line. This is not serious. If your left-hand opponent redoubles, which is exceedingly unlikely, bid two spades or gamble it out, depending on what you think of the opponents.

(2) ♠ Q J 10 8 7 4   ♡ A 5 4   ◇ K 9   ♣ A 2

   Double. You must regain the lead twice in order to run the spades. This double is a trifle riskier than the first case. However, you should expect to beat one notrump, and your double will probably produce a profit.

(3) ♠ A K Q J 7 4   ♡ 6 5 4   ◇ K 9   ♣ 8 2

   Bid two spades. You can take the first six tricks against the contract of one notrump, but the opponents are not in danger if they bid an escape suit. What's more, they're not in too much danger if they stay in one notrump.

✔ REQUIREMENTS FOR A TAKEOUT DOUBLE

The first requirement for a takeout double is the right

shape—ideally four or more cards in any unbid suit. That is, your best distribution is a singleton or void in the opponent's suit with either four or five cards in each of the unbid suits. This distribution is described as 4-4-4-1 or 5-4-4-0.

The only other requirement is the right *strength*, usually at least the value of an opening bid. More often you will have a better hand.

If the opening bid is one diamond and you are next with:

(1)   ♠ Q J 8 4   ♡ K Q 9 3   ◊ 5   ♣ K 7 6 2

Double. You have the right shape for a double of one diamond (you would have *horrible* shape for a double of any other suit, and you would therefore pass) and adequate strength. You count 11 points in high cards and 3 points for the singleton in support of partner's best suit, whatever that may be. This is minimum value for a takeout double.

Assume that your partner has some such miserable hand as four hearts to the jack and perhaps the queen of clubs, with poor distribution. He will have to bid one heart in response to your takeout double. Will he be in trouble?

Not at all. He will probably manage to scramble home with six or seven tricks. This is not a very good result for the opponents, with their 26 points in high cards.

You may have a far better hand for your takeout double:

(2)   ♠ K J 8 4   ♡ K Q 9 3   ◊ 5   ♣ A Q 6 2

Now you have 15 points in high cards plus 3 points for the singleton. Your partner needs very little to make a game.

Your strength may be increased even more:

(3) ♠ A K 8 4   ♡ A Q 9 3   ◊ 5   ♣ A Q 6 2

If partner responds in spades or hearts you will raise to three of his suit.

If the hand gets much better, you make an immediate cue-bid in the opponent's suit instead of doubling for a takeout. That is, over an opening bid of one diamond you bid *two diamonds*. This asks your partner to bid his best suit and is forcing to game.

You would make such a bid with:

(4) ♠ A K J 4   ♡ A Q J 3   ◊ 5   ♣ A Q J 2

You need slightly less in high cards if you have 5-4-4-0:

(5) ♠ K Q J 4   ♡ A Q J 3   ◊ ——————   ♣ A Q J 3 2

Now that we've seen the upper and lower limits of the takeout double in its standard form, let's look at a few variations.

Sometimes you make a shaded takeout double. This is particularly common when the opponents have a part score, as we have seen. For example, over an opening bid of one diamond:

♠ K 8 7 3   ♡ Q J 8 3   ◊ 5   ♣ K 7 6 2

This is a pretty poor takeout double, but it's not likely to cause much trouble for the doubler's side. It is safer to shade a takeout double than any other aggressive move—provided that you have the right distribution.

This brings us to the next type of variation—a takeout double with inferior distribution. Over an opening bid of one diamond:

(1) ♠ K Q 8 4   ♡ A 7 4   ◇ 6 2   ♣ Q J 7 5

Double. You have 12 points in high cards and 1 point for the doubleton. The support for hearts is somewhat shabby, but it is better to compete than to pass with such a good hand.

(2) ♠ K Q   ♡ A Q 4   ◇ 6 2   ♣ Q 9 7 5 4 2

Pass. Your partner has a right to expect good support for his best suit when you make a takeout double. It's not a crime to have only 3-card support but that's the limit. When you have only 2-card support for an unbid major suit, you just don't have a takeout double. If you have a long suit, overcall. If the suit is not good enough—as in this case—PASS.

The inferior distribution is all right when you have a very powerful two-suited or one-suited hand. Again, over an opening bid of one diamond:

(1) ♠ A K J 9 4   ♡ A Q J 7 3   ◇ 5   ♣ K 2

Double. If partner responds in a major suit, you will raise to game. If he responds in clubs, you will bid spades first, and hearts later if you get the chance.

(2) ♠ A K J 9 8 4   ♡ A Q J   ◇ 5   ♣ K Q 2

Double. If partner responds in spades, you will raise to game. If he responds in hearts or clubs, you will bid spades.

A weaker two-suited hand may be the basis of a takeout double when the opponents bid the other two suits:

SOUTH	WEST	NORTH	EAST
1 ◇	Pass	1 ♠	Double

East should have fine support for the two unbid suits, but he doesn't need a real powerhouse. He should have some such hand as:

♠ 5 2   ♥ A J 9 5   ♦ 7 3   ♣ A K J 8 5

East wants to compete in hearts or clubs, and wants his partner to choose the suit.

After an original pass, a player may double to indicate that he has the right distribution even if the wrong strength. For example:

EAST	SOUTH	WEST	NORTH
Pass	1 ♦	Pass	1 ♠
Double			

East should have a 5-5 two-suiter to make up for the fact that his high cards are not enough for an opening bid:

(1)   ♠ 5 2   ♥ K Q 9 5 2   ♦ 3   ♣ K Q 7 4 3

When you are not vulnerable against vulnerable opponents you may shade the strength even further, provided that you have good enough distribution:

(2)   ♠ 2   ♥ Q J 9 5 2   ♦ 3   ♣ K J 7 4 3 2

    You know that the hand belongs to the other side. You intend to sacrifice at five clubs or five hearts (if necessary) if you can find a reasonable fit for clubs or hearts in partner's hand.

✓ WHEN NOT TO DOUBLE

In general, double when you want your partner to choose the suit. Shade the strength if you must, but don't shade the distribution.

Don't double when *you* want to name the suit regardless of your partner's preference. *Don't* double when you have three or more cards of the opponent's suit.

For example, over an opening bid of one diamond:

(1)   ♠ A Q J 9 4   ♡ A 7 3   ♢ 4   ♣ Q 8 6 3

Bid one spade. Why ask partner to choose a suit when you have a very strong wish to play the hand at spades? If partner bids hearts or clubs without being forced to do so, you can then afford to raise.

(2)   ♠ A 9 8 6   ♡ A 7 3 2   ♢ K 5 4   ♣ Q 3

Pass. If you double for takeout, your partner may respond in clubs and then where will you be?

(3)   ♠ A Q J   ♡ A 7 3 2   ♢ K J 4   ♣ Q 9 3

Bid one notrump (see Chapter 3, How to Handle Your Notrumps). Your bid describes your strength and your distribution. If you use a takeout double instead of bidding one notrump, you won't know what to do next even if your partner responds in a major suit.

We have seen some rather weak examples of the takeout double, but its primary purpose is to take the hand away from the opponents. With just a bit of luck you hope to bid and make a game.

For this reason there is strong emphasis on support for the major suits. If you double a *minor suit,* you should have 4-card support for each of the majors. It is a flaw to have only three cards in one of the majors. It is a crime to have *less* than 3-card support in one or both of the majors.

If you double a *major suit* for takeout, you should have good 4-card support for the other major. It is a serious flaw to have only 3-card support in the unbid major. It is dangerous madness to have any less.

✓ IN SHORT

A takeout double asks partner to bid his best suit.

For a takeout double you need:

- Right strength—about the value of an opening bid
- Right shape—shortness in the opponent's suit, length in the others

A double is meant for takeout when:

1. Partner has not bid.
2. This is the first opportunity to double that suit.
3. It is made at the level of one or two.

Doubles of high opening bids

- A double of a bid of three is for takeout, but partner may pass if he has defensive values.
- A double of four is for penalty, but partner may take out if he has offensive values.
- A double of four spades or five of any suit is for penalty. Partner bids only at his own risk.

Double an opening bid of one notrump when you expect to defeat it with a near-solid suit.

AFTER A TAKEOUT DOUBLE

The Opening Bidder	The Doubler's Partner
√ Responding in Notrump	√ After Partner Passes
√ Free Responses	√ After Partner Raises
√ After a Redouble	√ After Partner Redoubles
√ The Penalty Pass	√ After Partner Bids a New Suit
Rebids by the Doubler	In Short
Opening Bidder's Partner	

A TAKEOUT DOUBLE sets the stage for a bidding struggle. Each side has staked out a claim to the final contract, for the opening bidder and the doubler have announced about equal strength.

The spotlight now swings to the other two players. With their limited strength they must play a leading role in finding the answers to these questions:

1. Whose hand is it—ours or the enemy's?

2. Which is our best suit—or is notrump the spot?

3. How high can we go—to get the biggest plus score (if it's *our* hand) or the smallest minus score (if it's *their* hand)?

Each of the four players has his own way of describing his hand. Each must be given individual attention in this chapter.

154

The Doubler's Partner

The doubler's partner has been asked to bid a suit. He should not sidestep his responsibility merely because he has a poor hand. The weaker the hand, the more essential the takeout.

Whenever possible, moreover, the doubler's partner should convey some idea of his strength. He should indicate whether he has a good hand, a fair hand, or a poor hand.

Take a typical bidding situation:

SOUTH	WEST	NORTH	EAST
1 ♡	Double	Pass	?

How does East indicate his approximate strength?

The textbooks won't give you a sensible answer to this question. Instead we must examine the rules followed by the best players:

- A non-jump response shows 0 to 8 points.
- A jump response shows 9 to 11 points.
- A cue bid in the opponent's suit followed by a *minimum* rebid shows 12 or 13 points.
- A cue bid in the opponent's suit followed by a *jump* rebid shows 14 points or more.

Here are some examples of correct responses by East, based on the typical bidding situation just given:

(1) ♠ J 6 5 2   ♡ 7 4 3   ◇ 9 8 2   ♣ 8 4 2

Bid one spade. This is about as bad a hand as you are likely to hold. Never mind. The responsibility is partner's, not yours.

(2)   ♠ K J 5 2   ♡ 7 4 3   ◊ K 9 8 2   ♣ 4 2

Bid one spade. Almost, but not quite, good enough for a jump response. Your count is 7 points in high cards and 1 point for the doubleton.

(3)   ♠ K J 5 2   ♡ 7 4 3   ◊ K J 9 8   ♣ 4 2

Bid two spades. A minimum jump response. This jump bid is invitational but not at all forcing. Don't be afraid to jump in a 4-card suit; partner has promised good support.

(4)   ♠ Q 7 6 5 2   ♡ 7 4   ◊ A K 9 8   ♣ 4 2

Bid two spades. Maximum value for a jump response. You count 9 points for high cards, 1 point for the doubleton in clubs, and 1 point for the fifth spade. Count nothing for shortness in the *opponent's* suit, since there is a very strong likelihood that your partner is counting for his own shortness in that suit.

(5)   ♠ K J 5 2   ♡ 7 4 3   ◊ A K 9 8   ♣ 4 2

Bid two hearts. This cue bid in the opponent's suit is forcing for one round and shows at least 12 points. In this case you have the minimum value of 12 points. Presumably West will bid two spades, and you will show your minimum by raising to *three* spades. This permits partner to get out of the auction below game if he has doubled with more tripe than tricks.

(6)   ♠ K J 5 2   ♡ 7 4   ◊ A K 9 8   ♣ K 4 2

Bid two hearts. You will not settle for less than a game. If partner bids two spades, you will jump to four spades.

Now for a slight word of warning. Probably most of the players in your regular game follow the textbooks instead of the leading experts. They treat any jump response as forcing to game; and they have never heard of such a thing as a response in the opponent's suit. If you can, convert one or two to the method described here. With the rest of them, adopt their method and do your best.

√ RESPONDING IN NOTRUMP

When do you respond in notrump to your partner's takeout double? Seldom. Your partner has asked you to bid a suit, probably because he has a singleton or void in the opponent's suit. The last thing he wants to hear from you is a response in notrump.

When you respond one notrump you should have reason to believe that the hand will play there safely and well. You should have *two* stoppers in the opponent's suit and about 7 to 10 points.

Do not bid one notrump merely because your only long suit has been bid by the opening bidder. In such a situation respond in your cheapest 3-card suit. You cannot respond in notrump with either a good hand or a bad hand, for if you do, guesswork will take the place of system.

A response of *two* notrump is so rare as to be almost unheard of. Your partner's takeout double should be based on at least 10 or 11 points in high cards. You need about 11 or 12 points in high cards to be safe at two notrump; and you also need two sure stoppers in the opponent's suit.

√ FREE RESPONSES

If the opener's partner bids or redoubles, you are relieved of your responsibility to bid. With any weak hand you may pass instead of bidding your suit. If you have modest values, however, you should show them instead of passing.

SOUTH	WEST	NORTH	EAST
1 ♡	Double	2 ♡	?

If East has a borderline jump bid, he may content himself with a simple response. The fact that he makes it *freely* indicates that his hand is not worthless.

East can respond in the unbid major with as little as a 5-card suit headed by K-J and no side strength. (This is not recommended when the doubler is an erratic player with a marked tendency to overbid. The recommended action with such a partner is to find yourself another game!)

✓ AFTER A REDOUBLE

Similar principles are observed when the opener's partner redoubles:

SOUTH	WEST	NORTH	EAST
1 ♡	Double	Redouble	?

East may pass with a bad hand, leaving it up to the doubler to rescue himself. In such a situation East's pass does *not* indicate satisfaction with the redoubled contract. West must run for safety unless he expects to defeat the contract all by himself.

East can help his partner by bidding when he has something to say, but not otherwise. For example, East can well afford to bid any suit of real merit, such as K-J-x-x-x or better. East can afford to bid a weaker 5-card suit if it is the cheapest possible response. This may indicate a cheap way out of the redouble, and it doesn't prevent the doubler from following his own inclinations if he has a better rescue in mind.

If East bids a 4-card suit in this position, he should have something like two honor cards at the head of his suit. Even then he should avoid bidding such a suit if his bid deprives the doubler of safe rescues.

SOUTH	WEST	NORTH	EAST
1 ◊	Double	Redouble	?

(1) ♠ 8 5 2   ♡ 7 4 3   ◊ 8 6 3   ♣ 9 7 5 4

Pass. Your partner dug this hole; let him dig himself out.

(2) ♠ Q 5 2   ♡ K 7 4 3   ◊ 8 6 3   ♣ 7 5 4

Pass. You're not worried about the outcome, but there's no need to respond in hearts. If West rescues himself in spades, you'll be quite content. Just let him make his natural rescue; a heart bid may merely serve to confuse him.

(3) ♠ 5   ♡ 10 7 4 3 2   ◊ 8 6 3   ♣ 7 5 4 2

Bid one heart. You hate to step in with so ghastly a hand, but you must do something to prevent partner from bidding spades.

✓ THE PENALTY PASS

When should you pass your partner's takeout double for penalties? Only when you expect to draw trumps and defeat the contract. For this purpose you need five or more trumps headed by a good sequence, such as Q-J-10-9-2.

You cannot afford to double a one-bid and then let de-

clarer win tricks by ruffing with all of his small trumps.
You must plan to draw trumps—just as though *you* were
the declarer.

If the opening bidder passes, you expect your partner
to lead a trump if he has any. You will thereafter lead
trumps at each opportunity. This policy will do you no
good if you have a flabby trump holding such as
Q-7-5-3-2.

Take a typical hand:

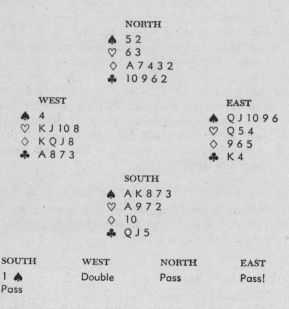

NORTH
♠ 5 2
♡ 6 3
◇ A 7 4 3 2
♣ 10 9 6 2

WEST
♠ 4
♡ K J 10 8
◇ K Q J 8
♣ A 8 7 3

EAST
♠ Q J 10 9 6
♡ Q 5 4
◇ 9 6 5
♣ K 4

SOUTH
♠ A K 8 7 3
♡ A 9 7 2
◇ 10
♣ Q J 5

SOUTH	WEST	NORTH	EAST
1 ♠	Double	Pass	Pass!
Pass			

East has the right hand for a penalty pass—a *solid* trump
holding and prospects of side entry. Nevertheless the
defense depends on the opening lead.

If West opens the king of diamonds, South makes his
doubled contract. He wins the first trick with dummy's

ace of diamonds, ruffs a diamond, cashes the ace of hearts, and gives up a heart.

The defenders now lead trumps, but it is too late. South wins the trump shift, ruffs a heart in dummy, and ruffs another diamond in his own hand. He now has six tricks safely stashed away, with the ace of trumps still in his hand.

The score goes the other way if West opens his single-ton trump—relying, of course, on East's penalty pass.

South wins the first trick with the king of spades, takes the ace of diamonds, and ruffs a diamond. He continues with the ace of hearts and a low heart.

East overtakes the second round of hearts with his queen in order to lead a second trump. This takes the last trump out of dummy and also wrecks South's chance of ruffing another diamond. Thus the contract is set two tricks.

The trump lead would accomplish nothing, however, if East had something like ♠ Q-9-8-7-6 to South's ♠ A-K-J-10-3. South would win the first trump trick with a "free finesse," cash the ace of diamonds, and ruff a diamond. Then he would lead the ace of hearts and a low heart. East would have to lead a trump, giving South another finesse. South would then have seven sure tricks —his five trumps and two side aces.

Rebids by the Doubler

The doubler's rebids depend on the strength of his own hand and the strength (if any) shown by his partner's response.

SOUTH	WEST	NORTH	EAST
1 ♡	Double	Pass	2 ♡
Pass	?		

West can bid in comfort. East has at least 12 points and probably has a good fit for the unbid major. Slam is unlikely, but possible.

SOUTH	WEST	NORTH	EAST
1 ♡	Double	Pass	2 ♠
Pass	?		

East shows 9 to 11 points for play at spades. West can afford to raise with 14 or 15 points in support of spades (including at least four trumps). West should pass with only 13 points or so. The jump response is invitational but not forcing.

SOUTH	WEST	NORTH	EAST
1 ♡	Double	Pass	1 ♠
Pass	?		

East can have only 0 to 8 points, so West must proceed with caution if at all. West need not consider a further bid unless he has about 18 points in support of spades. Even with so fine a hand he should raise only to *two* spades. West can raise to *three* spades with 20 points, and to *game* with about 23 points.

Here we can see the advantage of using an *invitational* jump response to the takeout double. The doubler finds out very quickly just where he stands.

A non-jump response shows 0 to 8 points. The doubler can pass with hands of 15 to 17 points. He won't miss a game if partner has maximum (8 points); and he won't be in trouble if partner has minimum (0 points). Life is simple.

Now see how complicated life can be if a jump response is forcing to game. A non-jump response may be made with 10 points. The doubler cannot relax with hands of 15 to 17 points, for he may miss a game. But if he bids with such hands, he may discover that his partner has a completely worthless hand—and then the one extra bid is the one that lands him in the soup!

When the doubler bids a new suit he shows a very good hand. If he had a mediocre takeout double, he would pass his partner's response. If he didn't like his partner's suit, he wouldn't have doubled to begin with; he would have overcalled in a good suit of his own.

SOUTH	WEST	NORTH	EAST
1 ♡	Double	Pass	2 ♣
Pass	2 ♢		

West should have some such hand as:

♠ K Q 6 4   ♡ 5   ♢ A K J 10 7 2   ♣ K 3

This is the sort of hand that some players use for a *strong* jump overcall.

When the doubler's rebid is in the opponent's suit, he is making a cue bid; he does not show real length or strength in the enemy's suit.

SOUTH	WEST	NORTH	EAST
1 ♡	Double	Pass	1 ♠
Pass	2 ♡		

West wants to get to game in *spades*. He is trying to show that his hand was very nearly good enough for an *immediate* cue bid of two hearts over one heart. He should have some such hand as:

♠ K Q J 5   ♡ ———   ♢ A K J 7 2   ♣ Q J 10 4

West didn't want to bid two hearts at his *first* turn because he didn't want to guarantee a game if his partner responded in clubs, or even in diamonds. Now that East has responded in spades, West wants to force to game and suggest a slam.

Very fine for a well-oiled partnership. Very dangerous if your partner is unreliable. Whenever you bid a suit that you don't really have, remember that your partner may decide to drop you there.

Opening Bidder's Partner

Your partner's opening bid of one in a suit has been doubled for takeout. What should you do?

With support for partner's suit—
• Redouble with 10 points or more.
• Raise partner's suit with less than 10 points.

Without support for partner's suit—
• Redouble with 10 points or more and strength in only two of the unbid suits.
• Pass and double later with strength in all suits.
• Bid a new suit with a good suit and a mediocre hand.
• Bid one notrump with 8 or 9 points, balanced distribution.
• Pass any bad hand.

SOUTH	WEST	NORTH	EAST
1 ♡	Double	?	

(1)   ♠ 5 2   ♡ K J 7 4   ◇ A Q 6 3   ♣ 8 7 5

Redouble. At your next turn you will show heart support as cheaply as possible. The redouble followed by a *simple* (non-jump) raise shows about 10 to 12 points in support of partner's suit.

(2) ♠ 5 2   ♡ K J 7 4   ◊ A Q 6 3   ♣ Q 7 5

Redouble. At your next turn you will *jump*-raise in hearts. This shows 13 points or more in support of partner's suit and is forcing to game.

(3) ♠ K J 5 2   ♡ 7 4   ◊ A Q 6 3   ♣ Q 7 5

Pass. You expect to double for penalties at your next turn. A redouble at this stage will warn the opponents that they are in trouble; East can then pass with a bad hand. If you just pass quietly, East must bid and West may make a *further* bid, and you'll have a chance to double at the level of two or three.

(4) ♠ K Q 5 2   ♡ 7 4   ◊ A K J 6   ♣ 8 7 5

Redouble. You cannot double the opponents if they bid clubs. If your partner doubles clubs, you will be happy as a lark. The redouble asks your partner to double any contract that he can handle, and to pass anything else around to you. The redouble is used with good support for partner's suit or with strength in *only two* of the unbid suits.

(5) ♠ 5 2   ♡ 7 4   ◊ A K J 6 3   ♣ Q J 7 5

Bid two diamonds just as though there had been no takeout double. In a sensible bidding system a response in a new suit should be forcing for one round, just as though the double had not occurred. Unfortunately you will find that many experienced players treat this as a weak bid. This is, of course, sheer nonsense; but when such a player is your partner you have to know what his bids mean and how he will interpret your bids.

(6) ♠ 5 2   ♡ 7 4   ◊ K J 7 6 3 2   ♣ Q 7 5

Pass. Don't start to "rescue" your partner before you are hurt.

(7)   ♠ K 5 2   ♡ 7 4   ◇ K J 7 6   ♣ Q 8 7 5

Bid one notrump. This shows balanced distribution, poor support for partner's suit, and about 8 or 9 points. With less strength you would pass; with more, you would redouble or pass. You want to show your values while it is cheap to do so.

(8)   ♠ 5 2   ♡ K J 7 4   ◇ 7 6 3 2   ♣ 8 7 5

Bid two hearts. The simple raise over a takeout double shows trump support and a very poor hand. It is a feeble shutout bid, but it also indicates to partner definite but limited values for a sacrifice bid.

(9)   ♠ 5 2   ♡ K J 7 4   ◇ K 6 3 2   ♣ 8 7 5

Bid three hearts. The jump raise over a takeout double shows good trump strength with about 7 to 9 points in support of partner. With a really good hand you would redouble first and raise later.

(10)   ♠ 5   ♡ K J 7 4 2   ◇ K 6 3 2   ♣ 8 7 5

Bid four hearts. The jump to four of partner's suit remains the same whether the intervening player bids, passes, or doubles for takeout. It shows five trumps, a singleton or void suit, and not more than 9 points in high-card strength (usually much less).

The Opening Bidder

When your opening bid has been doubled for takeout you know that at least one opponent has fair strength. It is quite possible that the hand "belongs" to the opponents. If you bid incautiously, you may dip deep into the red ink.

Your further action, if any, will depend partly on the strength of your hand and partly on what has happened by the time your second turn comes. You are particularly influenced by what your partner does.

✓ AFTER PARTNER PASSES

You also will pass any minimum hand. If partner is playing a waiting game, let him spring his trap; if he is "busted," stay out of the auction.

If you have a good hand, you may rebid a strong suit of six or more cards, bid a new suit (showing at least nine cards in your two bid suits), or counter with your own takeout double (showing good support for the unbid suits). Counting points for distribution, you should have at least 16 points for any bid in this position.

✓ AFTER PARTNER RAISES

Remember that partner has a weak hand with good trump support. (If he has a good hand, he would redouble first and raise later.) Add your own points to those shown by partner to see how high you can bid safely. You must also consider the advisability of a sacrifice bid if the opponents reach a game. If your partner's raise shuts out the next opponent, it is often a good idea for you to go on to three (or even four) of your suit in order to shut the doubler out.

✓ AFTER PARTNER REDOUBLES

In general, pass unless you have the chance to double a suit you like. If both the doubler's partner and you have passed, the doubler at his next turn will probably get out with a bid of his own; if that bid is passed around to you, you must either double or make some rebid of your own. You and your partner should be able to pass the buck back and forth without worrying about a premature end to the auction. Your purpose is to double the opponents if they are in trouble, but to bid on if they have found a safe suit. There is one exception to this general rule: you may bid instead of passing if you have opened a borderline hand because of unbalanced distribution. Your bid in this situation says that you are not interested in doubling the opponents.

✓ AFTER PARTNER BIDS A NEW SUIT

If your partner is a sensible player, he has a fair hand and expects you to keep the bidding open. Rebid normally if the intervening player passes—almost as though the takeout double had not taken place. As usual, you may pass a minimum hand if there is a bid by the intervening player; the bidding will be kept open by that opponent's action.

In Short

After the takeout double has been made:

• The doubler's partner should tend to bid optimistically.

• The doubler should be very cautious unless his partner shows unmistakable signs of strength.

- Opener's partner should raise or redouble with trump support, should bid with real values, should pass with a bad hand.

- Opening bidder should avoid getting back into the auction if partner passes; any free rebid shows about 16 points or more (counting distribution).

13th DAY
ᴧᴧᴧᴧᴧᴧᴧᴧᴧᴧᴧᴧᴧᴧᴧᴧ

SHUTOUT BIDS

√ Risk Versus Gain	√ The Case Against Strong Three-
√ Shutout Bids of Three or	Bids
More	√ Responding to a Shutout Bid
√ Examples of Shutout Bids	√ Defending Against Shutout Bids
	√ In Short

WHAT CAN YOU do when the opponents hold most of the aces and kings?

Usually, not much. You cannot fight cannons with cream puffs.

When you have the right kind of hand, however, you can use a shutout bid to make life difficult for the opponents.

That is all you should expect. Even if you have the right kind of hand and make the right kind of bid, the opponents still have all their aces and kings. They may still stumble into their best contract.

In general, shutout bids show a loss. Keeping silent, however, shows a bigger loss. You must expect the opponents to make a profit on their preponderance of aces and kings. Your aim is to reduce that profit.

A shutout bid is largely a sacrifice bid in advance. You make your sacrifice at a high level before the opponents start to bid instead of after they have reached their best contract.

Your sacrifice bid is *too expensive* if you are unable to win a reasonable number of tricks. It is *foolish* if the opponents have no good contract of their own.

To put it another way, there are two general requirements for a sound shutout bid:

1. *A long suit,* preferably topless, that should win at least five tricks.
2. *No defense,* that is, no aces, kings, or queens outside of the trump suit—and preferably no ace in the trump suit itself.

    ♠ Q J 10 9 6 4 3   ♡ 5 2   ◊ 4   ♣ 9 6 3

Bid three spades, particularly if you are non-vulnerable against vulnerable opponents. You have the right kind of long trump suit. You have no defense. This is the ideal hand for a shutout bid.

✔ RISK VERSUS GAIN

Isn't this kind of bid risky?

Yes, it is.

Isn't it possible to be doubled and suffer a penalty of 700 points?

Yes, that is possible.

Do not lose your courage, gentle reader. In the long

run, this risky kind of bid will save you *thousands* of points.

Look back on your own experience. What usually happens when an *opponent* opens with three of a suit? Sometimes you bid a suit of your own; sometimes you double and your partner bids a suit. Or perhaps your partner bids or doubles. But in any case you very seldom let the opponents play the hand in their original shutout bid.

If you *never* double for penalties in this situation, the opponents have managed to throw difficulties in your path at no cost to themselves. It would surely be *much* easier for you to bid your cards without their interference.

What happens when a double is allowed to stand? Perhaps you collect only a measly 100 points. Even 300 points is not enough if you have been talked out of a game.

How often will you collect 500 or 700 points? Only when the dummy turns up with, at most, one useful ace, king, or queen. When that happens, it is likely that *both* opponents have no defense. Why aren't you bidding your laydown slam instead of settling for a penalty of 500 or 700 points?

Occasionally, it is true, the dummy shows up with an assortment of queens and jacks that are useless to the declarer at his shutout bid but that would have stopped the opponents from making any slam—or perhaps even from making any game. This is the only real disaster that can overtake the right kind of shutout bid. And fortunately for those who like to make shutout bids, this kind of disaster is quite rare.

The sort of thing that usually takes place is far more likely to be what happened in the finals of the annual contest for the Vanderbilt Cup a few years ago:

South dealer
East-West vulnerable

NORTH
♠ 5 2
♡ 9 8 6 4
◇ Q J 10 5
♣ Q J 4

WEST
♠ A K 8
♡ A Q 10 3
◇ K 7 3
♣ A 8 7

EAST
♠ 7
♡ K J 7
◇ A 9 8 6 2
♣ K 10 5 2

SOUTH
♠ Q J 10 9 6 4 3
♡ 5 2
◇ 4
♣ 9 6 3

SOUTH	WEST	NORTH	EAST
3 ♠	Double	Pass	5 ◇
Pass	6 ◇	Pass	Pass
Pass			

There was a bad trump break, and North won two
trump tricks for down one. As it happened, North had
the typical disaster hand, but his opponents didn't know
it. Instead of collecting, they shelled out.

Even if East-West had managed to make a penalty
double stick, they would have scored no triumph. North
would have provided a club trick, and South would have
escaped with a penalty of only 500 points. This is less
than the value of the vulnerable East-West game.

Is this truly a triumph for the shutout bid of three
spades? After all, isn't it possible that East would get to
six diamonds even if South had passed to begin with?

It is possible, but not likely. At the other table of this match the bidding was:

SOUTH	WEST	NORTH	EAST
Pass	1 ♡	Pass	2 ◊
Pass	3 NT	Pass	Pass
Pass			

A spade lead would have held West to eleven tricks at most, but North actually led the queen of clubs. West won with the ace of clubs and returned the suit to finesse dummy's ten. He won twelve tricks without a struggle, scoring 690 points. Since his teammates were plus 100 at the first table, the total gain on this hand was 790 points—most of it traceable to the opening bid of three spades.

Mind you, the profit could not be foreseen. It was possible for East-West to stop at three notrump or at five diamonds. Had they done so, they might have earned themselves an even break, nothing more.

The important thing to remember about the shutout bid is that it gives the opponents a problem. They can seldom earn a bonus for solving the problem; they often suffer a severe penalty for coming up with the wrong answer.

✓ SHUTOUT BIDS OF THREE OR MORE

In practically all systems the opening bid of three or more in a suit is a shutout bid. The exact requirements vary with:

* The height of the bid
* Vulnerability
* Position at the table

In all cases the bidder should have a long suit but no defense.

An opening bid of three is usually based on a 7-card suit. An opening bid of four promises either an 8-card suit or perhaps a 7-4 two-suiter. An opening bid of five in a minor is usually a very weird hand—something like an 8-4 or 7-5 two-suiter. Since opening bids of four or five are often doubled for penalties, they should be more solid than three-bids.

Vulnerability has a sobering effect on your shutout bids. When you are not vulnerable against vulnerable opponents, you can usually get away with even an outrageous bid. When neither side is vulnerable, you have less to gain and can therefore seldom afford to attempt an atrocity. When only your side is vulnerable, do not preempt at all unless your distribution is so freakish as to tempt you beyond your power to resist. When both sides are vulnerable, be bold but sober; even timid opponents can be provoked into doubling for penalties.

As dealer or second hand after a pass, as we have seen, your shutout bid is based on a topless suit. In third or fourth position, however, you may occasionally have a suit headed by top cards. After your partner has passed, there is little danger of missing a game or slam; and you can therefore concentrate on keeping the opponents out.

By a roundabout route we have come to one of the important principles of shutout bidding. In your first- or second-hand shutout bids you must guarantee a topless suit without high cards on the side *so that your partner will know whether to pass, raise, or sacrifice.* Once you have made your shutout bid you must forever after hold your peace. If further action is necessary, your partner will know what to do—provided you have told him the truth. Do not be alarmed if the opponents bid a slam; perhaps your partner is lurking in a corner with the setting trick. He will not thank you for getting back into the auction and thus incurring a disastrous penalty against a slam that wasn't going to come home.

√ EXAMPLES OF SHUTOUT BIDS

What do you say as dealer on each of the following hands?

(1) ♠ 8 3   ♡ Q J 10 7 6 5 2   ◇ 9 4   ♣ 6 2

Bid three hearts unless vulnerable against non-vulnerable opponents. You would make the same bid after one or two passes. In fourth position, however, you would pass and ask who had passed with an opening bid!

(2) ♠ 8 3   ♡ A Q J 7 6 5 2   ◇ 9 4   ♣ 6 2

Pass, regardless of vulnerability. Aces and shutout bids do not mix. In third position, however, you would bid three hearts in equal or favorable vulnerability (when non-vulnerable against vulnerable opponents).

(3) ♠ 8 3   ♡ A K Q 7 6 5 2   ◇ 9 4   ♣ 6 2

Bid one heart. Do not pre-empt with 2 Quick Tricks. However, in third or fourth position you may bid three hearts. Improve the distribution slightly (to 7-3-2-1 instead of 7-2-2-2), and you might well bid *four* hearts in third position, except, of course, in unfavorable vulnerability (when vulnerable against non-vulnerable opponents).

(4) ♠ 3   ♡ Q J 10 8 7 6 5 2   ◇ 9 4   ♣ 6 2

Bid four hearts only in favorable vulnerability. Bid three hearts if vulnerable. It's a little too easy for the opponents to make a penalty double stick when you open with a four-bid. Your partner might provide a trick, and you might still go for an 800-point ride.

(5)   ♠ 3   ♡ K Q J 8 7 6 5 2   ◇ 9 4   ♣ 6 2

Bid four hearts in equal or favorable vulnerability. If the worst happens, you may still go for that 800-point ride, but this is very unlikely. Your bid will probably have its proper pre-emptive effect.

(6)   ♠ 3   ♡ K Q 10 9 7 6 2   ◇ J 10 9 4   ♣ 2

Bid four hearts if not vulnerable. You expect to win six hearts and a diamond. You need an eighth playing trick for a *vulnerable* four-bid.

(7)   ♠ 3   ♡ 2   ◇ Q J 10 9 7 6 2   ♣ J 10 9 4

Bid four diamonds if not vulnerable. With a tolerant partner you might even make this bid when both sides are vulnerable. The need for a shutout bid is greater when *both* major suits are available to the enemy. Moreover, the opponents are not so quick to pass a double of four clubs or four diamonds. The combination of greater need and lesser risk should just about persuade you to risk the vulnerable four-bid—provided that a bad result won't completely wreck your partnership.

(8)   ♠ 3   ♡ ———   ◇ K Q 10 9 7 6 3 2   ♣ J 10 9 4

Bid five diamonds in equal or favorable vulnerability. This bid should advertise a real freak.

✓ THE CASE AGAINST STRONG THREE-BIDS

Some players like to reserve the opening bid of three in a suit for solid 7-card suits—A-K-Q-x-x-x-x or better. There is something to be said for this when you are vulnerable against non-vulnerable opponents. If you're never going to pre-empt, anyway, in this vulnerability, you might just as well set up high requirements.

There's nothing really wrong with strong three-bids in other situations, just as there's nothing wrong with using a twenty-ton tank as a runabout. It's just wasteful.

If you use the three-bid with a strong hand, you give up the chance to use it with a weak hand. (The late Ely Culbertson once tried to popularize a "Two-Way Three-Bid," but gave up after a chaotic year or two.) The question is: Which type of three-bid is more useful in the long run?

You get the weak hand far oftener than the solid suit. Moreover, you can usually describe your solid suit after opening with a one-bid; the weak hand must usually be opened or abandoned.

The arguments are clear and decisive. Among the leading players, the battle has been won by the *weak* bid. Nevertheless there are many stanch *strong* three-bidders in *social* bridge circles (as distinguished from *tournament* and *serious* rubber-bridge circles). If your partner likes strong three bids, let him have his way—and make your own three-bids strong when you play with him. Even a poor system is better than none at all.

One thing is sure: you cannot afford to make weak three-bids with a partner who insists on overestimating your strength. Unless your partner understands exactly what your bids mean and what he should do, you must revert to strong three-bids. You can handle the opponents, but a stubborn partner is the gravest risk of all.

✔ RESPONDING TO A SHUTOUT BID

In general, *don't.*
When your partner has made a weak bid of three in

a suit, you seldom have a hand good enough for a serious raise. When he has opened with four of a major, you practically never have enough strength for a slam.

You must learn to pass a strong hand quickly and calmly, to entice your left-hand opponent into the auction. If you pass with obvious reluctance, your opponent will know enough to stay out. The auctions that follow a shutout bid are very puzzling and can be very painful. Do not solve the puzzles or relieve the pain of the opponents by indicating the nature of your hand. It's quite all right to read the riot act to your partner when the hand is over—what does the idiot mean by pre-empting when his partner has the best hand at the table!—but show no trace of this while the auction is going on. A tranquil pass may produce points by the thousand!

There are, nevertheless, hands with which you want to take further action. Assume that your partner has only a queen-high 7-card suit—nothing more. When do you want to bid more?

You want to raise seriously when you can produce five sure tricks in trumps and aces. This may be slightly reduced if you have a good trump fit and an already established side suit.

For example, after partner has opened with three hearts, you would raise to four hearts with:

(1)　♠ A 9 5　　♡ K 4　　◊ K Q 8 3　　♣ A K 7 3

Put this opposite a 7-card heart suit and three doubletons, and it will just barely make a game. The average player might try for a slam with this hand if he didn't understand just how terribly weak a shutout bid is.

The other type of hand for a serious raise:

(2)　♠ 9 5 2　　♡ K 4 3　　◊ A K Q 8 3 2　　♣ A

Declarer should manage to hold the loss down to two spades and the ace of trumps. If he has three small spades, which is possible, he may go down at game even with this magnificent dummy!

Not all raises are serious. If you have very little defense and know from your partner's bid that he likewise has no defense, you may raise to game or beyond game to fool the enemy or, at any rate, complicate their task.

For example, partner opens as dealer with three hearts. The next player passes, and you hold:

(1) ♠ 5 2 ♥ K 8 4 3 ♦ 9 8 3 2 ♣ 6 5 2

Bid four hearts. The opponents must have enough material for at least a small slam, perhaps a grand slam. You cannot expect to steal the hand, but perhaps you can talk them out of a slam. Be sure to bid no more, for you will only push them into a slam that they will make.

(2) ♠ 5 2 ♥ K 8 4 3 ♦ Q J 9 8 3 2 ♣ 5

If vulnerability is favorable, jump to *six* hearts! Partner will probably go down four or five, but the opponents surely have a slam. If vulnerability is equal, bid four notrump as though trying for a slam. Partner will show no aces, and you will bid five hearts—if the opponents fail to enter the auction. You may even get away undoubled!

The point is that you know what the opponents can make, when you can trust your partner's bidding. It is up to you to take evasive action, and almost any action is reasonable.

Incidentally, experts treat any response in a new suit as a force for one round. The opening bid is horribly weak, of course, but the responder accepts responsibility for the final contract. The theory is that the responder will simply pass if he has a bad hand, but he will bid a suit of his own if he is looking for a slam or trying to confuse the enemy.

Only very experienced players can be trusted in this

situation. In the normal game your partner will open
with three hearts, for example, and cheerfully pass when
you make such a response as three spades or four diamonds.

You might bid a short suit in response to your partner's
opening three-bid if you were trying to "steal" the suit
from the opponents. For example, with either of the last
two hands you might bid three spades on your worthless
doubleton! This would be fine if your partner could be
trusted to bid again, but you might not enjoy being down
nine at 100 points per trick if your partner dropped you
at three spades. You wouldn't mind being down nine at
50 points per trick (not vulnerable, not doubled) because
the opponents surely have a slam against you.

Ideally (for your side) the bidding should go:

PARTNER	YOU
3 ♥	3 ♠
4 ♥	Pass

The opponents have to be rather naïve to believe this
kind of auction. An astute opponent could listen to an
auction like this without even looking at his cards and
know that somebody was trying to steal the teeth out
of his head. However, knowing this and combating it
are not equally easy. An occasional smart-aleck bid of this
kind may give the opponents an acute case of the heebie-
jeebies.

Occasionally responder's new suit is meant as the first
step in a move toward slam. For example, in this auction:

OPENER	RESPONDER
3 ♥	4 ♦
4 ♥	4 ♠
?	

If responder knows what he is doing, he is trying to get to a slam in hearts. He has controls (aces) in diamonds and spades, but the slam is makable only if opener has a singleton club.

Responder should have some such hand as:

♠ A 9 3   ♥ A K 4   ♦ A K Q 8 3   ♣ 6 2

Opener should jump to *six* hearts if his hand is:

♠ 8 2   ♥ Q J 10 8 7 6 2   ♦ 6 5 2   ♣ 3

At any rate, that is the *theory*. You're not likely to have many partners that you'd trust enough to jump to six hearts. In *practice,* responder must bid a slam or stay out of it; he will get no help from the opener.

✓ DEFENDING AGAINST SHUTOUT BIDS

There is no sure-fire defense against shutout bids. Most experts act against a three-bid or a weak two-bid much as if it were a one-bid—but with more caution.

- A double is for takeout. Partner may pass a double of three for penalties with balanced distribution and two or more high cards, even without special length or strength in the bid suit.
- An overcall promises a good suit and reasonable safety.
- A jump overcall promises a good suit and a good hand; very little should be needed from partner.

(See also the *Fishbein Convention* and *Cheaper Minor for Takeout* in the 33rd Day, *Modern Bidding Conventions.*)

If the opening shutout bid is passed around, fourth hand should reopen on any hand worth an opening bid. A double is for takeout; if fourth hand has enough trump strength to defeat the opening shutout bid, he must pass and take his profit.

Doubles of four-bids are for penalties.

√ IN SHORT

An opening bid of three or four in a suit shows:

- A topless suit of seven cards or more
- No high cards in the side suits

Responder needs a very powerful hand or a very fine trump fit to raise a three-bid to game. Responder should not consider slam unless he has virtually a strong two-bid of his own, including at least three aces.

Don't use weak three-bids with a partner who doesn't understand them (even if he says he does). Reserve them for partners you are quite sure of.

14th DAY

mmmmmmmmmm

WHEN TO SACRIFICE

√ The Value of Game	√ Discouraging a Sacrifice
√ Advantages of Sacrifice Bidding	√ Bid or Double?
√ How Much Will You Be Set?	√ The Forcing Pass
√ Encouraging a Sacrifice	√ In Short
√ The Advance Sacrifice	

ONE OF THE objects of the game is to lose a minimum with bad cards. In many cases all you can do is to sit tight and defend to the best of your ability against an opponent's contract. Sometimes, however, you can deliberately overbid and give the opponents less for beating you than they could make at their own best contract. Such a deliberate overbid is called a *sacrifice* bid.

Is it sporting to sacrifice, and thus deprive the opponents of the fun of playing at a contract of their own?

This depends on the kind of game you play in. If the other players are all elderly maiden ladies, it is somewhat cruel to steal their hands from them. In any other kind of game, the players can all have more fun and a keener battle if sacrifice bids are accepted as part of the game, like the cards or the scorepad.

✓ THE VALUE OF GAME

To know when to sacrifice and how much you can profitably afford, you must know the value of game.

At the beginning of a rubber, the side that wins a game scores 100 points (or slightly more) below the line. Nothing else appears on the scorepad. Is this the full value of the game?

Not at all. The value of that game is roughly 300 points outside of what is written down on the scorepad.

If the opponents score the next game, their game is likewise worth about 300 points—for they have canceled your advantage.

If your side wins not only the first but also the second game of the rubber, the second game is worth about 400 points. The two-game bonus for rubber is 700 points; you mentally count about 300 for the first game and the other 400 for the second game.

When both sides have a game, the rubber game is worth exactly 500 points. As it happens, this is written down on the scorepad when the second game is scored.

It isn't necessary to remember all of these figures in

actual practice. For rubber-bridge purposes it is enough to assume that any game is worth about 500 points, counting both the bonus and the trick score. (In tournament bridge any non-vulnerable game is worth 300 points, any vulnerable game 500 points; the trick score is added to these figures.)

You can afford to suffer a penalty of 500 points to prevent the opponents from making a game. This means that you can go down three tricks non-vulnerable or two tricks vulnerable. Anything less is a bargain; anything more, an overpayment.

A vulnerable small slam is worth about 1400 points, all told. A non-vulnerable small slam is worth about 1000 points. You can afford to sacrifice up to these amounts if your opponents are good enough to bid their slam and skillful enough to make it. In practice, you should seldom sacrifice more than 700 points against a non-vulnerable slam or about 900 points against a vulnerable slam. Let the opponents earn their big scores for themselves; perhaps declarer will find a way to go down.

✓ ADVANTAGES OF SACRIFICE BIDDING

The advantages of judicious sacrifice bidding are:

- If doubled, your loss is smaller than the value of the opponents' game.
- If the opponents bid on instead of doubling, they may go down.
- In either case the opponents are strained to the breaking point.

How can you tell that your sacrifice bid is going to be *judicious?*

You must consider two questions:

- How sure is the opponents' game?
- How many tricks will you be set?

The sureness of the opponents' game depends on a number of factors.

Do you and your partner have enough defensive tricks to defeat the game? Always consider the possibility of getting ruffing tricks.

Is declarer going to run into unfavorable distribution? This is always a possibility when both sides can bid up to a high level.

Is the declarer-to-be a skillful player? A poor player can show unsuspected talent in finding a way to lose a cold contract.

When you are considering an *advance* sacrifice, you must also wonder whether the opponents will bid their game if left to their own devices.

As you might imagine, you don't want to sacrifice against a phantom game or against a game that the actual declarer is likely to flub. If you have doubts about the sureness of the game, you may be willing to sacrifice 300 points but not 500 points. In general, you give up 500 points only against a game that you have no doubts about.

✓ HOW MUCH WILL YOU BE SET?

Calculating how many tricks you will be set is a very difficult art. You can avoid disasters by sacrificing only when the partnership has a very sound trump suit and when the excellence of your distribution leads you to believe that the penalty will be on the low rather than the high side. Avoid sacrifice bids with doubtful trump suits or balanced distribution; these are the hands that sometimes run up to penalties of 900 or 1100 points!

Let's see some examples to put these principles into practice. You are West. Neither side is vulnerable. The bidding has been:

SOUTH	WEST	NORTH	EAST
1 ♠	2 ◇	2 ♠	3 ◇
4 ♠	?		

(1)   ♠ 8 7 3 2   ♡ 6   ◇ A K J 9 8 4   ♣ 9 2

Bid five diamonds. You have very little defense against four spades. Even if you get a heart ruff and a diamond trick—surely all you can expect from this hand—you cannot feel sure that your partner will contribute two other tricks. If you can boost the opponents to *five* spades, however, you will have a fair chance to defeat the contract.

The trump suit is sound, and the distribution is excellent. Partner must be very short in spades, and you are short in hearts. In fact, if partner is void of spades and has a useful high card in hearts or clubs, you may even *make* five diamonds.

(2)   ♠ 8 7   ♡ 6 3 2   ◇ A K J 9 8 4   ♣ 9 2

Pass. You did your all when you bid two diamonds. Do not sacrifice with balanced distribution.

(3)   ♠ 8 7   ♡ K J 3   ◇ Q J 9 8 4 2   ♣ A 9

Pass. You have excellent defense against four spades. You may well take three tricks yourself, and your partner should turn up with a trick or so. Don't sacrifice against a doubtful game.

✓ ENCOURAGING A SACRIFICE

When your opponents are confirmed sacrifice bidders it's a shame to deprive them of the chance to do their stuff. Whenever they bid and raise a suit against your side, think of bidding game with great confidence—whether you can make it or not. A certain kind of opponent will go for the sacrifice without asking questions.

SOUTH	WEST	NORTH	EAST
1 ♠	2 ◊	2 ♠	3 ◊
?			

Bid game on any sound opening bid. One opponent or the other will probably take a stab at five diamonds.

Similarly in slam auctions, particularly when you are vulnerable against non-vulnerable opponents:

SOUTH	WEST	NORTH	EAST
1 ♠	2 ◊	3 ♠	4 ◊
?			

If you have a reasonable number of aces, bid a slam without further ado. You seldom have to play the hand, for the opponents usually take the push to seven diamonds. If you do play the hand, it isn't a total loss: you may make the contract, after all. If not, you at least have got "advertising value" from your jump, which may make it easier for you to "buy" the next slam hand. The opponents may think that you are bluffing again.

✓ THE ADVANCE SACRIFICE

The best kind of sacrifice is bid *before* the opponents reach game. For example:

SOUTH	WEST	NORTH	EAST
1 ♠	2 ◇	2 ♡	5 ◇!

East has:

  ♠ 8732 ♡ 4 ◇ Q9732 ♣ A64

East can be reasonably sure that the opponents have a game in hearts. West would have doubled one spade if he had length in hearts, the unbid major, as well as in diamonds.

If East waits until the game is bid and then bids five diamonds, the opponents will have a better idea of what to do. They will double or bid on—according to which is better for them.

East can get a better result by taking his sacrifice *at once* instead of waiting. South, who surely has undisclosed heart support, will feel compelled to bid five hearts instead of doubling five diamonds. Now the opponents are in a shaky contract. Partner may get a spade ruff and a trump trick, and you will get your ace of clubs.

✓ DISCOURAGING A SACRIFICE

When the bidding indicates that a sacrifice bid is in the wind, you can sometimes stave it off by making some meaningless forcing bid:

SOUTH	WEST	NORTH	EAST
1 ♠	2 ◇	2 ♠	3 ◇
?			

  ♠ AQJ984 ♡ Q32 ◇ 4 ♣ AK5

Bid three hearts! No danger of being dropped, since this bid is forcing. The idea is to confuse the opponents either during the bidding or during the play. Perhaps they will think enough of their heart strength to give up the sacrifice at five diamonds.

Another way of discouraging the sacrifice is to allow yourself to be *pushed* to game instead of bidding it at once. In the situation given above, you might bid only *three* spades at your second turn.

If West bids four diamonds, you will then bid four spades. Now the opponents may think that you are over-board and that it isn't necessary to sacrifice.

What if West passes? Then *North* may bid four spades. True, North may pass and you will miss a game. The danger of playing cat-and-mouse is that the mouse may get away.

Much the same tactics, with the same danger, may be employed when the idea is to get to a slam without forcing the opponents to sacrifice.

SOUTH	WEST	NORTH	EAST
1 ♠	2 ◇	3 ♠	4 ◇
?			

♠ A Q J 9 8 4   ♡ K 3 2   ◇ 4   ♣ A K 5

Partner surely has enough material to make six spades a laydown. If you bid the slam, the opponents are likely to sacrifice. If you bid only four spades, the opponents will probably bid five diamonds, giving you another chance.

Perhaps if you then jump to six spades, the opponents may decide that you are just stabbing at the slam. Why should they sacrifice against so uncertain a contract?

Some experts, iron of nerve, allow themselves to be pushed first to five spades and only then to six spades! Sometimes they even get doubled at a cold contract that they intended from the very outset to bid! But it must be admitted that they often get dropped at five spades.

Incidentally, make a mental note that five spades and five hearts are usually shaky contracts. If the declarer had any substantial extra strength, he would bid a slam.

When you have pushed the opponents to five of a major, *get out of the auction;* you have done your job. The opponents are a trick above game but will get only 30 points extra for their courage. Their risk is far greater than their gain. When you have the opponents at a disadvantage, don't try one more push. There is an old Wall Street saying that applies to bridge as well: Sometimes the bulls win and sometimes the bears win, but the hogs *never* win!

✓ BID OR DOUBLE?

When the opponents compete against you at a fairly high level you must often choose between doubling them and making a further bid of your own. Your choice depends partly on your cards and partly on how clear it is that the opponents are beyond their depth.

If the opponents are clearly overboard, you may double even though your hand has little defensive value. If the opponents may have a play for their contract, however, your double should show positive defensive values.

We can see the difference in a few auctions:

SOUTH	WEST	NORTH	EAST
1 ♠	2 ◊	2 ♠	3 ◊
4 ♠	5 ◊		

West is not clearly overboard. He may have a very fine play for his contract even though North and South have full value for their bids. If both East and West had passed on the first round, however, it would be reasonable to assume that the five-diamond contract is a stretch. Two passing partners should not have a good play for eleven tricks.

SOUTH	WEST	NORTH	EAST
1 ♠	2 ◇	3 ♠	Pass
4 ♠	5 ◇		

West is almost surely overboard. Only a very fine and very crafty player would bid two diamonds at his first turn on a hand that was good for eleven tricks!

When the opponents are clearly sacrificing, a player should bid on if he has substantial extra strength but should double if he has good defensive values or has already overbid his hand slightly. Take the last auction:

SOUTH	WEST	NORTH	EAST
1 ♠	2 ◇	3 ♠	Pass
4 ♠	5 ◇	?	

(1) ♠ K 9 7 3   ♡ A J 10 7 3   ◇ 4   ♣ A J 10

Bid five spades (with a fine partner, five hearts). It is hard to imagine a hand with which South cannot easily make five spades—provided that he has no wasted strength in diamonds. Slam is still not out of the question, but you cannot afford to bid it single-handed. Partner may have worthless doubletons in hearts and diamonds, for example, and will then lose a heart and a diamond.

(2) ♠ K Q 7 3   ♡ Q J 10 7   ◇ 4 2   ♣ K J 3

Double. Your jump to three spades was based on minimum values, and you cannot afford to encourage a contract of five spades. Among other things, your partner may have a doubleton diamond that duplicates your own. You are both counting a ruffing value that doesn't exist. You have a trifle of defensive strength in hearts and clubs, but these are not really the backbone of your double. What you really mean is, "Partner, don't bid any higher."

✓ THE FORCING PASS

Sometimes you don't really know whether to bid or double. What then? If the opponents are clearly overboard, you can pass and leave the decision to your partner. Since your partner should know, just as you do, that the opponents are beyond their depth, he can fall back on a double if he cannot see his way clear to a further bid.

In the last auction we saw that North can bid five spades with maximum values and will double with minimum values. He may, instead, have a hand of middling value:

    ♠ K973   ♡ KQ107   ◇ 42   ♣ KQ3

North should pass. He cannot bid five spades with this aceless hand. He should not settle for a penalty that may come to only 300 points. It is safe to pass, for South will know what to do. South can bid five spades if he has two or three aces and a singleton diamond. If South lacks such clear values, he will double.

The forcing pass is used differently when the opponents have sacrificed against a slam. The pass then shows ace or void in the enemy's suit and asks partner whether he can afford to bid a grand slam in the light of this information:

SOUTH	WEST	NORTH	EAST
1 ♠	2 ◇	3 ♠	4 ◇
6 ♠	7 ◇	?	

(1) ♠ K 9 7 3   ♡ A Q 10 7 4   ◊ ———   ♣ Q J 3 2

Pass! This promises the ace or void in diamonds, together with values that may yield a fine play for the grand slam. South is invited to bid again if his only concern is with diamonds. If South has other problems, however, he should double and collect his sure profit.

(2) ♠ K J 7 3   ♡ A Q 10 7 4   ◊ 2   ♣ K J 3

Double. This is compulsory since North cannot control the first round of diamonds. (Remember that a pass would *guarantee* ace or void in diamonds.)

√ IN SHORT

Be on the alert to sacrifice against a sure game or slam. You can afford to pay out 500 points against a game, slightly more against a slam.

Don't sacrifice with a doubtful trump suit or with balanced distribution.

15th DAY
wwwwwwwwwwwww

PENALTY DOUBLES—LOW CONTRACTS

√ Light Doubles	√ In Short
√ Doubling into Game	

THE PENALTY DOUBLE is the most important call in contract bridge. Without it, you couldn't keep optimistic

opponents from bidding game or slam on every hand.
With it, you get your biggest profits.

If you are a newcomer to the game, do not be misled
by the maiden-aunt type of experienced player who
thinks that penalty doubles are rough and unsporting.
They are the soul of the game. Double your opponents
with amiable ferocity; accept their doubles with resigna-
tion but no resentment.

One other myth should be exploded—that of the sancti-
ty of your partner's penalty doubles. Some years ago
the late H. T. Webster took great delight in drawing
cartoons that pilloried the wretch who took out his
partner's business double. After a few of these cartoons
had appeared, the notion somehow got about that it
was morally wrong or at the very least a breach of
etiquette to bid after your partner had doubled the
opponents for penalties.

Experts have never paid much attention to this myth.
If he has a good reason, an expert takes out a *double*
just as though partner had shown his strength by a *bid*.
And the doubler, if he is likewise an expert, not only
expects this treatment but scolds his partner for letting
the double stand if his hand clearly called for a takeout.

Here we must say something about tentative and
authoritative doubles. We have all heard some doubles
timidly quavered and others viciously snapped out. We
shouldn't really hear this sort of thing; all doubles should
be made in the same tone of voice. Certainly we shouldn't
allow partner's tone to persuade us one way or the other.
We will go into this subject in more detail at the end of
this book, in Chapter 34, Manners, Morals and Laws,
but here we can make the mental note that it is improper to indicate by your tone what kind of double you
are making; it is even more improper to allow your
partner's tone to influence you if his voice control happens to slip.

✓ LIGHT DOUBLES

The problem of whether or not to let partner's double stand is most acute in low-level overcalls. For example:

EAST	SOUTH	WEST	NORTH
1 ♠	2 ◊	Double	Pass
?			

If East's opening bid consists of

(1) ♠ A 9 6 3 2   ♡ A 4   ◊ K 9 3   ♣ K J 8

he will be delighted with the double. East has excellent defense against a contract of two diamonds doubled, and can expect to tear poor South limb from limb.

If East's opening bid, instead, consists of

(2) ♠ A K Q J 6 3   ♡ J 1 0 8 4   ◊ ——   ♣ 9 8 5

he will dislike the double. East has practically no defense against diamonds, and should expect to see South make two diamonds doubled if he is allowed to play that contract.

In expert partnerships West is expected to make very light doubles of such overcalls as two diamonds, two clubs, or one of anything. East, the opening bidder, is expected to use his judgment on whether or not to let the double stand.

One argument in favor of the light double of these low contracts is that declarer does not score game if he makes his doubled contract. The unsuccessful double costs something, but it is not disastrous. If the double works well, it picks up a large number of points.

Another argument is that many unenlightened citizens cling to the custom of overcalling on hands that would make even a garbageman blanch.

For example:

```
                    NORTH
                    ♠ K Q J 5
                    ♡ J 10 8 3
                    ◇ 5
                    ♣ 10 9 5 2

    WEST                              EAST
    ♠ 4                               ♠ A 9 6 3 2
    ♡ K Q 6 2                         ♡ A 4
    ◇ J 7 6 4                         ◇ K 9 3
    ♣ A 6 4 3                         ♣ K J 8

                    SOUTH
                    ♠ 10 8 7
                    ♡ 9 7 5
                    ◇ A Q 10 8 2
                    ♣ Q 7
```

EAST	SOUTH	WEST	NORTH
1 ♠	2 ◇	Double	Pass
Pass	Pass		

Of course South should be given thirty days on
bread and water for that overcall of two diamonds.
But how can South be punished adequately unless
West is permitted to double with a light hand? (And
East lets the double stand with Hand 1, shown
earlier.)

Once the double is made, South suffers in pro-
portion to his crime. West opens a spade, and East
takes the ace. East returns the nine of spades for
West to ruff.

West reads this as a signal to return a heart. (In
leading for a ruff, you lead a high card to ask for
a return in a high suit; you lead a low card for a
low suit.) East takes the ace of hearts and returns
the deuce of spades for another ruff.

West now cashes the king and queen of hearts, allowing East to discard a club. West cashes the ace of clubs and leads a club to East's king.

By this time South has been stripped down to his five trumps. East leads another spade, and South must still lose two more trump tricks.

South wins only three tricks and is therefore down five. If he is not vulnerable (would *anybody* make that overcall when vulnerable?), the penalty will be 900 points—just about what the whole rubber is worth. What is more, South cannot write off part of the loss as the value of an East-West game. East and West would probably have stopped below game and might well have gone down if they had bid a game.

Now see what happens if East has the other kind of hand (shown as Hand 2 earlier in the chapter):

NORTH
♠ 9 5 2
♡ A 3
◇ K 9 5 3
♣ K J 10 2

WEST
♠ 4
♡ K Q 6 2
◇ J 7 6 4
♣ A 6 4 3

EAST
♠ A K Q J 6 3
♡ J 10 8 4
◇ ——————
♣ 9 8 5

SOUTH
♠ 10 8 7
♡ 9 7 5
◇ A Q 10 8 2
♣ Q 7

The South and West hands remain unchanged.

Only East and North have changed. If East passes the double of two diamonds, he will eventually regret it.

South will lose three spades, one heart, and one club. He will not lose a trump trick, since he can cash his ace, discovering East's void, and then finesse through West's jack. Hence South will score 80 points below the line and 50 points above the line for making the doubled contract. Counting the value of the part score, South shows a profit of about 200 points on his miserable overcall.

South's full profit is really much greater. East-West can make game in either spades or hearts. Assuming that the game is worth about 500 points, South has gained 700 points by the combination of his overcall and East's leave-in.

This sort of loss can be avoided by the opening bidder if he treats the double as a *suggestion* rather than as a command.

He accepts the suggestion if his hand is good for defense (a couple of trumps and strength in two or three suits); he rejects the suggestion if his hand is better for offense (singleton or void in trumps, strength concentrated in a long suit or suits).

The light double (of two diamonds or any lower overcall) promises:

- About 10 points in good defensive values
- Prospects of at least one trump trick
- Shortness in the opener's suit
- About 1½ Quick Tricks (or more) in the unbid suits

If the doubler has greater trump strength, he can reduce the other requirements slightly, but he should never get far below 1½ Quick Tricks in the unbid suits. There is no great advantage in doubling the only contract you can beat. What will you do if the opponents run to a new suit? And what if your partner doubles the new suit, counting on you to provide a couple of defensive tricks?

To put it another way, the light double shows general strength of about 10 points, just as though the responder had made a response at the level of two. This permits the partnership to go on if the opener has a lopsided hand, but prevents the opponents from escaping if the opener has good defense.

The opener should take out the double when he has a void or singleton in the doubled suit (except perhaps a singleton ace or king) or when his strength is concentrated in one or two long suits.

If he decides to take the double out, the opener rebids his suit to show a minimum hand but a good suit; jumps in his suit to show a self-sufficient suit; bids a new suit to show a two-suiter of some kind; may even bid the opponent's suit to force to game and show a void in the doubled suit.

Now let's take a look at some examples of the light double:

EAST	SOUTH	WEST	NORTH
1 ♠	2 ◇	?	

(1) ♠ 8   ♡ A 7 3 2   ◇ Q 10 4 3   ♣ K 8 5 2

Double. You have only 9 points in high cards, but you have prospects of *two* trump tricks. If an opponent or your partner bids a new suit, you will know what to do. An ideal light double.

(2)   ♠ A 3 2   ♡ 8 7   ◊ Q 10 4 3   ♣ K 8 5 2

Bid two spades. The strong support for partner's suit steers you away from the double. If you get any later chances to double, you will be delighted. On some hands you get the chance to show your support and also your defensive strength.

(3)   ♠ 8   ♡ 9 7 3 2   ◊ A J 10 9 8   ♣ 8 5 2

Pass. Why scare the opponents out of the only contract you can beat? If two diamonds is passed around to your partner, he may reopen the auction with a (takeout) double. You will be delighted to pass such a double. But don't double on your own when your only strength is in the enemy's suit.

(4)   ♠ 8   ♡ A Q 3 2   ◊ 10 4 3   ♣ K Q 9 8 5

Double. Do this only with a very reliable partner. Your trump trick is non-existent, but your side strength may make up for it. No other call is really attractive, but you might bid three clubs if you cannot trust your partner to treat your double as a mere suggestion.

Should the opener accept the double? Let's take a few cases.

The bidding has been:

EAST	SOUTH	WEST	NORTH
1 ♠	2 ◊	Double	Pass
?			

(1)   ♠ K Q 9 6 4   ♡ K 9 3   ◊ J 8 5   ♣ A 2

Pass. You have all the defensive value your partner can reasonably expect. You may or may not defeat two diamonds; it is as good a way as any to try for a juicy score.

(2) ♠ A K Q 9 6 4   ♡ K 9 3   ◇ 2   ♣ J 8 5

Bid two spades. Too much of your high-card strength is in spades. If you had more diamonds, you might be tempted to let the double stand despite your concentrated spade strength.

(3) ♠ K Q 9 6 4   ♡ K J 9 8 3   ◇ 5   ♣ A 2

Bid two hearts. Your defense against diamonds is poor. You may well have a game at hearts.

(4) ♠ A Q 9 6 4   ♡ K Q J 9 3   ◇ 5   ♣ A 2

Bid three hearts. The jump shows the power as well as the distribution.

(5) ♠ A Q 9 6 4   ♡ K Q J 3   ◇ ——————   ♣ A J 10 2

Bid three diamonds. You are more interested in game or slam at one of your suits than in defense against any low diamond contract. Partner will be very bullish if he has good outside strength and weak diamonds.

✓ DOUBLING INTO GAME

When you double an opponent at two hearts or any higher bid, you give him a game if he makes his contract. Your double may be the opponent's only way of scoring game.

If this kind of double goes sour, it costs you at least 500 points. Hence you avoid highly speculative doubles

in this situation. You must have a *real* trump trick or
two, not just prospects of a trick. If in doubt, you can
pass and accept the undoubled penalty.

EAST	SOUTH	WEST	NORTH
1 ♠	2 ♡	?	

(1)   ♠ 8   ♡ Q 10 4 3   ◇ A 7 3 2   ♣ K 8 5 2

Double. You will probably get two trump tricks and
your two high cards in the side suits. You should
beat two hearts if partner can provide the two or
three defensive tricks promised by his opening bid.
This is about as light a double as you can afford
to make.

(2)   ♠ 8   ♡ 10 4 3   ◇ A Q 3 2   ♣ K Q 9 8 5

Bid three clubs. You cannot afford to double without a
real trump trick. You are not delighted with your
high bid on a possible misfit hand, but you have too
much strength to pass.

(3)   ♠ 8   ♡ 10 4 3 2   ◇ A Q 3 2   ♣ Q J 8 5

Pass. You have enough hearts to worry declarer but
not enough to be sure of beating him. If your partner reopens the bidding with a (takeout) double,
you will pass for penalties.

It follows that the opening bidder has less responsibility to take out this kind of double. He can afford to
pass when he has three defensive tricks even though he
may have a worthless singleton in the opponent's suit. If
void of the doubled suit, however, the opening bidder
should find a rebid of some kind.

The opening bidder should be alert to double any

rescue bid if he has three or more cards in that suit headed by the queen or better. His partner has promised some length and strength in the unbid suits by his double, and there is no escape for the enemy.

EAST	SOUTH	WEST	NORTH
1 ♠	2 ♡	Double	3 ♣
?			

(1)   ♠ A K J 8 5   ♡ 4 2   ◇ K 7 4   ♣ Q 8 6

Double. Clubs will probably be as bad for the opponents as hearts—and one trick higher.

(2)   ♠ A K J 8 5   ♡ 4 2   ◇ K Q 4   ♣ 8 6 5

Pass. You will be delighted if partner doubles, but there is no need to bid his cards for him. If his cards are predominantly red, he will not want to double—and if he doesn't, you shouldn't.

(3)   ♠ A K J 8 5 3   ♡ 4   ◇ K Q 8 4 2   ♣ 6

Bid three diamonds. There is a fine chance for game at diamonds or spades, but you shouldn't expect to get rich against a low club contract.

✓ IN SHORT

- Double the opponent's overcall of two diamonds or less LIGHT with:
  - . . about 10 points in good defensive values
  - . . prospects of at least one trump trick
  - . . shortness in opener's suit
  - . . at least 1½ Quick Tricks in the unbid suits

- Double any higher bid with:
  - . . sound—not shaded—values for a light double
  - . . a *sure* trump trick or two
- The opener should take the double out if he has:
  - . . a void or singleton in the doubled suit
  - . . strength concentrated in one or two long suits

16th DAY

PENALTY DOUBLES—HIGH CONTRACTS

√ Game Doubles	√ Slam Doubles
√ Counting Tricks for a Double	√ Other Lead-Directing Doubles
√ Inferential Doubles	√ In Short
√ Doubles of Three Notrump	

√ GAME DOUBLES

WHEN THE OPPONENTS get to a normal game contract you don't have to worry about doubling them into game— they've already bid it. Nevertheless your double is not "free."

An opponent who fulfills a *doubled* game contract scores at least 150 points more than if undoubled. If he wins an overtrick, his gain from the double goes up to about 250 or 350 points. If he is confident enough to re-double, his gain may go up to 600 points or more. Clearly, a double that may cost you 600 points is not *free*.

A further warning about doubles of game bids. Sometimes the double tells declarer just how to make his contract.

NORTH
- ♠ 10 4
- ♡ 8 3
- ◇ A K J 6 4
- ♣ A 7 6 5

WEST
- ♠ K J 9 8
- ♡ 9 5 4
- ◇ 8 7
- ♣ Q J 10 4

EAST
- ♠ 2
- ♡ A 7 2
- ◇ Q 10 5 3 2
- ♣ K 9 3 2

SOUTH
- ♠ A Q 7 6 5 3
- ♡ K Q J 10 6
- ◇ 9
- ♣ 8

SOUTH	WEST	NORTH	EAST
1 ♠	Pass	2 ◇	Pass
2 ♡	Pass	2 NT	Pass
4 ♡	Pass	4 ♠	Pass
Pass	Double (?)	Pass	Pass
Pass			

West leads the queen of clubs, and declarer wins in dummy with the ace. He continues with a heart to the king.

When West fails to produce the ace of hearts, South can be pretty sure that West has doubled on the basis of great trump strength. West would make his three trump tricks if he had had the good sense to keep quiet, but his double will cost him a trump trick if South is a player of real competence.

At the third trick South leads a low trump toward dummy. West cannot gain by ducking, so he steps up with the jack of spades. His best defense is to lead a club to make South ruff.

South cannot afford to lead another low trump, for back would come another club to "punch" him again. South would eventually lose control of the hand by this line of play.

Instead, South leads a diamond to dummy's king and returns a heart from dummy. East takes the ace of hearts and leads another club. South must ruff, and now the position is:

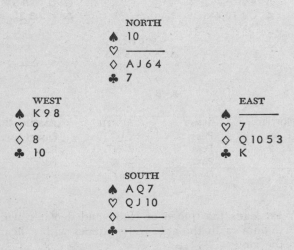

NORTH
♠ 10
♡ ———
♢ A J 6 4
♣ 7

WEST
♠ K 9 8
♡ 9
♢ 8
♣ 10

EAST
♠ ———
♡ 7
♢ Q 10 5 3
♣ K

SOUTH
♠ A Q 7
♡ Q J 10
♢ ———
♣ ———

South leads his good hearts. Sooner or later West must ruff, and dummy will over-ruff (unless West has wasted his king of spades). South then ruffs any card from dummy (even the ace of diamonds), not caring what West does.

If West over-ruffs, it reduces him to the singleton king of spades. No matter what West returns, South can easily ruff, lead out the ace of spades, and claim the rest.

Somewhat complicated, but a good declarer would feel

his way, step by step, if West let the cat out of the bag with a penalty double of four spades.

If any player adopted such a line of play without being doubled, he should be complimented on his eyesight. East and West should sit up straighter and hold their cards closer to the vest.

Normally, in the absence of a double, declarer would win the first trick in dummy with the ace of clubs and return a low trump. Down one from there on!

You can avoid such "giveaway" doubles by adopting two simple rules for your doubles of game contracts:

- Never double without at least one trump trick.
- Never double for a *one*-trick set. Always have reason to expect a set of *two* tricks or more.

The reserve of one trick will take care of the times when the double helps declarer to play the hand well.

✓ COUNTING TRICKS FOR A DOUBLE

When you are considering a double of a game contract, count your own defensive tricks first and then add the tricks promised by your partner's bids (if any). Double if the total includes at least one trump trick and will put declarer down two or more.

Start by counting your trump tricks. If the bidder is on your right, it is reasonable to assume that you are behind most of the missing high trumps. This is particularly true if dummy has never raised the suit. If the bidder is on your left, your trumps are in bad position; the high cards are all *over* them. The position of your trumps may seriously affect their value.

Count something extra for a holding of four or more

trumps unless you have already counted the combination at its highest possible value. Declarer will have trouble getting the trumps out, and even four worthless trumps may have a high nuisance value.

When dummy has raised the trump suit he may have a high honor count and you cannot be sure of favorable position. The best course is to count your trumps at full value and then deduct a trick for safety's sake.

In counting values in the side suits, just count up your Quick Tricks. Assign a slightly higher value to high cards in declarer's side suit if he has bid one. Beware of counting more than one trick in a suit of six cards or more.

Count on your partner for two or three tricks for an opening bid of one in a suit; for four tricks for an opening bid of one notrump (16 to 18 points). Count on him for only one defensive trick if he has made an overcall; for two or three tricks if he has made a takeout double. Count on him for nothing at all if he has made a shutout bid—and in that case watch out for freakish distribution.

Test yourself on the three examples that follow. You are West, sitting behind declarer.

NORTH	EAST	SOUTH	WEST
1 ♣	1 ◇	1 ♠	Pass
2 ♠	Pass	4 ♠	?

(1)   ♠ Q 10 6 3   ♡ K 7 4   ◇ 6 2   ♣ K 8 5 3

Pass. You can count only one sure trump trick (since North has raised in spades) and 1 Quick Trick (the two kings) for your own hand. Count partner for one trick for his overcall. The total is only three tricks, which will not defeat the contract. You need two more probable tricks for a sound double. Don't be amazed if you beat four spades with this hand, but also don't double.

(2) ♠ K 10 9 3   ♡ K 7 4   ◇ 6 2   ♣ K 8 5 3

Double. You count two trump tricks, 1 Quick Trick, and something for the nuisance value of your four trumps. Your length in clubs may also have a nuisance value. Partner's one trick brings the total up to four defensive tricks plus nuisance values. This is just about enough for a somewhat scratchy double. If your partner makes sound overcalls, your double is a good one; if he tends to overcall on garbage, your double is doubtful.

(3) ♠ K 10 9 3   ♡ K 7 4   ◇ 6 5 3 2   ♣ K 8

Pass. Your length in diamonds may reduce your partner's trick-taking power. The double is now definitely below scratch.

✓ INFERENTIAL DOUBLES

Sometimes you can double on what you *imagine* rather than on what you see. The reliability of such doubles depends on the quality of your imagination.

Every experienced player is familiar with auctions of this kind:

OPENER	RESPONDER
1 ♠	2 ♠
3 ♠	4 ♠
Pass	

Clearly neither partner has any real conviction. Probably declarer will have a reasonable play for his contract if he gets good breaks. He will go down if he runs into bad breaks.

If one defender has five trumps but no side values, he may be reluctant to double for fear of locating the trumps. His partner, with considerable side strength and *no* trumps, should double. He knows that declarer will run into a bad trump break. The double may induce declarer to begin trumps from the wrong hand, and this alone may be worth a trick.

Another typical spiritless auction:

OPENER	RESPONDER
1 ♠	1 NT
2 ♡	2 ♠
3 ♠	4 ♠

Responder has dragged his feet at every step. Opener was not strong enough to make a jump bid of three hearts at his second turn or of four spades at his third turn. Surely this contract is headed for the rocks if trumps break badly, particularly if the hearts are also sour.

You might well double with:

(1)   ♠ 8 7 5 3 2   ♡ 4   ◇ Q J 10 4   ♣ A 9 5

You can see that the trumps are breaking badly, and you suspect that your partner has length and probably strength in hearts. This hand may play very badly for declarer.

You would not dream of doubling with:

(2)   ♠ 8 7 5   ♡ 5 4 2   ◇ K J 10 4   ♣ A Q 9

Declarer is going to get good breaks in both of his key suits. This is probably just what he needs to make his contract.

You would double with trump shortness:

(3)   ♠ ——   ♡ Q J 9 4   ◇ Q J 10 4   ♣ K J 9 5 2

Your partner surely has trump length, and declarer will run into a bad trump break and a troublesome heart break. He is almost surely headed for defeat.

The inferential double is made on the smell of blood when the opponents bid as though they are (or may be) in trouble. If they are going to run into bad breaks, both opponents should know it. There is no need to double until they stop bidding; then the last opponent should apply the ax.

√ DOUBLES OF THREE NOTRUMP

When the *opening leader* doubles three notrump he means only that he expects to defeat the contract. He should have a pretty clear idea of where to find the setting trick.

If the doubler goes into a trance before choosing his opening lead, he has picked the wrong time to double. In this situation a good double is based on an establishable suit and sure side entries. When you have this kind of double you know what you intend to lead. A double based solely on general strength serves only to tell declarer how to play the hand. Such a double almost always costs you a trick or two—often the *setting* trick.

When the *non-leader* doubles three notrump he asks his partner to lead a particular suit. (This is the expert practice. Non-experts often double on general principles in this situation.)

The double asks for a lead in:

- The suit bid by the *defenders* if they have bid only one suit
- The suit bid by the *doubler** if each defender has bid a different suit

---

* A few experts reverse this. Their theory is that the leader almost invariably opens his partner's suit rather than his own in the absence of a double. Hence the double is not necessary to get such a lead. They double to ask the leader to open his *own* suit. I have adopted this practice myself, but use it only with partners with whom it has been thoroughly discussed.

• The first suit bid by the *dummy* if neither defender has bid a suit

For example:

SOUTH	WEST	NORTH	EAST
1 ♣	1 ◇	1 NT	Pass
3 NT	Double	Pass	Pass
Pass			

West wants a diamond opening lead. Only one suit has been bid by the defenders, and that is the suit to lead. Likewise:

SOUTH	WEST	NORTH	EAST
1 ♣	1 ◇	1 ♠	Pass
1 NT	Pass	3 NT	Double
Pass	Pass	Pass	

East wants a diamond lead. Presumably East has a supporting honor or two in diamonds and wants to make sure the suit is set up before West's entries are knocked out. For example, East might have:

♠ J 10 4 2   ♡ 5 3   ◇ Q 10 4   ♣ Q J 7 3

When *two* suits have been bid:

SOUTH	WEST	NORTH	EAST
1 ♣	1 ◇	1 ♡	1 ♠
3 ♣	Pass	3 NT	Pass
Pass	Double	Pass	Pass
Pass			

West wants a diamond lead, not a spade. West might have:

♠ 5 3   ♡ 8 3   ◇ K Q J 10 9 6   ♣ K 7 4

He expects to set up the diamonds with one lead. Then he can sit back and wait to get in with the king of clubs in order to run the diamonds. If any other suit is opened, the king of clubs will be knocked out before the diamonds have been set up, and then it may be impossible to defeat the contract.

When *no* suit has been bid by the defenders:

SOUTH	WEST	NORTH	EAST
1 ♣	Pass	1 ◊	Pass
1 NT	Pass	3 NT	Double
Pass	Pass		

East wants a diamond lead. Neither defender has bid, so East's double calls for the first suit bid by dummy. Possibly dummy has bid a weak suit in the hope of discouraging a lead; or perhaps dummy's bid was normal enough, but East has the rest of the suit massed behind him.

An exception to the rule:

SOUTH	WEST	NORTH	EAST
1 ♣	Pass	1 ♠	Pass
2 ♣	Pass	2 ◊	Pass
2 ♡	Pass	2 NT	Pass
3 NT	Double	Pass	Pass
Pass			

What is the meaning of West's double? Which suit should East lead?

West can hardly want a lead in a suit that dummy has bid *and rebid*. In this case the double must request a lead in dummy's other bid suit. West must have reasonable club strength, and the chances are that he can support a lead in any suit that East really wants to open.

✓ SLAM DOUBLES

In a very weak game a defender may profitably double any slam on the theory that declarer may get rattled and fumble a cold contract. This is too much to hope for in a good game.

When good players voluntarily bid a slam, they should be able to win eleven tricks pretty surely and they should have a reasonable play for the twelfth trick. You won't get rich doubling such slams.

Since the double is hardly needed in its ordinary meaning, it has been given a special° meaning: "Partner, make an unusual lead to defeat this slam!"

The normal lead, except for the double, would be a suit bid by the defenders or an unbid suit. The double demands an *abnormal* lead.

Some players rigidly limit the meaning of an abnormal lead to the first suit bid by dummy. This is better than no convention at all, but it doesn't cover the many situations in which the leader's partner is ready to ruff the opening lead in some other side suit.

The slam double more often than not shows ability to ruff. The defender must get his ruffing trick immediately, since otherwise his trumps will be drawn. If the defender's double is based on high cards, there is less urgency; he will usually get his tricks even if the wrong suit is opened. For this reason he does not need to double.

In rare cases declarer may be warned by the double and may run out to six notrump to escape the ruff. Curiously enough, this is seldom done; declarer may be worried about one of the unbid suits and may not be quite sure that the double is based on ruffing power.

° This idea was first suggested almost thirty years ago by Theodore A. Lightner, and such doubles are sometimes called Lightner Doubles.

The opening leader can usually tell which suit his partner is ready to ruff, for he is usually quite long in the suit. Occasionally, of course, he guesses wrong, but the ability to call for an unusual lead pays big dividends in the long run despite the occasional losses.

What happens when the non-leader can defeat the slam with the *normal* lead? In this case he doesn't double. He should be quite satisfied to get even a small profit on such a hand.

In the rare cases when the non-leader can be sure of defeating the contract with *any* lead, he can double and enjoy his partner's problem about the choice of lead. A player who has the ace-king of trumps, for example, can afford to double and welcome *any* opening lead with a smug smile.

✓ OTHER LEAD-DIRECTING DOUBLES

It is possible to double almost any artificial bid in order to indicate a favorable opening lead. Among the bids that you might double for this purpose are:

* Response of two clubs to one notrump (Stayman Convention)
* Blackwood responses
* Cue bids made on the way to slam

For example:

SOUTH	WEST	NORTH	EAST
1 NT	Pass	2 ♣	Double

East wants a club opening lead if South eventually becomes the declarer.

SOUTH	WEST	NORTH	EAST
1 ♠	Pass	3 ♠	Pass
4 NT	Pass	5 ♦	Double

East wants a diamond opening lead against South's final bid.

SOUTH	WEST	NORTH	EAST
1 ♠	Pass	3 ♠	Pass
4 ♣	Pass	4 ♡	Double

East wants a heart opening lead against South's final bid.

In all such cases the doubler should have real length and strength in the suit he is doubling. Otherwise an alert opponent may redouble and settle for an overtrick or two instead of pursuing his original plan. Even if this doesn't happen, few things are more destructive of partnership morale than to demand a particular lead only to discover that almost any other lead would have produced a better result.

The opening leader may get some help from the fact that *no such double* was made during the auction. For example:

SOUTH	WEST	NORTH	EAST
1 ♠	Pass	3 ♠	Pass
4 ♣	Pass	4 ♡	Pass
6 ♠	Pass	Pass	Pass

West may have no clear idea of what to lead. He knows that East is not positively enthusiastic about a heart lead since East failed to double the cue bid of four hearts. West may therefore choose between clubs and diamonds on this basis. If South is a crafty bidder, a club opening may be the killing lead.

√ IN SHORT

To avoid giveaway doubles of game bids, double only with:

- At least one sure trump trick
- An expectation of defeating the contract two tricks

Double game contracts reached by hesitant bidding when you know declarer is going to get bad breaks

A double of three notrump by the leader's partner calls for a lead in

- The suit bid by the defenders if there is only one
- The suit bid by the doubler if both defenders have bid
- Dummy's first bid suit (unless rebid) if defenders have not bid

Slam doubles by the opener's partner call for an abnormal lead—usually for a ruff.

REOPENING THE BIDDING

√ Bid or Double?
√ Responding to a Reopening Bid
√ Opening Bidder's Rebids
√ Reopening After a Raise

√ The Unusual Notrump
√ Non-Fit Auctions
√ In Short

WHAT HAPPENS in your bridge game when the bidding threatens to die an early death?

SOUTH	WEST	NORTH	EAST
1 ♡	Pass	Pass	?

Does East pass with a happy sigh? Or does he find some excuse to bid or double even if he has only 8 or 9 points in high cards?

In 99 games out of 100 East will pass as quickly as he can. And he will be dead wrong.

In the hundredth game East will seek almost *any* excuse to bid or double. And he will be right.

The danger of reopening the bidding is that the opponents will suddenly discover that they can bid and make a game after all. This does happen, but very seldom. Players who bid so erratically are far more likely to get themselves overboard on being given a second chance. If they do bid a game, they will probably have no play for it.

The advantages of reopening the bidding are:

• You may make a part score of your own instead of having one scored against you.

218

- You may indicate a favorable lead and therefore put up the best defense even if you are outbid.
- You may push the opponents one trick too high.
- You may close the jaws of a trap on the bidder.

How light should you reopen? Obviously it's too risky to reopen with an utterly worthless hand. It's reasonably safe to set your bottom limit at 8 high-card points. (There is no upper limit.)

This is a very low bottom limit, and perhaps we should start by listing a couple of exceptions:

1. Don't bother to reopen with a very weak hand (8 or 9 points) if you have three or more cards in the opponent's suit. It is unlikely that your partner has passed a good hand with length in the bidder's suit—not *everybody* at the table can have length in this suit. If your partner doesn't have a good hand, you can afford to pass.

2. Don't reopen *vulnerable* with only 8 or 9 points unless you have a reasonably strong suit.

✓ BID OR DOUBLE?

When you do reopen, what sort of move do you make? Should you double, or should you bid a suit or notrump?

The double is the ideal reopener. If your partner has made a "trap" pass with strength in the opponent's suit, he can pass your double for penalties. Even at a contract of only one, declarer can lose a lot of blood!

However, it is necessary to set up a few standards. The double should be reserved for hands of 11 points or more in high cards. With hands of 8 to 10 points you bid a suit or one notrump, whichever better describes your hand. With a very strong suit and about 10 points in high cards, make a jump bid in your suit.

For example:

SOUTH	WEST	NORTH	EAST
1 ♡	Pass	Pass	?

(1)   ♠ K Q 7 5   ♡ 4 2   ◇ A 8 4 2   ♣ 9 6 3

Bid one spade. Show your 8- to 10-point value by a minimum bid.

(2)   ♠ Q J 7 5   ♡ 9 6 4 2   ◇ K J 4   ♣ Q 2

Pass. You have 9 points in high cards but only ½ Quick Trick. Moreover, your length in hearts makes it likely that partner is short in hearts. Why didn't he double or overcall? Probably because he has a poor hand—in which case you will be better off passing.

(3)   ♠ K Q 7 5   ♡ Q J 10 4   ◇ A J 4 2   ♣ 4

Pass, especially if the opponents are vulnerable. You will almost surely make a plus score against one heart. If you double, partner will probably bid clubs, and you may wind up in the ash can.

(4)   ♠ K J 7 5   ♡ 4 2   ◇ A J 4 2   ♣ Q 5 4

Double. The reopening double shows 11 points or more. You expect to pass at your next turn unless your partner takes drastic action.

(5)   ♠ K Q J 9 7 5   ♡ 4   ◇ K 4 2   ♣ 7 6 3

Bid two spades. You have only 9 points in high cards, but your suit is very powerful.

(6)   ♠ 9 7 5   ♡ Q J 4   ◇ K J 2   ♣ K 10 6 3

Bid one notrump. This rare reopening bid shows limited values (less than the 11 points needed for a double) with a stopper in the opponent's suit. (Not to be confused with the normal overcall of one notrump, which shows 16 to 18 points.)

(7) ♠ A K J 7 5   ♡ 2   ◇ A J 4 2   ♣ Q J 4

Double. If partner responds in clubs or diamonds, you
expect to show the spades. This rebid will show a
good hand, not just a reopening hand.

❡ RESPONDING TO A REOPENING BID

Your partner has reopened the bidding after the opening bid has been passed around to him. What do *you* do?

First, count your own points and add those shown by
partner's bid. Get a general idea of where you belong—
in a part score or in a game.

If you belong in a part score, look for a safe hole to
crawl into. If you belong in a game, look for some way
to show your strength and distribution. With a strong
hand always consider the possibility of passing a double
for penalties.

SOUTH	WEST	NORTH	EAST
1 ♡	Pass	Pass	1 ♠
Pass	?		

(1) ♠ A J 6 3   ♡ 5 3   ◇ Q 7 4   ♣ J 10 8 5

Pass. Partner has only 8 to 10 points in high cards, and
you have only 8 points. Game should be out of the
question, but you should be able to make one or
two spades. If partner had reopened with a double,
you would have bid one spade.

(2) ♠ A J 6 3   ♡ 5 3   ◇ K 7 4   ♣ K 10 8 5

Bid two spades. Game is possible if partner has maximum values—10 points in high cards with good distribution. If partner had reopened with a double,
you would have jumped to two spades—encouraging
but not forcing.

(3)　♠ A J　　♡ K J 5 3　　◇ K 7 4　　♣ K 10 8 5

>*Bid three notrump.* You were hoping to trap South, but your partner wasn't strong enough to reopen with a double. There should be a good play for game even though partner may have only 8 or 9 points. You know where all the high cards are and should be able to play the hand to best advantage. If partner had reopened with a double, you would have passed for penalties (and licked your chops).

(4)　♠ 6 3　　♡ 5 3　　◇ 8 7 4　　♣ K Q 8 5 3 2

>*Pass.* Partner has only 10 points at most, and you have only 5 points. This hand belongs to the opponents, who have 25 points to your 15. You have managed to get past the strong hand, and the weak responding hand will probably pass—allowing your side to steal the hand. If you bid two clubs—probably a safer contract than one spade—you will give the strong opponent a second chance to get back into the auction. Use the point count to see when you should leave well enough alone.

✓ OPENING BIDDER'S REBIDS

The opening bidder can seldom afford any rebid whatever. His partner, who could not respond to the opening bid, has a ghastly hand—less than 6 points, perhaps less than one miserable jack.

For this reason the opening bidder should give up immediately with any balanced hand.

If the opening bidder has a two-suiter of considerable solidity, he may show the second suit. If he has a three-suiter of some kind, he may be able to make a takeout double.

SOUTH	WEST	NORTH	EAST
1 ♡	Pass	Pass	1 ♠
?			

(1) ♠ 6   ♡ K Q J 9 4   ◇ A K Q 8 5   ♣ A 2

Bid two diamonds. Game is not completely out of the question, since partner may have four or more small diamonds and the king of clubs. At any rate you can afford to compete for the part score.

(2) ♠ ———   ♡ K Q J 9 4 2   ◇ A K Q 8 5   ♣ K 2

Bid three diamonds. The jump rebid is not forcing since you failed to open with a forcing two-bid, but it strongly suggests game in one of your long suits.

(3) ♠ 6   ♡ K Q J 9 4   ◇ A K 8 5   ♣ K Q 2

Double. If partner has length in diamonds or clubs, you are willing to compete in *his* suit. Despite the power of the hand, you cannot afford to make any further aggressive moves. You have now told your full story, and the rest is up to your partner. He must be allowed to get out if he has a really fearful collection of small cards.

(4) ♠ A K 8 5   ♡ K Q J 9 4   ◇ 6   ♣ K Q 2

Pass. You already know that partner cannot raise hearts. The chances are that a double by you at this point would inspire partner to bid diamonds and the opponents to double.

(5) ♠ A 8 5   ♡ K Q J 6 3   ◇ K 6   ♣ A 5 2

Pass. You might have opened with one notrump to begin with, but you were lucky that you didn't. You would probably make only your two aces and two hearts at notrump. If you climb back into the auction, you are inviting trouble without any hope of getting a good result.

✓ REOPENING AFTER A RAISE

As we have seen, it usually pays to reopen the bidding when the opening bid of one in a suit is passed. It may likewise be advisable to reopen when the opponents stop at *other* low contracts.

Let's begin with the clearest case:

SOUTH	WEST	NORTH	EAST
1 ♡	Pass	2 ♡	Pass
Pass	?		

If West is a good player, he reopens about eighty per cent of the time. He passes chiefly when he has length in hearts and therefore cannot think of a better spot, or when he has good reason to believe that the opponents have misjudged their strength. If West is short in hearts, he may reopen with some astonishingly weak hands. For example:

    ♠ Q J 7 6 3   ♡ 2   ◇ K 9 5 4   ♣ 9 8 2

West should bid two spades! Without a quiver, too.

Let's see why this is both advisable and safe.

The deck always contains exactly 40 points in high cards; never more, never less. Whatever isn't held by the side that opens the bidding must be held by the other side.

If the opener's side has 20 points in high cards, the other side has the remaining 20 points. If the opener's side has 22 points, the other side has 18 points. Simple mathematics, but very useful.

If the opener and his partner have a fit in a suit, the

opponents have a fit in some *other* suit. (This is not an absolute certainty, but the odds in favor of an 8-card fit are very high.)

What do you know about the opener's side when the opening bid is raised to two and dropped right there? The opener has a near-minimum bid, and the reopener has a weak hand. Their combined count, in high cards alone, is seldom more than a point or so above 20. Moreover, the opener and his partner have a fit.

Now we can see what we know about the strength of the opponents. They must have within a point or so of 20 points between them. At worst, their high-card total is 18 points. And they have a fit, somewhere or other.

These facts should be known to everybody at the table. The opening side's opponents almost invariably have the material for a competitive bid of some kind.

Sometimes this material is fairly evenly divided between the two partners; sometimes one has most of it, and the other has a poor hand. If the player who is last to speak (West, in our last example) happens to have the bulk of the partnership assets, it is easy for him to speak up. If West has a poor hand, he can take comfort from the knowledge that his partner surely has strength; it is West's duty to speak up despite his weakness.

What is accomplished by this reopening bid? Not as much as when the opening bid was followed by two passes, but quite enough.

In rare cases the reopening side finds a good part score. In *very* rare cases, they may get to a sound game. Sometimes they are able to push the opponents high enough to double them.

These are, however, the exceptions. The chief function of the reopening bid is to boost the opponents from the level of two up to the level of three. Here they may well be defeated; at two, they were safe.

The difference between letting them make a comfortable two hearts and beating them is about 150 to 200 points (when you include the hidden value of the part score). This is worth a bit of effort and a small risk.

You can afford to take this risk only with a partner who understands the theory and knows that in many cases *you have already bid his cards for him.* If the opponents are driven to the level of three, he must have the self-discipline to pass. The job has been done. He must not double the opponents or bid further except with most unusually appropriate cards.

√ THE UNUSUAL NOTRUMP

In a few very distinct situations a player may bid two notrump as a sort of takeout double. The ordinary takeout double asks partner to bid a major suit if he can. The Unusual Notrump bid asks partner to choose between the two minors.

SOUTH	WEST	NORTH	EAST
1 ♡	Pass	2 ♡	Pass
Pass	2 NT		

West should have some sort of weak two-suiter in clubs and diamonds. East should respond in whichever minor suit he can better support.

A similar situation:

SOUTH	WEST	NORTH	EAST
1 ♡	Pass	1 NT	Pass
2 ♡	Pass	Pass	2 NT

East should have a fairly good two-suiter in clubs and diamonds. West should respond in the minor he prefers. One word of warning about misuse of the Unusual

Notrump. This convention, invented by Alvin Roth about fifteen years ago, became suddenly popular among tournament players in 1956 and 1957. Since then it has been cruelly abused—so that a player can practically never bid notrump for a natural purpose once the opponents have opened the bidding! His partner always insists on taking out into some mangy minor suit.

Better not to use the convention at all than to overwork it to this extent.

V NON-FIT AUCTIONS

As we have seen, when the opener's side discovers a fit and stops short, the other side always has the material and a fit for a competitive bid of some kind. This is not necessarily true when the opener's side stops short *without* discovering a fit.

For example:

SOUTH	WEST	NORTH	EAST
1 ♡	Pass	1 ♠	Pass
2 ♡	Pass	Pass	?

No fit has been discovered. North-South may have 23 or 24 points in high cards between them. East-West may have only 16 or 17 points without a fitting suit.

Much the same is true if an opening bid of one notrump is passed. Also, if one or two suits are bid and the partners stop at one notrump or at two of an unraised suit.

In all such situations a reopening bid may run into trouble. The reopener should have a good reason for entering the auction—such as a strong suit or unusual strength, preferably both. That is why we noted on the preceding page that in one case the reopening bid of two notrump showed a *strong* two-suiter; East would stay out of the auction altogether unless he had an excellent reason for coming in.

The force of this principle is even stronger when the opponents bid *three* suits and stop short at two of an un-raised suit:

SOUTH	WEST	NORTH	EAST
1 ♡	Pass	1 ♠	Pass
2 ♢	Pass	2 ♠	Pass
Pass			

North and South may have a galloping misfit. If West gets into the auction, he will get the opponents out of trouble and himself into it—in one move.

✓ IN SHORT

Avoid letting the opponents play a hand at one of a suit. Reopen with a double to show 11 points or more in high cards; reopen with a bid to show 8 to 10 points. Pass with less than 8 points or with length in the bid suit.

Avoid selling out when the opponents find a fit (by a bid that is raised) and stop at the level of two. Your side is safe with some sort of competing bid at the level of two (possibly at the level of three). The idea is to boost the opponents up to three of their suit. If your partner does the boosting, do not "punish" him by doubling the opponents or making a further bid.

Do not be so eager to reopen the bidding when the opponents have failed to find a fit. A misfit for one side usually is accompanied by a misfit for the other side.

SECOND REVIEW AND SELF-TESTING QUIZZES

9th Through 17th Days

THIS COMPLETES the section on COMPETITIVE BID-DING. Now it is time to rate yourself on how well you have grasped this phase of bidding.

Turn to page 473 and answer questions 91 through 155 on a separate piece of paper, and then compare with the answers which begin on page 492.

Rate yourself on this basis:

> 60 or more right ....excellent
> 55–59 right ....good
> 50–54 right ....fair
> Below 54 right ....a rereading is in order

To get the maximum benefit from this book, take each incorrect answer and go back to the chapter that dealt with that subject. Fix the correct bid in your mind now, so you will know how to use it when you meet the same situation at the bridge table.

III

THE PLAY OF

THE CARDS

SIMPLE FINESSES

√ The Principle of the Finesse	√ Two-Way Finesses
√ Finessing Against the Ace	√ Finessing Against the Jack
√ Finessing Against the King	√ Double Finesses
√ When to Lead High	√ Triple Finesses
√ Finessing Against the Queen	√ Finessing an Opponent's Lead

√ THE PRINCIPLE OF THE FINESSE

THE FINESSE, one of the basic maneuvers of bridge, is an attempt to win a trick with a card that is not the highest card of its suit *after one opponent has already played to the trick.*

The most familiar example:

1. NORTH
(dummy)
♠ 3 2

WEST
♠ 6 5

EAST
♠ K 4

SOUTH
♠ A Q

The deuce of spades is led from the North hand.*
East plays the four.

---

* In all the examples in this chapter, South is declarer and North is dummy.

South now takes the finesse by playing the queen. This is an attempt to win a trick with the queen after East has played. South hopes that the king is in the hand of the opponent who has already played, for this is the only outstanding card that can beat the queen.

This happens to be the case. South's queen wins the trick. East cannot now take back his low spade and play the king to win the trick. He has already committed himself. He had to play before South, and this gave South the advantage. South thus wins two tricks, since his ace is good for the second trick.

East could not gain by playing his king (instead of the low spade) on the first trick. South would then win with the ace and would be able to win the next trick with the queen.

The shoe is on the other foot if we exchange the East-West hands:

2. NORTH
    (dummy)
    ♠ 3 2

WEST   EAST
♠ K 4   ♠ 6 5

        SOUTH
        ♠ A Q

The deuce is led from the North hand, and East plays low. Now South cannot win a trick with the queen; he must commit himself before West does, and this time *West* has the advantage. If South plays the queen, West wins with the king; if South, instead, plays the ace, West saves his king for a later trick.

Here we can see many of the basic principles of the finesse.

If the high card is in favorable position, the finesse succeeds; if it is in unfavorable position, the finesse fails.

You lead toward the hand containing the card you are trying to promote. (It would be even better to have the suit led by your left-hand opponent, so that you play last to the trick and are sure to win. This is popularly known as a "free" finesse.)

✓ FINESSING AGAINST THE ACE

The finesse against the king is the most familiar type, but it is equally possible to finesse against almost any high card. Here are two examples of a finesse against the ace:

3. NORTH
   (dummy)
   ♠ 3 2
   SOUTH
   ♠ K 4

4. NORTH
   (dummy)
   ♠ 4 3 2
   SOUTH
   ♠ K Q 5

In Diagram 3, the deuce is led from the North hand. If East plays low, South plays the king. This wins the trick if the ace is held by East.

In Diagram 4, the deuce is led from the North hand. If East plays low, South plays the king. If the king wins the trick, South must get back to the North hand by way of some other suit in order to lead another low spade. In this way South *repeats* his finesse and thus gets a trick with the *queen* of spades as well as the king.

✔ FINESSING AGAINST THE KING

We have already seen one example of a finesse against the king. Here is a different type:

5. NORTH	6. NORTH	7. NORTH
(dummy)	(dummy)	(dummy)
♠ Q J	♠ Q J 10	♠ Q J 4
SOUTH	SOUTH	SOUTH
♠ A 2	♠ A 3 2	♠ A 3 2

In Diagram 5 the queen of spades is led from North. If East plays low, South plays low also—letting the queen of spades "ride" for a finesse. The queen wins the trick if East happens to have the king. East cannot gain by playing his king, since then South plays the ace.

In Diagram 6 the first trick is the same. If the queen wins the first trick, the finesse is repeated by leading the jack. Declarer wins all three tricks if the king is favorably located.

In Diagram 7 the queen is led, as before. Even if this wins the first trick, the finesse cannot be repeated. The new situation is:

7A. NORTH
(dummy)
♠ J 4
SOUTH
♠ A 3

If the jack is led from the North hand, East *covers* with the king. This forces out South's ace, and South has no other trick in the suit. If, instead, a low card is led from the North hand, East likewise plays low.

South has to play the ace, and East's king is good for a later trick.

Two related situations:

8. NORTH
   (dummy)
   ♠ Q 2
   SOUTH
   ♠ A 3

In Diagram 8 there is no finessing position. There is no advantage in leading the queen since the king will surely cover—no matter which opponent holds it. South's only chance to win two tricks is to lead the ace in the hope that the king will fall—a very remote chance.

There is a better chance if one of the opponents leads spades. For example, suppose West leads a low spade. South should play dummy's queen at once; it wins the trick if West happens to hold the king. If *East* leads a low spade, South should play low in the hope of winning the trick with dummy's queen. This comes to pass if East has led from the king.

9. NORTH
   (dummy)
   ♠ Q 3 2
   SOUTH
   ♠ A 5 4

In Diagram 9 South cannot gain by leading the queen from dummy. The finesse should be taken in a different way. South leads out the ace and then leads a low spade toward the queen. If West happens to hold the king of spades, dummy's queen is good for a trick sooner or later.

✔ WHEN TO LEAD HIGH

In the cases we have been discussing it is sometimes correct to lead the queen, and sometimes correct to lead *toward* the queen. When do you lead a high card for a finesse, and when do you lead toward the high card?

Lead an honor for a finesse only when you would be pleased to see the honor covered by a higher card.

You can gain nothing if your other cards in the suit are all very small. You gain only when you have one or more supporting honors that become worth more when the higher cards are played off.

It is proper to lead the queen for a finesse when you have the jack to support the queen. It is even better when you have the ten as well as the jack.

However, you don't automatically lead the queen for a finesse just because you have the jack. For example:

10. NORTH
(dummy)
♠ Q J 3 2

WEST   EAST
♠ K 10 9 8   ♠ 7 6

SOUTH
♠ A 5 4

It would be proper to lead the queen of spades from the North hand if you need exactly two spade tricks. If you need *three* spade tricks, you will not be pleased to see the queen covered by the king. That would leave only your ace and jack as winning cards. Since you would not be pleased by a cover, you do not lead the queen.

The correct play is to get to the South hand in another suit and then lead a low spade from the South hand toward the dummy. West plays low, and dummy wins with the jack. You return a small spade to the ace and lead another spade toward dummy. West can take his king, but dummy's queen is good for a later trick.

√ FINESSING AGAINST THE QUEEN

Finesses against the queen occur very frequently:

11. NORTH	12. NORTH	13. NORTH
(dummy)	(dummy)	(dummy)
♠ 4 3 2	♠ A 3 2	♠ 5 4 3 2
SOUTH	SOUTH	SOUTH
♠ A K J	♠ K J 4	♠ A K J 7 6

In Diagram 11 the deuce of spades is led from the North hand. If East plays low, South finesses the jack. This wins the trick if East has the queen.

If South finds it convenient to do so, he may lead out the ace of spades before going over to dummy to lead a low spade. The advantage is that the queen may fall, after which no finesse is necessary.

In Diagram 12 the ace of spades is played (optional) and then a low spade. If East plays low, South finesses the jack.

In Diagram 13 a low spade is led to the ace. South doesn't need to finesse at this point. If East fails to follow suit, it is clear that a finesse will fail. If West fails to follow suit, it is clear that a finesse will succeed.

If both opponents follow suit, South should next lead out the king of spades instead of finessing. The play for the *drop* is more likely to work than the finesse.

When should you finesse for a queen? The old rule of thumb is still a good guide: *With eight, ever; with nine, never.*

Finesse for a missing queen when you have eight cards of a suit between your hand and the dummy. Play for the drop when you have nine or more cards.

The finesse for the queen may likewise be taken in these three positions:

14. NORTH	15. NORTH	16. NORTH
(dummy)	(dummy)	(dummy)
♠ 4 3 2	♠ J 10 9	♠ J 10 4
SOUTH	SOUTH	SOUTH
♠ K J 10	♠ K 3 2	♠ K 3 2

In Diagram 14 a low spade is led from the North hand. If East plays low, South finesses the ten. If East has the queen, South's ten either wins the trick or forces out the ace.

If necessary, South will get back to dummy with another suit and will lead a second low spade. This time South will finesse the jack. If East happens to hold the queen, South wins two of the three tricks.

In Diagram 15 the jack of spades is led from dummy. If East plays low, South lets the jack of spades ride for a finesse. The jack either wins the trick or forces out the ace if East happens to hold the queen.

If necessary, South will get back to dummy with another suit and will lead the ten of spades. If East has the queen, South wins two of the three tricks.

In Diagram 16 the first trick is the same. Then, however, there is no longer a finessing position. If declarer continues by leading the ten of spades, East covers with the queen. South wins one trick but cannot win another. South's best chance is to lead

the low spade from dummy the second time in the
hope that East's queen will then fall. A poor chance,
but better than none.

If South needs only one trick in spades, he must
guess whether or not to play the king the first time.
The king is the winning play if East has the ace but
not the queen. In many situations of this kind South
must simply guess. Very often, however, South has
a clue that points to the right play. A fairly large
part of bridge skill consists in observing all the clues
in order to eliminate guesswork.

✓ TWO-WAY FINESSES

17. NORTH
(dummy)
♠ A 10 2
SOUTH
♠ K J 3

18. NORTH
(dummy)
♠ A J 10
SOUTH
♠ K 3 2

South need not lose a spade trick if he knows (or
can guess) which opponent has the queen.

In Diagram 17, for example, a low spade is played
from North. If East has the queen, South's jack
should be finessed. If West has the queen, declarer
should go up with the king and return a spade to
finesse the ten.

In Diagram 18 South should begin the suit by
leading the jack from the North hand. The only advantage, a substantial one against average opponents, is that East may be foolish enough to play the
queen. If East plays low, South can decide whether
to let the jack ride or to put up the king and finesse
the ten on the way back.

An opponent who knows enough not to cover the

jack with the queen may nevertheless have to stop and think about it. This pause for thought locates the queen for declarer.

It is quite proper for declarer to base his play on an opponent's hesitation, but quite improper for an opponent to stage a false hesitation to deceive declarer. This topic is discussed more fully in Chapter 34, Manners, Morals and Laws.

✓ FINESSING AGAINST THE JACK

Finesses against the jack are less common than those against the queen or king, but still common enough.

19. NORTH (dummy)	20. NORTH (dummy)	21. NORTH (dummy)
♠ 4 3 2	♠ 4 3 2	♠ K 3 2
SOUTH	SOUTH	SOUTH
♠ A K Q 10	♠ K Q 10	♠ Q 10 4

In Diagram 19 South can lead out the ace and king of spades in the hope of dropping the jack. Then, if he considers it necessary, he can get to dummy with another suit to lead a spade toward the Q-10. If East plays low, South can finesse the ten.

Actually this is usually the wrong play. South's best chance is to lead out all three top spades in the hope of dropping the jack. In some hands, however, South may have good reason to believe that East has considerable length in spades, and then the eventual finesse is the correct play.

In Diagram 20 North first leads the deuce of spades. If East plays low, South puts up the king. This wins the trick if East has the ace.

In this case South will return to dummy with another suit and will lead another low spade with the intention of playing the queen if East plays low again.

If the first play of the king loses to the ace, South gets back to dummy with another suit and leads a spade to finesse the ten. This gives him two of the three tricks in the suit if East has the jack.

In Diagram 21 the king of spades may be played first (optional). Either at trick one or two a low spade should be led from dummy, and South finesses the ten from his hand. This gives him two tricks if East has the jack, regardless of which opponent has the ace. (If possible, South should begin this combination by leading a low card toward dummy's king.)

✓ DOUBLE FINESSES

A double finesse is taken against *two* missing honors.

22. NORTH	23. NORTH	24. NORTH
(dummy)	(dummy)	(dummy)
♠ 4 3 2	♠ 4 3 2	♠ 4 3 2
SOUTH	SOUTH	SOUTH
♠ A Q 10	♠ A J 10	♠ K J 5

The deuce of spades is led in Diagram 22, and South finesses the ten. If this wins, South returns to dummy and leads another spade to finesse the queen. South wins all three tricks if East has both the king and jack of spades.

If the first finesse loses to the jack, South returns to dummy to finesse the queen of spades. He will still win two tricks if East has the king.

If the first finesse loses to the king, no further finesse is necessary.

In Diagram 23 a low spade is led from dummy, and South finesses the ten. This loses to the queen or king (unless East happens to hold both of the missing honors). South will later return to dummy and lead another low spade to finesse against the honor that is still missing. Declarer will win two of the three tricks unless West started with both honors.

In Diagram 24 a low spade is again led from dummy. If East plays low, South finesses the jack. If this loses to the ace, no further finesse is necessary.

If the jack loses to the queen, South returns to dummy and leads another spade toward the king. South will make one trick in the suit if East has *either* the ace or the queen; South will make two tricks if East has *both* the ace and queen.

✓ TRIPLE FINESSES

Some triple finesses—taken against *three* missing high cards—are fairly simple:

25. NORTH (dummy)	26. NORTH (dummy)	27. NORTH (dummy)
♠ 4 3 2	♠ 4 3 2	♠ 4 3 2
SOUTH	SOUTH	SOUTH
♠ K 10 9	♠ Q 10 5	♠ A J 9

In Diagram 25 a low spade is led from dummy. If East plays low, South finesses the ten. This may drive out the ace and solve South's problem.

If the first finesse loses to the queen or jack, South returns to dummy and leads another low spade toward his hand. If East again plays low, South may have to guess whether to play the king or the nine. The better play against average opponents is the nine, since East is not likely to play low twice if he has the ace.

In Diagram 26 a low spade is led from dummy. If East has both ace and king, he is likely to play the king. South can later return to dummy and lead another spade toward the queen.

If East plays low on the first spade, South finesses the ten. This may lose to the jack, in which case South will not win a spade trick. However, if the finesse of the ten knocks out the ace or king, South still has a chance. He returns to the dummy and leads a spade toward the queen. He wins a spade trick if East has ace-jack or king-jack.

In Diagram 27 declarer starts with a low spade from dummy. If East plays low, South finesses the nine.

South hopes that East's spade holding includes either the king-ten or queen-ten. If so, the nine will drive out West's picture card. South will later return to dummy to finesse the jack.

⋎ FINESSING AN OPPONENT'S LEAD

Most finesses can be taken just as easily when an opponent leads, and in many cases this improves your position:

28. NORTH (dummy)	29. NORTH (dummy)	30. NORTH (dummy)
♠ A J 2	♠ K 3 2	♠ 10 3 2
SOUTH	SOUTH	SOUTH
♠ Q 4 3	♠ Q 10 4	♠ A J 4

In Diagram 28 West leads a spade. South should play low from the dummy. If West has led from the king, South will win the first trick with the queen and can later win another finesse with dummy's jack. South will thus get all three spade tricks.

If South is left to develop the suit for himself, he can win a finesse with dummy's jack but then has no further finesse. Unless West started with the doubleton king of spades, South can win only two spade tricks. (If West has only two spades, South can finesse dummy's jack and then lead out the ace to drop the king. This is the standard way to play this combination.)

In Diagram 29, if West leads a spade, South is sure to win two of the three tricks. South plays low from the dummy at the first trick.

If East plays the ace, South wins the king and queen. If East plays the jack, South wins the queen and can win another trick with the ten or king. If East plays low, South wins with the ten and can win another trick with the queen or king.

If South must develop the spades by himself, he wins two tricks only if East has the jack. (South has other chances to win two tricks, since West may have the singleton ace or the doubleton ace-jack, but these possibilities are very slim.)

In Diagram 30 West leads a low spade. Dummy plays low. Now East must play a picture card to prevent the jack from winning. South takes the ace and must later win a second trick with the jack or the ten.

If South must lead spades for himself, he has only a slim chance of winning two tricks in the suit.

MORE ABOUT FINESSES

√ Eliminating a Guess
√ How Many Finesses?
√ Guessing the Doubleton
√ More Doubletons
√ One Last Doubleton
√ The Ruffing Finesse

√ Complex Ruffing Finesses
√ Saving Entries
√ When to Cover an Honor
√ Which Honor to Cover?
√ Tips in General

WE MOVE NOW from the finesses that every player should know, described in the previous chapter, to the finesses that only very fine players know. This will not exhaust the subject, for there must be hundreds of finesses, but it will give you a good idea of what to think about when you see an unfamiliar finessing situation at the table.

√ ELIMINATING A GUESS

1. NORTH
   (dummy)
   ♠ Q 10 9
   SOUTH
   ♠ A 3 2

2. NORTH
   (dummy)
   ♠ Q 10 9 8
   SOUTH
   ♠ A 4 3 2

3. NORTH
   (dummy)
   ♠ Q 10 8 4 3
   SOUTH
   ♠ A 9 2

All of these combinations are essentially the same; the *average* player begins each by taking the ace and then leads toward the queen. If neither the king nor jack has appeared by this time, our hero must guess whether to finesse the queen or the ten.

If the king and jack are in different hands, South

loses two tricks if he guesses wrong—and he guesses wrong half the time.

The way to eliminate the guess is to take *two* finesses toward the ace. Declarer first leads the ten from dummy and lets it ride for a finesse. If it loses to the king, no further finesse is necessary. If it loses to the jack, South gets back to dummy and leads the queen for a second finesse.

If the honors are split, *one* of the finesses will surely succeed. South is not at the mercy of a bad guess.

What if West has both the king and jack? Then our recommended play has failed (we never guaranteed it as one-hundred-per-cent sure). But the old-fashioned play of cashing the ace first loses if East has both the missing honors. These two possibilities cancel each other out in the long run. The big advantage of taking two finesses is that it eliminates the guess when the two honors are divided.

If the bidding indicates that West is far more likely than East to have spade strength, it is no longer a question of eliminating a guess. You *use* the evidence you have by leading low to the ace and back toward the queen.

✓ HOW MANY FINESSES?

4. NORTH
   (dummy)
   ♠ Q 10 9 2
   SOUTH
   ♠ A 8 7 6 5

5. NORTH
   (dummy)
   ♠ J 10 9 2
   SOUTH
   ♠ A 8 7 6 5

These two situations look alike but should be treated differently.

With *nine* spades, in Diagram 4, you do *not* take

two finesses. That would lose two tricks if West had the doubleton K-J or K-J-x. The best play is to lead out the ace and then lead low toward the queen. There will be no guess at the second trick. You win unless West started with a singleton small card.

In Diagram 5 you don't have the queen, and the right play is to *take* two finesses. If you lose the first, don't give up and cash the ace. The only time the ace play works and the two finesses fail is when West has specifically the doubleton king-queen. But the plan of taking two finesses succeeds if West started with *either* the singleton king *or* singleton queen. (In all other cases the choice of plays is immaterial; either they both fail or they both win.)

If you do not have the entries to North to take two finesses, don't even try one. Bang down the ace and then continue with a small one to the jack. This holds the loss to one trick unless either opponent originally had K-Q-x.

✓ GUESSING THE DOUBLETON

6. NORTH
(dummy)
♠ A J 9
SOUTH
♠ Q 5 4 3 2

7. NORTH
(dummy)
♠ A J 2
SOUTH
♠ Q 9 5 4 3

In each of these diagrams South begins with a low card, finessing dummy's jack. If this first finesse wins, South must then guess how to proceed.

If West started with a doubleton king, declarer should next cash the ace of spades. This will drop the king, whereupon South can draw the last spade with his queen.

If West started with K-x-x, then East's holding

was 10-x. After the first finesse works, South must get back to his hand with another suit in order to lead the *queen* of spades for the next spade finesse. This finesses through West's king and captures the ten at the same time. (If West plays low, South's queen wins the trick; if West covers with the king, dummy wins with the ace, East's ten falls gracefully, and the nine is then good.)

If West started with K-10-x or with four trumps, this sequence of plays will not work. South can only play for the most likely combination that will permit him to run the suit without loss.

South may be able to guess the position from bidding or playing clues. His problem may be made easier if either player drops the eight on the first spade trick. Unless the eight is a false card or signal, the player who drops it probably has started with the doubleton K-8 or 10-8 of spades. South decides which holding will help him (if East, 10-8; if West, K-8) and plays accordingly.

✓ MORE DOUBLETONS

8. NORTH	9. NORTH
(dummy)	(dummy)
♠ A 4 3 2	♠ A 3 2
SOUTH	SOUTH
♠ Q 9 8 7	♠ Q 9 8 7 4

Again in Diagrams 8 and 9 we have a two-part play. First, lead a low card from North toward the nine. This gives you two chances right off: with a doubleton king most Easts will jump up with the king, and your ace and queen will then clear the suit. Or East may *tell* you he has the king doubleton by agonizing before playing low. (Some Easts even give the show away with a holding of king and *two* others.) You cross them up, of course, by playing the queen instead of the nine.

Even if East does not have the king, he may have J-10-x and play low. Since he will probably make this play without undue hesitation, you go through with your original play of the nine, and are rewarded when it draws the king from West. Again, your ace and queen can mop up the suit.

But let's assume that nothing wonderful happens, and your nine loses to West's jack or ten. Then you must fire your second salvo. The direction of this shot depends upon your guessing the doubleton— just as in Diagrams 6 and 7.

If you figure West for the doubleton, you hope he has only the king remaining, and you lead a low card to the ace to drop it.

If East looks like a man with a doubleton (who can guess with a *woman?*) you hope it was originally J-x or 10-x (remember, you already cooked his goose if he had the *king* doubleton). You therefore lead the queen to finesse against West's king and pick up East's lone ten or jack on the same trick.

The odds on this two-part play are far superior to the fifty-fifty chance of first cashing the ace and then leading low to the queen. Try the latter play only when the bidding or playing clues give you reason to believe East holds the king.

✓ ONE LAST DOUBLETON

10. NORTH
(dummy)
♠ J 9 2
SOUTH
♠ A 8 5 4 3

The best play to lose only one trick in spades is to lead low toward the jack, hoping West has the doubleton ten, with or without a higher honor.

If West has K-10 or Q-10, he will probably step up with his picture card. Later you will get to dummy and lead the jack through East, finessing through East's Q-x or K-x and capturing the ten. What if West plays the ten at the first trick? You then cover with dummy's jack, forcing out East's picture card; later you lead out your ace to capture West's now blank honor.

If West started with 10-x or 10-x-x, he will almost surely play his low card at the first trick. You finesse dummy's nine, forcing out an honor from East.

You now have to guess whether West started with two or three cards in the suit. If you guess right, you can pick up the rest of the suit without further loss. (For West's 10-x you lead the jack next; for West's 10-x-x you just lead out the ace to drop East's now lone honor.)

✔ THE RUFFING FINESSE

The *ruffing finesse* is another way of finessing against an ace:

11. NORTH	12. NORTH
(dummy)	(dummy)
♠ K 2	♠ K Q
SOUTH	SOUTH
♠ ——	♠ ——
♡ 3 2	♡ 3 2

In both diagrams hearts are trumps. Only a few cards of each hand are shown.

In Diagram 11 North leads the deuce of spades,

and South ruffs with a low heart. If the ace of spades falls on this trick, dummy's king of spades is good for a later trick. This is an establishment play, not a true finesse.

In Diagram 12 North leads the king of spades. If East plays the ace, South ruffs; and dummy's queen is good for a later trick. If East plays a low spade instead of the ace, South discards instead of ruffing. The king wins this trick if East happens to hold the ace of spades; but the king loses if West has the ace. Even if the finesse loses, dummy's queen is good for a later trick.

∨ COMPLEX RUFFING FINESSES

All of the complex finesses discussed thus far have been in two stages. One or both of the stages may be ruffing finesses.

13. NORTH	14. NORTH
(dummy)	(dummy)
♠ J 10 3 2	♠ Q J 10 9
SOUTH	SOUTH
♠ A 9	♠ ——
♡ 2	♡ 3 2

In each case hearts are trumps and only South has any trumps left.

In Diagram 13 North leads the deuce of spades, and South finesses the nine. If, as is probable, this finesse loses, South later clears the ace of spades out of the way and gets back to dummy to lead the jack of spades through East. If East covers with the remaining picture, South ruffs and gets back to dummy to cash the ten of spades. If East plays a low spade on dummy's jack, South discards immediately. This sequence of plays succeeds if East had one or both of the missing spade honors. Even if both finesses lose, South has set up dummy's ten of spades, on which he may be able to discard a loser.

In Diagram 14 North leads the queen of spades. If East covers, South ruffs; otherwise South discards. In either case South gets back to dummy to lead the jack of spades through East for a second ruffing finesse.

In both cases South needs plentiful entries to dummy and must be able to make useful discards if no honor appears from the East hand.

Here is an advanced two-stage finesse in a complete hand, taken from a recent Open Pair Championship:

```
                    NORTH
                 ♠ K J 9 8 6
                 ♡ 9 3
                 ◇ A K 6
                 ♣ 10 6 2

      WEST                           EAST
   ♠ 10 7 3 2                     ♠ A Q 4
   ♡ 10 8 7                       ♡ 6 5
   ◇ 9 8                          ◇ J 10 4 2
   ♣ J 9 7 3                      ♣ A K Q 8

                    SOUTH
                 ♠ 5
                 ♡ A K Q J 4 2
                 ◇ Q 7 5 3
                 ♣ 5 4
```

NORTH	EAST	SOUTH	WEST
1 ♠	1 NT	Double	2 ♣
Pass	Pass	3 ♡	Pass
3 ♠	Pass	4 ♡	Pass
Pass	Pass		

West opened the nine of diamonds, and South won with the queen to preserve dummy's entries. He next drew three rounds of trumps. South could count nine tricks in top cards and needed one additional trick.

Since East had bid one notrump, it was clear that he held all the missing high cards except perhaps one jack. East therefore surely held both the ace and queen of spades.

From the opening lead declarer assumed diamonds wouldn't break 3-3. Therefore South decided to go after the tenth trick in spades, playing West for the ten of spades. A complex finesse was required.

South led the singleton spade and finessed dummy's nine. The finesse *against the ten* succeeded, for East had to win with the queen of spades.

East promptly cashed two top clubs, but South ruffed the third club. The time was now ripe for the second stage of the spade finesse. Declarer led a diamond to dummy and returned the king of spades through East for a ruffing finesse.

East put up the ace of spades, and South ruffed. Declarer got back to dummy with another diamond and cashed the jack of spades for a discard of his small diamond and thus fulfilled the contract.

V SAVING ENTRIES

When entries are scarce it is necessary to conserve them in finessing. The next two positions show how this can be done:

15. NORTH
    (dummy)
    ♠ 9 3 2
    SOUTH
    ♠ A J 10 8

16. NORTH
    (dummy)
    ♠ J 9 3
    SOUTH
    ♠ A Q 10 2

Declarer should begin by leading the deuce of spades from dummy in Diagram 15, finessing the jack. The first finesse loses, but North regains the lead in another suit and leads the nine of spades.

If East has the remaining spade honor and does not cover, dummy's nine of spades holds the trick. (South drops his eight on this trick.) Declarer therefore stays in dummy to continue with a further spade finesse. No other entry to dummy is needed.

The point of this series of plays is to save North's high card for the finesse you hope *succeeds*—rather than waste it on the finesse you expect to *lose*.

In Diagram 16 declarer should first lead the *nine* of spades from dummy. If the king covers, South wins all four tricks with the four honor cards.

If the nine wins the first trick, declarer can continue with the jack and can hold the lead by playing the ten from the South hand. Now the finesse can be continued from dummy without the need of a side entry.

Declarer cannot be sure of winning all four tricks if he begins by leading the jack. If he plays the deuce from his own hand, he is obliged to win the second trick in the South hand. Then if there is no side entry to the North hand, South may lose a spade trick.

South may lose a trick if he begins with the jack from dummy and plays the ten from his own hand. When he next leads the nine of spades from dummy, East covers with the king. South still has the deuce of spades in his hand and will lose it unless the spades break 3-3.

When you don't hold the nine in either hand, you may wonder whether to lead high or low for the first finesse. For example:

17. NORTH	18. NORTH	19. NORTH
(dummy)	(dummy)	(dummy)
♠ Q 4 3	♠ J 4 3	♠ 10 4 3
SOUTH	SOUTH	SOUTH
♠ A J 10 2	♠ A Q 10 2	♠ A Q J 2

The question is whether you should lead the honor
or a small card from the North hand for the first
finesse.

Given plentiful entries to the North hand, you
should lead low; this is immediately rewarded if
East has the singleton king. If East plays low and
the first finesse works, you get back to dummy and
lead a low card again; this works well if East has a
doubleton king. If two finesses succeed and the king
has not appeared, you can lead out the ace in the
hope that the spades will break 3-3. If so, your last
spade will be good.

If you begin by leading the honor from dummy,
you not only need to find the king with East but
in order to make all four tricks you must get a 3-3
break. The odds are almost 2 to 1 against getting
this 3-3 break.

However, if you have no entry to North, you must
lead the honor at the first trick for lack of a better
play. This will succeed if East has K-x-x. Leading
low gives you only one finesse, which will work only
if East has K-x. The odds are more than 2 to 1
that East has K-x-x rather than K-x.

A further advantage of leading the honor when
North is entryless is that a successful finesse will
give you three tricks in the suit. Even if the fourth
trick does not materialize, you may still be better off getting three fast spade tricks than only
two.

✔ WHEN TO COVER AN HONOR

We have assumed in most of these examples that an opponent will cover an honor when it is to his advantage to do so, and that he will play low in all other cases. This gives the defenders credit for more skill than most players have.

The average player has heard somewhere the old whist saying "Cover an honor with an honor." Put an honor in front of his nose, and he will promptly cover it if he can.

This makes life simple for both sides, but it isn't good bridge. The old whist rule must be brought up to date for modern bridge.

Cover an honor only to set up a card in your own hand or a probable card in your partner's hand.

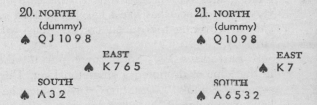

In both diagrams the queen of spades is led from dummy. Should East cover with the king?

In Diagram 20 East cannot gain by covering. The ace would capture the king, and then dummy's J-10-9-8 would all be good. If East refuses to cover, South will eventually have to play the ace on a small card. Then East's king will be high.

There are other advantages in playing low. For one thing, South may have only a singleton ace. For

another, East cannot be sure that South has the ace.
It would be disastrous to put up the king if *West*
had the singleton ace.

Even if East has K-x or K-x-x, he should not play
his king. He cannot gain by giving up his king. If
East plays a low card without apparent thought,
South may decide to play the ace rather than take
the finesse.

In Diagram 21 East should usually play his king.
His partner may have J-x, in which case the cover
is necessary to produce a spade trick for the defenders.

If North leads the ten of spades instead of the
queen, East should *not* cover. West's jack, if he has
it, can cope with dummy's ten; there is no need for
East to become active.

The situation may be altered if South has bid and
rebid spades very aggressively. In this case there is
very little chance that West has J-x, so East cannot
gain by covering the queen (or the ten) with his
king.

If East plays low, South may put up the ace
in the hope of dropping a singleton king. This may
even be South's "percentage" play, since he may
have eleven spades between his own hand and the
dummy.

It must be observed once more that South will not
be tempted to play the ace if East does some obvious soul-searching before playing low. In situations
of this kind a player should look at the dummy and
his own hand and decide *in advance* whether or not
to cover if the high card is led. Then, if the low play
is indicated, he can play the low card with speed
and nonchalance.

√ WHICH HONOR TO COVER?

When dummy has a sequence of honors, East should be careful not to cover with his only honor until the *last* card of the sequence is led. This rule is most important when the defenders have two honors between them.

22. NORTH
(dummy)
♠ Q J 9 2

WEST
♠ 10 8 7

EAST
♠ K 4 3

SOUTH
♠ A 6 5

When North leads the queen of spades, East must *not* cover. The queen will win the first trick, but then the defenders can play to get an eventual spade trick.

If North continues with the jack, East covers with his king. This follows the rule, since the jack is dummy's last honor in the sequence. South can win with the ace, but then West's ten will be good.

If North continues with a low spade, East also plays low, and he or his partner must then win a spade trick.

The defenders may never get a spade trick if East covers the first honor with his king. South wins with the ace and can then finesse through West. Dummy will have J-9 behind West's 10-8.

If East has K-10-x, he is sure to win a trick whether he covers the first or the second honor. But if East has the doubleton K-10, his only chance to get a trick is to cover the first honor; South may finesse the nine on the second round.

What if East holds the doubleton K-x? He should still play low on the first honor. His best chance is that South will lead the jack from dummy at the second trick (playing West for 10-x originally).

The next two situations come up frequently; a little study here will save you countless tricks later.

23. NORTH
(dummy)
♠ J 10 2

WEST
♠ Q 8 7 6

EAST
♠ K 9 3

SOUTH
♠ A 5 4

Declarer, seeking two spade tricks, leads the jack from dummy. If East makes the mistake of covering, South wins with the ace and returns a spade toward dummy's ten. The ten will give declarer his second trick sooner or later.

East can prevent this by following the rule about honors in sequence. Since the jack is not the *last* honor, East plays low. West wins the first trick with the queen. Now the ten cannot win a trick no matter what South does.

East would cover if he had both the king and the queen. The rule about covering the last card of a sequence applies only to a *single* honor in the defender's hand.

A similar situation:

24. NORTH
(dummy)
♠ 10 3 2

WEST
♠ Q 8 7 6

EAST
♠ K 9 4

SOUTH
♠ A J 5

If North leads the ten, East must cover with the king. South can win with the ace but can never win a trick with the jack.

It would cost East a trick to play low when the ten is led from the North hand. The ten would ride, losing to the queen. Declarer would later get to dummy to lead another spade toward his A-J.

These last two North-South holdings were not included earlier as *finessing* situations because their success depends partly on an opponent's error (or on finding *both* honors in East's hand).

When the suit is fairly long, however, declarer need not rely on a defensive error:

25. NORTH
(dummy)
♠ J 4 3 2
SOUTH
♠ A 10 6 5

South assumes that the honors are divided between the two defenders and that one opponent has a doubleton. The question is, Which opponent has the doubleton?

If West has the doubleton, South leads a low spade from his hand. West probably will step up with his honor, after which declarer can eventually finesse through East for the other honor. (If West fails to step up with his honor, dummy uses the jack to force out East's honor, and South later leads out the ace to capture West's honor.)

If *East* has the doubleton, declarer begins the suit by leading low from dummy. East plays low (his best defense), and South finesses the ten. This forces out West's honor. South later leads out the ace, capturing East's honor.

If declarer has no reason to play one defender for the doubleton rather than the other, he should lead low toward the ace-ten. This will work if East has the doubleton or *both* of the missing honors.

As in many situations, declarer is best off if the opponents lead the suit for him. If West leads up to the ace, declarer captures an honor and still has the jack and ten left. If East leads through the ace, declarer has the material for a true finesse when North regains the lead.

Friendly opponents can also help you out by leading first in these combinations:

26. NORTH	27. NORTH	28. NORTH
(dummy)	(dummy)	(dummy)
♠ Q 3 2	♠ K 2	♠ K 3 2
SOUTH	SOUTH	SOUTH
♠ J 5 4	♠ J 4 3	♠ A 10 9

In Diagram 26 South may be unable to get a spade trick if he leads the suit himself. If either opponent leads spades, however, South is sure of a trick. He plays low from the second hand, and third hand must play the ace or king to win the trick. Now declarer uses one honor to force out the other top spade, and this establishes his other honor for a trick.

In Diagram 27 a lead by South or North may give the opponents all of the spades. If the opponents lead spades, however, declarer is sure of a trick. If West leads a low spade, for example, declarer plays low from dummy. East must play the queen (or ace) to win the trick. Now the king will force out the ace if it hasn't been played and thus set up South's jack.

If East leads first, he gives declarer a "free finesse" and the king must make.

In Diagram 28 declarer can win only two spade tricks if he leads the suit himself (unless he is lucky enough to find a doubleton Q-J or a singleton honor). But if an opponent leads the suit, South has an excellent chance to win all three tricks. Suppose West leads a *low* spade. North plays low and captures an honor with the ace. South then leads the ten for a finesse through West. If the honors are split, South is sure to win all three tricks. Try it with East on lead, and it works out the same way.

If an *honor* is led by an opponent in this situation, you have to decide who has the other honor. You can set up a finesse against either opponent easily enough. But outguessing the opponents requires a certain skill. One hint: it takes a good player or a dub to lead an unsupported honor; if you judge your opponent to be somewhere between, play him for the other honor.

✔ TIPS IN GENERAL

- Give the opponents a chance to go wrong.
- Try to eliminate your own guesswork.
- Decide what you're hoping for—and its likelihood—BEFORE you finesse.

www.www.www

WHEN *NOT* TO FINESSE

√ A Dangerous Suit	√ Delayed Finesse
√ A Dangerous Shift	√ Time Is Opportunity
√ Beware the Singleton	√ Trump Control
√ A Blocked Suit	√ Other Reasons
√ Prefer the Long Suit	

WE HAVE JUST GONE THROUGH two long chapters full of situations with which the successful player must be familiar. If many of the finessing positions were new to you, come back and review them when you have finished reading the book.

Now we can get back to using *judgment* instead of memory. It's more enjoyable, and the benefits are more lasting.

Having learned *how* to finesse, we must now decide *whether* to do so. A finesse is a tool; and you don't use a tool without rhyme or reason, just because it happens to be lying about.

∤ A DANGEROUS SUIT

For example, let's consider the following typical situation:

1. NORTH
    ♠ A Q 4
    ♡ 8 3 2
    ◇ 6 4
    ♣ A 10 9 6 3

WEST   EAST
♠ 9 5   ♠ K J 10 6 2
♡ Q 10 5 4   ♡ J 9 7
◇ J 9 8 5   ◇ Q 3 2
♣ 5 4 2   ♣ K 8

                SOUTH
                ♠ 8 7 3
                ♡ A K 6
                ◇ A K 10 7
                ♣ Q J 7

SOUTH	WEST	NORTH	EAST
1 NT	Pass	3 NT	Pass
Pass	Pass		

West leads the nine of spades, hoping to strike his partner's good suit since he has no suit of his own that is worth developing. It happens to be a lucky shot.

South can, if he likes, finesse dummy's queen of spades. If he does, he will be sorry.

East would win with the king of spades and return the jack of spades to force out dummy's ace. Sooner or later South must try the club finesse, losing to East's king. And then East takes the rest of his spades, defeating the contract.

This unpleasantness can be avoided if South refuses the spade finesse at the first trick. Instead, declarer wins the first trick with dummy's ace of spades.

South gets to his hand with a heart or a diamond and tries the club finesse. If the finesse succeeds, any line of play at all will bring home nine tricks; but the finesse loses.

Now what can East do? If he leads spades, dummy's queen will be set up. If East leads anything else, South can win and run his tricks. He makes his contract with one spade, two hearts, two diamonds, and four clubs.

The point is that it doesn't pay to take a finesse when it may give an opponent the chance to establish a whole suit or even just a trick that you cannot afford to lose. Look to see what will happen if you refuse the finesse. Perhaps you can retain a stopper in the dangerous suit by grabbing the trick.

√ A DANGEROUS SHIFT

A slight change in the hand gives us another point:

2. NORTH
♠ A Q J
♡ 8 3 2
◇ 6 4
♣ A 10 9 6 3

WEST
♠ 10 9 5 2
♡ K 7 5
◇ J 9 8 5
♣ 5 2

EAST
♠ K 6 4
♡ J 10 9 6 4
◇ 10 3 2
♣ K 8

SOUTH
♠ 8 7 3
♡ A Q
◇ A K Q 7
♣ Q J 7 4

SOUTH	WEST	NORTH	EAST
1 NT	Pass	3 NT	Pass
Pass	Pass		

West leads the deuce of spades, and South has it in his power to finesse dummy's jack or queen. If he does, he goes down.

East wins the first trick with the king of spades and sees at a glance that no lasting happiness can come from this suit. He therefore shifts to the jack of hearts.

Now South is in the soup. It does him no good to refuse *this* finesse. For this reason he finesses the queen of hearts, losing to the king. Back comes a heart, and South's ace must go.

South cannot make nine tricks without tackling the clubs. East gets in with the king of clubs and takes the rest of the hearts. Down two.

Watch the difference if declarer refuses the spade finesse at the first trick. Instead, he wins with dummy's ace of spades.

South gets to his hand with a diamond to take the club finesse. East wins with the king of clubs and shifts to the jack of hearts.

South can afford to try the heart finesse, losing to the king. Back comes a heart, and South runs his tricks—one spade, one heart, three diamonds, and four clubs. Just enough for game.

The finesse in spades is the best play to develop spade tricks, but it happens that the spade tricks are not essential to the contract. Loss of the spade finesse gives an opponent the chance to shift to a more productive suit.

✓ BEWARE THE SINGLETON

A new reason for refusing a finesse comes up at suit contracts:

3. NORTH
♠ 9 3
♡ A 10 5
◇ K 7 4
♣ A Q J 10 6

WEST
♠ 8 7 2
♡ 8 7 6 2
◇ Q 8 5 3 2
♣ 7

EAST
♠ 6 5
♡ 9 4 3
◇ J 10 9
♣ K 9 8 5 2

SOUTH
♠ A K Q J 10 4
♡ K Q J
◇ A 6
♣ 4 3

NORTH	EAST	SOUTH	WEST
1 ♣	Pass	2 ♠	Pass
3 ♣	Pass	4 NT	Pass
5 ♡	Pass	5 NT	Pass
6 ◇	Pass	6 ♠	Pass
Pass	Pass		

South's jump to two spades is forcing to game and hints at slam ambitions. South next uses the Blackwood Convention and discovers that North has two aces and one king. Since one king is missing, South stops at a small slam.

West opens the seven of clubs. If South finesses, East wins with the king of clubs and returns a club. West ruffs and defeats the slam then and there.

Clearly, declarer should not take the club finesse at the first trick. He should put up the ace of clubs and draw trumps. He can give up the club trick later. In fact, he can take the first twelve tricks if he makes sure of drawing trumps.

At trump contracts beware of the singleton opening lead. If you can afford to do so, refuse finesses until you have drawn trumps.

Incidentally, note that six notrump is a better spot for this hand. South could take the club finesse and try for an overtrick with complete safety, since there is no trump factor to worry about.

✓ A BLOCKED SUIT

Just to show that not all of these situations occur at the first trick, we now show a different reason for refusing a finesse.

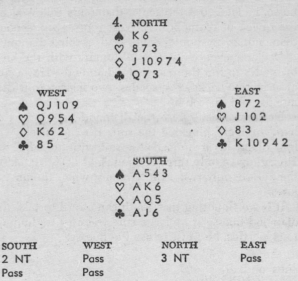

4. NORTH
♠ K 6
♡ 8 7 3
◇ J 10 9 7 4
♣ Q 7 3

WEST
♠ Q J 10 9
♡ Q 9 5 4
◇ K 6 2
♣ 8 5

EAST
♠ 8 7 2
♡ J 10 2
◇ 8 3
♣ K 10 9 4 2

SOUTH
♠ A 5 4 3
♡ A K 6
◇ A Q 5
♣ A J 6

SOUTH	WEST	NORTH	EAST
2 NT	Pass	3 NT	Pass
Pass	Pass		

West opens the queen of spades, and declarer unwisely wins in dummy with the king of spades in order to lead the jack of diamonds for a finesse. The finesse loses, and South is in trouble.

West leads the jack of spades, forcing out the ace. Now South finds his diamond suit is "blocked." The only sure outside entry to dummy—the spade king— was wasted at trick one, so dummy cannot be reached for the long diamonds. Result: declarer makes only two tricks in each suit.

It does South no good to lead out the jack of clubs. East refuses this trick, saving his king to kill dummy's queen.

How easy it becomes if South wins the first spade trick in his hand. Then, disdaining the diamond finesse, he leads out the ace of diamonds followed by the queen of diamonds. If West refuses the second diamond, as he should, South leads a third diamond.

Declarer eventually gets to dummy with the king of spades to run the rest of the diamonds. He makes at least nine tricks—two spades, two hearts, four diamonds, and one club.

Declarer must refuse the diamond finesse in this hand to avoid blocking the suit. He can surely win four diamonds if he leads the suit without a finesse. He can make only three diamonds, at best, by taking the finesse; only two, as it happens, when the finesse loses.

It is worth noting that South can afford to take the diamond finesse if he has a sure re-entry to dummy. Lacking this, he must refuse the finesse.

✓ PREFER THE LONG SUIT

An unwise finesse in our next hand might cost you a slam:

5. NORTH
♠ K 9 8 2
♡ J 10
◇ J 9 8 7 3
♣ Q J

WEST
♠ 4
♡ K 9 8 5 2
◇ 5
♣ 10 9 8 7 3 2

EAST
♠ 3
♡ 7 6 4 3
◇ K Q 10 6 4
♣ 6 5 4

SOUTH
♠ A Q J 10 7 6 5
♡ A Q
◇ A 2
♣ A K

SOUTH	WEST	NORTH	EAST
2 ♠	Pass	3 ♠	Pass
4 NT	Pass	5 ♣	Pass
5 NT	Pass	6 ◇	Pass
6 ♠	Pass	Pass	Pass

North's raise to three spades is a bit doubtful despite the fact that he has points galore. He has only one king and no aces. The eventual slam contract is, however, quite reasonable.

West opens the ten of clubs, and South wins with the king. At first glance it may appear that South must sooner or later try the heart finesse. This is, however, a short-sighted glance.

South should lead the ace of spades at the second trick, drawing both of the missing trumps. Then South cashes the ace of diamonds and gives up a diamond trick.

If both opponents followed suit to the second round

of diamonds, South would be home without much trouble. Only two diamonds would remain unaccounted for. South could surely get to dummy three times with trumps—twice to ruff diamonds and the third time to cash the last diamond, discarding the queen of hearts.

As it happens, West discards a club on the second diamond, and it looks for a moment as though the 5-1 diamond break is fatal to South's plan. But then South sees that East must use the ten of diamonds to win the second trick in that suit. The original plan can still be followed.

East takes the ten of diamonds and returns a heart. South must *not* finesse; the finesse offers only a fifty-fifty chance while the diamond suit is a sure thing. South therefore puts up the ace of hearts and leads a trump to dummy's eight.

Back comes the eight of diamonds. East must cover with the queen to prevent dummy's eight from winning the trick. South ruffs and leads a trump to dummy's nine.

The nine of diamonds is now led. Again, East must cover, this time with the king. (If East failed to cover at either of these tricks, South would discard his queen of hearts at once.) South ruffs and leads a trump to dummy's king.

Now dummy's jack of diamonds is led. East follows suit with the six of diamonds, and South discards the queen of hearts. The rest is easy.

What would happen if the six and seven of diamonds were exchanged? In that case it would be impossible to establish a diamond in the North hand. South would see the whole story on leading out the second round of diamonds, and he would fall back on the heart finesse as a last resort.

The important point about a finesse in a *short* suit is that you can often postpone your decision until you have tried one or two other possibilities. If nothing else works, you can try the finesse. It is wrong to try the finesse first, for then you are wholly dependent on that single play. You cannot always postpone the decision when the finesse is in a *long* suit since you may have to develop the rest of the suit.

✓ DELAYED FINESSE

Sometimes you decide against a finesse because some other play *in the same suit* gives you a better chance for your contract:

```
              6.  NORTH
                  ♠ K Q 5 2
                  ♡ K J 5 2
                  ♢ 8 4
                  ♣ A 5 4
    WEST                              EAST
    ♠ 9 6                             ♠ J 4
    ♡ 10 9 8 6                        ♡ Q 4
    ♢ K 7 5 2                         ♢ J 10 9 6 3
    ♣ Q J 10                          ♣ K 9 8 3
                  SOUTH
                  ♠ A 10 8 7 3
                  ♡ A 7 3
                  ♢ A Q
                  ♣ 7 6 2
```

SOUTH	WEST	NORTH	EAST
1 ♠	Pass	3 ♠	Pass
4 ♢	Pass	4 ♠	Pass
Pass	Pass		

South can afford to make one gesture in the direction of slam, but when the cue bid of four diamonds meets with no encouragement, South is content to stop at game.

West opens the queen of clubs, and South can count on winning five trumps and four top cards in the side suits. Where is the tenth trick?

There are finesses in hearts and diamonds. Another possibility is dummy's fourth heart. If South tries both finesses, however, he may lose a heart, a diamond, and two clubs.

Declarer should take the first trick with dummy's ace of clubs. Otherwise East might be brilliant enough to overtake with the king of clubs and lead a diamond. This would force South to commit himself before he knows what he wants to do.

Declarer next draws trumps and develops the hearts in a strange way. He takes the king of hearts first, then the ace of hearts.

If the queen of hearts fails to drop, South plans to lead a third heart toward dummy's jack. This will give him a third heart trick whenever West has the queen of hearts (in which case the finesse would likewise work); whenever the hearts are 3-3; and also whenever East has the doubleton queen of hearts.

In this case East has the doubleton queen, and South has no further problem. He does not lose a heart trick, so he can afford to lose two clubs and a diamond.

As the cards lie, South goes down if he makes the "normal" play of taking an early heart finesse. Both finesses lose, and the hearts break badly. In effect, however, South's best play is a late lead toward the jack of hearts—or a delayed finesse.

✓ TIME IS OPPORTUNITY

When the opening leader has missed his best bet, beware of taking a finesse that gives him time to shift:

                    7. NORTH
                        ♠ K 7
                        ♡ K 7 2
                        ◇ A K J 9 4
                        ♣ K 6 5

       WEST   EAST
       ♠ A J 5   ♠ Q 9 8 6 4 2
       ♡ Q 10 6   ♡ 5 3
       ◇ 5 2   ◇ Q 8 6
       ♣ A Q J 7 4   ♣ 9 2

                        SOUTH
                        ♠ 10 3
                        ♡ A J 9 8 4
                        ◇ 10 7 3
                        ♣ 10 8 3

WEST	NORTH	EAST	SOUTH
1 ♣	1 NT	Pass	2 ♡
Pass	3 ♡	Pass	Pass
Pass			

When this hand was played in a national tournament, West opened the five of diamonds. A club lead would have been better for his side, but West hated to lead from his club combination even though North's notrump overcall made it clear that the king was behind him.

South saw that he could not afford to lose the lead prematurely. Disdaining all finesses, he went up with the king of diamonds, took the king and ace of hearts, cashed the ace of diamonds, and gave up a diamond.

Now declarer was safe. Nothing could prevent him from getting a club discard on one of dummy's long diamonds.

As the hand was played, East returned a club on winning with the queen of diamonds. West took the ace of clubs and returned the queen of clubs to dummy's king. Declarer then led a good diamond from dummy to discard his last club. West ruffed with the queen of hearts, but it was too late. South lost only one trick in each suit.

Try taking a finesse, and see what happens.

Suppose South takes a diamond finesse at the first trick. East wins and returns a club. West takes the ace of clubs and leads the queen of clubs to dummy's king. South can draw two rounds of trumps and go back to diamonds, but West ruffs the third diamond (before any discard is available) and takes a second club trick and the ace of spades.

Suppose South refuses the diamond finesse but tries the heart finesse. West wins with the queen of hearts and goes right after the clubs. When East gets the queen of diamonds he returns a spade, giving West the chance to take the ace of spades and a second club trick.

The point is that South must not give the opponents time to attack the clubs. He must develop his own tricks first—without a finesse.

✓ TRUMP CONTROL

Sometimes you cannot afford to take a finesse for fear of losing control of trumps:

8. NORTH
♠ K 4
♡ 10 7
♢ A K J 8 4
♣ A 5 3 2

WEST
♠ Q 10 8 7
♡ A 9 3
♢ 7 5
♣ Q J 10 9

EAST
♠ 5 2
♡ 6 5 2
♢ Q 10 9 6
♣ K 8 7 4

SOUTH
♠ A J 9 6 3
♡ K Q J 8 4
♢ 3 2
♣ 6

NORTH	EAST	SOUTH	WEST
1 ♢	Pass	1 ♠	Pass
2 ♢	Pass	3 ♡	Pass
3 ♠	Pass	4 ♠	Pass
Pass	Pass		

West opens the queen of clubs, and dummy wins with the ace. Declarer leads back the ten of hearts to force out the ace, and West leads another club, forcing South to ruff.

It is now time to do something about the trumps. South leads a trump to dummy's king and a trump back.

Should he finesse the jack?

See what happens if he does. West wins with the queen of spades and leads back a third club. South must ruff—and now South has only one trump while West has *two*. South goes down one trick and is lucky not to go down more.

How different if South refuses the trump finesse. He takes the ace of spades and abandons the trumps.

This leaves two trumps in the West hand and two trumps in the South hand. South leads hearts until West ruffs. Now South stays ahead of West. Declarer ruffs another club and leads his last heart to punch out West's last trump. South loses the ace of hearts and two trump tricks, but easily wins the rest.

√ OTHER REASONS

There are other reasons to refuse a finesse. For example, you may have all thirteen tricks without risking the finesse. You will find other reasons if you keep on the alert when you play bridge.

In addition, you will find some other plays of this nature in Chapter 23, and in the material on Safety Plays in Chapter 28.

22nd DAY
᠊᠊᠊᠊᠊᠊᠊᠊᠊᠊᠊᠊᠊᠊᠊᠊᠊᠊᠊᠊᠊᠊᠊᠊

THE HOLD-UP PLAY

√ The Basic Idea	√ Hold-Up at Suit Contracts
√ When Not to Hold Up	√ Hold-Up by Defender
√ Blocking the Enemy's Suit	√ In Short
√ Defense Against Hold-Ups	

√ THE BASIC IDEA

THE TIME TO take a trick is when it does you the most good—not necessarily at your first opportunity.

Why should you refuse to take a trick? Usually because you want to cut the communications between your opponents. Here is the basic idea:

1. NORTH
♠ 8 4
♡ 7 3 2
◇ A Q J 6 2
♣ A Q 5

WEST
♠ Q 10 7 5 2
♡ Q 9 8
◇ 8 4 3
♣ 10 2

EAST
♠ K J 3
♡ J 10 6 4
◇ K 7
♣ J 9 8 3

SOUTH
♠ A 9 6
♡ A K 5
◇ 10 9 5
♣ K 7 6 4

NORTH	EAST	SOUTH	WEST
1 ◇	Pass	2 NT	Pass
3 NT	Pass	Pass	Pass

Opening lead: ♠ 5

West leads the five of spades, and East plays the king. South has the chance to take the ace of spades immediately, but he should not do so. He should *hold up* his ace until the third round of spades.

Let's see what happens both ways—if he takes the ace and if he holds up.

Suppose South takes the first trick with the ace of spades. He counts his tricks: one spade, two hearts, and at most four tricks in clubs. He needs at least two tricks in diamonds. Sooner or later, therefore, South must try the diamond finesse.

Since there is no good reason to postpone the play,

South tries the diamond finesse at once. East wins with the king of diamonds and returns the jack of spades. East then leads his last spade, and West continues with the rest of the spades.

The defenders take one diamond and four spades, defeating the contract.

Now let's go back to the first trick and see what happens if South holds up his ace of spades. East wins the first trick with the king of spades.

East continues with the jack of spades, and South refuses the trick again. In for a penny, in for a pound.

East leads his last spade, and South takes the ace. The hold-up play has been completed.

South's next step is to try the diamond finesse, since his fundamental plan for the hand is unchanged. The finesse loses to East's king. After all, the hold-up play hasn't changed the location of any cards.

Nevertheless, there is a big difference. After East takes his king of diamonds he cannot return a spade. He'd like to, mind you, but he just doesn't have a spade to lead. *And that's exactly why South held up the ace of spades until the third round of the suit: to exhaust East's spades.*

It doesn't matter what else East leads. Declarer easily takes the rest of the tricks, making his contract with an overtrick.

Now let's ask a few other questions. What would happen if East still had one more spade even after South held up the ace of spades as long as he could? In that case the eight missing spades would be divided 4-4; and the defenders would take only three spades and the king of diamonds. South would still make his contract.

What would happen if East had five spades and West had only three? In that case South would be

defeated. He would congratulate West on making a
brilliant opening lead (usually a player opens his
own long suit rather than guess at his partner's long
suit) and would comfort himself with the thought
that the contract was unmakable.

In short, the hold-up play doesn't guarantee your
contract. It improves your chances—which is reason
enough to use it.

Let's take another case:

2. NORTH
♠ 10 6
♡ A Q J
◇ Q J 10 9 7
♣ A J 10

WEST   EAST
♠ J 9 7 5 3 2   ♠ K 8
♡ 7 3   ♡ 9 8 5 4 2
◇ K 8 5   ◇ A
♣ 5 2   ♣ 9 7 6 4 3

SOUTH
♠ A Q 4
♡ K 10 6
◇ 6 4 3 2
♣ K Q 8

NORTH	EAST	SOUTH	WEST
1 ◇	Pass	2 NT	Pass
3 NT	Pass	Pass	Pass

Opening lead: ♠ 5

West leads the five of spades, and South hopefully
plays the ten from dummy. This would hold the
trick if West had led from a suit headed by king-
jack.

There is no such luck. East plays the king of
spades at the first trick.

What should South do?

His impulse is to grab the trick before the mice get at it. If he does so, he loses his contract.

Let's see what happens. South wins the first spade trick and leads a diamond. (Or he may lead a heart or a club to dummy and return a diamond from dummy.) East wins the first diamond with the ace and returns his low spade.

It is now too late for South to hold up his high spade. If South plays low, West overtakes with the nine or jack of spades in order to lead a third spade. One way or the other, South's queen of spades is knocked out.

West still has the king of diamonds, and his long spades are established. Whenever South leads another diamond, West will pounce on the trick with his king and will run all of his spades. At best, South can take only eight tricks; if he leads a second diamond before taking his tricks, he will be down two.

South makes his contract if he holds up at the very first trick, letting East win the first trick with the king of spades.

East continues with his other spade, and South wins the trick. When East is given a diamond trick, he cannot lead a spade.

As a result South manages to preserve his second stopper in spades. He can win any club or heart return and knock out the king of diamonds while the spades are still stopped.

South loses only one spade and two diamonds, making his contract with an extra trick.

As this hand demonstrates, *it is sometimes necessary to refuse the first trick even when you have two stoppers in the enemy's suit*. (This happens when you must give up the lead *twice* in order to develop your own tricks.)

√ WHEN NOT TO HOLD UP

The advantages of the hold-up play are so great that you may be tempted to refuse the first trick for the rest of your bridge career. This would be going too far.

• *There's no need to hold up, for example, when you can take all of your tricks on the run.* The hold-up is necessary only when you must give up a trick or so in the course of developing your suits—and when you want to control what is led back at that time.

• *Another bad time to hold up is when you're better off in the suit that has been led than in some other suit.* If you refuse the first trick, the opponents may switch to their other good suit. (If you're that badly off in two suits, maybe you've bid the hand too optimistically. Even so, you must make the best of a bad situation.)

• *Sometimes you refuse to hold up because it can't possibly do any good.* For example, you hold A-x opposite dummy's x-x. Holding up one trick does not exhaust the cards held by either defender; it merely tells the opponents that they have opened a good suit and that they have you on the ropes. You may fare better by taking the first trick and proceeding with your plan. The opponents may think you have other tricks in their suit, and they may switch to something else—or they may hand you your contract by discarding unwisely on your tricks.

• *Sometimes you take the first trick in order to make sure of a second trick in the suit.* For example, suppose you hold A-J-10 in the suit that is opened. When the king or queen is played by the opponent at your right, you win with your ace. Later on you will get a second trick in the suit. If you refuse the first trick, you will probably win only one trick—the ace.

✓ BLOCKING THE ENEMY'S SUIT

In a certain kind of hand you must refrain from holding up in order to keep the enemy's suit blocked. This is true, in general, when you have A-x opposite 9-x-x-x (or better) in the other hand. Here is how it works:

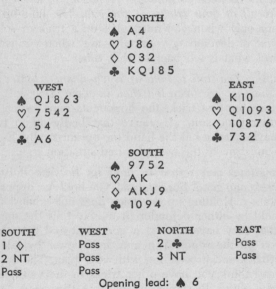

```
                3. NORTH
                ♠ A 4
                ♡ J 8 6
                ◇ Q 3 2
                ♣ K Q J 8 5
     WEST                              EAST
  ♠ Q J 8 6 3                       ♠ K 10
  ♡ 7 5 4 2                         ♡ Q 10 9 3
  ◇ 5 4                             ◇ 10 8 7 6
  ♣ A 6                             ♣ 7 3 2
                SOUTH
                ♠ 9 7 5 2
                ♡ A K
                ◇ A K J 9
                ♣ 10 9 4
```

SOUTH	WEST	NORTH	EAST
1 ◇	Pass	2 ♣	Pass
2 NT	Pass	3 NT	Pass
Pass	Pass		

Opening lead: ♠ 6

West opens the six of spades, and South's problem is whether or not to hold up.

Suppose declarer refuses the first trick. East wins with the king of spades and returns his other spade to dummy's ace. South must knock out the ace of clubs, whereupon West runs the rest of his spades, defeating the contract.

But if declarer puts up dummy's ace of spades at

the first trick, he will block the spade suit and make his contract.

What is East to do? If he plays the ten of spades, he has the blank king left. Declarer knocks out the ace of clubs at the second trick. West leads another spade, and East takes the king. End of spade suit. South wins eleven tricks.

East can do a trifle better if he drops the king of spades under dummy's ace. Declarer knocks out the ace of clubs, and West can take the queen and jack of spades. Then South's nine stops the suit. Declarer wins ten tricks.

How does South know that this is going to happen? Strangely enough, he can tell that the spades will block just by looking at dummy and his own hand.

To begin with, South doesn't worry about any 4-3 division of the seven missing spades. He can comfortably afford to give up three spade tricks and the ace of clubs. Only a 5-2 break worries South.

Assume that East has only two spades, since this is the only dangerous combination. Both of East's spades must be honor cards. Otherwise West would have three honors at the head of his suit, and in that case he would have led an honor rather than a small card. (West would lead the king of spades from K-Q-J or K-Q-10, the jack from K-J-10, the queen from Q-J-10.) If East has two honor cards in spades, the play of the ace from dummy is sure to block the suit.

The play of the ace is recommended, likewise, if South has *any* four small spades. East may have the doubleton K-Q, or he may have K-x and fail to drop the king to unblock. If East can unblock and is clever enough to do so, South needs the nine or better at the head of his four cards in order to stop the suit from being run against him.

It isn't necessary to work this problem out at the table each time you get it. Whenever you have A-x in one hand opposite any four cards in the other hand, play the ace immediately on the opening lead of a small card. This is your best chance to keep the suit blocked.

There is one other situation in which it is improper to hold up: when you can't afford to refuse the first trick for fear of never getting another chance at it. For example, if you get the chance to win the first trick with K-x or Q-x-x in your own hand and only small cards in the dummy, you'd better take the trick. One trick is better than none.

✓ DEFENSE AGAINST HOLD-UPS

This fact gives the defenders the chance to frighten you out of a hold-up play in certain situations:

```
              4.  NORTH
                  ♠ 8 3
                  ♡ K 9 6 4
                  ◇ A Q J 7 6
                  ♣ A 8
  WEST                              EAST
  ♠ J 9 7 4 2                      ♠ A Q 6
  ♡ 5 2                            ♡ J 10 8 3
  ◇ 8 3 2                          ◇ K 5
  ♣ 6 4 2                          ♣ J 10 9 5
                  SOUTH
                  ♠ K 10 5
                  ♡ A Q 7
                  ◇ 10 9 4
                  ♣ K Q 7 3
```

NORTH	EAST	SOUTH	WEST
1 ◇	Pass	2 NT	Pass
3 NT	Pass	Pass	

Opening lead: ♠ 4

How is this hand usually played? East wins the first trick with the ace of spades and returns the queen of spades. South holds up the king. East leads his last spade, and South takes the king.

Sooner or later South tries the diamond finesse. East wins with the king of diamonds—but cannot return a spade. South therefore makes his contract.

Do you pin a medal on South for holding up the king of spades? Not at all. East is the one who gets a decoration, but it isn't a medal.

At the first trick East should play the *queen* of spades, not the ace! South has to win the trick. If he doesn't he may never win a spade trick at all. After all, South doesn't know who has the ace of spades. West may have opened from A-J-x-x-x.

In short, South is scared out of a hold-up play. He wins the first trick with his king of spades.

East gets in with the king of diamonds, leads out the ace of spades, and then leads his low spade. West takes the rest of the suit, defeating the contract. Thereupon East and West smile tolerantly at South, agreeing that there was no way for him to know that he was being swindled.

It's all right for East to smile smugly; he wasn't running any risk. If West had the king of spades, East would win the first trick with the queen, and he could then continue with the other spades. If South had the king of spades, he was getting nothing that didn't belong to him; East might just as well give him the trick when it will do declarer the least good.

East's play would be riskier, but just as correct, if he played the jack at the first trick from A-J-x. If South has K-x-x, he takes it at once rather than hold up. If South has Q-x-x, he wins an undeserved trick, but the contract will still be defeated.

There's no need to make this kind of play when you have *four* cards in your partner's suit. Declarer cannot hold up long enough to exhaust your suit. The disadvantages of playing the queen are first, the king may be singleton, and second, your partner may win the first defensive trick and shift to some other suit.

If you have A-Q-x of your partner's suit and a high card or two on the side, your partner probably has nothing outside of his suit. This is the right time to play the queen at the first trick. However, if you have no high cards outside of partner's suit, your best bet is to take the ace immediately and then return the queen. The hand is hopeless if your partner likewise has no high cards; and if your partner does get in with a side suit, you want him to know that his suit is established.

Incidentally, when you do play the queen from A-Q-x, don't give the matter deep and obvious thought. If declarer knows that you have the ace he will hold up his king. If you want to deceive an opponent, be deceptive rather than transparent.

✓ HOLD-UP AT SUIT CONTRACTS

The hold-up play is most useful at notrump contracts, in which you are interested in shutting out a complete suit. The play is also useful at suit contracts, but then you usually hope to save one trick rather than a whole suit.

5. NORTH
♠ 6 2
♡ A 9 8 2
♢ A 5 4
♣ Q J 10 9

WEST
♠ 7
♡ K Q J 4 3
♢ Q J 9 6 2
♣ 7 4

EAST
♠ A 8 4 3
♡ 10 7 6
♢ K 10
♣ A K 8 2

SOUTH
♠ K Q J 10 9 5
♡ 5
♢ 8 7 3
♣ 6 5 3

EAST	SOUTH	WEST	NORTH
1 ♣	3 ♠	Pass	Pass
Pass			

Opening lead: ♡ K

West opened the king of hearts, and dummy's ace won. There wouldn't be much sense in holding up the ace of hearts at a suit contract.

Declarer led a low spade from dummy, and East played low. This wasn't a hold-up play; East simply wanted to get value for his ace of trumps.

South won with the king of spades and returned the queen of spades. West discarded a low heart, and East took his ace of trumps.

East returned another heart, and South ruffed. Declarer next led a club, and West played the seven.

East won with the king of clubs and did some thinking. He was pretty sure that the seven of clubs was the beginning of a signal, showing a doubleton. If so, South had three clubs. He was already known to have six spades and one heart. That accounted for ten of his thirteen cards, and the other three had to be diamonds.

East saw that he had to attack diamonds at once. If East woodenly led his last heart, South would ruff and draw trumps. He would then lead a club to set up two club tricks in dummy, with the ace of diamonds as a sure entry to the club tricks. South would then make five spades, two clubs, and two red aces.

To thwart this plot, East tucked his last heart back into his hand and led the king of diamonds instead.

If you've been waiting for a hold-up play, here it comes. Declarer cannot afford to take the ace of diamonds immediately. If he does, East will take the next club and lead his other diamond, whereupon West will overtake with an honor and play another high diamond. South will lose two clubs, two diamonds, and a trump.

Declarer holds up dummy's ace of diamonds, allowing East to win the trick with the king. East leads his other diamond, and dummy wins with the ace.

For the sake of argument, suppose that declarer now leads another club from dummy. What is East to do?

If East wins the trick, he cannot prevent declarer from leading another club to dummy. Then South will be able to discard his last diamond on one of dummy's high clubs.

East must therefore hold up the ace of clubs. The hold-up play is useful to the defenders as well as to the declarer. Now if South leads a third club, East can take the ace and exit safely with a heart or a trump. South will be able to take his trumps, but he will eventually have to lose a diamond to West.

South should see all of this coming. When East holds up the ace of clubs, South should not lead a third club from dummy. Instead, he leads a heart from dummy, ruffing in his own hand. This takes the last heart out of East's hand.

Now South draws two more rounds of trumps. Finally, he leads his last club. East is down to two cards, the ace and a small club. He cannot prevent dummy from making one of the two clubs, and South thus makes the contract.

The hand is a battle of hold-ups, and South wins the battle by depriving East of a safe exit.

✓ HOLD-UP BY DEFENDER

The defensive hold-up, which we have just seen at a suit contract, is more useful at notrump. The idea, usually, is to stop declarer from getting the full benefit of dummy's long suit.

6. NORTH
♠ J 6
♡ K Q J 10
♢ 7 6 3
♣ 6 5 3 2

WEST
♠ 8 5 3 2
♡ 9 6 4 2
♢ K Q 9 8
♣ 10

EAST
♠ K 9 7 4
♡ A 8 7
♢ 2
♣ J 9 8 7 4

SOUTH
♠ A Q 10
♡ 5 3
♢ A J 10 5 4
♣ A K Q

SOUTH	WEST	NORTH	EAST
1 ◊	Pass	1 ♡	Pass
2 NT	Pass	3 NT	Pass
Pass	Pass		

Opening lead: ♠ 2

Declarer puts up the jack of spades at the first trick, hoping that West has led from the king. As it happens, East produces the king of spades, and South wins with the ace. There is, of course, no need for a hold-up in spades since South can win all three tricks in the suit.

South leads a heart, and East holds up his ace, allowing dummy to win with the ten of hearts. This is the defensive hold-up in action. If East took the first heart trick, declarer would be able to win tricks with dummy's other three hearts. He would make three spades, three hearts, three clubs, and one diamond, and thus make his contract with an over-trick.

Declarer returns a diamond from dummy after winning a trick with the ten of hearts. He cannot be sure of bringing home two heart tricks, so he must take the opportunity to test the diamonds. He finesses the ten of diamonds from his hand, losing to West's queen.

West returns a spade, and South wins with the ten. Now South lays down the ace of diamonds. If both opponents follow suit, South will give up one more diamond trick and make his contract with three spades, one heart, three diamonds, and three clubs.

As it happens, however, East shows out on the second round of diamonds. Now South is limited to one diamond trick and therefore needs a second heart trick to make his contract.

South leads another heart, playing the jack from dummy. Should East win the trick or should he hold up his ace once more? If East takes the trick, South may have another heart and may therefore take a total of three heart tricks. If East holds up, South manages to steal a second heart trick and therefore makes the contract.

How does East know what to do?

In the average game East just guesses. Sometimes he guesses right, sometimes wrong.

In an expert game East *knows* what to do. When the first heart is led, West is supposed to start a *high-low* signal if he has two or four cards in the suit; but West plays his lowest heart if he has an *odd* number of cards in the suit.

In this case West has four hearts. He plays the *nine* of hearts (the higher the signal, the clearer it is) the first time that suit is played. This tells East that his partner has either two or four hearts.

East works it out from there. South has the rest of the suit—either two cards or four cards. If South has four hearts, no hold-up play will work. If South has two hearts, East must hold up exactly once and no more.

Now make a slight change in the hand. Give South the six of hearts, and give West the queen of clubs in exchange. Now South and West have three hearts each. South needs three heart tricks for his contract.

When South leads the first heart, West plays the deuce. This, obviously West's lowest heart, indicates that West has an odd number of cards in the suit. East can tell that West and South have three hearts each. East therefore waits until the third round of hearts to take his ace.

✓ IN SHORT

The hold-up play is a refusal to take a trick until the second or third opportunity in order to cut the enemy's communications.

It is used by declarer:

- Most commonly at notrump to prevent the run of the enemy's suit
- At a suit contract to save one trick

Declarer should *not* hold up when:

- He has enough tricks on the run
- He is more afraid of another suit
- The hold-up can't possibly help him
- The hold-up would cost him a second trick in the suit
- He can block the enemy's suit by taking the first trick

The defenders can use the hold-up:

- To prevent the run of declarer's or dummy's suit
- To frighten declarer out of his own hold-up play

The defender who has only small cards should signal his partner when to grab the trick:

- A high-low shows an even number of cards
- Lowest card first shows an odd number of cards

KEEPING THE DANGEROUS OPPONENT OFF LEAD

√ Watch for the Hyena!	√ The Double Duck
√ The Deep Finesse	√ Loser-on-Loser
√ The Duck	√ In Short

√ WATCH FOR THE HYENA!

ONE OF THE most important things to learn about bridge is how to tell your friends from the hyenas. Once you've learned the difference, you act one way toward your friends and quite another way toward the other jokers.

Let's look at an example, and then we can talk about general principles.

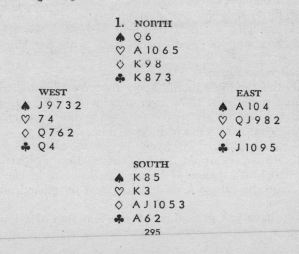

```
                    1. NORTH
                       ♠ Q 6
                       ♡ A 10 6 5
                       ◊ K 9 8
                       ♣ K 8 7 3
      WEST                                    EAST
    ♠ J 9 7 3 2                             ♠ A 10 4
    ♡ 7 4                                   ♡ Q J 9 8 2
    ◊ Q 7 6 2                               ◊ 4
    ♣ Q 4                                   ♣ J 10 9 5
                       SOUTH
                       ♠ K 8 5
                       ♡ K 3
                       ◊ A J 10 5 3
                       ♣ A 6 2
```

SOUTH	WEST	NORTH	EAST
1 ◇	Pass	1 ♡	Pass
1 NT	Pass	3 NT	All Pass

Opening lead: ♠ 3

West opens the three of spades, and you study the dummy for a moment or two before you play the first card.

You are sure to win one spade, two hearts, two diamonds, and two clubs—a total of seven tricks.

You need two additional tricks for your contract, and one glance is enough to tell you that they must come from your long diamond suit.

Your first step is to play the queen of spades from dummy. This wins a trick if West has led from the ace of spades.

What's more, your only chance to win a trick with that queen of spades is to play it immediately.

So far everything is familiar. Where is the hyena? Don't be impatient. You'll see one in a moment.

East pounces on the first trick with his ace of spades. East then leads the ten of spades, and you refuse the trick, applying a lesson that you learned a few pages ago. You win the next spade trick with the king of spades.

Enter the hyena!

By this time you should know that West has led from a long spade suit. If he ever regains the lead, he will take the rest of his spades, defeating the contract. In short, West is a hyena of hideous hue.

What about East? No hyena he, as one of our leading news magazines would put it. Your hold-up play has exhausted East's spades. If East gains the lead, he can do no harm; he cannot lead a spade, and no other lead is dangerous.

You have just gone through the first step of a lesson

that most bridge players never learn. *You have discovered that one opponent may be dangerous while the other opponent is safe. This is true in a tremendous number of hands.*

The second step is to "take measures." These come in all shapes and sizes, from simple to extreme. Just remember that you can't take even the simplest measure until you know what you're up against.

In this case you have a simple problem to solve: how to develop at least four diamond tricks without letting West gain the lead.

You have just won the third trick with the king of spades. You must now lead the jack of diamonds from your hand for an immediate finesse. If West plays a low diamond (as he should), you must play low from the dummy, letting the jack ride.

As the cards lie, this finesse wins. You continue with a small diamond, finessing dummy's nine. Then you take dummy's king of diamonds and return to your hand to lead out the ace of diamonds.

The rest is easy.

When you lead the jack of diamonds for a finesse, you don't know who has the queen. Perhaps East will win the trick. That doesn't bother you. You have already decided that East is the *safe* opponent. East will make some harmless return, and you will still make your contract.

You would go down if you played the diamonds the other way. Suppose you won the first diamond trick with dummy's king and then led the nine of diamonds from dummy. You would be unable to develop the diamonds without giving West his queen—and then West would gleefully take the rest of his spades.

You cannot even afford to win the first diamond trick with the ace before leading the jack of diamonds for a finesse. That would give you three diamond tricks, but you need *four* to assure your contract.

In bridge player's lingo, you have a "two-way finesse" in diamonds. If you think West has the queen, you can finesse through him; and if you think East has the queen, you can take your finesse the other way. But there is only one correct way to finesse once you recognize the hyena!

In some hands your only problem is to guess which opponent holds the queen. But in hands like the example you don't care who has the queen. *You finesse in such a way as to keep the dangerous opponent out.*

Here's a different solution to the same problem:

2. NORTH
♠ Q 6
♡ A 8 5
◇ A K J 6 3
♣ 10 9 5

WEST
♠ A J 9 3 2
♡ 9 6 2
◇ 7 2
♣ K 8 4

EAST
♠ 10 7 4
♡ J 10 4 3
◇ Q 8 4
♣ 7 3 2

SOUTH
♠ K 8 5
♡ K Q 7
◇ 10 9 5
♣ A Q J 6

SOUTH	WEST	NORTH	EAST
1 ♣	Pass	1 ◇	Pass
1 NT	Pass	3 NT	All Pass

Opening lead: ♠ 3

West opens the three of spades, and you count your sure tricks: one spade, three hearts, two diamonds, and one club. You need two additional tricks.

One glance is enough to show you that you can develop two additional tricks either in diamonds or in clubs. Which suit should you tackle?

You don't know yet. Choosing the suit comes under the heading of taking measures. First you must find the hyena.

You play the queen of spades from dummy, and East plays the four of spades.

Enter the hyena!

You now know that West has led from a long spade suit headed by the ace. (If East had the ace of spades, he would use it to take the first trick away from dummy's queen.)

However, *West* is still your friend. If West is allowed to win a trick, he cannot continue the attack on spades without giving you a second spade trick. And if West leads anything else, you can surely handle it.

East is the hyena. If East wins a trick, he will lead a spade through your king; and then West will defeat the contract with the rest of his long suit.

You have a choice of finesses, but not in the same suit. Your problem is much the same, however: to develop two additional tricks without allowing the dangerous opponent to gain the lead.

You solve the problem by tackling the clubs rather than the diamonds. Either suit is best developed by a finesse. *You must pick the finesse that will surely shut out the dangerous opponent.*

At the second trick, therefore, you lead the ten of clubs from dummy for a finesse. Then or at the next trick, West will take his king of clubs. West may lead a heart or a diamond, but cannot afford to lead another

spade. You will take your nine tricks and fold your tent.
You would go down if you tackled the diamonds instead
of the clubs. East would win a trick with the queen of
diamonds and would lead a spade through your king.
That would be the end of you.

Before we leave these two examples, let's take a second
look at the spade suit. In both hands you have Q-6 in
the dummy opposite K-8-5 in your own hand. In both
cases you play the queen from dummy at the first trick.

In the first hand East wins the first trick with the ace
of spades. You hold up your king of spades as long as
possible, and *West* becomes the dangerous opponent.

In the second hand dummy's queen of spades wins
the first trick. This makes *East* the dangerous opponent.

It's instructive to see what happens if you switch the
spades from one hand to the other. That is, West will
have A-J-9-3-2 of spades in the first hand, and J-9-7-3-2
in the second hand.

Now when you put up the queen of spades in the
first hand, it wins the trick. You see that *East* is the
dangerous opponent. Hence you must play the diamonds
in such a way as to keep East out. You lead the king of
diamonds from dummy and then lead the nine of diamonds for a finesse through East.

There is a similar reversal in the second hand. When
you put up the queen of spades, East wins with the ace.
You must hold up your king of spades and treat *West*
as the dangerous opponent. For this reason you tackle
the diamonds instead of the clubs.

You cannot look at the dummy and decide immediately which opponent is dangerous. You must see what
happens to the queen of spades before you know who
is your friend and who is your enemy.

√ THE DEEP FINESSE

Sometimes it is so important to keep the dangerous opponent out of the lead that you must take an unusually deep finesse.

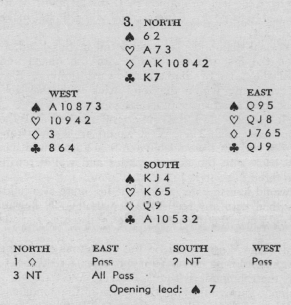

3. NORTH
    ♠ 6 2
    ♡ A 7 3
    ◇ A K 10 8 4 2
    ♣ K 7

WEST
♠ A 10 8 7 3
♡ 10 9 4 2
◇ 3
♣ 8 6 4

EAST
♠ Q 9 5
♡ Q J 8
◇ J 7 6 5
♣ Q J 9

SOUTH
♠ K J 4
♡ K 6 5
◇ Q 9
♣ A 10 5 3 2

NORTH	EAST	SOUTH	WEST
1 ◇	Pass	2 NT	Pass
3 NT	All Pass		

Opening lead: ♠ 7

You count your sure tricks: one spade, two hearts, three diamonds, and two clubs. One additional trick is needed, obviously from dummy's long diamond suit.

You play a low spade from the dummy, and East plays the queen. You win with the king of spades and realize that *East* is the dangerous opponent. If he wins a trick later on, East will lead a spade through your jack, and the jig will be up.

Your problem is to develop the diamonds in such a way as to keep East out.

The method is to lead a club (or a heart) to dummy and return a low diamond. When East plays low, you must finesse the nine of diamonds from your hand.

You are willing to lose this deep finesse if West happens to have the jack of diamonds. If this happens, West will be unable to do any damage, and you will still make your contract.

The normal diamond play would fail in this hand. If you won the first diamond trick with the queen and then led the nine of diamonds toward dummy, East would eventually win a diamond trick with the jack. Then the spade return would beat you.

Switch the ace and the queen of spades, and the situation is reversed. Then West would be leading from Q-10-8-7-3, and East would have A-9-5. East would win the first trick with the ace of spades and would return a spade through your K-J.

You would finesse your jack of spades, more as a hold-up play than with any real hope of winning the finesse. West would take the queen of spades and return a spade to your king.

At this stage West would be the dangerous opponent, and East would be safe. Your problem would be to develop the diamonds without allowing West to win a trick. Hence you would take the queen of diamonds and let the nine of diamonds ride through West for a deep finesse. As in our first example you have a two-way finesse, and *you finesse through the dangerous opponent.*

✓ THE DUCK

Sometimes your method of keeping the dangerous opponent out is just a matter of playing a low card at the right time.

4. NORTH
♠ 7 4
♡ A K 5 4
◇ 8 7 4 3
♣ A Q 6

WEST
♠ K J 9 6 3
♡ J 10 8
◇ J 10 6
♣ 7 3

EAST
♠ Q 8 5
♡ Q 9 3
◇ Q 5
♣ 9 8 5 4 2

SOUTH
♠ A 10 2
♡ 7 6 2
◇ A K 9 2
♣ K J 10

SOUTH	WEST	NORTH	EAST
1 ◇	Pass	1 ♡	Pass
1 NT	Pass	3 NT	All Pass

Opening lead: ♠ 6

You count your sure tricks: one spade, two hearts, two diamonds, and three clubs. One additional trick is needed. You make the mental note that you must try to establish one of the low cards in diamonds, or possibly even in hearts.

Having come to this conclusion, you refuse the first and second spade tricks. You win the third spade trick and come to the next conclusion: *West* is the dangerous opponent. You are willing to give a trick to East, however, since he is out of spades by this time.

How can you establish a low diamond without allowing West to gain the lead?

If you weren't worried about a dangerous opponent, you might lead out the ace and king of diamonds and then give up one diamond trick. That wouldn't work in this case, for West would take the jack of diamonds and the rest of his spades.

Another way to set up a diamond is just to lead a low diamond from your hand to start the suit. That likewise wouldn't work in this case. West would step up with the ten of diamonds and would take the rest of the spades.

What can you do if you can't lead high and you can't lead low?

Lead a heart to dummy's king and return a diamond. If East puts up the queen, you will duck, allowing him to hold the trick. Your idea is to give up one diamond trick *to East,* and this is as good a time as any to do it.

What if East plays his *low* diamond? Then you must win the trick with the ace. Get back to dummy with a club and lead another diamond through East. When East plays the queen, duck. Play your low card and let East win the trick.

What if East is able to play a low diamond the first time and another low diamond the second time? You must win both tricks and lead a third diamond from your hand in the hope that East rather than West will have to win the trick. All you can do is your best. You cannot always get a guarantee from the bank that your plan will work.

Why did you go to all the trouble of getting to the dummy for each diamond lead? If you led the ace or king of diamonds from your hand, East might double-cross you by dumping his queen! This clever unblock would allow *West* to gain the lead sooner or later with a diamond in order to run the spades. (Just because you have identified *West* as the hyena on this hand doesn't mean that you can afford to give your safe-deposit key to *East!*)

Now go back to your first attempt to reach dummy. You led a small heart. If West played the three of hearts, you would have played a low heart from dummy. Your object would be to duck the trick into the East hand. Later on if this plan worked, you would take the top hearts in the hope of winning a trick with dummy's last heart. Your plan failed because West played the eight of hearts and you couldn't afford to duck this card. (East also would duck, and your dangerous opponent would be in the lead.)

The hand might be something like this:

<pre>
                    4A. NORTH
                    ♠ 7 4
                    ♡ A K 5 4
                    ◇ 8 7 4 3
                    ♣ A Q 6
    WEST   EAST
 ♠ K J 9 6 3   ♠ Q 8 5
 ♡ 10 8 3   ♡ Q J 9
 ◇ Q J 10   ◇ 6 5
 ♣ 7 3   ♣ 9 8 5 4 2
                    SOUTH
                    ♠ A 10 2
                    ♡ 7 6 2
                    ◇ A K 9 2
                    ♣ K J 10
</pre>

West leads the six of spades against your contract of three notrump. You hold up your ace of spades until the third trick, discarding a small diamond from dummy.

Now you lead a low heart. West plays the three, and you play low from dummy. This ducks the trick to East, who wins with the nine.

East returns a diamond, and you must win. You lead a heart to dummy's king and return a diamond, hoping that East will have to play the queen.

As it happens, East plays a low diamond. You win with the king of diamonds and think of leading a third diamond. But first you can try the hearts. You lead a heart to dummy's ace and heave a sigh of relief when both of the missing hearts fall on this trick. Dummy's last heart is now good, and you take it. The three clubs now give you the game contract.

✔ THE DOUBLE DUCK

In some hands you make a whole career out of keeping the dangerous opponent off lead.

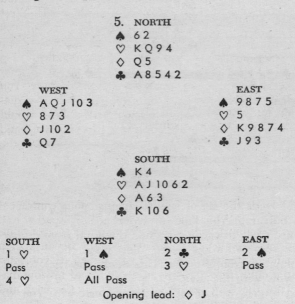

```
                    5.  NORTH
                        ♠ 6 2
                        ♡ K Q 9 4
                        ◇ Q 5
                        ♣ A 8 5 4 2

        WEST                              EAST
        ♠ A Q J 10 3                      ♠ 9 8 7 5
        ♡ 8 7 3                           ♡ 5
        ◇ J 10 2                          ◇ K 9 8 7 4
        ♣ Q 7                             ♣ J 9 3

                        SOUTH
                        ♠ K 4
                        ♡ A J 10 6 2
                        ◇ A 6 3
                        ♣ K 10 6
```

SOUTH	WEST	NORTH	EAST
1 ♡	1 ♠	2 ♣	2 ♠
Pass	Pass	3 ♡	Pass
4 ♡	All Pass		

Opening lead: ◇ J

Your first step at a trump contract is to count *losers:* two spades, one diamond, and one club.

Clearly, you must plan to set up dummy's long clubs

in order to get rid of a spade or two. In the meantime you must keep East out to prevent him from leading a spade through your king.

How can East gain the lead? Perhaps with a diamond, perhaps with a club. You must handle both of those suits with great care.

It's easy to see who has the king of diamonds when you're looking at the entire hand. At the table you wouldn't have this advantage, but you still should know all about the diamonds.

West's spades have been bid and raised. If he wanted to make a dangerous lead, he would lead a spade. West certainly wouldn't lead a diamond from the king out of a clear sky. Clearly, West is leading a diamond in the hope that this suit will be safer, not riskier, than spades.

Since East surely has the king of diamonds, you cannot gain anything by playing the queen from dummy. You must duck in dummy. East naturally plays a low diamond (if he played his king, neither he nor West would ever win a diamond trick); you duck in your own hand as well. This allows West to win the first trick with the jack of diamonds.

What is the reason for this play? You must lose one diamond trick sooner or later. You must make sure of losing that trick to *West*, not to East. You have just done so.

Why can't you play the queen of diamonds from dummy and capture the king with your ace? Because then East's nine of diamonds would be an entry. If you later gave up a club trick to West, he would lead his low diamond (not the ten), and East would win the trick and push a spade through you.

West is a little surprised to win the first trick with the jack of diamonds, but leads another diamond for lack of anything better. This time, of course, you win with the ace of diamonds.

You next draw three rounds of trumps, ending in dummy, and lead a low club toward your own hand. East plays low, and you play the ten of clubs from your hand.

This is more a ducking play than a finesse. You want to give up a trick, but you want to make sure the trick is won by *West*.

Your play works. West wins with the queen of clubs. As soon as you regain the lead you can take the king and ace of clubs, after which dummy's remaining clubs will be good. If West fails to take his ace of spades at this moment, you will get rid of *both* of your spades on dummy's clubs. Even if West takes his ace, however, you will still make your contract.

✓ LOSER-ON-LOSER

Sometimes you must give up a trick to the *dangerous* opponent if you develop a suit normally. The loser-on-loser play may give you a useful play to develop the suit abnormally.

6. NORTH
♠ A 9 7 3
♡ Q J
◇ 5 4
♣ A 8 7 6 4

WEST
♠ 8
♡ A K 8 5 3
◇ A 8 6 3
♣ J 5 2

EAST
♠ 2
♡ 9 7 6 4 2
◇ Q J 10 9
♣ K Q 10

SOUTH
♠ K Q J 10 6 5 4
♡ 10
◇ K 7 2
♣ 9 3

SOUTH	WEST	NORTH	EAST
4 ♠	Pass	Pass	Pass

Opening lead: ♡ K

South's opening shutout bid was very effective. His opponents could have made five hearts if allowed to play the hand. As it was, South bid and made a game of his own.

West won the first trick with the king of hearts, and South counted losers: one heart, two diamonds, and one club. The problem was to set up dummy's long clubs without allowing *East* to gain the lead. East was dangerous because he would surely lead a diamond, and the defenders would get their two diamond tricks.

After winning the first trick with the king of hearts, West shifted to a low club.

Now put yourself in South's seat and see if you can find the way to make the contract.

You can't afford to play a low club from dummy. East will win and lead a diamond at once.

You must step up with dummy's ace of clubs. *Then what?* Lead the queen of hearts from dummy and discard your nine of clubs! This is known as discarding a loser on a loser.

Your loser-on-loser play gives the defenders a second heart trick but robs them of their club trick. More important, it gives the trick to the *safe* defender and shuts the dangerous opponent out.

West accepts the heart trick and leads a trump, his best defense. You win with dummy's nine of spades, ruff a club, return to dummy with the seven of spades, and ruff another club.

By this time, fortunately, you know that the clubs are established. You can get back to dummy with the ace of spades to discard two diamonds on the last two clubs. Then you cheerfully give up one diamond trick.

What would you do if the clubs failed to break so favorably? You would then have to lead a diamond from dummy toward your king in the hope that East had the ace. You never gave up that chance of making your contract.

✓ IN SHORT

When you plan the play of a hand, consider which opponent is dangerous. If one opponent is quite safe, develop your suits so that the friendly enemy is the only one to win the lead. Be sure to keep the dangerous opponent out.

24th DAY
~~~~~~~~~~~~~~~~~~~~~~~~

WHEN TO DRAW TRUMPS

✓ No-Problem Hands	✓ Trumps as Stoppers
✓ Leaving the Master Trump Out	✓ Defending the Trump Suit
✓ Forcing Out the Master Trump	✓ Trumps for Communication
✓ Ruffers in Dummy	✓ Protecting a Side Suit
✓ Defense Against Ruffs in Dummy	✓ Making Sure of a Discard
✓ The Cross-Ruff	✓ In Short

THE AVERAGE DECLARER's first move is to draw trumps—provided only that he's not playing a notrump contract. This is sometimes a good idea—perhaps even more often than not. Often enough, however, it is a fatal error.

Declarer's best first move at any contract is to *think*. If he thinks along the right lines, he usually sees whether or not on this particular hand it would be wise to draw trumps.

No single general rule covers all cases, but I have devised a simple little rule that has steered many pupils in the right direction.

Draw trumps only when you can see no possible problem.

✓ NO-PROBLEM HANDS

You get many of these no-problem hands. Some of them look like this:

1. NORTH
♠ J 7 5
♡ Q 10 7 4
◇ A Q J 3
♣ K 7

WEST
♠ A K 9 6 4
♡ 6 2
◇ 7 2
♣ Q J 8 4

EAST
♠ Q 10 2
♡ 8 5
◇ K 10 8 4
♣ 10 9 5 2

SOUTH
♠ 8 3
♡ A K J 9 3
◇ 9 6 5
♣ A 6 3

SOUTH	WEST	NORTH	EAST
1 ♡	1 ♠	3 ♡	Pass
4 ♡	Pass	Pass	Pass

West leads the king of spades, and East signals encouragement by playing the ten. West obediently continues with the ace of spades and then a third spade.

South ruffs the third spade and sees that there is no conceivable problem. Hence he draws trumps, ending in his own hand. Two rounds of trumps are enough but South would have drawn three trumps if necessary.

South then tries the diamond finesse. East casually refuses the first diamond on the sound theory that it doesn't pay to accept the first trick of a repeatable finesse. As it happens, this does not embarrass South.

Declarer returns to his hand with the ace of clubs to repeat the diamond finesse. This time East takes his king and returns a club.

South eventually trumps his last club with one of dummy's trumps. He loses only two spades and one diamond.

There was nothing much to this hand. That's why it was safe for South to draw trumps. The only reason for drawing trumps is to prevent an opponent from ruffing a diamond. (If South had not drawn trumps, West would eventually have ruffed the third diamond trick for down one.)

The need for drawing trumps is even more urgent when you have a really *long* side suit to safeguard. Such hands are very welcome, but they offer very little in the way of diversion or instruction.

✓ LEAVING THE MASTER TRUMP OUT

When you are drawing trumps you may set up an opponent's card as the master trump. Should you lead a trump to force out this master trump, or should you ignore it?

2. NORTH
♠ A Q J 3
♡ A 7 2
◇ K 6
♣ Q 6 3 2

WEST
♠ 9 8 2
♡ Q 6 4
◇ 5 3 2
♣ J 10 9 8

EAST
♠ 10 7 5 4
♡ J 3
◇ A 10 9
♣ A K 7 4

SOUTH
♠ K 6
♡ K 10 9 8 5
◇ Q J 8 7 4
♣ 5

NORTH	EAST	SOUTH	WEST
1 NT	Pass	3 ♡	Pass
4 ♡	Pass	Pass	Pass

West leads the jack of clubs, holding the trick. He continues with another club, and South ruffs.

Declarer leads a diamond to the king, and East wins with the ace. East leads the ace of clubs, and South ruffs again.

Up to this time South has had problems. Therefore he has not drawn trumps. Since there is no further problem (except the possibility of a 4-1 trump break, which would almost surely be fatal), South is ready to draw trumps.

South leads a trump to dummy's ace and another to his own king. This leaves only one trump out—the queen. Should South lead a trump to knock out the queen, or should he ignore it?

South must abandon trumps. If he leads a third trump,

West will win and all the trumps will be gone—dummy's and declarer's as well as West's. (Don't forget that South has been forced to ruff twice.) West will lead his last club, East will win with his king, and South will be down one.

Instead of leading a third trump, South must lead out his high diamonds and continue with good diamonds and high spades. West may trump whenever he likes, but South will still have control of the hand with a trump in his own hand and another in dummy. The defenders can get only a trump, a diamond, and a club, and South makes his game contract.

✓ FORCING OUT THE MASTER TRUMP

In general, you take the trouble to force out the master trump when you want to prevent the opponents from interrupting you while you are running an entryless long suit.

3. **NORTH**
♠ 7 6 3
♡ A 3 2
♢ 5 2
♣ A K J 8 4

WEST
♠ Q J 10 9
♡ 7 6
♢ K 7 6 3
♣ 10 9 2

EAST
♠ 8 4 2
♡ Q J 4
♢ J 10 9 8 4
♣ 6 5

SOUTH
♠ A K 5
♡ K 10 9 8 5
♢ A Q
♣ Q 7 3

NORTH	EAST	SOUTH	WEST
1 ♣	Pass	2 ♡	Pass
3 ♡	Pass	4 ♣	Pass
4 ♡	Pass	4 NT	Pass
5 ♡	Pass	5 NT	Pass
6 ◇	Pass	6 ♡	Pass
Pass	Pass		

West opens the queen of spades, and South wins with the king.

South has no problem, so he draws trumps.

The right course is to take the ace of hearts and the king of hearts, and then force out the queen of hearts by leading a third round of trumps.

Now nothing can stop South. He wins any return (refusing the diamond finesse, of course, if East leads a diamond), and runs the clubs. On dummy's last two clubs, South can discard the low spade and the queen of diamonds.

South would lose his slam if he drew just two rounds of trumps and then tried to run the clubs. East would ruff the third round of clubs—before South could get any discard at all. South would be unable to get back to dummy for the last two clubs and would go down two tricks instead of making the slam.

⫟ RUFFERS IN DUMMY

One of the most important reasons not to draw trumps is that you want to ruff losing cards in the dummy. In most hands of this sort you plan to draw trumps after ruffing your losers.

4. NORTH
♠ 9 6 2
♡ 6
◇ Q 8 7 3
♣ A J 6 5 3

WEST
♠ J 10 7
♡ Q J 10 7 5
◇ 10 6 4
♣ 8 2

EAST
♠ 5 3
♡ K 9 4 2
◇ K J 9
♣ K Q 10 9

SOUTH
♠ A K Q 8 4
♡ A 8 3
◇ A 5 2
♣ 7 4

SOUTH	WEST	NORTH	EAST
1 ♠	Pass	2 ♠	Pass
4 ♠	Pass	Pass	Pass

North is not exactly proud of his trump support, but he's not strong enough to bid two clubs, and a one-no-trump response is no good with a singleton in the other major. Two spades is the least of evils.

West leads the queen of hearts, and South wins with the ace. South must not draw trumps because he wants to ruff his low hearts with dummy's otherwise worthless trumps.

South leads a low heart at the second trick and ruffs in dummy. He returns to his hand by leading a trump to the ace. (Only two hearts are to be ruffed in dummy, and this releases one of dummy's trumps for this job of getting to the South hand.)

South next ruffs his last heart with dummy's last trump. The job has been done, and now South wants to get back to his hand to draw the rest of the trumps. Fortunately South can get back with the ace of diamonds.

Now South can lead out the king and queen of trumps

to draw the enemy's teeth. At the end South cheerfully gives up two diamonds and a club. The contract is safe.

✓ DEFENSE AGAINST RUFFS IN DUMMY

The time-honored defense against ruffers in the dummy is to lead trumps. If the defenders get several chances to lead trumps before declarer can get back and forth to take his ruffing tricks, dummy's trumps may be removed—and the ruffing tricks with them. If dummy had only two trumps in Hand 4, for example, an opening trump lead would immediately cook declarer's goose.

But dummy actually has three trumps. Suppose West opens the jack of spades anyway. South can ruff the losing hearts in dummy but runs into new trouble.

South wins the first trick with the queen of spades and cashes the ace of hearts. He ruffs a heart with dummy's second trump and returns to his hand with the ace of diamonds. South ruffs his last heart with dummy's last trump.

Now what? South wants to get to his hand to draw trumps, but there is no convenient way for him to do so. The opening trump lead has disrupted South's communications.

Declarer cashes the ace of clubs and leads a low club from dummy, as good a try as any other. East wins with the nine of clubs and continues with the king of clubs.

This is very awkward for declarer. If South ruffs low, West will overruff; if South ruffs high, West's ten of spades will become established.

South tries to postpone the day of reckoning by discarding a losing diamond. A good idea, but West likewise discards a diamond. East leads the queen of clubs, and once more South and West discard diamonds.

Now East leads the king of diamonds, and the jig is up. No matter what South does, West will take the setting trick with the ten of spades.

✓ THE CROSS-RUFF

The cross-ruff gives declarer *two* excellent reasons for not drawing trumps. He needs the trumps *in his own hand* as well as in *dummy*.

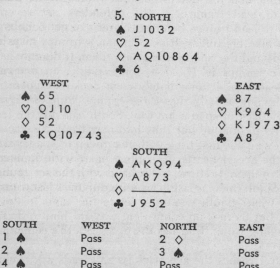

5. NORTH
♠ J 10 3 2
♡ 5 2
◇ A Q 10 8 6 4
♣ 6

WEST
♠ 6 5
♡ Q J 10
◇ 5 2
♣ K Q 10 7 4 3

EAST
♠ 8 7
♡ K 9 6 4
◇ K J 9 7 3
♣ A 8

SOUTH
♠ A K Q 9 4
♡ A 8 7 3
◇ ———
♣ J 9 5 2

SOUTH	WEST	NORTH	EAST
1 ♠	Pass	2 ◇	Pass
2 ♠	Pass	3 ♠	Pass
4 ♠	Pass	Pass	Pass

West opens the queen of hearts, and South counts his tricks: five trumps in his own hand, two red aces, and three ruffing tricks in the dummy—if he can get them.

Can he ruff three times in the dummy? Yes, if he tries to ruff clubs.

South wins the first trick with the ace of hearts and returns a club. East takes the ace of clubs and leads a trump in the hope of reducing dummy's ruffing power.

South must win the trump return in his own hand. He ruffs a club with dummy's three of trumps and breathes a little easier when this gets by. The rest of dummy's ruffs will be executed with high trumps, so there will be no danger of an over-ruff.

Now declarer must provide for entry back to his own hand. He cashes the ace of diamonds, carefully discarding a heart, and ruffs a diamond with the four of spades. South heaves a big sigh of relief when this small trump wins. No further over-ruffs need be feared.

Declarer continues on his merry way, ruffing clubs in the dummy and diamonds in his own hand. He gives up two heart tricks at the end, but the contract is safe.

There are several interesting points in this cross-ruff. Declarer was ready to ruff diamonds, but dummy wasn't ready to ruff clubs. South had to give up a trick to prepare the cross-ruff.

South had to lead a club rather than a heart. He needed three ruffs in dummy and could confidently expect to ruff three clubs. He couldn't expect to ruff three hearts for the very good reason that after playing two rounds of hearts he would have only two hearts left. You can't ruff two cards three times.

South had to discard a heart on dummy's ace of diamonds. Every one of his clubs was needed for another purpose—the ruffs in dummy.

Why couldn't South get his three ruffing tricks by ruffing two hearts and one club or two clubs and one heart? He would have to give up a heart trick and also a club trick to get the cross-ruff under way. The opponents would lead a trump back each time, and dummy would thus get only two ruffing tricks.

The standard defense against a cross-ruff is to lead a trump at each opportunity. The defenders would have no difficulty in spotting the best line of defense once they had caught a glimpse of dummy.

In fact, West could have defeated the contract by opening a trump instead of leading the queen of hearts. The defenders would win a club trick fairly soon and would then lead another trump, limiting the dummy to two ruffing tricks.

√ TRUMPS AS STOPPERS

Sometimes you refrain from drawing trumps because you need dummy's trumps to stop the enemy's long suit. You don't really plan to ruff anything in dummy, but you must keep the means of doing so.

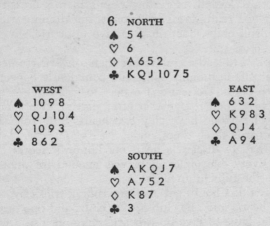

6. NORTH
♠ 5 4
♡ 6
♢ A 6 5 2
♣ K Q J 10 7 5

WEST
♠ 10 9 8
♡ Q J 10 4
♢ 10 9 3
♣ 8 6 2

EAST
♠ 6 3 2
♡ K 9 8 3
♢ Q J 4
♣ A 9 4

SOUTH
♠ A K Q J 7
♡ A 7 5 2
♢ K 8 7
♣ 3

North opened with one club, and South eventually got to six spades by a wild auction that is better forgotten. Wild as the bidding was, South managed to wind up at a makable contract (although six clubs would have been safer).

West opened the queen of hearts, and South won with the ace. South could ruff a heart or two in the dummy if he liked, but this would be a short-sighted plan.

Just see how it works out. South ruffs a heart in dummy, gets back with the king of diamonds, and ruffs another heart. Now what? When South knocks out the ace of clubs he must still lose a heart.

Nor can South draw trumps right away, for East will get in with the club ace and take *three* hearts. What then? South must let a trump or two stay in dummy until the ace of clubs has been knocked out—to keep the hearts at bay.

At the second trick South leads a club to force out the ace. No matter what East returns, South can win and draw trumps. Then he can get to dummy with the ace of diamonds to run the clubs. The long suit gives South all the tricks he needs for the slam contract.

✓ DEFENDING THE TRUMP SUIT

Your opponents will sometimes try to wrest control of the hand from you by forcing you to ruff, thus running you out of trumps. You may be able to defend yourself against this type of attack by leaving a trump in the dummy.

```
                    7.  NORTH
                        ♠ Q 7 6
                        ♡ 7 5 4
                        ◇ K 6 3
                        ♣ A 8 7 2
        WEST                              EAST
        ♠ 9 8 5 2                         ♠ 4
        ♡ K Q J 6                         ♡ A 10 9 3 2
        ◇ 10 7                            ◇ Q J 9 5 2
        ♣ 9 4 3                           ♣ K 6
                        SOUTH
                        ♠ A K J 10 3
                        ♡ 8
                        ◇ A 8 4
                        ♣ Q J 10 5
```

SOUTH	WEST	NORTH	EAST
1 ♠	Pass	2 ♠	Pass
3 ♠	Pass	4 ♠	Pass
Pass	Pass		

West opens the king of hearts and continues with the queen of hearts. You ruff with the three of spades and draw two rounds of trumps with the ace and jack.

When East discards a diamond on the second trump you must pause for thought. A problem has reared its ugly head.

You cannot afford to draw the rest of the trumps. That will take out all of *your* trumps as well as West's. If the club finesse loses, you will be defenseless against the rest of the hearts. You cannot even afford to draw a third trump. The reason will soon become very clear.

Instead, you lead the queen of clubs for a finesse. East wins with the king of clubs and leads a third heart. You cannot afford to ruff, for that will leave you with fewer trumps than West.

You must discard a low diamond on the third heart. After all, this diamond must be lost sooner or later no matter how the hand is played.

Now East must abandon the hearts. *Dummy's* last trump will ruff if East leads a fourth heart. This will relieve your own trumps from the attack. And this is, of course, your reason for leaving a trump in the dummy.

No matter what East leads, you can win and draw trumps. Then you can safely take your club and diamond tricks.

✓ TRUMPS FOR COMMUNICATION

Sometimes you must draw trumps piecemeal because the trumps offer the most convenient way of getting to the right hand at the right time.

8. NORTH
♠ A 5
♡ Q 10 9 6
◇ A Q J 10
♣ 6 3 2

WEST
♠ J 10 9 6 2
♡ 3
◇ K 9 8 3
♣ A 8 7

EAST
♠ K Q 7 3
♡ 5 4 2
◇ 7 5
♣ Q J 10 9

SOUTH
♠ 8 4
♡ A K J 8 7
◇ 6 4 2
♣ K 5 4

SOUTH	WEST	NORTH	EAST
1 ♡	Pass	3 ♡	Pass
4 ♡	Pass	Pass	Pass

West leads the jack of spades, and declarer must win at once with dummy's ace. Otherwise East would overtake with the queen of spades in order to lead through the king of clubs, and that would be the end of poor South.

South is fairly sure to lose a spade and at least two clubs, so he cannot afford to lose a diamond trick. In planning the play of the hand, therefore, South must assume that the diamond finesse will succeed.

Look ahead, and see what happens if South begins by drawing three rounds of trumps. He can then take a diamond finesse. This puts him in dummy. How is he to get back to his hand for more diamond finesses?

Dummy still has a trump. South gets to his hand with a fourth round of trumps and takes a second diamond finesse.

Now there is no convenient way for South to reach his hand. He must cross his fingers and either bang down the diamond ace, hoping the king drops, or lead a club from dummy and hope for the best. Neither play works, and the opponents promptly take three clubs and a spade, defeating the contract.

South should see from the start that he has a problem of communication. Hence he does not hasten to draw all of the trumps. He *thinks* first.

Instead of using *only the fourth trump* as a way to reach his hand, South uses *earlier trumps* as well.

At the second trick, declarer gets to his hand by leading the six of trumps to his own seven. Then he leads a diamond to finesse the queen.

Next, declarer returns to his hand by leading the nine of hearts from dummy to his own jack. Then he leads a diamond and finesses dummy's jack.

Declarer continues the process by leading the ten of hearts to his own king. Then he leads his last diamond and finesses dummy's ten. Since three rounds of trumps have been drawn by this time, East cannot ruff the diamond. South has been slow about it, but he has managed to draw the trumps in time.

Declarer can now lead dummy's ace of diamonds to discard a losing spade or a losing club. Three tricks remain to be lost in either case since the ace of clubs is in unfavorable position. The contract, however, is quite safe.

✓ PROTECTING A SIDE SUIT

It may be all right to draw trumps when you have a solid side suit, but not when your side suit needs establishment. This is very obvious when you must ruff your side suit in dummy during the process of setting it up.

Even if you don't expect to ruff the side suit in dummy, a bad break may cause you to change your mind. If you have already drawn dummy's trumps, you are helpless against a bad break in the side suit; if dummy still has a trump or two, the situation may not be beyond repair.

9. NORTH
♠ 4 3 2
♡ 7 4 2
♢ K 8 7
♣ K 10 9 2

WEST
♠ 9 8
♡ Q J 9 8
♢ 9 6 4 2
♣ J 7 3

EAST
♠ Q J 10
♡ 10
♢ J 10 5 3
♣ A Q 6 5 4

SOUTH
♠ A K 7 6 5
♡ A K 6 5 3
♢ A Q
♣ 8

SOUTH	WEST	NORTH	EAST
1 ♠	Pass	1 NT	Pass
3 ♡	Pass	3 ♠	Pass
4 ♠	Pass	Pass	Pass

West opens the nine of spades. He fears that dummy is short in hearts, and he aims to reduce dummy's ruffing power and thus protect his heart tricks.

South wins with the king of spades and should do some thinking before proceeding. He has problems in all three of the side suits.

South would like to clear the ace and queen of diamonds and then get to dummy somehow in order to discard the singleton club on the king of diamonds. The trouble is that there is no way to reach the dummy. South must therefore regretfully abandon this tempting idea.

Now South considers the hearts. If the suit breaks normally, South can take the top hearts and give up one heart to clear the suit. Then South will lose one heart, one trump (if that suit also breaks normally), and one club.

What if the hearts break 4-1? Then South may have to lose two heart tricks. This is one trick more than he can afford. If South draws trumps, he will surely lose two hearts, one trump, and a club.

South can make his contract, however, if he refrains from drawing trumps. Microscopic as dummy's trumps are, they are just strong enough to save the day.

At the second trick, South leads out the ace of hearts. Then he overtakes the queen of diamonds with dummy's king in order to return a heart toward his hand. This, as we shall see, protects declarer against a singleton heart in the *East* hand. (There is no practical way to guard against a singleton heart in the *West* hand.)

What is East to do? If East ruffs, South can play low. Thus East wastes his sure trump trick° on a heart that South was going to lose anyway.

If East does ruff, he will probably return a diamond (as good a return as any). South wins and leads out the ace of trumps. Thanks to East's ruff, South can thus draw all of the missing trumps in only two rounds. Now he cashes the king of hearts and ruffs a heart with dummy's remaining trump. This assures the contract, plus an overtrick.

Assume that East does *not* ruff the second round of hearts. When East discards, South puts up the king of hearts to win the trick. Then he gives up a heart.

West wins and leads a second trump. South wins with

° If East started with two trumps, declarer could not make the hand. East could use an otherwise useless trump to ruff, and West would still have a sure trump trick.

the ace of spades and leads a fourth round of hearts, ruffing with dummy's carefully preserved last trump. East can over-ruff if he likes, but only by using his sure trump trick. Regardless of East's play, South loses only one trump, one heart, and one club.

✔ MAKING SURE OF A DISCARD

Sometimes you must postpone trump plays until you have made some urgent play in a side suit, such as getting a fast discard.

10. NORTH
♠ 8 7 3
♡ 8 7 5
◇ K Q J
♣ Q J 10 9

WEST
♠ J 10 9 2
♡ A 3
◇ 8 7 4 3
♣ 6 3 2

EAST
♠ Q 6 5
♡ K 4
◇ A 10 9 5 2
♣ 8 7 4

SOUTH
♠ A K 4
♡ Q J 10 9 6 2
◇ 6
♣ A K 5

SOUTH	WEST	NORTH	EAST
1 ♡	Pass	1 NT	Pass
3 ♡	Pass	4 ♡	Pass
Pass	Pass		

West opens the jack of spades, and South wins with the king. South counts his losers and sees that he has a problem. If he doesn't watch out, he will lose a spade, two trumps, and a diamond.

South *thinks* before he draws trumps. If South leads a trump at the second trick, East will take the king of hearts and return a spade. South takes the ace of spades and, let us say, returns another trump. West takes the ace of trumps and a spade, and then leads a diamond to East's ace, defeating the contract.

Instead of leading trumps at the second trick, South should lead a diamond to force out the ace. Back comes a spade, and South takes the ace. Now South leads a low club to dummy's queen in order to discard the losing spade on a high diamond. *Only then* is it safe for declarer to begin drawing trumps. From this point on South has no problems.

✓ IN SHORT

Draw trumps when you have no problems in the play of a hand. This is particularly desirable when you have a long, solid side suit.

Postpone the drawing of trumps when you can foresee problems in the play of the cards, particularly when you need to:

- Ruff losing cards with dummy's low trumps
- Cross-ruff
- Stop the opponents' dangerous suit
- Stop the attack on your trump suit
- Keep a way of getting back and forth
- Establish a side suit
- Make sure of a discard first

As a rule, you should not force out the opponents' master trump unless you need to run an entryless established suit without interruption.

HOW THE EXPERTS COUNT

√ Counting Trumps   √ Counting for the Defense
√ The Right Way to Count   √ Counting for the Plan
√ Sources of Information   √ In Short

ACCORDING TO SOME definitions, the ability to count is what distinguishes man from the beasts. I can't vouch for zoology in general, but it's certainly true of bridge players.

You can sit down in any bridge game in the world, and in five minutes you can tell the players from the dilettantes. The players invariably count.

✓ COUNTING TRUMPS

The newcomer to bridge makes a big forward step when he begins to count trumps. Up to that time he leads out trumps until nobody is able to follow suit; then he knows that trumps are all out. He is on a par with the driver who backs up his car until he hears glass.

The novice usually begins to count in the natural but unhelpful fashion. He draws one round of trumps and mentally counts "four" because four trumps appeared on the trick. He counts four more trumps in his own hand and three more in the dummy. That comes to eleven. Two more trumps are out.

Our hero draws another round of trumps. One opponent discards. He says to himself "seven," and hastily counts his own and dummy's trumps again.

He draws a third round of trumps, saying "ten" to himself. Now there are three trumps between his own hand and dummy, so he knows that all the trumps have been drawn.

It is a lot better than not counting at all. But it's harder than the right way and not as useful.

√ THE RIGHT WAY TO COUNT

You should begin to count before you even touch the trumps. You see five trumps in your own hand and four in the dummy. That accounts for nine trumps, leaving four out. Those four may be divided 4-0, 3-1, or 2-2. You think this out consciously to begin with; it becomes automatic and quite effortless after a short time.

You now draw the first round of trumps. Both follow. You dismiss the 4-0 break from mind. The trumps are sure to break 3-1 or 2-2. You aren't busy counting, for your work has already been done.

You draw a second round of trumps. If both follow, you know that trumps have broken 2-2 and that they have been drawn. If one opponent shows out, you know that the break is 3-1 and that a third round is necessary to draw trumps from the opponent who started with three.

Try it a few times, and you'll see that this method of counting is easier. But its big advantage is that it starts you thinking about each opponent's *original thirteen* cards. Not the cards that are left in his hand, but *the hand he held during the bidding.*

Pretty soon you'll get to the point where you're willing to count a second suit in this painless way. That will add to your picture of each opponent's original hand.

What is so important about knowing an opponent's original hand?

When you have worked out *one* opponent's full hand, you can then, in effect, see 39 cards. The remaining 13 cards of the deck are easily worked out—and they constitute the hand of the *other* opponent. You can play the hand as though all the cards were face up on the table!

Sometimes you can't be sure of every detail of an opponent's hand. Instead, you may say to yourself, "Perhaps his full hand to start with was such-and-such. He would have bid the hand just as he did, if that was his hand. Ah, but he would not have had a problem at the second trick. He would have known just what to do. Therefore he could not have had that hand. By the process of elimination, he must have had thus-and-so."

It will seem much less mysterious if you watch it in operation. Here is a rather extreme, but instructive, example:

1. NORTH
♠ J 10 5
♡ K Q J
◇ K Q J
♣ A 10 3 2

WEST
♠ 8
♡ 9 3 2
◇ 10 9 8 6 3
♣ J 8 7 5

EAST
♠ 9 7 6 4 3 2
♡ 8 7 5 4
◇ 5 2
♣ 6

SOUTH
♠ A K Q
♡ A 10 6
◇ A 7 4
♣ K Q 9 4

SOUTH	WEST	NORTH	EAST
2 NT	Pass	7 NT	Pass
Pass	Pass		

West opens the ten of diamonds. You count your tricks and discover that you need four club tricks to make the grand slam. The only danger is that one of the opponents may hold J-x-x-x of clubs.

How should you play the hand? Remember, at the bridge table you see only your own hand and the dummy.

Counting gives you the answer.

You begin by drawing three rounds of diamonds. On the third diamond East discards a spade. You now know that West started with five diamonds; East with only two.

If you were a flighty player, you might now say to yourself, "West is long in diamonds, so he won't also be long in clubs." Thereupon you would take the king and ace of clubs—and down you would go.

Since a spade has been discarded, try running the three spades before you make up your mind about the clubs. On the second spade West discards a diamond. On the third spade West discards another diamond.

Now you add something to your picture. West started with five diamonds and only one spade. East started with six spades and only two diamonds.

Hold on. Eight of East's thirteen cards are accounted for. He started with exactly five cards in hearts and clubs combined.

The way to find out about the clubs is to tackle the hearts. You run three rounds of hearts and both opponents follow to all three rounds. You cannot be sure which opponent has the last heart.

You do know that East started with five cards in hearts and clubs. At least three of those cards were hearts, so East clearly started with either one or two clubs.

Now, at last, you know just what to do about the clubs without the slightest guesswork. The grand slam is absolutely guaranteed.

You lead out the king of clubs and then take the queen of clubs. If East had two clubs, it means clubs have broken favorably and your slam is home. East actually follows to only one round of clubs, and then he discards a spade.

The rest is easy. You lead a club toward dummy's ace-ten and take the proven finesse to make your grand slam.

Not all counting is so unusual. Even in a routine game contract you may get help from counting out the hands of the opponents. Nor can you always get a dead certainty, but it pays to play with, rather than against, the odds.

2. NORTH
♠ K 5 4
♡ K 10 5
♢ K 10 4
♣ A K 5 3

WEST
♠ Q J 10 6
♡ 6 3
♢ Q 9 8 3 2
♣ 10 6

EAST
♠ A 9 8
♡ 7 4 2
♢ 7 6
♣ Q J 9 8 2

SOUTH
♠ 7 3 2
♡ A Q J 9 8
♢ A J 5
♣ 7 4

NORTH	EAST	SOUTH	WEST
1 NT	Pass	3 ♡	Pass
4 ♡	Pass	Pass	Pass

West opens the queen of spades, and the defenders swiftly take three spade tricks and then get out safely with a club.

South needs the rest of the tricks and has to guess which opponent has the queen of diamonds. If he tosses a coin, he has a fifty-fifty chance of being right. If he plays the hand correctly, the odds will be five to two in his favor.

Declarer wins the fourth trick in the dummy with the king of clubs and draws three rounds of trumps. West discards the deuce of diamonds on the third trump.

If West is an artless player, declarer should feel that West does not have the queen of diamonds. West cannot have a card of any importance other than the queen of diamonds. In this position a guileless player saves as much "protection" as possible for the queen of diamonds.

A good player tends to discard a diamond quickly and cheerfully if he *does* have the queen. The idea is to convince a naïve South that West does *not* have the queen.

Declarer may ruminate over this, but while ruminating he takes the ace of clubs and ruffs a club. West discards the last spade.

Now South sums up his counting. West started with exactly four spades, two hearts, and two clubs. Hence West is known to have exactly five diamonds to fill out the thirteen original cards.

This leaves two diamonds for East.

South still cannot be sure who has the *queen* of diamonds. Since the suit is split 5-2, the odds are five to two that West (the *long* hand) has the queen. This is not certainty, but it is a lot better than a mere guess.

South may decide to disregard the odds. If West is the sort of player who would *never* discard a diamond away from the queen, South may come to the conclusion that East has Q-x of diamonds.

In the absence of any special knowledge, South should

follow the odds. He cashes the ace of diamonds and then finesses through West for the queen.

✓ SOURCES OF INFORMATION

Thus far we have seen declarer get an absolute count on various suits by leading the suits to see how soon an opponent fails to follow. This is the best, but not the only, evidence.

Sometimes you get a tentative count on a player's hand from his bidding. If he bids two suits very vigorously, for example, you expect him to show up with 5-5 or perhaps 6-5 in those suits; if he bids notrump, you expect him to show up with balanced distribution; and so on.

Sometimes you get a count on one suit because of the nature of the lead. A fourth-best lead is made from a suit of four or more cards. The leader has three cards higher than the lead and in some cases may have a card or cards lower than the lead. You may be able to read the exact situation.

For example, a player who leads the deuce has no cards lower than the lead. He has led from a 4-card suit. (Occasionally a player leads the bottom of a 3-card suit. On rare occasions, a player leads fifth-best or sixth-best in the hope of deceiving declarer.)

A player who leads the three and later plays the deuce has led from a 5-card suit. A player who leads the five from a long suit and later plays the three and deuce has led from a 6-card suit. And so on.

You may get information from the signals of the opponents. If a defender signals his partner that he has a doubleton, declarer should be aware of the signal, too. Similarly with the trump echo or the distributional echo. (See Chapter 30.)

√ COUNTING FOR THE DEFENSE

Most of the same information is available to the defenders as well. For example:

3. **NORTH**
♠ Q 10 9 4
♡ K 7 3
◊ 10 5 2
♣ 10 7 5

WEST	EAST
♠ 8 5	♠ 7 3 2
♡ 8 2	♡ 9 6 4
◊ A K 9 6 3	◊ Q J 7
♣ A Q 8 4	♣ J 9 6 2

SOUTH
♠ A K J 6
♡ A Q J 10 5
◊ 8 4
♣ K 3

SOUTH	WEST	NORTH	EAST
1 ♡	2 ◊	Pass	Pass
2 ♠	Pass	3 ♠	Pass
4 ♠	Pass	Pass	Pass

West opens the king of diamonds, and East signals with the queen. This shows either the singleton queen or a Q-J combination. In either case the opening leader is implored to lead a *low* card at the second trick.

Why is East so interested in having a low diamond led at the second trick?

South's bidding indicates five hearts and four spades. There are only four cards (at most) for South to hold in the minor suits. East hopes to take those four cards away from declarer before he can draw trumps and get discards.

West has bid diamonds at the level of two and should have at least five diamonds. Hence, since there are three in dummy and three in the East hand, East knows that South cannot have more than two diamonds.

It boils down to this. East wants to win a diamond trick in order to lead a club through South. East must win the diamond at the *second* trick or never.

West obediently leads a low diamond at the second trick, and East wins with the jack.

East returns the deuce of clubs. South puts up the king, and West wins with the ace.

Now West has a problem. Should he try to cash the ace of diamonds or the queen of clubs? South has only one more card in the minor suits. Is it a diamond or a club?

A careless West might decide to play East for the doubleton Q-J of diamonds. If West tries to cash the ace of diamonds, South ruffs, draws trumps, and runs the hearts. He discards two clubs from dummy on the good hearts, assuring his contract.

A careful West would notice that East returned the *deuce* of clubs at the third trick. This shows no more than four cards in the suit. West therefore knows that South must have a second club. He cashes the queen of clubs and defeats the contract.

✓ COUNTING FOR THE PLAN

Thus far we have seen how a count will tell you which way to finesse. It may, instead, show you which plan to adopt.

4. NORTH
- ♠ 6
- ♡ A 7
- ◇ 1 0 9 5 4 2
- ♣ K Q J 9 6

WEST
- ♠ ———
- ♡ 8 4 3
- ◇ K Q J 7 3
- ♣ 1 0 8 7 3 2

EAST
- ♠ Q 7 5 3
- ♡ K Q J 1 0 9 6 2
- ◇ 6
- ♣ 4

SOUTH
- ♠ A K J 1 0 9 8 4 2
- ♡ 5
- ◇ A 8
- ♣ A 5

SOUTH	WEST	NORTH	EAST
2 ♠	Pass	3 ♣	3 ♡
3 ♠	Pass	4 ♡	Pass
6 ♠	Pass	Pass	Pass

West opens the king of diamonds, and South wins with the ace. South leads out the ace of spades, and West discards a small heart.

The time has come for South to scratch his head and look up at the ceiling. This has been known to help.

Should South try to run the clubs in the hope of getting a fast diamond discard? This will work if East has three or more clubs. (He would ruff the third club *low* if he had only two clubs.)

Or should South force out the queen of spades and draw trumps? This will work if East started with exactly one diamond.

South should *count* to choose his plan. East is known to have had exactly four spades in his original hand. He should have at least six hearts, perhaps seven, for his overcall of three hearts. That accounts for ten or eleven cards, and East has already followed suit to a diamond. *East cannot possibly hold three clubs!*

South doesn't know whether or not East started with a singleton diamond, but there is no other hope. South cannot possibly get a fast discard on the clubs.

Therefore South draws trumps and crosses his fingers. As the cards lie, this line of play brings in the slam.

Try a defensive hand:

5. NORTH
♠ J 10 9
♡ K 10 7 4
◇ Q 9
♣ A J 9 6

WEST
♠ Q 8 6 2
♡ 5 2
◇ A 8 6 3 2
♣ 7 3

EAST
♠ K 7 4 3
♡ Q J 9 3
◇ K 4
♣ 10 4 2

SOUTH
♠ A 5
♡ A 8 6
◇ J 10 7 5
♣ K Q 8 5

SOUTH	WEST	NORTH	EAST
1 ♣	Pass	1 ♡	Pass
2 ♡	Pass	3 ♣	Pass
3 NT	Pass	Pass	Pass

West leads the three of diamonds, dummy plays the nine, and East wins with the king.

East is tempted to return his partner's suit automatically, but stops to count first.

West has led the *three* of diamonds, and the deuce is nowhere in sight (from East's point of view). It is reasonable to assume that West has the deuce. This means that West has led fourth-best from a 5-card suit.

East places the diamonds: five with his partner, two with dummy, and two in his own hand. Evidently South has four diamonds. Just as evidently it will take East-West a long time to grow fat on the diamonds.

Is any other suit better? South has bid clubs, so presumably he has four of those. He might bid a 3-card club suit with *some* hands, but not when he has four diamonds. Hence East places declarer with four cards in each of the minor suits.

South raised hearts but then bid notrump. Clearly a 3-card raise. If South had only two hearts, he wouldn't raise at all; if he had four hearts, he would go back to the major suit instead of bidding notrump.

By now East has accounted for *eleven* of declarer's cards. South can have only two spades.

This is what East was looking for. Spades should be more productive than diamonds.

East therefore shifts to the three of spades at the second trick. South plays low, and West wins with the queen.

West returns the deuce of spades, and declarer plays the jack from dummy. East knows better than to cover. He plays a low spade, and South must win with the ace.

South has only seven tricks in top cards. He must go after the diamonds to win nine tricks. Then West takes the ace of diamonds and leads a spade to defeat the contract with three spades and two diamonds.

✓ IN SHORT

Practice counting until you can count all four suits with little effort. Develop the stamina for this by counting one or two suits and eventually one or two hands per session. Increase this gradually until you can count *all* hands.

Build up a picture of the *original* hands of your opponents. If you don't have *sure* information, use the bidding and other clues to build up a *tentative* count.

When the evidence is all in you will be able to play the rest of the hand as though your opponents had put their cards face up on the table.

26th DAY

PLANNING YOUR PLAY

√ Study the Dummy	√ Dummy Reversal
√ Planning a Trump Contract	√ Notrump Planning
√ Counting Winners	√ Get the Whole Loaf

WE HAVE SEEN examples of planning in most of the chapters on play, and we shall see others. This is as it should be, for planning pervades the entire field of play; you cannot bottle it up in one chapter and have done with it. The purpose of this chapter is merely to remind you of the principles of planning.

√ STUDY THE DUMMY

Before you start, make a resolution:

Study the dummy for at least a few seconds before you play the first card.

The *habit* of thinking is almost as important as the

thinking itself. If you *always* spend a few seconds think-ing about your next few moves, you will get far better results than the brilliant player who takes the trouble to plan only two or three times per session.

Now for a word of encouragement. Novices work much harder than experts. The novice thinks about a dozen wrong things before he gets an idea that applies to that particular hand. It's hard work to consider and reject all these wrong turnings. The expert may not see the right play immediately, *but he knows which way to look*. The chief purpose of this chapter—and of this book—is to teach you which way to look. You'll still have to do your own thinking, but you won't have to do so much *aimless* think-ing.

✓ PLANNING A TRUMP CONTRACT

In the play of most trump contracts you begin by count-ing your *losers*. Particularly at high contracts, your losers stand out clearly and there are few of them to count.

If you can afford to give up these losers, go ahead with the play of the hand. If you cannot afford to lose the full number, look for a way to dispose of some of the losers.

What can you do to reduce the loss?

Here is a little check list of the most important methods:

- Take a finesse in some suit.
- Play to drop an honor if a finesse seems wrong.
- Ruff a loser in the dummy or, rarely, in your own hand.
- Take a *fast* discard on an extra top card.
- Take a *slow* discard by setting up a long suit.
- Look for a throw-in or a squeeze. (See Chapter 28.)

These are the general plans for the hand. You must also consider smaller items:

- Should you hold up for a trick or two?
- Must you keep a particular opponent out of the lead?
- Is it necessary to nurse entries to one hand or the other?
- Can you afford to draw trumps—and if so, when?

Let's try some of these out on an illustrative hand.

```
                    NORTH
                 ♠ 5 4 2
                 ♡ 8 4
                 ◇ A K 6 5 3
                 ♣ A 5 2
      WEST                          EAST
   ♠ 9 6                         ♠ Q J 10
   ♡ Q J 10 5 2                  ♡ K 7 6
   ◇ 10 7                        ◇ Q J 9 4
   ♣ K 9 8 7                     ♣ J 10 4
                    SOUTH
                 ♠ A K 8 7 3
                 ♡ A 9 3
                 ◇ 8 2
                 ♣ Q 6 3
```

SOUTH	WEST	NORTH	EAST
1 ♠	Pass	2 ◇	Pass
2 ♠	Pass	4 ♠	Pass
Pass	Pass		

West opens the queen of hearts, and the dummy is put down on the table. Of course you're going to play a small heart from the dummy—*eventually*. In the meantime stop and think.

You expect to lose one trump (if the suit breaks normally), perhaps two hearts, no diamonds, perhaps two clubs. Total: five losers, two more than you can afford.

Next step: What can you do to reduce the loss?

You can ruff one heart in dummy. You can lead a club from dummy toward the queen (a type of finesse) in the hope that East has the king. If both maneuvers work, you will eliminate two of the five losers.

Any other ideas? What about setting up a long suit? That may be surer than leading a club toward the queen.

You decide to work on dummy's diamonds. You will—sooner or later—take the top diamonds and ruff a diamond. If the suit breaks 3-3, the last two diamonds in dummy will be good.

What if the diamonds break 4-2? Then you must get back to dummy to ruff another diamond. Finally, you must get back to dummy to cash the last diamond.

This is the general plan. Next you look to see if you have enough entries to dummy. You may need two entries outside of diamonds. The ace of clubs is one. The heart ruff is the other.

Now you can proceed. With a little practice you can do thinking of this kind in less time than it takes to read the words.

You refuse the first heart trick. This kind of hold-up is a simple device that allows *you* to decide when to ruff the third heart. If you take the heart ace at once and lead a heart back, the opponents might just be shrewd enough to lead a third heart promptly. This would force you to ruff the heart in dummy before you are ready to do so.

At the second trick West continues with a heart, and you take the ace. You plan to ruff only one card in dummy, so you can afford to draw exactly two rounds of trumps. You therefore lead out the ace and king of trumps.

Both opponents follow suit on both rounds of trumps. That is a relief. You wouldn't enjoy a bad trump break to add to your other problems.

Now it is time to try out the diamonds. You cash dummy's ace and king, and both opponents follow suit. This is fortunate. Diamonds may break 3-3; they cannot break worse than 4-2.

You lead a low diamond from dummy and ruff in your own hand. West discards a heart.

Now you ruff your last heart with dummy's last trump. This play was always part of your plan, but you didn't want to make it until you had done some work on the diamonds.

You are in position to ruff another diamond, which sets up dummy's last diamond. Finally you lead a club to dummy's ace and cash the last diamond. East may ruff or not, as he pleases. You discard a club and fulfill the contract either way.

This was a difficult hand with a large amount of planning. Most hands are much simpler.

✔ COUNTING WINNERS

Before we go on to a discussion of planning at no-trump, we should spend a moment or two on counting *winners* at a trump contract.

Sometimes your losers don't stand out from the rest of the hand. This is particularly true at very low contracts. In such situations count your winners. If the count doesn't seem high enough at first glance, try to add to it by developing extra winners.

Count your winners also whenever you may want to ruff two or three times in your own hand. In cross-ruffs, a count of the *winners* will help you far more than a count of the losers.

You can easily see how this would work in a cross-ruff.

NORTH
♠ K Q 2
♡ A 7 6 2
◇ 6
♣ Q J 6 3 2

SOUTH
♠ A J 10 9 4
♡ 8
◇ A 7 4 3
♣ 8 5 4

West opens a low heart against your contract of four spades.

You can count eight trump tricks if you ruff diamonds in the dummy and hearts in your own hand. Add the two red aces and you have ten tricks. Simple enough.

How could you ever count losers in such a hand?

There is another way of counting trump tricks when the hand is not a complete cross-ruff. Think of one hand as the *long* trump hand, and count the trump tricks you expect to win with that hand. Then add the number of ruffing tricks you expect to get in the *other* hand.

For example, take the cross-ruff described. You expect to win your own five trumps plus three ruffs in the dummy. Take the earlier hand in this chapter. You expect to make four of your own five trumps plus one ruff in the dummy.

√ DUMMY REVERSAL

Sometimes you plan to ruff several times in your own hand, leaving dummy as the long trump hand. In such hands, known as dummy reversals, it is easier to count your winners than your losers.

```
                    NORTH
                 ♠ K Q 2
                 ♡ A 7 6 2
                 ◊ A Q J
                 ♣ 8 5 4

      WEST                        EAST
   ♠ 8 6 3                     ♠ 7 5
   ♡ K J 9 3                   ♡ Q 10 5 4
   ◊ 10 8 6 5                  ◊ 9 3 2
   ♣ A Q                       ♣ K J 10 9

                    SOUTH
                 ♠ A J 10 9 4
                 ♡ 8
                 ◊ K 7 4
                 ♣ 7 6 3 2
```

NORTH	EAST	SOUTH	WEST
1 NT	Pass	3 ♠	Pass
4 ♠	Pass	Pass	Pass

West leads the three of spades, and you count your losers. Four club losers—one more than you can afford.

What can you do about it? You can't hope to ruff a club in dummy. Every time you lead a club, back will come a trump.

It looks as though your only chance is a 3-3 club break—with the odds almost 2 to 1 against you.

Now think of ruffing out dummy's hearts. Perhaps you can establish *dummy's* hand instead of your own. After all, dummy has only *three* club losers.

It may be easier to count winners. You have four tricks in the red suits and need six trump tricks. You can get them by taking the three trumps from dummy as the long hand and adding three ruffs from your own hand.

Once you make the plan, the execution is simple. Take the first trump in your own hand. Lead a heart to the ace and ruff a heart. Trump to dummy's queen. Heart ruff.

Diamond to dummy. Last heart ruff with your own last trump.

Now you lead another diamond to dummy and cash dummy's king of trumps. This draws West's last trump. Strangely enough, you are out of trumps and can discard a losing club on dummy's king of spades!

This gives you the first nine tricks, and you promptly cash the last high diamond to fulfill the game contract.

✓ NOTRUMP PLANNING

Planning a notrump contract is often simpler than planning a trump hand. You begin by counting winners. If the first count doesn't reveal enough winners, look for a way to bring in additional tricks.

Most notrump contracts develop into a race. Can you set up and cash your own tricks before the opponents set up and cash theirs? Always consider this question when you are wondering which suit to attack.

```
                    NORTH
                  ♠ K 6
                  ♡ 10 4
                  ◇ K 7 6 4 2
                  ♣ K 7 4 3
    WEST                              EAST
  ♠ Q J 10 7 2                     ♠ 9 5 3
  ♡ K J 7                          ♡ Q 6 3 2
  ◇ Q 9 5                          ◇ J 10 8
  ♣ 10 2                           ♣ Q J 5
                    SOUTH
                  ♠ A 8 4
                  ♡ A 9 8 5
                  ◇ A 3
                  ♣ A 9 8 6
```

SOUTH	WEST	NORTH	EAST
1 NT	Pass	3 NT	Pass
Pass	Pass		

West opens the queen of spades, and you count your winners. Seven tricks, all in aces and kings.

What should you do to develop two additional winners?

The longest suit in the combined hands is clubs. If you cash the top clubs and give up a club, you can probably develop an extra trick in clubs. The odds are slightly better than 2 to 1 in favor of a 3-2 club break.

This would be excellent if your contract were only *two* notrump. As matters stand, however, you need *two* additional tricks, not just one. The clubs are a waste of precious time.

What about diamonds? If you take the top diamonds and give up a diamond, you will develop two additional diamond tricks—provided that the suit splits 3-3. The odds are almost 2 to 1 against this favorable break.

This is unfortunate, but a poor chance is better than none at all. You must go after the diamonds to have any reasonable chance for the contract.

As the cards lie, the diamonds break and you make the game contract. If you had failed to count, you probably would have gone after the clubs—and you would have gone down like a little gentleman.

✓ GET THE WHOLE LOAF

Everybody knows the old saying about half a loaf. Remember, however, that a whole loaf is better than half a loaf.

Try to plan your plays so that you have *all* the chances for the contract instead of just part of the chances.

Here is a simple example:

<pre>
              NORTH
         ♠ K 10 8 7 6 2
         ♡ 3 2
         ◇ 8 5
         ♣ Q 10 8

              SOUTH
         ♠ A Q J 9 5
         ♡ K 4
         ◇ A Q
         ♣ A K J 9
</pre>

West leads a club against your contract of six spades.
How should you plan the play?

If you count winners, you have eleven sure tricks: six
trumps, a diamond, and four clubs. You can make the
slam if you get a trick with either the king of hearts or
the queen of diamonds.

If you want to count losers, you can expect to discard
one red card from dummy (after drawing trumps) on
your fourth club. If you discard a heart, you will have a
possible loser in each red suit; if you discard a diamond,
you will have no diamond losers but two possible heart
losers.

It comes to the same thing. Should you lead a heart
toward the king or should you finesse the queen of diamonds?

You can do *both* if you plan properly.

First, let's look at the *wrong* way. Draw trumps, get
to dummy, and take the diamond finesse. If this loses, the
opponents will take the ace of hearts and beat you. It
will be too late then to discover that the other play
would have worked.

Now see the *right* way. Draw trumps and run the
clubs, discarding a heart from dummy. Reach dummy
with a trump and lead a heart toward your hand.

If the ace is played by East, you can later discard a diamond from dummy on the king of hearts. No need for the diamond finesse.

Suppose the ace of hearts is *unfavorably* located. West takes the ace of hearts and returns a heart. You trump in dummy (after all, this is why you discarded a heart on the fourth club) and now take the diamond finesse. If the king of diamonds is well placed, you can still make your slam.

In short, you will make the slam if either the ace of hearts or the king of diamonds is favorably located.

If both cards are badly placed? There is no disgrace in going down. The only shame consists in choosing a bad line of play when something better is available.

And this is just what you *won't* do if you take the lesson of this chapter to heart.

27th DAY
mmmmmmmmmmmm

WATCH YOUR ENTRIES

√ Preserving an Entry	√ The Defenders' Entries
√ The Duck	√ In Short
√ Destroying an Entry	

AS WE HAVE SEEN in our wanderings amid finesses, it is often of the greatest importance to lead from one hand rather than from the other. For this purpose it is necessary to win a trick in the hand where you want the lead next.

1. NORTH	2. NORTH	3. NORTH
♠ J 10 2	♠ A 10 2	♠ A Q 10
♡ 4 3 2	♡ 4 3 2	♡ 4 3 2
SOUTH	SOUTH	SOUTH
♠ A K Q	♠ K Q J	♠ K J 2
♡ A J 10	♡ A J 10	♡ A J 10

The contract is notrump, and the lead is in the South hand.

Declarer wants to lead hearts twice from the dummy to take two finesses. How does he get to dummy in order to lead hearts?

If South must rely on the spade suit, he will be sadly disappointed in Diagram 1. He must win all three spade tricks in his own hand.

In Diagram 2 South can overtake one of his own spades with dummy's ace. This enables him to lead hearts just once from the dummy. Better than nothing, of course, but not enough unless South is rather lucky with the hearts.

In Diagram 3 South has a very flexible spade suit. He can win one, two, or three spade tricks in the dummy—just as he wishes.

To win just one spade trick in the North hand, South leads low to the ace. Later he plays dummy's ten under the jack, and the queen under the king.

To win two tricks in dummy, he leads low to the queen and then plays his jack under dummy's ace, saving the king to win one trick in his own hand. (There are other ways, too.)

To win all three tricks in dummy, South leads low to the ten, plays the jack under dummy's queen, and still has the ace. This also can be done in other ways.

In all cases declarer wins exactly three spade tricks. The only difference lies in the number of *entries* to the dummy. Each entry gives declarer the right to lead from dummy.

We can see the principle in operation in a full hand:

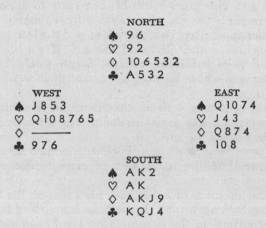

```
                    NORTH
                    ♠ 9 6
                    ♡ 9 2
                    ◇ 10 6 5 3 2
                    ♣ A 5 3 2
    WEST                          EAST
    ♠ J 8 5 3                     ♠ Q 10 7 4
    ♡ Q 10 8 7 6 5                ♡ J 4 3
    ◇ ─────                       ◇ Q 8 7 4
    ♣ 9 7 6                       ♣ 10 8
                    SOUTH
                    ♠ A K 2
                    ♡ A K
                    ◇ A K J 9
                    ♣ K Q J 4
```

South manages to bid himself up to seven notrump, a rather ambitious contract. West opens the seven of hearts, and South has his chance to be the hero or the goat.

Declarer wins the first trick with the king of hearts and hopefully lays down the ace of diamonds. South has a moment of elation when West (sadistically) discards the queen of hearts. (It pays to discard "red on red" and "black on black," especially late in a session. It isn't *your* fault if hearts and diamonds look alike to a careless or sleepy opponent.)

South recovers in time to complete the trick and do some planning. He needs all five diamond tricks to fulfill the contract. Entries to the dummy are more precious than rubies.

South cashes the king and queen of clubs, noting with satisfaction that both opponents follow suit both times.

The suit is sure to break 3-2, and the grand slam is now assured.

The next step is to overtake the jack of clubs with dummy's ace. This gives South his first entry to dummy.

Declarer leads the ten of diamonds from dummy—an *entry-maintaining* play. East plays low, and the lead stays in dummy for another diamond finesse. (If a low diamond had been led from dummy, South would have been obliged to win in his own hand; the situation would then be hopeless.)

Declarer continues with another diamond from dummy, finessing the jack from his hand. The king of diamonds then clears the suit.

Now how does South get back to dummy for the fifth diamond? He leads the four of clubs to dummy's five!

After the top cards of a suit have been played, the low cards have their own rank. Little fleas have littler fleas.

Having arrived in the dummy with the five of clubs, declarer cashes the last diamond in order to discard his losing spade. He then claims the rest of the tricks.

Nothing very difficult about this play, of course, except the *idea*. It might not occur to a beginner that dummy's five of clubs could be of any importance; he might even play it carelessly from dummy under his own king or queen.

In much the same way, *any* card that wins a trick is an entry. It may be an obvious high card, a spot-card (as in the last example), a successful finesse, or a ruffing trick. The card may have importance as an entry quite apart from its value as a trick.

✓ PRESERVING AN ENTRY

Sometimes an entry is of value only at a late stage of

the hand. If you use the entry up too soon it may be worthless to you.

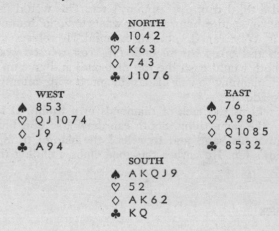

NORTH
- ♠ 10 4 2
- ♡ K 6 3
- ♢ 7 4 3
- ♣ J 10 7 6

WEST
- ♠ 8 5 3
- ♡ Q J 10 7 4
- ♢ J 9
- ♣ A 9 4

EAST
- ♠ 7 6
- ♡ A 9 8
- ♢ Q 10 8 5
- ♣ 8 5 3 2

SOUTH
- ♠ A K Q J 9
- ♡ 5 2
- ♢ A K 6 2
- ♣ K Q

West leads the queen of hearts against a contract of four spades. Hearts are continued, and South must ruff the third round.

South takes care to ruff with a *high* spade. All of his spades are "equals," of course, but he must save the nine of spades to lead to dummy's ten—*when the right time comes.*

South plans to knock out the ace of clubs, cash his other high club, and then get to dummy by leading the *third* round of trumps to dummy's ten. This will leave him in position to discard two low diamonds on dummy's jack and ten of clubs.

South does not want to reach dummy *early* with the ten of spades. He must first get two rounds of clubs and two rounds of trumps out of the way.

After ruffing the third heart South leads out just one high trump. This is all that he can afford at this moment. Then he shifts to the king of clubs.

If South had taken two rounds of trumps, West might be clever enough to take the ace of clubs immediately and lead a third trump to dummy's ten. This would use up the ten of spades before South wants to be in dummy.

As it is, West can do nothing harmful. He refuses the first club and takes the second. (If West refused *both* clubs, South would cash the top diamonds and give up a diamond, planning to ruff his last diamond with dummy's ten of spades.)

West returns the jack of diamonds or a trump. It all comes to the same thing. South can draw a second high trump from his hand and then lead the nine of trumps to dummy's ten. He cashes the good clubs, fulfilling the contract.

✓ THE DUCK

One of the most valuable ways of saving an entry until needed is known as the "duck"—by no means a rare bird to bridge players.

```
                         NORTH
                      ♠ K Q
                      ♡ 10 8 4
                      ◇ 7 6 2
                      ♣ A J 5 3 2
        WEST                              EAST
     ♠ J 10 8 6                        ♠ 9 5 3 2
     ♡ K 7 5                           ♡ J 9 3 2
     ◇ J 9 5 3                         ◇ Q 10
     ♣ 8 6                             ♣ K Q 10
                         SOUTH
                      ♠ A 7 4
                      ♡ A Q 6
                      ◇ A K 8 4
                      ♣ 9 7 4
```

West leads the jack of spades against a contract of three notrump.

Dummy's queen takes the first trick.

South counts his immediate winners: three spades, one heart, two diamonds, and one top club. Two additional tricks are needed, and South can expect to win them with dummy's long club suit.

If declarer is thoughtless about entries, he may go slam-bang after the clubs, cashing the ace, and then giving up a club. This will cost him a cold game contract.

East would win the second club and return a spade to dummy's king. Now the dummy is dead. If declarer leads a third club, dummy's last two clubs will become established, but there will be no way to reach them. South will go down at least one trick.

South can avoid this sad fate by proper play of the clubs.

On winning the first spade in the dummy, declarer leads a *low* club rather than the ace. In bridge lingo, declarer *ducks* a club to the opponents.

Back comes a spade to dummy's king, and declarer ducks another club to the opponents. That is, he leads a second low club from the dummy.

East wins again and leads a third spade to South's ace. South leads his third club and at last puts up dummy's ace.

This play captures the only outstanding club and puts the lead in dummy at the same time. Declarer is thus in position to cash dummy's two remaining clubs.

And so South makes his contract instead of going down two.

The *duck* gives the opponents nothing that they are not entitled to get; it merely gives them their tricks sooner rather than later.

✓ DESTROYING AN ENTRY

The hold-up (Chapter 22) and avoidance plays (Chapter 23) are methods of destroying entries. Another way to destroy an entry is to knock it out before your opponent is ready to use it.

This type of play is very common at notrump contracts:

```
                    NORTH
                 ♠ 8 5
                 ♡ 7 6 2
                 ◇ A 10 9 4
                 ♣ J 6 5 2
     WEST                          EAST
  ♠ J 9 7 6 2                   ♠ Q 10 4
  ♡ A 10 9 4                    ♡ 8 3
  ◇ 6 5                         ◇ K 8 3 2
  ♣ 7 3                         ♣ Q 10 9 8
                    SOUTH
                 ♠ A K 3
                 ♡ K Q J 5
                 ◇ Q J 7
                 ♣ A K 4
```

West leads the six of spades against a contract of three notrump.

South counts winners and sees that he needs five tricks in the red suits to make his contract. Even if the diamond finesse works, South will still have to tackle the hearts sooner or later.

Which suit should South tackle first—hearts or diamonds?

With luck, South can make four diamond tricks; three tricks are sure. In hearts South can make only three tricks at best.

Nevertheless, South must go after the hearts first!

South wins the first spade and leads the king of hearts. If West refuses the first heart, South must lead the queen of hearts next. He must make sure of two heart tricks since he cannot depend on getting more than three diamonds.

West cannot gain by refusing hearts a second time. He takes the ace of hearts and leads another spade.

East puts up the ten of spades, and South must hold up. East leads his last spade, and South takes his remaining top spade.

Now South can afford to lead the queen of diamonds for a finesse. The finesse loses, but East cannot lead a spade and cannot do any other mischief to declarer. South therefore makes his contract with two spades, two hearts, three diamonds, and two clubs.

South will go down if he starts the diamonds first. East takes the king of diamonds and returns the ten of spades. A hold-up does South no good, for West will take care to establish the spade suit and will gain the lead with the ace of hearts in time to defeat the contract.

In short, South's plan of play is to knock out West's ace of hearts before the dangerous spade suit has become established.

South is not worried about the king of diamonds. If West has that card, it will not be an entry; a finesse will capture it. The ace of hearts is a sure entry and must be spoiled.

√ THE DEFENDERS' ENTRIES

All of declarer's entry plays are available to the defenders as well. They can make entries, preserve them, destroy them. The chief difference is that they cannot see their combined resources, and simple declarer plays become difficult defensive plays.

For example:

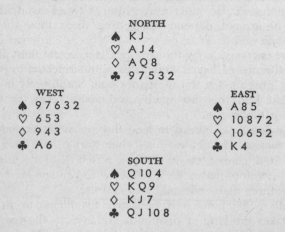

NORTH
♠ K J
♡ A J 4
◇ A Q 8
♣ 9 7 5 3 2

WEST
♠ 9 7 6 3 2
♡ 6 5 3
◇ 9 4 3
♣ A 6

EAST
♠ A 8 5
♡ 10 8 7 2
◇ 10 6 5 2
♣ K 4

SOUTH
♠ Q 10 4
♡ K Q 9
◇ K J 7
♣ Q J 10 8

West opens the three of spades against a contract of three notrump. East takes the ace and returns a spade to dummy's king.

South has eight tricks and needs only one club trick to make his contract. At the third trick he leads the deuce of clubs from the dummy.

Only a very fine player would defeat this contract. East must put up the king of clubs!

When this holds the trick East returns his last spade. West's suit is established, and he gains the lead with the ace of clubs in time to defeat the contract with the spades.

South will make his contract if East plays *second hand low* on the first club trick. *West* has to win the trick, and his only entry to the long spades has been knocked out. South has nothing more to fear.

There are only a few hundred players in the whole

country good enough to rise with the king of clubs when the first club is led from dummy. Exchange the ace and king of clubs, and perhaps a few thousand Easts would be skillful and alert enough to play second hand *high* by putting up the ace of clubs.

If East and West could see each other's cards (as declarer can see dummy's cards), the correct club play would be very simple. Millions could be expected to preserve West's entry until his suit was established.

When you think about it, the play of putting up the king of clubs is not as hard as it looks. East's king is worthless unless West has club strength. East must just know this play and be alert to execute it.

Some other defensive entry plays are easier. For example, it is routine for experienced players to duck or hold up against declarer.

Here is one of the most familiar situations:

```
                    NORTH
                  ♠ K 6 4
                  ♡ 8 3
                  ◇ K 1 6
                  ♣ A Q J 7 2
     WEST                            EAST
   ♠ 7 3 2                        ♠ Q J 8 5
   ♡ K 9 6 4 2                    ♡ A 10 5
   ◇ 7 3                          ◇ 9 8 5 4
   ♣ 8 4 3                        ♣ K 6
                    SOUTH
                  ♠ A 10 9
                  ♡ Q J 7
                  ◇ A Q 10 2
                  ♣ 10 9 5
```

West leads the four of hearts against a contract of three notrump.

East takes the ace of hearts and returns the ten of

hearts. South puts up the queen of hearts at the second trick, and West . . .

What *does* West do?

If West is an inexperienced player, that queen of hearts will panic him into taking the king. End of defense. South eventually loses the club finesse and wins ten tricks.

West must refuse the second round of hearts. He must *duck*. Now South must try the club finesse, losing to East's king. East leads his last heart, and West takes the king of hearts—*and two more heart tricks*. Down one.

How does West know that South has the jack of hearts? If *East* had the jack of hearts as well as the ten, he would return the jack. (He would then hold A-J-10-5 of hearts, and he would take the ace first and return the jack.) Since East cannot hold the jack of hearts, South must have it.

How does West know that East will have another heart to lead later on? Perhaps West will never get his king of hearts if he doesn't take it at once.

This is possible but not likely. Sometimes the spot cards tell the story. South plays the seven of hearts at the first trick. It isn't likely that he started with Q-J-7-5, for the seven would be too good a card to waste.

When the spot cards fail to tell the story, West must simply hope. West should risk having the king of hearts put to sleep in order to preserve the best chance to defeat the contract.

√ IN SHORT

Any card that wins a trick is an entry, enabling the player to lead to the next trick. This right to lead may be far more important than the trick that earned the right.

When entries to a hand are scarce they should be saved until they are most useful.

If you cannot destroy an opponent's entry by shutting out the trick, force the opponent to take the trick before it is useful to him.

28th DAY

EXPERT PLAYS

√ Safety Plays	√ The Trump Coup
√ The Throw-In Play	√ The Squeeze

EVERY EXPERIENCED PLAYER should be familiar with the basic plays presented in the earlier chapters. In this chapter, however, we come to more advanced plays. They can be much easier than most players suspect.

√ SAFETY PLAYS

Sometimes your chief problem is to guard against a bad break in a key suit, often the trump suit. It helps to know how to play some of the more common combinations in the safest possible manner. After you have examined a few types of safety plays, you may grasp the general idea and be able to improvise a safety play at the table when you are faced by an unfamiliar combination of cards.

1. NORTH
♠ K 10 3 2

2. NORTH
♠ K 9 2

3. NORTH
♠ A 4 3 2

SOUTH
♠ A Q 9 5 4

SOUTH
♠ A Q 10 4 3

SOUTH
♠ K Q 9 6 5

How should South play these spade suits to lose no tricks?

In Diagram 1 declarer must win the first trick in the hand with the two top cards—the South hand. If either opponent fails to follow suit, declarer will be in position to finesse through the other opponent.

It would be wrong to win the first trick with dummy's king. If West had all of the missing spades, declarer would then have to lose a trick.

In Diagram 2 South has only eight spades in the combined hands. Both opponents will follow to the first trick even though one opponent may have J-x-x-x. South must give up the notion of finessing through West (unless East is known to be extremely short in spades). The important thing is to win the second spade trick in dummy so as to be able to finesse through East if West fails to follow suit on the second round.

This means that South wins the first trick in the hand with the two top cards, just as in the first example. He wins the second spade with dummy's king. By this time he will know whether or not to finesse on the third round of spades.

In Diagram 3 only four spades are missing. If *West* has all four of them, he cannot be prevented from winning a spade trick. If *East* has all four spades, declarer can pick them up by taking two finesses through East.

The correct technique is to win the first trick in the hand with the single top card—in this case the ace. If West fails to follow suit, dummy must lead spades twice through East.

4.	NORTH	5.	NORTH	6.	NORTH
	♠ J 3 2		♠ K J 2		♠ K 9 2
	SOUTH		SOUTH		SOUTH
	♠ A K 9 5 4		♠ A 9 5 4 3		♠ A J 5 4 3

The problem in Hands 4, 5, and 6 is to limit the spade loss to one trick. The danger arises if one of the opponents has Q-10-x-x or the singleton queen.

In Diagram 4 South cashes the ace of spades and then leads a low spade toward dummy's jack. If West started with Q-10-x-x, he can take his queen, but then South can clear the suit with dummy's jack and his own king.

If *East* started with Q-10-x-x, West will show out. The jack is played to force out the queen. Dummy later leads a spade through East for a finesse of the nine.

In the next two hands the solution is to cash the honor above the jack. In Diagram 5 the first trick is taken by dummy's king. South gets to his hand in another suit and leads a spade toward dummy's jack. The situation is then exactly as in Diagram 4.

In Diagram 6 South leads out the ace of spades and then leads low toward the K-9. If West plays low, the nine is finessed. If East can win this trick, the suit will break 3-2 and dummy's king will later capture the last card. If West has started with Q-10-x-x, dummy's nine will win. West can put in the ten, but then dummy will win and return the nine to force out the queen.

If *East* has Q-10-x-x in Diagram 6, West will show out at the second trick. Dummy wins with the king and returns a spade toward the jack. This holds East to one trick.

7.	NORTH	8.	NORTH	9.	NORTH
	♠ K 3 2		♠ 4 3 2		♠ K 9 2
	SOUTH		SOUTH		SOUTH
	♠ A 10 6 5 4		♠ A K 10 6 5		♠ A 10 6 5 4

The problem in these three cases is to limit the loss to one spade trick. The danger is a 4-1 break.

In Diagram 7 South can guard against four spades in the East hand only. If *West* has four spades, he will get two tricks.

South leads a low spade to dummy's king and returns a spade through East. If East plays low, South finesses the ten. South is not worried about losing the finesse, for then the suit breaks 3-2 and South's ace will later clear the suit.

In Diagram 8 South cashes the ace and then gets to dummy to lead a spade through East. The situation is then just as in Diagram 7.

In Diagram 9 South can guard against four spades in *either* opponent's hand. If he judges that *East* is more likely to have spade length, South plays as in Diagram 7.

If South judges that *West* is more likely to have spade length, South cashes the ace of spades and then leads a low spade toward dummy. If West plays low, dummy's nine is finessed. In this position declarer needs the nine as well as the ten.

10. NORTH ♠ 4 3 2 — SOUTH ♠ A K J 10 5

11. NORTH ♠ K 3 2 — SOUTH ♠ A J 10 5 4

12. NORTH ♠ 3 2 — SOUTH ♠ A K J 10 5 4

In Diagram 10 South leads out the ace of spades in the hope of dropping a singleton queen. If only small cards fall, declarer can get to dummy to lead spades twice through East. Even if East has Q-x-x-x, the queen will be picked up.

In Diagram 11 South should lead a low spade to dummy's king in the hope of dropping a singleton queen. If only small cards fall, declarer can lead twice through East. This works if East has Q-x, Q-x-x, or Q-x-x-x.

It would not be as good a play to finesse through West. If South leads the jack for a first-round finesse, he may lose to the singleton queen. Moreover, if West has Q-9-x-x, he can get a trick by covering either the jack or ten. Hence a finesse through West works only if West has Q-x or Q-x-x and not if he has Q-x-x-x.

The finesse should still be taken through West if there is a special reason to keep him out of the lead or if West is known to have spade length or strength. In the absence of special reasons or information, the percentage play is to finesse through East.

In Diagram 12 dummy has only *two* small spades, not three. South will not be able to take two finesses if he cashes an honor first. South's best play is to take two finesses. This will work if West has the singleton 9, 8, 7, or 6, but will lose if West has the singleton queen. It is obviously better to provide for four cases than for just one.

13. NORTH	14. NORTH	15. NORTH
♠ 5 4 3 2	♠ 5 4 3 2	♠ 4 3 2
SOUTH	SOUTH	SOUTH
♠ A Q 10 7 6	♠ A Q 8 7 6	♠ A Q 7 6 5

In Diagram 13 if South needs *all* of the spades, he should lead from dummy and finesse the queen. This works if East has K-x or K-x-x; the finesse of the ten works only if East has K-J-x.

If South can afford to lose one spade trick, he should begin by leading out the ace. Then he can get to dummy and lead a low spade toward his hand.

This play eliminates the guess at the second trick. If South begins by losing the queen to the king, he must guess at the second trick whether to finesse against the jack or play for the drop.

In Diagram 14 the play is the same. If South needs all of the tricks, he finesses the queen. If he can afford to lose one trick, he first leads out the ace (which may drop the singleton king), and then gets to dummy to lead toward the queen.

In Diagram 15 South is sure to lose at least one spade trick under even the most favorable conditions. (If East has K-J, West will still make a trick with 10-x-x.) South should first lead out the ace of spades and then get to dummy to lead toward the queen. This will develop as many tricks as the "normal" queen finesse, and will guard against excessive loss if West has the singleton king.

If this is the trump suit, South must beware of taking the safety play when there is danger of a ruff. His duty, then, is to get the trumps out as quickly as possible; and the normal finesses will be best.

16. NORTH	17. NORTH
♠ K 9 3 2	♠ K 9 3 2
SOUTH	SOUTH
♠ A 10 6 5 4	♠ A J 6 5 4

In both cases the object is to limit the loss to one trick.

In Diagram 16 the best play is to lead low from either hand. If second hand shows out, go up and lead the suit back through the other opponent. If second hand follows with a low spade, finesse the nine or ten. (If the finesse loses, the suit will break no worse than 3-1, and all will be easy.)

The same play will work in Diagram 17, but you can make a try to win all the tricks. Win the first trick with the ace—the honor above the jack. If both opponents follow, you can lead to the other top card in the hope of getting a 2-2 break.

If East shows out, lead low toward the K-9. West can

be held to one trick. If West shows out, lead to the king
and then back toward the jack.

There are almost as many safety plays as there are finesses. Try to remember those shown in this chapter, and
then look for others in actual play.

✓ THE THROW-IN PLAY

One of the most useful of the expert plays is known
variously as the throw-in, the end play, the strip-and-
end play, and the elimination play.

All of these names are descriptive. You *strip* the hand
by *eliminating* the suits in which an opponent can make a
harmless lead. Then, usually near the *end* of the hand,
you *throw* an opponent into the lead. He must then give
you a trick because of his lead.

A simple example at notrump:

```
                    NORTH
                 ♠ Q 8 4
                 ♡ 10 4 2
                 ◇ 10 9 6 3
                 ♣ J 6 4

    WEST                         EAST
 ♠ 9 6 5                      ♠ J 10 7 3 2
 ♡ Q J 8 5 3                  ♡ K 7
 ◇ 8 5 2                      ◇ 7 4
 ♣ K 7                        ♣ 10 9 5 2

                    SOUTH
                 ♠ A K
                 ♡ A 9 6
                 ◇ A K Q J
                 ♣ A Q 8 3
```

SOUTH	WEST	NORTH	EAST
3 NT	Pass	Pass	Pass

West opens the five of hearts, and East is allowed to win the first trick with the king. East returns a heart, and South wins with the ace.

South must not hold up his ace of hearts a second time. He has a very important job in mind for the nine of hearts.

South can win eight tricks in top cards in his own hand. He cannot reach dummy to cash the queen of spades. If he tries to develop a second club trick, the opponents will take four hearts and a club.

What can South do to be saved? He can force West to yield the ninth trick.

After winning the second trick with the ace of hearts, South cashes his top spades and all four diamonds. This is the stripping process.

South then leads the nine of hearts. This is the throw-in.

West can take his heart tricks but must then lead a spade to dummy's queen or a club to South's ace-queen. Either way, South gets his ninth trick.

Here is a throw-in at a trump contract.

NORTH
♠ 7 5
♡ J 10 9 6 2
♢ K 8
♣ J 6 4 2

WEST
♠ K Q J 8 4
♡ 7
♢ 10 9 5 4
♣ K 7 5

EAST
♠ 9 6 3 2
♡ 5
♢ Q J 7 3
♣ 10 9 8 3

SOUTH
♠ A 10
♡ A K Q 8 4 3
♢ A 6 2
♣ A Q

SOUTH	WEST	NORTH	EAST
2 ♡	Pass	3 ♡	Pass
4 NT	Pass	5 ♣	Pass
5 NT	Pass	6 ◇	Pass
6 ♡	Pass	Pass	Pass

North didn't really have the values for his immediate raise to three hearts, but the final contract is a good one, nonetheless.

West opened the king of spades, and South won with the ace. He drew a round of trumps with the ace, cashed the top diamonds, and ruffed a diamond in dummy. This completed the stripping.

South then led a spade from dummy, executing the throw-in.

West was stuck. If West led a club, South would get a free finesse. If West led anything else, dummy would ruff and South would discard the queen of clubs. There was no way to defeat the contract.

South was lucky that he had the *ten* of spades. Switch the ten and nine of spades, and *East* would be careful to win the second round of spades. East would then lead through the ace-queen of clubs, and the slam would go sour.

Remember these elements of the throw-in play:

- The stripping—clearing away the suits that an opponent can safely return

- The throw-in card—a way of transferring the lead to your victim

- The finesse or ruff-and-discard—the situation that makes it costly for the victim to lead to you eventually

✔ THE TRUMP COUP

The trump coup is a way of taking a trump finesse without a trump. The method is shown in the following example:

```
                     NORTH
                   ♠ 4 3
                   ♡ A J 10
                   ◇ Q 9 4 2
                   ♣ K J 5 3
        WEST                           EAST
      ♠ 5                            ♠ J 7 6 2
      ♡ 9 8 7 6 4                    ♡ 5 3 2
      ◇ J 10 7 6                     ◇ 8 5
      ♣ 9 4 2                        ♣ Q 10 8 7
                     SOUTH
                   ♠ A K Q 10 9 8
                   ♡ K Q
                   ◇ A K 3
                   ♣ A 6
```

SOUTH	WEST	NORTH	EAST
2 ♠	Pass	3 NT	Pass
4 NT	Pass	5 ◇	Pass
5 NT	Pass	6 ◇	Pass
7 ♠	Pass	Pass	Pass

West opens the nine of hearts, and South wins with the king. Unable to see East's trumps, South leads out the ace and king of spades.

When West discards a heart on the second trump, South must pause for thought. How can he finesse through the guarded jack of spades with no trump to lead from the dummy?

Declarer begins a campaign to have the lead in the dummy at the twelfth trick. To accomplish this he must ruff twice, reducing to the same number of trumps as East.

South cashes the top clubs and ruffs a club. He next overtakes the queen of hearts with dummy's ace and ruffs another club. This completes the *trump-reduction* process.

Declarer cashes the ace of diamonds and leads a diamond to dummy's queen. This brings about the following position:

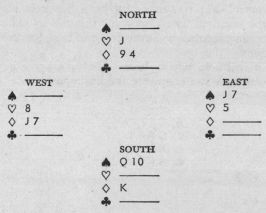

```
                    NORTH
                 ♠ ———
                 ♡ J
                 ◇ 9 4
                 ♣ ———
   WEST                           EAST
 ♠ ———                          ♠ J 7
 ♡ 8                            ♡ 5
 ◇ J 7                          ◇ ———
 ♣ ———                          ♣ ———
                    SOUTH
                 ♠ Q 10
                 ♡
                 ◇ K
                 ♣ ———
```

Dummy leads the jack of hearts. When East follows suit, South discards the king of diamonds.

The twelfth trick has now arrived, and the lead is in the dummy. No matter what dummy leads, East must play a trump. South wins both tricks, thus executing a trumpless trump finesse.

Now that we have observed the essential end position, we can see why South must ruff twice. He must get rid of excess trumps in order to let dummy lead at the twelfth trick. If South kept his trumps, he would be obliged to lead out of his own hand toward the end—and East would win a trump trick.

✓ THE SQUEEZE

The squeeze is the most complicated of all expert plays. There are dozens of squeeze positions, and scholars have written whole books on the squeeze.

It is quite unnecessary to know all of these positions. Mind you, it's very pleasant to say modestly that you have just executed a double trump squeeze by transferring a control—but you may still be a big loser at the end of the evening. The important thing is to bid sensibly and play accurately in the thousands of fundamental positions.

Since it will help you to know what a squeeze is, we may as well look at a couple of the basic positions:

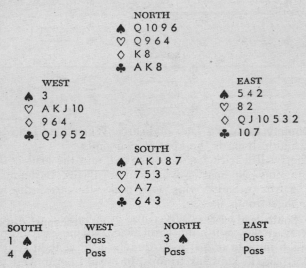

NORTH
♠ Q 10 9 6
♡ Q 9 6 4
◇ K 8
♣ A K 8

WEST
♠ 3
♡ A K J 10
◇ 9 6 4
♣ Q J 9 5 2

EAST
♠ 5 4 2
♡ 8 2
◇ Q J 10 5 3 2
♣ 10 7

SOUTH
♠ A K J 8 7
♡ 7 5 3
◇ A 7
♣ 6 4 3

SOUTH	WEST	NORTH	EAST
1 ♠	Pass	3 ♠	Pass
4 ♠	Pass	Pass	Pass

West opens the king of hearts, and East begins a signal by playing the eight. West continues with the ace of hearts, and East completes his high-low by playing the deuce.

West next leads the jack of hearts. South cannot gain by playing low from the dummy: East would discard, and West would lead another heart to kill dummy's queen. Hence declarer plays the queen of hearts from dummy, and East ruffs.

East returns the queen of diamonds. South wins, draws trumps, and cashes the remaining top diamond. South's one hope is that West holds the only guard to the club suit in addition to the heart guard. South therefore plays on the assumption that the cards are in the only position that will help. He runs the rest of the trumps. When the last trump is led the position is:

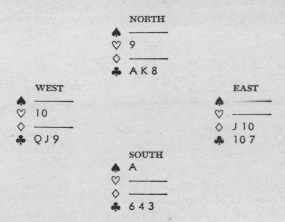

```
                      NORTH
                   ♠  —
                   ♡  9
                   ◇  —
                   ♣  A K 8

     WEST                              EAST
  ♠  —                               ♠  —
  ♡  10                              ♡  —
  ◇  —                               ◇  J 10
  ♣  Q J 9                           ♣  10 7

                      SOUTH
                   ♠  A
                   ♡  —
                   ◇  —
                   ♣  6 4 3
```

South leads the ace of spades, and West must discard. If West throws the ten of hearts, dummy's nine becomes good; dummy will throw the low club and will take the last three tricks with the top clubs and the heart.

If West, instead, throws a club, all of dummy's clubs become good. Dummy throws the nine of hearts and

wins the last three tricks with clubs. In this position South
may not know that all of the clubs will be good, since for
all he knows East may have a club stopper. South knows,
however, that the heart is not set up, and his only chance
is to keep the clubs and hope that a squeeze has indeed
taken place.

Here's a hand on which *both* opponents are squeezed:

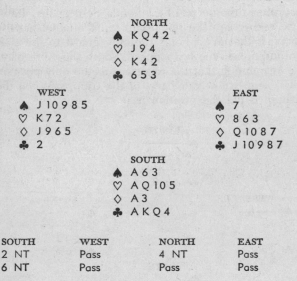

```
                    NORTH
                 ♠ K Q 4 2
                 ♡ J 9 4
                 ◇ K 4 2
                 ♣ 6 5 3
   WEST                              EAST
♠ J 10 9 8 5                      ♠ 7
♡ K 7 2                           ♡ 8 6 3
◇ J 9 6 5                         ◇ Q 10 8 7
♣ 2                               ♣ J 10 9 8 7
                    SOUTH
                 ♠ A 6 3
                 ♡ A Q 10 5
                 ◇ A 3
                 ♣ A K Q 4
```

SOUTH	WEST	NORTH	EAST
2 NT	Pass	4 NT	Pass
6 NT	Pass	Pass	Pass

Both players bid their cards to the hilt, but the final
contract is splendid. South will make the slam if the heart
finesse works or if either black suit breaks 3-3. The odds
are almost 4 to 1 that he will get one of these favorable
breaks.

As it happens, nothing is in South's favor—unless he
knows how to execute a double squeeze.

West opens the jack of spades. Declarer wins in dummy and leads the nine of hearts for a finesse. West re-

fuses the first heart but takes the king when declarer repeats the finesse. West then leads the ten of spades.

South wins with the ace of spades, as East discards the seven of clubs. This discard pleases South, so he leads a spade to dummy's king in order to encourage another club discard. This time, however, East discards a heart.

Declarer now tries out the clubs, discovering to his sorrow that this suit breaks just as badly as the spades. But he knows that East must keep a club to guard against his four; West must keep a spade to guard against dummy's four. If South plays correctly, he can squeeze both opponents out of their diamond stopper. South cashes the top clubs and then the top hearts, producing this position:

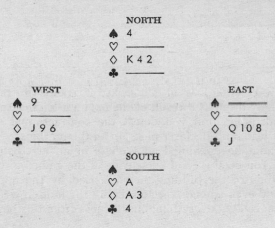

```
                        NORTH
                      ♠ 4
                      ♡ —
                      ◇ K 4 2
                      ♣ —
      WEST                                    EAST
    ♠ 9                                     ♠ —
    ♡ —                                     ♡ —
    ◇ J 9 6                                 ◇ Q 10 8
    ♣ —                                     ♣ J
                        SOUTH
                      ♠ —
                      ♡ A
                      ◇ A 3
                      ♣ 4
```

South leads the ace of hearts.

West is squeezed first. If West discards the spade, dummy's spade becomes good. Therefore West discards a diamond. Dummy can now part with the four of spades.

Now East is squeezed. If East discards the club,

South's club becomes good. Therefore East must also discard a diamond. Now the ace and king drop all the diamonds, and dummy wins the last trick with the four of diamonds!

29th D A Y

"IT'S YOUR LEAD"

√ Choosing the Suit

√ Choosing the Card

√ Touching Honors

√ Long Broken Suits

√ Short-Suit Leads

√ Leading Partner's Suit

√ Leading a Trump

√ Leading Against a Slam

√ Rule of Eleven

√ Illustrations

WHEN A CONTRACT is at all shaky, it stands or falls surprisingly often as a result of the opening lead. Attack the weak point, and you defeat the contract; make a friendly lead, and declarer picks up all the marbles.

Selecting the opening lead is more of an art than a science. You need a good knowledge of the game, an understanding of the bidding methods used by the opponents, and even a good nose to sniff out the hidden weakness. You can get everything but the nose from this book.

⁄ CHOOSING THE SUIT

It is customary to begin a discussion of opening leads with long lists of desirable and undesirable leading combinations. This is putting the cart before the horse.

In most hands you must first pick the *suit* that you want to open. Only then do you consider which card of that suit is the correct opening lead.

- If your partner has doubled to indicate a desired opening lead, follow instructions. Open the suit your partner wants led. (See Lead-Directing Doubles, pages 211–216.)
- In the absence of a lead-directing double, lead your partner's bid suit (if any).
- If your partner has not bid, lead your own bid suit when it offers a good attacking combination or if partner has raised you.
- If your side has not bid, lead an unbid suit. If more than one suit is unbid, lead the unbid suit in which you have the best attacking combination.
- If unbid suits are all undesirable (or if all four suits have been bid), lead through a suit bid by dummy.
- Lead a trump when it seems likely that declarer plans to ruff losers in the dummy.
- Avoid a trump lead when dummy's bidding indicates possession of a long, powerful suit.
- Lead a short suit, particularly a singleton, and try for a ruff if you have reason to believe that your partner has a fast entry and if you have some short but powerful trump holding, such as A-x-x or K-x-x.
- Lead a long suit when you have four or more trumps. You hope to make declarer ruff and thus weaken his trump control.
- Lead your longest and strongest suit against notrump unless an opponent has bid the suit. If your own hand is hopelessly weak, lead the suit that you think your partner is likely to welcome.

✓ CHOOSING THE CARD

When you have chosen the right *suit* to lead, it is usually easy to pick the right *card*.

With some holdings you should choose one card for a lead against notrump but another card for a lead against a suit contract.

Against notrump your aim is to set up your long suit. You are willing to give up one trick in order to set up several others.

Against a suit contract you avoid giving declarer an unearned trick because you may never get it back; he may be able to trump the suit when it is next led.

From most sequences of honors the lead is the same against notrump as against a suit contract—the top card of the sequence:

- From K-Q-J or K-Q-10 lead the king.
- From Q-J-10 or Q-J-9 lead the queen.
- From J-10-9 or J-10-8 lead the jack.

When your suit is headed by A-K your choice depends partly on the contract, partly on the rest of your cards in the suit, and partly on whether or not you have a sure side entry.

Against a suit contract you always lead the *king* from a suit headed by ace-king. (If the ace and king are your only two cards, you lead the ace first.)

Against a notrump contract you are interested not only in the two top cards but also in the rest of the suit. For this reason you usually lead the fourth-best card in the suit. You give up the first trick in the suit; if your partner gets in later, he will still be able to lead your suit and let you take the rest of it. If you try to take the early tricks in the suit, you may exhaust your partner's cards so that he will be unable to lead your suit when he later wins a trick.

You need not worry about your partner if your suit is headed by ace-king-queen-jack or even by ace-king-queen. Likewise, you lead out top cards first if you have a sure entry or two in a side suit; you can bring in the suit without your partner's help.

✓ TOUCHING HONORS

The lead from three touching honors is both safe and attacking. If you have A-K-Q, you win the first trick and have the chance to switch to a new suit if necessary. If you have K-Q-J, you force out the ace and set up two tricks for yourself. If you have Q-J-10, you force out a top card and still have two touching honors with which to renew the attack later.

The lead from *two* touching honors is far less safe. If you have A-K-x, for example, your lead may take the first step in setting up an opponent's queen. You would be better off leading another suit and setting up tricks for your own side rather than for declarer.

If you have K-Q-x, your king may lose to the ace and help declarer set up the jack or ten. For example, declarer may have A-x-x in his own hand and J-x-x in the dummy; he loses two tricks in the suit unless you help him by leading the king.

The lead of the queen from Q-J-x is also unsafe. Declarer may have K-10-x or A-10-x in the dummy, with the other top card in his own hand. He wins in his own hand and then finesses dummy's ten, losing no trick in the suit; if you had let the suit alone you would have won a trick.

The lead from a single honor is not bad if you have chosen your suit wisely. Even if you have chosen unwisely, you seldom give declarer a trick by your lead that he could not have won without your lead. Much the same is true when you lead a suit that consists entirely of small cards.

♥ LONG BROKEN SUITS

When you have a long broken suit, you are willing to lead some card of that suit against notrump. You tend to avoid such leads against a suit contract.

Against notrump, for example, you would lead:

- The queen from A-Q-J-x-x
- The jack from K-J-10-x-x or A-J-10-x-x
- The ten from A-10-9-x-x, K-10-9-x-x, or Q-10-9-x-x

When your broken suit does not contain sequences or near-sequences, you lead the fourth-best card:

- The deuce from A-Q-6-2, K-10-8-2, etc.
- The five from A-Q-6-5-2, K-10-8-5-3, etc.

A lead from a 5-card suit is more desirable (against notrump) than a lead from a 4-card suit.

All of these leads are undesirable against a suit contract. It is particularly unwise to lead low from an ace against a suit contract. (There is no such thing as *never* in opening leads, but the underlead of an ace against a suit belongs at the very end of your list of leads.)

♥ SHORT-SUIT LEADS

When leading a 3-card suit, lead an honor from honors in sequence: king from A-K-x or K-Q-x; queen from

Q-J-x; jack from J-10-x. With just *one* honor, lead the lowest card: deuce from K-6-2 or J-5-2, etc. When all three cards are lower than the ten some players lead the *top* card; but most experts lead the lowest. Since this is partly a matter of partnership understanding, try to find out your partner's preference.

When leading from a doubleton, lead the higher of the two cards. It is dangerous to lead from such combinations as K-x, Q-x, J-x, or even 10-x. Such a lead may relieve declarer of a guess or may give him a trick that he couldn't get without your kind help. When your doubleton is A-K, lead the ace first.

✔ LEADING PARTNER'S SUIT

You follow the usual rules when leading your partner's suit. Lead high from *any* doubleton. Lead your top honor when you have two or more touching honors in his suit: the king from K-Q-x, the queen from Q-J-x, etc. Lead *low* from other 3-card combinations, except that you lead the ace from A-x-x against a trump contract. (Some players lead the *top* of three worthless cards in partner's suit, but most experts lead the lowest card.) Lead fourth-best from a holding of four or more cards in partner's suit unless you have a sequence of honors at the head of the suit.

✔ LEADING A TRUMP

When do you lead a trump?
- Against a very low contract if your partner fails to reopen the bidding. You will usually be well off if you can get out all the trumps and thus reduce the hand to notrump. Avoid a trump lead, however, when the bidding indicates a possible misfit.

- If your partner passes your takeout double for penalties. Your partner wants to draw trumps, and even the slightest delay may cost several tricks.
- When dummy shows a decided preference for one of declarer's suits. The other suit will probably be ruffed in dummy unless you get the trumps out of the dummy with all possible speed.

✓ LEADING AGAINST A SLAM

Make a *safe* lead against a grand slam or against six notrump.

Make an *attacking* lead against six of a suit. Your object is to establish a trick quickly. If your side must be given an ace or a king in one of declarer's key suits (trump or the longest side suit), you will then be in position to cash the trick that was set up by your opening lead.

Avoid leading a trump against a small slam. This turns control over to declarer; he couldn't ask for a friendlier lead.

Avoid leading an ace except against a grand slam. (Even then, if the opponents know what they are doing, your ace will be ruffed and may set up tricks for declarer.) Exception: lead an ace when dummy's bidding is jumpy and may be based on a long solid suit. Your best chance is to take two tricks on the run. Declarer may be off two aces or the ace-king in your suit.

✓ RULE OF ELEVEN

When a player leads fourth-best, subtract the number of the card led from eleven. The remainder is the number of higher cards in the other three hands.

For example, West leads the seven of spades against a notrump contract. Dummy plays low from K-9-2. What should East play from A-J-5?

East should play the *five* of spades.

If the lead is fourth-best, South cannot beat the seven. Subtract 7 from 11, getting a remainder of 4. Dummy's K-9 and East's A-J account for all cards higher than the seven of spades in dummy, East, and declarer's hand.

There is another possibility: the lead may not be fourth-best. If West has led from the top of a worthless suit, the five of spades is as good a play as any from the East hand.

✓ ILLUSTRATIONS

In each of the following illustrative hands you are West. South is the declarer, and it is up to you to make the opening lead. Which card do you lead?

SOUTH	WEST	NORTH	EAST
1 NT	Pass	3 NT	Pass
Pass	Pass		

(1)   ♠ A J 7 6 2   ♡ K 8 4   ◊ J 10 5   ♣ 9 2

Lead the six of spades. In general, lead fourth-best from your longest and strongest suit against a no-trump contract.

(2)   ♠ A K 6 2   ♡ J 10 9 4   ◊ J 10 5   ♣ 9 2

Lead the jack of hearts. Save the top spades as entries to develop and run the hearts.

(3)   ♠ K J 6 2   ♡ K 10 8 4   ◊ J 10 5   ♣ K 2

Lead the jack of diamonds—the safest lead. Your own hand may provide enough high cards to defeat the contract if you avoid giving anything away. A passive defense is your best bet.

NORTH	EAST	SOUTH	WEST
1 ♣	1 ◊	1 ♡	Pass
2 ♡	Pass	4 ♡	Pass
Pass	Pass		

(1)   ♠ K J 8 4   ♡ 8 5 2   ◇ K 5   ♣ J 10 9 5

Lead the king of diamonds. In general, lead your partner's suit when he has bid.

(2)   ♠ 6 2   ♡ 8 5 2   ◇ A 5 4   ♣ Q J 10 8 5

Lead the deuce of hearts. The ace of partner's suit is not an ideal lead, for it may set up declarer's king. You can afford to lead trumps on the theory that declarer will not be happy if he has no chance to ruff away losing cards.

(3)   ♠ 6   ♡ A 5 2   ◇ 8 5 4 2   ♣ Q J 10 8 5

Lead the six of spades. Your object is to get spade ruffs. If partner has the ace of spades and a fast diamond entry, you get two ruffs. Even if he doesn't have the ace of spades, you can win the first round of trumps and put partner in with a diamond to give you a spade ruff.

SOUTH	WEST	NORTH	EAST
1 ♠	Pass	2 ♣	Pass
2 ♡	Pass	3 ♡	Pass
4 ♡	Pass	Pass	Pass

(1)   ♠ Q 10 7 3   ♡ 5 4   ◇ K J 8 2   ♣ Q 7 2

Lead the deuce of diamonds. Dummy's clubs will probably furnish discards unless you get the diamonds started promptly. If declarer tries to ruff spades in dummy, your partner may be able to over-ruff.

(2)   ♠ 8 3   ♡ 5 4 2   ◇ K J 8 2   ♣ Q 9 7 2

Lead the deuce of hearts. Declarer probably will want to ruff spades in the dummy, and your partner will have to follow suit. South will probably ruff clubs in his own hand, and *you* will follow suit. The best defense against a cross-ruff is to lead trumps early and often.

NORTH	EAST	SOUTH	WEST
1 ♣	Pass	1 ♠	Pass
2 ♣	Pass	2 ♡	Pass
2 NT	Pass	3 ♡	Pass
3 ♠	Pass	Pass	Pass

(1) ♠ 6 2   ♡ 8 3   ◊ A J 7 5 2   ♣ Q J 4 2

Lead the ace of diamonds. Your partner probably has four trumps. (Visualize the North-South hands from the bidding: North has five or six clubs, two spades, probably two hearts, probably two diamonds and one club.) The best defense is to lead the suit with which you can make declarer ruff.

(2) ♠ 6 2   ♡ 8 3   ◊ Q J 7 5   ♣ Q 10 5 4 2

Lead the queen of diamonds. The reasoning is the same as in the previous case. However, you are just a trifle worried about a cross-ruff.

(3) ♠ 6 3 2   ♡ 8   ◊ Q J 7 5   ♣ Q 10 5 4 2

Lead the deuce of spades. You are worried that declarer will ruff hearts in dummy and clubs in his own hand. You act to stop the cross-ruff. Since trumps are going to break evenly for declarer, there is no great virtue in trying to force him to ruff.

᠊ᠰᠰᠰᠰᠰᠰᠰᠰᠰᠰᠰᠰᠰᠰᠰᠰ

DEFENSIVE RULES—AND WHEN TO BREAK THEM

√ Second Hand Low
√ Third Hand High
√ Through Strength, Up to Weakness
√ Punch Declarer, Not Dummy
√ Count Your Tricks
√ Return Partner's Suit

√ Leading Trumps
√ The Come-On Signal
√ The Distributional Echo
√ The Trump Echo
√ The Suit-Preference Signal
√ In Short

AFTER THE OPENING LEAD has been made, you can study the dummy and look ahead to plan defensive maneuvers. If you see that a finesse will probably be taken through your king or queen, you can decide in advance whether or not to cover an honor. If you see that a lead will sooner or later be made through your ace, you can speculate in advance whether to play low or to hop up with the ace.

You will usually have time for this advance planning, since declarer will be studying the dummy to make his own plans. Even if declarer sets out at full speed, you can play your cards deliberately to prevent him from rushing you. You can often think about one suit while another suit is being played.

On many hands you will know exactly what to do about the defense. On some hands you may have to follow general principles.

As you become more and more proficient at defense, you follow general principles less and less. There are thousands of exceptions to the rules. Nevertheless, the rules will guide you to the right play more often than not. Follow them when you have nothing better in view.

√ SECOND HAND LOW

When you are second to play to a trick, it usually pays to play low. Don't waste your high cards by capturing only low cards with them.

For example:

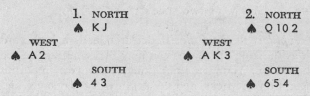

1. NORTH
♠ K J

WEST
♠ A 2

SOUTH
♠ 4 3

2. NORTH
♠ Q 10 2

WEST
♠ A K 3

SOUTH
♠ 6 5 4

When South, declarer, leads a low spade, West should play low.

In Diagram 1 South must guess whether to play the king or the jack from dummy. Put to the test, South may guess wrong. If West puts up the ace, however, there is no need for South to guess.

In Diagram 2 South plans to finesse dummy's ten. This finesse will lose to the jack, and the defenders will take all three tricks. If West plays the king on the first trick, South will probably realize what is going on; he will later lead toward dummy's queen and will win one of the three tricks.

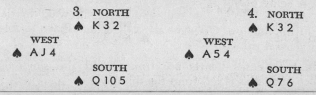

3. NORTH
♠ K 3 2

WEST
♠ A J 4

SOUTH
♠ Q 10 5

4. NORTH
♠ K 3 2

WEST
♠ A 5 4

SOUTH
♠ Q 7 6

When South leads a low spade toward the dummy West should play low.

In Diagram 3 West will make two spade tricks later if he ducks the first time. If West puts up the ace, however, declarer will win a trick with his own queen as well as dummy's king.

In Diagram 4 West should play low and allow dummy's king to win. The ace is used to capture South's queen. East will make a spade trick with some such card as the jack or ten. If West puts up the ace on the first spade, declarer wins two spade tricks.

Exceptions to the Rule: If declarer leads a high card, such as the king or queen, you may play your ace in second position. Your aces and kings have two important duties: to win tricks and to capture the enemy's high cards.

If declarer or dummy leads a singleton through you, take the trick at once if it is the setting trick. The cemeteries are full of bridge players who failed to take the setting trick when it was offered to them.

This does not, however, mean that you must hasten to play your ace in second position *whenever* a singleton is led through you. The general rule of *second hand low* usually applies. For example:

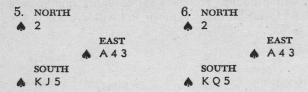

5. NORTH
♠ 2

                    EAST
                ♠ A 4 3

    SOUTH
♠ K J 5

6. NORTH
♠ 2

                    EAST
                ♠ A 4 3

    SOUTH
♠ K Q 5

In both cases hearts are trumps and the singleton deuce of spades is led from the dummy.

If East plays a low spade *casually* in Diagram 5, South will probably finesse the jack. This will lose to the queen, and South will never make a spade trick. If East plays the ace, South's king will later win a trick. If East plays low but does so with pain and travail, South will put up the king and thus win a spade trick.

Few defenders are skillful enough to play low in East's position. Fewer still can do it calmly enough to flummox an alert declarer. But when East does make the correct calm play, South will almost invariably finesse the jack on the assumption that East does not have the ace.

In Diagram 6 there is no deception. East plays low, and South wins one spade trick. If East plays his ace, South will later win *two* spade tricks.

In both cases East runs the risk of getting no spade trick at all when he plays low. In some cases East may have to weigh one risk against the other. In most cases East should simply play low without apparent thought.

When your partner opens his suit against a notrump contract you must be on the alert to help him set up and run his suit. If dummy makes an early lead through you, it often pays to step right up with your ace—or even with an unsupported king. (See the hand on page 360.) The idea is to win an *early* trick while you can still lead your partner's suit. Your partner's entries must be saved for later.

✓ THIRD HAND HIGH

If you are the third person to play to a trick, play as high as necessary to win the trick or to force out a top card. If you cannot beat a card already played, there is no need for you to play high.

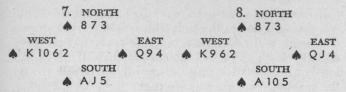

7. NORTH
♠ 8 7 3

WEST
♠ K 10 6 2

EAST
♠ Q 9 4

SOUTH
♠ A J 5

8. NORTH
♠ 8 7 3

WEST
♠ K 9 6 2

EAST
♠ Q J 4

SOUTH
♠ A 10 5

In both cases West leads the deuce of spades, and dummy follows with the three.

In Diagram 7 East should put up the queen. This will force out the ace. East will later lead the nine of spades through South, and South's jack will be captured by a finesse. If East fails to play high at the first trick, South can win at once with the jack and will win a second spade trick with the ace.

In Diagram 8 East should play the *jack*. When a defender has *touching* cards, he plays the lowest of them to do the job of winning or forcing out a higher card. If East had Q-J-10, he would play the ten.

When this rule is followed, West can often tell what is going on. In Diagram 7, for example, East plays the queen to force out the ace. West knows that East cannot have the jack of spades, since with Q-J East would play the jack. Therefore South must have the jack of spades, and West must wait for his partner to lead through the jack.

In Diagram 8 East plays the jack to force out the ace. This tells West who has the queen of spades. If South had the queen, he would be glad to win the first trick with it instead of using the ace for that purpose. Since South doesn't have the queen, East must have it.

Exceptions to the Rule: The chief exception to the rule of *third hand high* occurs when the defender must finesse behind the dummy.

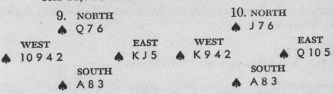

9. NORTH
♠ Q 7 6

WEST
♠ 10 9 4 2

EAST
♠ K J 5

SOUTH
♠ A 8 3

10. NORTH
♠ J 7 6

WEST
♠ K 9 4 2

EAST
♠ Q 10 5

SOUTH
♠ A 8 3

West leads the deuce of spades, and dummy plays low. In Diagram 9 East should finesse the jack. In Diagram 10 East should finesse the ten. There is, of course, no point in wasting the king or the queen in these two situations; the jack or the ten can do the same job.

In the cases just described, the finesses are very clear and comfortable. East can see the card he is finessing against and can therefore be quite sure that his finesse will work. Not all finesses behind the dummy are so obvious:

11. NORTH
♠ Q 7 6

WEST
♠ J 9 4 2

EAST
♠ K 10 5

SOUTH
♠ A 8 3

12. NORTH
♠ J 7 6

WEST
♠ Q 9 4 2

EAST
♠ K 10 5

SOUTH
♠ A 8 3

West leads the deuce of spades in both cases, and dummy plays low. East should finesse the ten in both cases. This will force out the ace. East must save his king to capture dummy's honor.

If East plays the king at the first trick, South wins with the ace and can lead toward dummy's honor to get a second trick.

Third hand should not play high in the situations in which it would be wrong to cover an honor. For example, West may have the bad luck to open a suit in which dummy holds Q-J-10-9-x. East, with K-x-x-x, should play low, exactly as he would if the suit had been led by dummy.

✓ THROUGH STRENGTH, UP TO WEAKNESS

When the dummy is at your left, lead through some strong but broken holding—such as A-Q-x, K-J-x, or the like. If your partner has one or more of the missing honors, he will be in favorable position.

When the dummy is at your right, lead up to dummy's weakness. If your partner has any strength in the suit, he will be in favorable position since he plays after declarer.

Exceptions:

1. There is no need to lead dummy's long suit in most hands; declarer will have to develop this suit for himself, and there is seldom an advantage in doing declarer's work for him. In such situations, do not lead through A-Q-x-x-x; try to set up a trick in some *shorter* suit.

2. Leading up to weakness in the *trump* suit may be a waste of time. Your partner will get his trump tricks whether or not you lead the suit. (Sometimes you want to make a *safe* lead and you don't mind "wasting time" by leading a trump.)

3. When dummy has a long suit that will be set up quickly, beware of general principles. Lead up to dummy's side ace to knock out an entry and to set up your tricks before declarer manages to discard his losers.

✓ PUNCH DECLARER, NOT DUMMY

It is often wise to "punch" declarer by leading a suit that he must ruff. If you can do this a few times in the

same hand, he may run out of trumps and lose control
of the hand.

It is seldom advantageous to make the *dummy* ruff.
In fact, this may be just what declarer wants to do on
his own account. Furthermore, if declarer also is void
of the dummy's void suit, he will be able to ruff in
dummy while discarding a loser from his own hand. This
play gives him an advantage that he could not produce
for himself.

A continued attack on declarer's trumps may ruin even
a very strong trump holding:

```
                    NORTH
                 ♠ 7 6 5
                 ♡ 10 8 4
                 ◊ A 7 6 5
                 ♣ K Q 6
   WEST                            EAST
 ♠ A 4 3 2                       ♠ ———
 ♡ K Q J 9                       ♡ 7 6 5 3 2
 ◊ 8 3 2                         ◊ K 4
 ♣ J 8                           ♣ A 10 7 5 3 2
                    SOUTH
                 ♠ K Q J 10 9 8
                 ♡ A
                 ◊ Q J 10 9
                 ♣ 9 4
```

SOUTH	WEST	NORTH	EAST
1 ♠	Pass	1 NT	Pass
3 ♠	Pass	3 NT	Pass
4 ♠	Pass	Pass	Pass

West opens the king of hearts, and South takes the
ace. South leads the king of spades, expecting no problems. West refuses the trick, and East discards a club.
South discovers that he has a problem after all.

South continues with the queen of spades, and West refuses the trick once more. This is fine defense, as we shall soon see.

South leads the queen of diamonds for a finesse, losing to the king. Back comes a heart, and South must ruff.

South leads a club, and dummy's king loses to the ace. Back comes a heart, and South is punched once more.

At this stage South has two trumps, and so has West. If South leads another trump, West will take the ace and will lead a fourth heart to punch out South's last trump. This will leave West with the last trump, and the contract is thus defeated since the defenders take two trumps, a diamond and a club.

If South decides not to lead a third trump, West will eventually trump the fourth diamond with his low trump. It is this low trump trick that defeats the contract.

Let's try it again with West taking the *first* or *second* trump with his ace. He would lead a second heart, forcing South to ruff.

South would take the diamond finesse, and back would come a third heart, forcing him to ruff again.

South would then knock out the ace of clubs, and East would be unable to continue the attack on South's trumps. If East leads a fourth heart, *dummy* can ruff. If necessary, South can get to his hand with a diamond to draw the rest of the trumps. The defenders get only *one* trump trick, and South makes his contract.

✓ COUNT YOUR TRICKS

As a defender, count the sure and probable tricks that your side can take. Keep in mind the number of tricks you need to defeat the contract.

Just knowing how many tricks you need may sharpen your wits and help you find the tricks.

NORTH
♠ K Q
♡ Q 9 6 5
◇ A J 9
♣ A Q J 8

WEST
♠ J 10 9 6
♡ K 7 2
◇ K 4 3 2
♣ 9 5

EAST
♠ A 7 5 3 2
♡ 4
◇ Q 10 6
♣ 7 4 3 2

SOUTH
♠ 8 4
♡ A J 10 8 3
◇ 8 7 5
♣ K 10 6

NORTH	EAST	SOUTH	WEST
1 ♣	Pass	1 ♡	Pass
3 ♡	Pass	4 ♡	Pass
Pass	Pass		

West opens the jack of spades, and East wins with the ace.

If East defends by general principles, he thinks of leading to dummy's weakness. This may induce him to lead a trump, since that is dummy's weakest suit. Another possibility is a spade return to dummy's blank king. When you can't lead up to weakness you often lead up to *solid* strength; this may not help you very much but at least it doesn't put your partner's high cards in the middle.

If East makes either a spade or a trump return, South easily fulfills the contract. Declarer loses a trick to the king of hearts, wins any return, and draws trumps. Then South runs the clubs, discarding one of his losing diamonds. Declarer loses one spade, one trump, and one diamond.

East can win a medal for his defense if he counts the

defensive tricks after winning the first trick with the ace of spades.

He knows that he needs four tricks to defeat the contract. One look at the dummy is enough to indicate that the defenders can win only the one spade trick. East hopes, but cannot be sure, that his partner has a trump trick. Clearly there is no club trick; even if West has the king of clubs, it will be finessed to death.

By the process of elimination, East sees that he needs two diamond tricks to defeat the contract. Not a single step in this chain of reasoning has been at all difficult, but the end product is a play that few defenders would be bold enough to make.

Seeing the need for two diamond tricks, East returns the six of diamonds at the second trick!

West plays the king, and dummy wins with the ace. Declarer tries the trump finesse, losing to the king. West then leads a diamond, and East takes the needed two tricks, defeating the contract.

✔ RETURN PARTNER'S SUIT

When your partner is the opening leader, he usually has a reason for choosing to lead a particular suit. Unless you have something definite in mind, it is usually a good idea to return his suit.

In the days of whist only two excuses were acceptable for failing to return partner's suit: not having any cards of the suit—and sudden death.

This is no longer true. Other excuses are accepted— particularly if your play succeeds. But you do have to have a reason of some kind.

It is particularly important to keep plugging away at one suit when defending against notrump. If you scatter your shots, you won't make much of an impression; if you concentrate your fire, you may put the enemy away underground.

This is not quite so important when you are defending against a trump contract. It may be important for each defender to lead a different suit, through broken strength and toward partner's strength.

✓ LEADING TRUMPS

We have already seen cases in which the opening lead should be a trump. If the leader has made a wise choice, both defenders usually know it. Each defender will be alert to lead trumps again at the first opportunity.

The same principle may hold good even if the opening leader is unable to lead a trump:

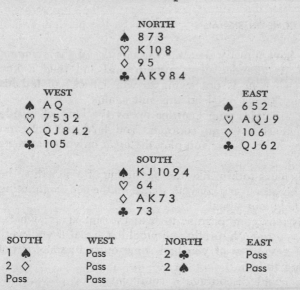

```
                        NORTH
                      ♠ 8 7 3
                      ♡ K 10 8
                      ◇ 9 5
                      ♣ A K 9 8 4
        WEST                              EAST
      ♠ A Q                             ♠ 6 5 2
      ♡ 7 5 3 2                         ♡ A Q J 9
      ◇ Q J 8 4 2                       ◇ 10 6
      ♣ 10 5                            ♣ Q J 6 2
                        SOUTH
                      ♠ K J 10 9 4
                      ♡ 6 4
                      ◇ A K 7 3
                      ♣ 7 3
```

SOUTH	WEST	NORTH	EAST
1 ♠	Pass	2 ♣	Pass
2 ◇	Pass	2 ♠	Pass
Pass	Pass		

West wanted to open a trump to protect his diamonds, but he couldn't afford to lead away from the doubleton ace-queen. For lack of anything better, he opened the deuce of hearts. He tackled the unbid suit in the hope that his partner could get in and return a trump.

So it worked out. East won the first heart with the jack and returned a trump to reduce dummy's ruffing power. West took the ace and queen of trumps and led another heart. East won and led a third trump.

Now South was a dead duck. He had already lost four tricks and could find no way to avoid the loss of two more. If the defenders had left a trump in the dummy, South would have ruffed a third round of diamonds (with the seven or eight of spades), thus getting his eighth trick.

∨ THE COME-ON SIGNAL

We have already seen many examples of the *come-on signal*. A defender plays a high card and then a low card (when he is not trying to win a trick) to tell his partner, "Come on—lead this suit again!"

For example, your partner opens the king of a side suit against a trump contract. You hold the 8-2, and dummy holds Q-x-x. You play the *eight* on your partner's king.

This looks to him like the beginning of a signal, so he leads his ace. You play your deuce on the ace, completing your *high-low* signal.

This tells your partner to lead the suit again, whereupon you ruff. Naturally you wouldn't signal if you were out of trumps or if you had some other reason for not wanting to ruff.

You could discourage a continuation by playing the

deuce (or, with other holdings, your lowest card) on your partner's king.

You usually signal encouragement when you have the queen as well as when you have a doubleton. For example, with Q-8-2 you play the eight on partner's opening lead of the king. This gives you your best chance to take three immediate tricks in the suit.

You would not encourage a continuation if dummy had only two cards of the suit. You do not signal just to show that you have the queen; your signal tells partner to lead the suit again. His not to reason why. But if you have told your partner to do the wrong thing, you may have to do some explaining.

It is sometimes possible to tell partner to come on and then to stop. For example, your partner leads the king, and you have 8-7-2. You play the seven first, clearly the beginning of a signal. At the next trick you play the eight. By *playing up* instead of high-low, you tell your partner not to lead the suit a third time.

How high should a signal be? As high a card as you can spare. Sometimes this is a very high card. With Q-10-3-2 you can usually afford to signal with the ten. With only Q-3-2 you can spare only the three.

Your partner must be on the alert to determine whether or not you have begun a signal. He does this by looking for cards that are lower than your play.

For example, he leads the king of spades and you follow suit with the seven. This is a high card, but it need not be a signal. If your partner can see the six and five in his own hand, the three and deuce in the dummy, and the four as declarer's play to the first trick, he knows that you played the lowest available spade. The seven is *not* a signal.

Take another example. Your partner leads the king of spades, and you follow suit with the three. The deuce of spades is not in your partner's hand, is not in the dummy, and was not played at the first trick. Who has that deuce? If *you* have it, you have begun a signal with that humble three of spades. If declarer has it, he is trying to make your partner believe that you started a signal.

In short, the situation is sometimes clear, sometimes not. Unfortunately for defenders, the world is full of crafty declarers who do their best to make a frigid "Stop" look like a passionate "Go Ahead."

√ THE DISTRIBUTIONAL ECHO

It is possible to signal how many cards you have in a suit instead of whether or not you want your partner to lead the suit again. You usually signal distribution in a suit led by the opponents rather than in a suit led by your partner.

The most common use of the signal is to tell your partner exactly when to take his ace in dummy's long suit, particularly when dummy has no side entries.

```
                    NORTH
                 ♠ K Q J 8 6
                 ♡ 7 3
                 ◇ 8 3 2
                 ♣ 9 6 2
     WEST                          EAST
  ♠ A 4 3                       ♠ 9 7 2
  ♡ J 10 8 4                    ♡ 9 6 2
  ◇ 7 4                         ◇ K 10 9 5
  ♣ Q 10 8 7                    ♣ K J 4
                    SOUTH
                 ♠ 10 5
                 ♡ A K Q 5
                 ◇ A Q J 6
                 ♣ A 5 3
```

SOUTH	WEST	NORTH	EAST
1 ♡	Pass	1 ♠	Pass
2 NT	Pass	3 ♠	Pass
3 NT	Pass	Pass	Pass

North would have an easy time at four spades, but even the best partnerships occasionally reach the wrong contract.

West opens the seven of clubs, and East wins with the king. East returns the jack of clubs, South plays low, and West overtakes with the queen. West then returns the ten of clubs, forcing out the ace.

South leads the five of spades, and West must hold off. If West takes the ace of spades at once, he can cash his last club for a total of four defensive tricks. South then wins the rest with four spades, three hearts, a diamond, and a club.

West plays low on the first spade, and East carefully plays the *deuce*. This play—the absence of a high-low—indicates that East has an *odd* number of spades (three or five). With an even number of spades (two or four), East would begin a high-low.

Because of this signal, West can see the whole picture. It is clear that East has three spades. This means that South started with only two spades. (If East has a singleton deuce, South has four, and the suit cannot be shut out. However, the bidding makes this very unlikely.)

Let us now return to declarer. He wins the first spade trick in dummy and returns a diamond, successfully finessing the queen.

South leads his other spade, and West knows enough to step right up with the ace of spades. Now he can cash his last club and get out safely with the jack of hearts.

South is lucky if he manages to go down only one. He cannot make the contract against sound defense. South might cash the three top hearts before leading the second spade. This would help if West started with only three hearts; but the play fails as the cards lie.

Just see what would happen if West had no way of knowing when to take the ace of spades. He might very well refuse the second spade trick. This would allow South to steal the contract.

Declarer wins the second spade in dummy and finesses the jack of diamonds. Now he makes two spades, three hearts, three diamonds, and a club.

✔ THE TRUMP ECHO

It is sometimes important to tell your partner how many trumps you hold. A high-low in the trump suit shows exactly three trumps.° If you fail to high-low in a situation that calls for the signal, you have either two trumps or more than three. Your partner can almost always tell which the case is.

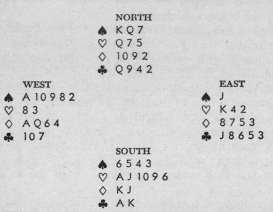

```
                    NORTH
                 ♠ K Q 7
                 ♡ Q 7 5
                 ◇ 10 9 2
                 ♣ Q 9 4 2
   WEST                          EAST
♠ A 10 9 8 2                  ♠ J
♡ 8 3                         ♡ K 4 2
◇ A Q 6 4                     ◇ 8 7 5 3
♣ 10 7                        ♣ J 8 6 5 3
                    SOUTH
                 ♠ 6 5 4 3
                 ♡ A J 10 9 6
                 ◇ K J
                 ♣ A K
```

° A high-low in a *side* suit should show an *even* number of cards, as we have seen.

SOUTH	WEST	NORTH	EAST
1 ♡	1 ♠	1 NT	Pass
2 ♡	Pass	Pass	Pass

South would have been better off if he had passed one notrump. He hoped to reach a good game contract, but succeeded only in getting out of a makable contract into one that went down.

West opened the ace of spades, and East dropped the jack. West naturally led a spade for East to ruff.

East ruffed with the four of hearts and returned a diamond. West won and led another spade. East ruffed with the deuce of hearts and once more returned a diamond.

West won and noted that his partner had echoed (played high-low) in trumps. This meant that East had a third trump. Hence it was safe to lead a fourth round of spades.

Declarer ruffed with dummy's queen of hearts, but East over-ruffed with the king. This was the setting trick

✓ THE SUIT-PREFERENCE SIGNAL

How did East know that a diamond return would work better than a club? Does he get credit for good guessing, or did West manage to signal the necessary information?

West managed to signal while leading spades.

How can you lead a spade that says, "Partner, return a diamond"? If this is possible, you must be able to lead some other spade that says, "Partner, return a club."

All of this is so.

When you lead a card for your partner to ruff, you may lead a *high* card or a *low* card. You lead a high card to ask for the higher side suit, a low card for the lower side suit. (The trump suit and your partner's void suit are ignored for the purpose of the signal—leaving just two side suits.)

In the hand just described, diamonds are the high side suit and clubs are the low side suit. West led the *ten* of spades at the second trick. This asked for a diamond return.

The next time West led a spade, he chose the *nine*. This once more asked for a diamond return.

This kind of signal is most useful in ruffing situations, but it is sometimes useful in other cases to show the location of side strength. Don't make the mistake of letting the suit-preference signal interfere with your basic *come-on* or *stop* signal.

√ IN SHORT

Try to work out, from the bidding and early play, an exact idea of declarer's hand. Then defend as though you could see all of the cards.

When you have only a vague idea of declarer's hand, follow these principles:

- Second hand low
- Third hand high
- Lead through strength and up to weakness
- Punch declarer, not the dummy
- Count the defensive tricks
- Return your partner's suit unless you have a good reason for shifting
- Use the high-low to signal strength or distribution
- Use the trump echo to show exactly three trumps
- Use the suit-preference signal to show where your likely entries are

DECEPTIVE PLAY

√ Falsecards	√ Inducing Discards
√ Inducing a Duck	√ Putting Declarer to the Guess
√ The Fake Finesse	√ The Defensive Hold-Up
√ A Feint Heart	√ In Short

NOBODY IS so good a player that he consistently gets from his cards all that is in them. Nevertheless, it is often possible to get *more* out of the cards than is really in them. The way to do this is to swindle your opponents.

We are talking now about honest swindles. If you can make a bid or play that throws the opponents off the track, more power to you. As we shall see in Chapter 34, Manners, Morals and Laws, you are *not* supposed to achieve your deceptive effects by your *manner* but only by the bid or by the card itself.

Let's take a simple example:

```
                    NORTH
                    ♠ 8 6 5
        WEST                        EAST
        ♠ A K 9 3                   ♠ J 10 4
                    SOUTH
                    ♠ Q 7 2
```

Hearts are trumps, and West leads the king of spades. East plays the four, his lowest spade, hoping to discourage a spade continuation.

If South likewise plays his lowest spade, the deuce, West can be sure that his partner has played a discouraging card. South is an honest citizen and the salt of the earth, but he is no bridge player.

✓ FALSECARDS

At the first trick, South should *falsecard* by playing the seven of spades. No anguish, no histrionics; just a calm seven of spades.

West notices that the deuce of spades has not appeared. Perhaps *East* has it. In fact, perhaps East started with Q-4-2 of spades.

West may talk himself into continuing the spades, whereupon South wins a trick with the queen.

There's nothing difficult or complicated about this type of falsecard. When you want the opponents to continue a suit, you "conceal" a low card—just as though you were beginning a high-low signal to your partner.

Sometimes your falsecard is a trifle more energetic:

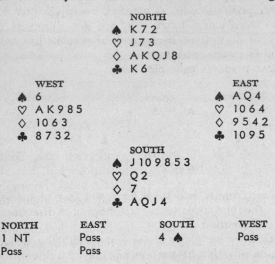

```
                    NORTH
                  ♠ K 7 2
                  ♡ J 7 3
                  ◇ A K Q J 8
                  ♣ K 6
     WEST                              EAST
   ♠ 6                               ♠ A Q 4
   ♡ A K 9 8 5                       ♡ 10 6 4
   ◇ 10 6 3                          ◇ 9 5 4 2
   ♣ 8 7 3 2                         ♣ 10 9 5
                    SOUTH
                  ♠ J 10 9 8 5 3
                  ♡ Q 2
                  ◇ 7
                  ♣ A Q J 4
```

NORTH	EAST	SOUTH	WEST
1 NT	Pass	4 ♠	Pass
Pass	Pass		

West opens the king of hearts, and South drops the queen! Poor West now fears that South is out of hearts. Can you blame West for leading a club through dummy's king?

This is, of course, just what South was hoping for. He grabs the king of clubs, cashes two top diamonds to get rid of the deuce of hearts, and eventually gives up two trump tricks.

A high card, such as the queen, has a certain *impact*. Your opponent may suspect that you're out stealing, but he is very reluctant to disbelieve your queen if he has any plausible shift.

The same sort of play may be executed by a defender:

```
                    NORTH
                  ♠ Q 7 5 4
                  ♡ A J 10 6 3
                  ◇ A 3
                  ♣ 8 6

   WEST                           EAST
 ♠ J 10 6 3 2                   ♠ 8
 ♡ 2                            ♡ Q 8 7 4
 ◇ K Q 10 6                     ◇ J 9 8 5 4 2
 ♣ J 10 4                       ♣ 7 2

                    SOUTH
                  ♠ A K 9
                  ♡ K 9 5
                  ◇ 7
                  ♣ A K Q 9 5 3
```

The scene was a national tournament, and South climbed up to six notrump. An ambitious bid, but absolutely ice-cold as long as the clubs break favorably.

The trouble was that South didn't know about the club break, and nobody told him.

West opened the king of diamonds, and declarer won in dummy with the ace. He led a club to the ace, and West calmly produced the *jack* of clubs.

So simple as to be corny, but very effective.

Naturally, South glared angrily at West. This got him nowhere, so South cashed the ace and king of spades in the hope of collecting some evidence.

South got some evidence. East discarded a diamond on the second spade. (If he had discarded a club, the cat would have been out of the bag, but East had a very good idea of what was going on.)

South reasoned that West had length in diamonds and five known spades, so might well have a singleton club. Declarer led a heart to dummy's ace, returned a club from dummy and finessed the nine from his hand.

West scooped in the ten of clubs and proceeded to run the rest of the diamonds. "I wouldn't have discarded one," East apologized, "if I'd known you had a club trick!"

✓ INDUCING A DUCK

One way to persuade an opponent to duck is to lead a card that he thinks his partner can win:

NORTH
♠ 9 4 3 2
♡ 7 5 3
♢ J 8
♣ K Q J 8

WEST
♠ A 5
♡ Q 10 6 4 2
♢ 7 6 4 3
♣ 7 4

EAST
♠ 7 6
♡ 8
♢ A 10 9 5 2
♣ A 6 5 3 2

SOUTH
♠ K Q J 10 8
♡ A K J 9
♢ K Q
♣ 10 9

SOUTH	WEST	NORTH	EAST
1 ♠	Pass	2 ♠	Pass
4 ♠	Pass	Pass	Pass

West leads the four of hearts, East puts up the eight, and South wins with the jack. South must start right out with the falsecard, hoping to conceal from West the fact that East started with a singleton heart. (South cannot be sure of this, but there is no harm in guarding against this danger.)

Now South wants to sneak one round of trumps past West. If South leads the king of spades, West naturally takes the ace of spades at once. If West then leads a heart, South is defeated.

South should try to induce a trump duck by leading some spade lower than the king. Perhaps West will play low in the hope that his partner will be able to win the trick.

Against a fine player, South should lead the *queen* of spades. West may worry about a possible singleton king of trumps in his partner's hand, and he may therefore duck the first trump. If so, South immediately leads another trump, and the contract is safe.

If West is not really a fine player, South may have a better chance if he leads the *jack* or even the *ten* of spades. These would be pretty obvious to an expert West, but there's no sense in making a five-dollar play against a ten-cent opponent.

√ THE FAKE FINESSE

One of the time-honored swindles, still good for a trick and a laugh, is the fake finesse:

```
                        NORTH
                    ♠ J 8 7
                    ♡ J 10 6 4 2
                    ◇ K 3 2
                    ♣ K 5
        WEST                            EAST
    ♠ 4 2                           ♠ 6 5 3
    ♡ Q 8 5 3                       ♡ A 9 7
    ◇ J 7 6                         ◇ A Q 9 4
    ♣ Q 10 3 2                      ♣ 8 6 4
                        SOUTH
                    ♠ A K Q 10 9
                    ♡ K
                    ◇ 10 8 5
                    ♣ A J 9 7
```

SOUTH	WEST	NORTH	EAST
1 ♠	Pass	1 NT	Pass
2 ♣	Pass	2 ♠	Pass
3 ♠	Pass	4 ♠	Pass
Pass	Pass		

West opened a trump, hoping to protect his clubs from ruffs in the dummy. It was a good idea and deserved a better fate.

Declarer went up with dummy's jack of spades and led the jack of hearts through East. The average good player in East's position automatically plays low in the hope that South will make the wrong guess if he has K-x of hearts.

In this case East did play low, and South won the trick with his singleton king.

Nothing else was needed. Declarer cashed the top clubs and cross-ruffed hearts and clubs to make sure of his ten tricks. East maintained a pained silence throughout.

♥ A FEINT HEART

When you want the opponents to lead trumps, make them think you want to get ruffing tricks in the dummy:

```
                         NORTH
                      ♠ K 3
                      ♡ A J
                      ◇ 8 7 4 2
                      ♣ K 10 9 4 2
        WEST                             EAST
     ♠ J 5 2                          ♠ A 7 4
     ♡ K Q 10 7                       ♡ 9 8 6 4 2
     ◇ J 10 6 3                       ◇ 9 5
     ♣ 8 5                            ♣ Q J 6
                         SOUTH
                      ♠ Q 10 9 8 6
                      ♡ 5 3
                      ◇ A K Q
                      ♣ A 7 3
```

SOUTH	WEST	NORTH	EAST
1 ♠	Pass	2 ♣	Pass
2 ♠	Pass	3 ♠	Pass
4 ♠	Pass	Pass	Pass

West leads the king of hearts, and you win in dummy with the ace. You expect to lose a heart, a club, and at least one trump. You have a better chance to limit the trump loss if you get the opponents to lead trumps.

At the second trick you return dummy's jack of hearts. Apparently you want to ruff a heart or two in dummy.

West takes the queen of hearts and may very well return a trump. If so, you are home.

√ INDUCING DISCARDS

The opponents tend to hold the suits that *you* keep and to discard from the suits that you show no interest in. Naturally, you can often paint the wrong picture for them. That is, you can carefully hold onto all cards of a suit that means nothing to you; and contrariwise, you can discard from a suit in which you are vitally inter-ested.

An example:

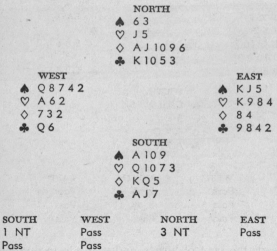

```
                    NORTH
                  ♠ 6 3
                  ♡ J 5
                  ◇ A J 10 9 6
                  ♣ K 10 5 3
    WEST                              EAST
  ♠ Q 8 7 4 2                       ♠ K J 5
  ♡ A 6 2                           ♡ K 9 8 4
  ◇ 7 3 2                           ◇ 8 4
  ♣ Q 6                             ♣ 9 8 4 2
                    SOUTH
                  ♠ A 10 9
                  ♡ Q 10 7 3
                  ◇ K Q 5
                  ♣ A J 7
```

SOUTH	WEST	NORTH	EAST
1 NT	Pass	3 NT	Pass
Pass	Pass		

West leads the four of spades, and you hold up your ace until the third round. What do you discard from dummy on the third spade?

When the hand was actually played, declarer discarded a low *club* from dummy. He needed only three club tricks for his contract and wanted to encourage the opponents to discard clubs also.

Declarer then ran the five diamonds. On the third diamond, East had to find a discard while everybody else was following suit. He incautiously discarded a club. On the next diamond he discarded another club.

South had no trouble in deducing that West had the queen of clubs.

✓ PUTTING DECLARER TO THE GUESS

As a defender you often have chances to lead through a king or a king-jack. The idea is to get a trick for your partner's queen (if he has it).

This is usually done after you have seen the dummy. In one famous hand the deception began with the opening lead:

```
                    NORTH
                  ♠ K J 3
                  ♡ 7
                  ◊ A Q 7 4
                  ♣ K Q 9 4 2
     WEST                              EAST
   ♠ A 5 4                           ♠ Q 10 7 6
   ♡ 8 4 3 2                         ♡ 10 5
   ◊ K 9 6                           ◊ J 10 5 3 2
   ♣ A 10 7                          ♣ 6 3
                    SOUTH
                  ♠ 9 8 2
                  ♡ A K Q J 9 6
                  ◊ 8
                  ♣ J 8 5
```

WEST	NORTH	EAST	SOUTH
Pass	1 ♣	Pass	1 ♡
Pass	2 ◊	Pass	3 ♡
Pass	3 NT	Pass	4 ♡
Pass	Pass	Pass	

The odd bidding was based on the fact that P. Hal Sims was South. His wife was North, and the hand was played against Ely and Josephine Culbertson in their 150-rubber match of 1935.

Sims did not encourage his partners to bid notrump, and Mrs. Sims did her best to get her husband to bid it. He not only declined to bid notrump but also refused to stay there when his partner bid it.

Mrs. Culbertson analyzed the bidding and came to the conclusion that the dummy would have broken spade strength and that declarer (since he had failed to bid notrump) would have no spade strength. She therefore led the four of spades.

Mrs. Culbertson's analysis was, as usual, quite correct. What's more, an opening lead away from the ace is so rare against a suit contract that Sims never for a moment considered playing dummy's king.

Sims played low from dummy, assuming that Mrs. Culbertson had led from the queen or queen-ten. Culbertson won the first trick with the ten of spades, carefully masking his surprise.

Culbertson returned a club to the ace, and Mrs. Culbertson calmly led the five of spades through dummy!

Sims, a giant of a man, glowered at the petite Mrs. Culbertson, snorted, and played the jack from dummy. He refused to believe that she could have had the effrontery to try to hornswoggle the great Hal Sims.

Naturally, Culbertson took the queen of spades and returned a spade to the ace, defeating the contract.

✓ THE DEFENSIVE HOLD-UP

As we have noted earlier, it seldom pays to grab your king promptly when declarer takes a *repeatable* finesse. This is the basic situation:

NORTH
♠ A Q J 10

WEST
♠ 6 5 4

EAST
♠ K 3 2

SOUTH
♠ 9 8 7

South leads a spade and finesses dummy's ten. East should casually play low.

East will get his king later on; such tricks don't run away. In the meantime South may misplay the hand on the assumption that the finesse is going to "work" the next time also.

For example, South may open up a dangerous suit to get back to his hand for a second spade finesse. Or he may give up some other line of play (that would succeed) on the assumption that the spades will come in.

The same principle is true, in general, when you have the ace behind the king-queen. For example:

NORTH
♠ K Q 10
♡ 9 5 2
♢ K J 6
♣ K J 9 6

WEST
♠ J 8 7 2
♡ J 8 6 3
♢ 10 7 4 2
♣ 3

EAST
♠ A 6 5
♡ Q 10 4
♢ 8 5 3
♣ Q 10 8 7

SOUTH
♠ 9 4 3
♡ A K 7
♢ A Q 9
♣ A 5 4 2

SOUTH	WEST	NORTH	EAST
1 NT	Pass	3 NT	Pass
Pass	Pass		

When this hand was played, West opened the deuce of spades. Declarer played the king from dummy, and East played the five of spades without apparent thought.

East didn't have to think because this is a situation that ought to be familiar to an expert. There is nothing to gain from taking the first trick unless you have to grab all of your tricks on the run.

Declarer led a club to the ace and returned a club toward the dummy. West discarded a diamond, and declarer saw that he would get nowhere with the clubs.

South won with the king of clubs in dummy, and decided to play for a second spade trick in order to make the contract. He got to his hand with a diamond and led a spade toward dummy.

West played low, and South wavered. If West were a bad player, he would either play the ace (if he had it) or show enough indecision to make it plain that he held the ace. Since West was a good player, South couldn't tell what was going on. West might play low very quickly even if he had the ace.

After much indecision of his own, South put up the queen of spades from dummy. Down one.

If East had taken the very first trick with the ace of spades, South would have finessed dummy's ten of spades later. This would have given him his contract.

✓ IN SHORT

When you are declarer you owe no duty of frankness to the opponents. When the situation calls for it you may falsecard, make phony discards, take fake finesses, and steal the teeth out of your opponents' heads.

When you are a defender, beware of fooling your partner as well as the declarer. Sometimes your partner is the only player at the table who doesn't know what is going on. But when your partner cannot be seriously misled, do what you can to lead declarer up the garden path.

Your object is to be a dependable partner, a dangerous opponent.

32nd DAY

THIRD REVIEW AND SELF-TESTING QUIZZES

19th Through 31st Days

You are now ready to try your hand on the last quiz and rate yourself as declarer and defender in the various situations covered in the lessons on THE PLAY OF THE CARDS of the preceding thirteen days.

Begin with question 156 on page 460 and work your way through to the last question, 199. Then check yourself against the answers that begin on page 479.

40 or more right	excellent
36—39 right	good
33—38 right	fair
Below 33 right	you need more study

Refer back to the chapters covering the material on which you had incorrect answers. A little study now will earn thousands of points later.

This includes the main part of the home-study course. Before closing the book and throwing yourself into the nearest bridge game, read the material for the 33rd and 34th days. These extra features—Modern Bidding Conventions and Manners, Morals and Laws—have been included to broaden your knowledge of the fascinating game of bridge.

Then turn to the 35th day, Final Review, which wraps up the full five-week course. However, note that an extra handy-reference section is included for post-graduate study.

IV

FINAL

TOUCHES

AND REVIEW

33rd DAY

MODERN BIDDING CONVENTIONS

√ The Blackwood Convention	√ Weak Jump Responses
√ The Gerber Convention	√ The Unusual Notrump
√ The Stayman Convention	√ Inverted Minor-Suit Raises
√ The Fishbein Convention	√ Jacoby Transfer Bid
√ Cheaper Minor for Takeout	√ The Texas Convention
√ The Landy Convention	√ The Drury Convention
√ Weak Notrumps	√ Italian Bidding Systems
√ Five-Card Majors	*The Roman Club*
√ Aces over Two-Bids	*The Neapolitan Club*
√ Weak Two-Bids	*Roman Blackwood*
√ Weak Jump Overcalls	

A BIDDING CONVENTION is a partnership understanding about the meaning of a bid or of a bidding sequence. Sometimes the partners agree that a bid is to indicate something very different from its natural meaning; sometimes the agreed-upon meaning is fairly close to the natural one.

Whenever two partners agree to use a bidding convention, they should explain it carefully to their opponents. In some cases it is necessary only to name the convention because the opponents are quite familiar with it. If you play mostly in the same game, it isn't necessary to say much about conventions, since the other players already know all about your little foibles.

An experienced player should familiarize himself with each of the widely used conventions. In some cases he will like the convention well enough to adopt it; in any case he will have a better idea of what his opponents mean by their bids.

√ THE BLACKWOOD CONVENTION

The Blackwood Convention begins with a bid of four notrump, which asks partner to show how many aces he holds. A later bid of five notrump may be used to ask partner how many kings he holds.

The method is described in full in Chapter 7, How to Bid Your Slams.

√ THE GERBER CONVENTION

A bid of four clubs is used to ask partner how many aces he holds. A later bid of five clubs asks partner how many kings he has. See Chapter 7, How to Bid Your Slams.

√ THE STAYMAN CONVENTION

In response to an opening bid of one notrump, two clubs is bid to find out whether or not the opener has four or more cards in a major suit. The object is to play the hand at the major suit if a good fit can be found.

See Chapter 3, How to Handle Your Notrumps.

√ THE FISHBEIN CONVENTION

SOUTH	WEST	NORTH	EAST
3 ◇	3 ♡		

West's bid of three hearts, when the Fishbein Convention is used, asks East to bid his longest suit (or to pass with heart length and a poor hand). In effect, therefore, this bid of the *cheapest suit* after a shutout bid is a take-out double. West might have:

♠ K Q 7 3   ♥ A J 10 4   ♦ 5   ♣ K Q 8 5

The double is reserved for *penalties*. A bid of three no-trump is natural, not for takeout. If the opening bid is three spades, the takeout bid is four clubs, not three no-trump.

The Fishbein Convention is used only in the *direct* position (immediately after the pre-emptive bid), not in the reopening position.

SOUTH	WEST	NORTH	EAST
3 ♦	Pass	Pass	3 ♥

East has a normal heart bid. If East doubled in this position, it is for takeout, not for penalties.

The Fishbein Convention is useful chiefly against the kind of player who opens with three of a horribly weak suit. Such players are encountered occasionally in tournaments but seldom in rubber bridge or home games. Against such players it is useful to be able to double for penalties.

If your opponents seldom or never open with a bid of three in a horribly ragged suit, the Fishbein Convention is useless. The normal takeout double is far more useful against opponents who bid normally.

✓ CHEAPER MINOR FOR TAKEOUT

This resembles the Fishbein Convention in that you bid a suit to get your partner to take out—after the bidding has been opened with a shutout bid. The double is reserved for penalties, as in Fishbein.

Instead of bidding the cheapest suit for takeout, you

use the cheaper of the two minor suits—clubs and diamonds.

SOUTH	WEST	NORTH	EAST
3 ♡	4 ♣		

West wants East to bid his best suit. East may pass, however, if he has club length and a poor hand.

This convention often allows you to bid three of a major suit as a natural bid. For example, over an opening bid of three diamonds you may bid either three spades or three hearts to show a good suit and a good hand. You might bid three hearts with:

♠ A 7   ♡ K Q J 9 7 3   ◇ 4   ♣ Q J 6 5

Partner is expected to raise if he has two or more trumps, with about an ace or a king anywhere in the unbid suits. If he has less, he may pass and the partnership is not in hot water.

The convention suffers from the same disadvantages as Fishbein. In addition, the takeout bid is usually four clubs (it can be three diamonds only if the opening bid has been three clubs), so that the partnership is almost always at game level.

It is somewhat more useful when used over weak two-bids, when the takeout bid is *three* clubs.

Neither the Fishbein Convention nor the Cheaper Minor is recommended to the casual player.

✓ THE LANDY CONVENTION

When your right-hand opponent opens with a weak no-trump (12 to 14 points), you bid two clubs to ask for a takeout.

SOUTH	WEST	NORTH	EAST
1 NT	2 ♣		

This bid does not promise club length. It asks partner to bid his best suit. Responder may pass with club length and a weak hand.

Most experts use the bid of two clubs with a hand of about 13 to 15 points. They double with 16 points or more.

The players in my own circle bid two clubs for takeout with scattered strength when there is no good suit to lead. They double to show a good attacking opening lead with enough high cards as entries to run the suit.

♠ Q J 10 9 7 4   ♡ K 5 2   ◇ A 3   ♣ A 2

Double the opening bid of one notrump. You will lead the queen of spades and expect to get four spade tricks, the two aces, and perhaps the king of hearts.

♠ K J 9 4   ♡ K J 5 4   ◇ A 9 3   ♣ A 2

Bid two clubs. You haven't the faintest notion of whether or not you can beat one notrump. You do expect to be fairly comfortable in partner's longest suit.

The Landy Convention is used by most players only over *weak* notrumps and only in the *direct* position.

SOUTH	WEST	NORTH	EAST
1 NT	Pass	Pass	2 ♣

East has a club suit. He is not asking for a takeout. If East had general strength, he would double.

Some players use Landy in either position. Some also use it against the strong notrump (16 to 18 points).

✓ WEAK NOTRUMPS

The opening bid of one notrump shows balanced distribution and only 12 to 14 points instead of the customary 16 to 18 points. The opening bidder does not promise stoppers in any particular number of suits and may have a worthless doubleton.

A typical opening bid of one notrump:

♠ K J 9 3   ♡ Q 8 5 2   ◇ 4 2   ♣ A K 4

The opening bidder should avoid opening on 12-point hands with less than 2 Quick Tricks, or on 12-point hands in general when vulnerable. (Some players use the weak notrump only when not vulnerable.)

The opener shows a hand of 15 to 17 points by opening in a minor suit and making a rebid of one notrump:

SOUTH	NORTH
1 ♣	1 ♡
1 NT	

South has a balanced hand, since otherwise he would rebid in a suit rather than in notrump. His hand is too good for an opening bid of one notrump and therefore must lie between 15 and 17 points. With 18 points South would jump to *two* notrump at his second turn.

Responder to a weak notrump should not consider game unless he has about 12 points or more (roughly an opening bid). With balanced distribution and 11 points responder should pass the opening bid and lie in wait for the last player. Many opponents consider it beneath their dignity to be kept out of the bidding by a weak notrump, but their dignity often costs them dear.

Responder should take out at once into a 5-card or longer major suit. The Stayman Convention (described in Chapter 3, How to Handle Your Notrumps) is used with hands of 11 points or more in high cards. Responder may raise the opening bid to two notrump with 12 points (or with 11 points and a strong 5-card suit); to three notrump with 13 points or more.

(The weak notrump is the keystone of the Kaplan-Sheinwold System, described quite fully in *How to Play Winning Bridge,* by Edgar Kaplan and Alfred Sheinwold.)

When playing against the weak notrump, avoid over-calling with mediocre balanced hands. Overcall with a mediocre hand only when you have very good distribution. (See the description of the Landy Convention earlier in this chapter.)

√ FIVE-CARD MAJORS

The opening bid of one in a major suit promises a 5-card or longer suit. With no major suit of five cards or more, a player may open in a 3-card (or longer) minor suit.

♠ A K 8 3   ♥ K J 9 4   ♦ J 9 4   ♣ K 3

Bid one diamond. Neither major suit may be bid. Since you must bid a minor suit, choose the longer minor. If partner can respond in a major, you will raise.

Responder always bids a major suit when he has four or more cards (no matter how weak) in either major. With four of each major, responder bids hearts.

SOUTH	NORTH
1 ♦	?

♠ J 5   ♥ Q 7 6 3   ♦ K 8 5 3   ♣ 8 4 2

Bid one heart. Show the 4-card major.

♠ Q J 5 4   ♡ Q 7 6 3   ◇ K 8   ♣ 8 4 2

Bid one heart. If partner has hearts, he will raise. If he has spades, he can conveniently bid one spade, and you will raise.

♠ Q J 5 4 2   ♡ A Q 6 3   ◇ 8   ♣ 8 4 2

Bid one spade. If partner fails to raise, you will bid hearts at your next turn. This sequence shows five spades, for otherwise you would have bid one heart first.

Most experts who promise 5-card major suits treat the response of one notrump as a force for one round.

SOUTH	NORTH
1 ♠	1 NT

South promises to bid again. A rebid in spades shows a 6-card suit. A rebid in hearts shows a biddable suit of four or more cards. If South does not have the requirements for a rebid in a major suit (or for a raise in notrump), he may bid a minor suit (even a 3-card suit if necessary).

SOUTH	NORTH
1 ♠	1 NT
?	

♠ A J 9 7 5 4   ♡ A 9 4   ◇ K 5   ♣ 5 2

Bid two spades. The 6-card suit may be rebid.

♠ A Q J 5 4   ♡ A 9 4 2   ◇ K 5   ♣ 5 2

Bid two hearts. Shows at least a 4-card suit.

♠ A Q J 5 4   ♡ A 9 4   ◇ K 5 2   ♣ 5 2

Bid two diamonds. For lack of any other rebid, the 3-card minor is chosen.

♠ A Q J 5 4   ♥ 5 2   ♦ A 9 4   ♣ K 5 2

Bid two clubs. When you have a choice of 3-card minors, prefer clubs. This gives partner a maximum of leeway.

At his second turn, responder may pass the new suit or may return to the 5-card major. If, instead, responder bids a new suit, this shows a long suit but a poor hand. Responder may rebid notrump with 10 points or more.

SOUTH	NORTH
1 ♠	1 NT
2 ♣	?

♠ 6   ♥ 8 5 3   ♦ J 9 6 3   ♣ A J 9 6 3

Pass. Even though opener may have only three clubs you like that suit far better.

♠ 6   ♥ K 5 3   ♦ J 9 6 3   ♣ A J 9 6 3

Bid three clubs. This shows club length, spade short-ness, and 10 points or more (counting high cards and distribution).

♠ 6 2   ♥ 8 5 3   ♦ J 9 6 3   ♣ A J 9 6

Bid two spades. Partner surely has a 5-card spade suit. Your doubleton is enough support for a low contract.

♠ 6   ♥ 8 5 2   ♦ Q J 9 6 4 3   ♣ A J 9

Bid two diamonds. This shows long diamonds, short spades, and a poor hand.

Five-card majors are highly recommended to all play-ers. This convention combines beautifully with the weak notrump.

✓ ACES OVER TWO-BIDS

In response to a strong two-bid, responder bids any suit of which he has the ace. With more than one ace, responder makes some drastic bid—but practically no two experts agree on what he should do.

The convention is useful when the opening bidder has a solid suit with clearly defined losers and perhaps a void suit. In such situations the opener is delighted to find out which ace (if any) his partner has.

When the opener has the more common type of strong two-bid he is interested first in his partner's suit lengths. Only after a good trump suit has been found does the opener want to know about aces.

This is one of the very few conventions that I refuse to play, even at a partner's request. I have never heard a fine analyst say a good word for it, but a few successful players swear by it.

✓ WEAK TWO-BIDS

(See also pages 83–87, Chapter 6, Two-Bids—
Strong and Weak)

An opening two-bid in spades, hearts, or diamonds shows a good suit but slightly less than a normal opening bid's total strength.

The opening bid of *two clubs* is reserved for game-going hands in all suits. Partner's negative response is two diamonds.

The best defense against a weak two-bid is to treat it much like a one-bid, with a takeout double or overcall. Some players use Fishbein or Cheaper Minor Suit, described earlier in this chapter.

✓ WEAK JUMP OVERCALLS

(See also pages 133–135, in Chapter 10, Overcalls)

A single jump overcall shows a fairly good suit (usually topless) with no side strength worth mentioning. It is intended to rob the opponents of bidding room.

As in the case of all shutout bids (see Chapter 13, Shutout Bids), the idea is to show a defenseless hand. Partner can then judge the defensive value of the partnership and decide whether or not to sacrifice at a higher level.

One of the chief advantages of using weak jump overcalls is that your non-jump overcalls are then known to be fairly strong. Partner can raise a non-jump overcall with a light hand—almost as though it were an opening bid.

Used boldly, weak jump overcalls are very valuable. If you're going to wait for a very powerful distributional hand for such a bid, however, give it up and use the jump overcall for strong hands.

✓ WEAK JUMP RESPONSES

The jump takeout in a new suit (which in most systems is a very strong bid, forcing to game) may be used, instead, to show a long topless suit and no side strength whatever.

SOUTH	NORTH
1 ◇	2 ♠

North has some such hand as:

♠ Q J 10 6 5 3 2   ♡ 5 4   ◇ 8 6   ♣ 5 2

If the spades and clubs were reversed, North would jump to three clubs.

This convention works quite well with this kind of hand opposite an opening bid. In ordinary systems, responder has no way of showing a topless suit with no side strength. If responder bids, his partner almost surely assumes he has more strength; if responder passes he misses a good chance to rob the opponents of bidding room, and may even miss a good contract at his long suit. A further advantage of using the convention is that the responder is known to have strength when he makes a non-jump response in a new suit and merely rebids his suit at the next opportunity; if he had just length in his suit, he would have made a jump response to begin with.

There are grave disadvantages also. It becomes difficult to handle the very powerful responding hands, since you cannot show your strength by way of a jump response. These hands are about as infrequent as the topless long suits just discussed, but they are far more important since they usually involve small or grand slams.

Another disadvantage for average players is the difficulty of remembering that the jump shows a weak hand. If you forgetfully make the jump with a powerful hand and your partner obediently passes, you may play a slam hand at a part score!

⩗ THE UNUSUAL NOTRUMP

A competitive bid of one or two notrump, usually made as a reopening bid to induce partner to bid a minor suit. (See Chapter 17, Reopening the Bidding.)

⩗ INVERTED MINOR-SUIT RAISES

A raise from one to two of partner's minor suit shows a strong hand (forcing for one round).

A raise from one to three of partner's minor suit shows a weak hand (shutout bid).

This convention, invented by Edgar Kaplan, has two distinct advantages over "standard" bidding:

- The partnership has ample room for exploration with strong hands.
- The opponents are robbed of bidding room when the hands of the bidding side are weak.

After partner's opening bid of one diamond, for example:

♠ 8 7   ♥ 7 5 2   ♦ A J 8 5   ♣ K Q 8 2

Bid two diamonds. If partner is interested in notrump, he can bid a suit that he can stop, and you will then show the clubs.

♠ 8 7   ♥ 7 5 2   ♦ K J 8 5 3 2   ♣ 8 2

Bid three diamonds. You promise good diamond support but nothing else. If this is enough for partner, he can go on. Your own intention is to interfere with the bidding of the opponents.

✓ JACOBY TRANSFER BID

In response to an opening bid of one notrump, the responder bids the suit lower than his true suit. This asks the opener to bid the responder's true suit.

RESPONSE	OPENER MUST REBID
2 ♦	2 ♥
2 ♥	2 ♠
2 ♠	3 ♣
3 ♣	3 ♦

One advantage is that the strong hand (16 to 18 points) is concealed and gets the advantage of the opening lead. Another is that the responder can make a transfer bid and then raise the forced rebid. This invites a game but does not force to game.

When responder has a freakish hand that may gain from being concealed, he can respond to the notrump bid with a jump to three (in any suit but clubs) as a normal forcing bid.

This bidding device, invented by Oswald Jacoby, is recommended for use with the strong notrump provided that the partners can remember what they are doing. Like the Texas Convention, below, it suffers more from the players' faulty memory than from any technical defect.

✔ THE TEXAS CONVENTION

In response to an opening bid of one notrump, a jump to four diamonds asks the opener to bid four hearts; a jump to four hearts asks the opener to bid four spades. (A jump to four clubs is the Gerber Convention.)

Like the Jacoby Transfer Bid, this convention is often forgotten in the heat of the fray. Not recommended for casual partnerships.

✔ THE DRURY CONVENTION

A bidding device invented by Douglas Drury to enable a player to find out whether or not a third-hand or fourth-hand opening bid is sound.

SOUTH	WEST	NORTH	EAST
Pass	Pass	1 ♠	Pass
2 ♣			

The bid of two clubs asks North to state whether or not he has a sound opening bid. If North has a substandard hand, he bids two diamonds; otherwise he makes some other bid to describe his hand.

Few players have adopted the Drury Convention.

✓ ITALIAN BIDDING SYSTEMS

Two very complicated and artificial bidding systems —the Neapolitan Club and the Roman Club—are used by the Italian bridge team, winners of the world championship for three years in a row. To play either system well it is necessary to memorize many bids that mean things very different from what they seem to mean.

It may be desirable to know the general idea of each of these systems in case some enterprising pair uses one of the systems *against* you. The summaries that follow are based on those that were presented by the American Contract Bridge League to assist spectators at the 1959 World Championship.

THE ROMAN CLUB

This system has been played in world championships by Walter Avarelli and Giorgio Belladonna.

Opening bid

One club—Artificial, showing one of three hand types:
1. Weak notrump, balanced hand, 12 to 16 points
2. Balanced distribution, 21 to 25 points
3. Unbalanced strong hand, equivalent of forcing two-bid

Conventional responses:

One diamond—less than 8-9 points
Two notrump—more than 16 points
Opener's rebid reveals nature of one-club opening:

Type A—Simple suit bid, or one notrump, or raise of
partner's response

Type B—Jump rebid in notrump

Type C—Jump rebid in suit, which requires responder
to show length by "step" responses

Other Opening Suit Bids of One: Suit of at least four
cards, forcing for one round; artificial response in next
higher-ranking suit indicates minimum hand. Response
in any other suit shows 9-11 points; response of one notrump shows 12-16; jump to two notrump, more than 16
points.

Opener's Rebid: Reverse bid or jump in original suit
shows strength. Rebid of one notrump after a negative
response shows 5-card length in responder's suit. In general, opener's second suit is always playable; his first suit
need not be.

Opening Bid of One Notrump: Balanced hand, 17 to
20 points. Responder may pass with 0 to 5 points. Response of two clubs asks for the size of the notrump;
opener bids two diamonds to show 17 or 18, or two
hearts to show 19 or 20 points. Response of two in any
suit but clubs is forcing to game; opener rebids by
"steps" to show his strength and whether or not he has
support for responder's suit.

Opening Bids of Two in a Suit: Two spades shows a
two-suiter, in spades and clubs; two hearts, in hearts and
clubs. Two diamonds shows a three-suiter (4-4-4-1 or
5-4-4-0) of 17 points or more; two clubs shows a three-
suiter of 16 points or less. Two notrump shows a two-
suiter in diamonds and clubs.

Opening Bids of Three in a Suit: Solid suit with a side
ace or king. Invites response of three notrump.

Jump Overcall: Weak two-suiter, including suit higher
than the one named.

Jump Overcall of Two Notrump: Strong two-suiter.

THE NEAPOLITAN CLUB

This system has been played in world championships by Pietro Forquet, Guglielmo Siniscalco, Eugenio Chiaradia, and Massimo D'Alelio.

One Club: Artificial. At least 17 points in high cards or a strong distributional hand; forcing for at least one round.

Responses to One Club Show Controls: (Ace-2; King-1) one diamond shows 0; one heart, 1; one spade, 2; one notrump, 4; two clubs, 3; two diamonds, 5; two notrump, 6 or more. Response of two spades or two hearts shows 6-card suit without controls; three hearts or three spades shows 7-card suit; four hearts or four spades shows 8-card suit.

One Diamond, One Heart, One Spade: 12 to 17 points, 4-card or longer suit.

Responses: Pass with less than 6 points. Response in new suit is forcing for one round. If responder bids two suits, his second suit is playable; his first suit need not be. Jump raise of opener's suit shows 9 to 12 points, not forcing. Jump response of two notrump shows 11 or 12 points, not forcing.

Opening Bid of One Notrump: 12 to 17 points, with length in clubs but in no other suit. Responder may bid two clubs with weak hand that includes two or more clubs.

Opening Two Clubs: 12 to 17 points. Two-suiter, in clubs and another suit. Response of two diamonds is non-committal and asks opener to show his other suit.

Opening Two-Bid in Other Suit: Weak two-bid, similar to those described in Chapter 6, Two-Bids—Strong and Weak.

Opening Two Notrump: Long solid suit other than clubs. Response of three clubs asks opener to show suit.

Three Clubs: Similar to opening bid of two notrump, but with clubs as real suit.

Rebid in Second Suit: Reverse and jump rebids shows strength and playable length in the second suit. The first suit, in such cases, need not be playable.

ROMAN BLACKWOOD

The Roman responses to the Blackwood Convention attempt to identify the aces held by the responder. The bids of four and five notrump are exactly the same as in standard Blackwood, but the responses are different:

Number of Aces	*Response to 4 NT*
None or three	5 ♣
One or four	5 ◇
Two matching aces	5 ♡
Two unmatched aces	5 ♠

The matching aces are:

hearts and diamonds (both red)
spades and clubs (both black)
spades and hearts (both major suits)
diamonds and clubs (both minor suits)

The unmatched aces are:

spades and diamonds, or
hearts and clubs

After the response to four notrump, a bid of five notrump guarantees that the partnership holds all of the aces, and asks for kings. The responses follow the same scheme:

Number of Kings	*Response to 5 NT*
None or three	6 ♣
One or four	6 ♦
Two matching kings	6 ♥
Two unmatched kings	6 ♠

Roman Blackwood may give the partnership important information when the response shows two aces or (more especially) two kings. If a player has one ace and gets a response of five spades to four notrump, he knows just which two aces his partner has:

Single Ace	*Responder's Aces*
spades	hearts-clubs
hearts	spades-diamonds
diamonds	hearts-clubs
clubs	spades-diamonds

When the response is five hearts, the aces are not completely identified but one ace is known:

Single Ace	*Responder's Aces*
spades	hearts-diamonds or diamonds-clubs
hearts	spades-clubs or clubs-diamonds
diamonds	hearts-spades or spades-clubs
clubs	spades-hearts or hearts-diamonds

The information thus gained may permit the partnership to play the hand safely at six notrump rather than six of a suit. This is important in match-point tournament play, but not in rubber bridge.

When a response of six spades or six hearts is made to five notrump, however, the advantage may be far greater. With one king missing, the partnership may still safely bid a grand slam when the missing king is not in a *key* suit (trumps or the longest side suit). Contrariwise, the partnership may decide to stay out of a risky grand slam when it is clear that the missing king is in a key suit.

If one partner is using standard Blackwood and the other is using Roman Blackwood, the opponents will be greatly amused. Never take it for granted that you are playing Roman Blackwood unless you and your partner have agreed to do so and have notified the opponents of your intention.

34th DAY
mmmmmmmmmm

MANNERS, MORALS AND LAWS

√ Bridge Etiquette	√ Reading the Opponents
√ Kibitzing	√ Bridge Laws
√ Table Talk	√ Simplified Digest of New Official
√ Bridge Language	Bridge Laws—Revised 1963
√ Intonation	√ Losing and Winning

IF YOU ALWAYS PLAYED BRIDGE with the same small group, you could make up your own rules and set your own standards of conduct. Who could object if you played all slam hands standing up or counted all spade hands at double their normal value?

Actually, we all play bridge with acquaintances and strangers as well as with close friends. The only way to avoid friction is to stick to an accepted code of etiquette, ethics, and laws in all bridge games.

There is such a generally accepted code. All good players know it. Most casual players don't. As a result the casual bridge player sometimes finds himself in an awkward position even though he had the best intentions in the world.

This is not of earth-shaking importance. If you always act reasonably and with good will, no other reasonable people of good will can find fault with you.

Still . . . it doesn't hurt to know—just in case somebody someday is *un*reasonable.

✓ BRIDGE ETIQUETTE

Certain practices have become traditional with bridge players; certain others are viewed with disfavor.

For example, you're supposed to wait until the dealer finishes dealing and begins to pick up his own cards before you pick up any of your cards. The idea is that he should have as much time as anybody else to study his hand.

In some games you see the dummy put trumps down before the opening lead is made. No law or tradition or point of etiquette ever required the dummy to put trumps (or any other cards) down on the table before the opening lead. This is a good habit to *break*, if you have it; it gives the opening leader an undeserved advantage.

When you are the dummy, don't look at either opponent's hand. Don't ask your partner to pass his hand across the table so that you can follow what he is doing. Above all, don't get up from your chair and stand behind the declarer while he plays the hand.

However, if you get up, when dummy, to bring refreshments to the players, nobody will hate you for sneaking a quick look at your partner's hand before you go off to do your chores.

In all other cases, sit still and try to look placid and relaxed. It's good for the soul.

√ KIBITZING

There is etiquette even for the kibitzer. Sit behind one player and sit still. Don't look at one hand and then at another; you give the impression that the first hand wasn't good enough to interest you.

As a kibitzer, avoid saying anything at all during the bidding or play—no matter how strong the provocation. Once, in a national tournament, a kibitzer doubled an especially horrible contract, and it has remained an exploit celebrated in verse and song—largely because it is so unusual for a kibitzer ever to utter a word.

If you happen to kibitz a serious match, maintain your silence even between hands. The players need freedom from distraction to keep concentrated.

If you are kibitzing friends in a casual game, you're the best judge of what to say and how to say it. But if there's any doubt, you can't go wrong by saying less rather than more.

√ TABLE TALK

Table conversation in general varies with the players and the game. As a mere man, I wouldn't dream of saying how much conversation is proper in a ladies' afternoon game.

In a serious game, general conversation is not welcome. If you want to find out where one of the other players buys his cigars or if you have a particularly juicy bit of gossip to pass on, let it wait until the game is over.

What about post mortems? How fully should you discuss the bidding or play of the hand just concluded?

Not to exhaustion. Don't tear a hand or a player to bits. If your partner has bid a hand like a lunatic and has played it even worse, just say "Bad luck" and let it go at that. If he is a good player, he will be grateful for your restraint; if he is not, give him a copy of this book and save your breath.

√ BRIDGE LANGUAGE

The language of bridge is limited to exactly fifteen words:

> pass, double, redouble
> one, two, three, four, five, six, seven
> notrump, spades, hearts, diamonds, clubs

That is all.

Do not say "Bye" or "Bye me" when you mean *pass.* When a contract has been doubled, do not say "Content."

When you are doubling a contract, don't say "I'll double that one," or "Double one spade," or anything else of the sort. Only one word—*double*—is proper.

If your accent is British or Bostonian, your "Pass" may sound like "Heart." In that case it is permissible to adopt the British practice of saying "No bid" rather than "Pass." If you do this, make it a point to say "No bid" always; never say "Pass."

Do not say "Club" or "Spade" when you mean "One club" or "One spade." You might accidentally get into the habit of saying "Club" for a mediocre hand and "*One* club" for a strong hand—which would be very severely censured if anybody noticed it. All of this can be avoided if you limit yourself to the approved bridge language.

✓ INTONATION

It is the most natural thing in the world for people to act like human beings—even in a bridge game. The better the player, the less human he must act.

When the average player gets a strong hand, he sits up and looks cheerful. He bids in a hearty voice. He doubles an opponent in a thunderous tone.

All of this is reversed when our hero has a poor hand. He slumps in his chair or glances away from the table. He looks pained or fearful. He bids, if he must, in an anguished whisper.

All very human—and all very revolting to the expert! The expert wants everybody to make every bid in the same tone of voice, with the same expression.

Bridge is a game of skill and judgment, not a contest of histrionics. You are entitled to base your judgment on your partner's bid, but not his tone of voice; on the card he has played, but not the manner in which he has played it.

We all occasionally slip. But when we do, our partner should not take advantage of the information that has been improperly conveyed by our intonation. If necessary, partner must lean over backward in order to be upright.

For example, suppose both sides have been bidding on a hand. At some point you double the opponents. As it happens, your double sounds very doubtful. Your partner is not entitled to take advantage of that note of doubt. If he has a borderline hand, he should pass your double—just as he would if you had doubled with vim and venom. He is entitled to take your double out only if he has absolutely clear-cut grounds for action.

In a casual game nobody lives up to this strict code of ethics. Nobody complains, partly because the tone of doubt may be bad judgment to begin with; and the partner is usually a million miles away in a world of his own and doesn't hear his partner's tone of voice.

In an expert game everybody is expected to live up to the code. (When a player doesn't he may be regarded as a petty crook.) Everybody is "at the table" all of the time, and nobody is tone deaf.

In a mixed game of experts and amateurs, the wind is tempered to the shorn lamb. He is forgiven for his violations because everybody realizes that he doesn't know the code. The transgressing *expert,* however, gets black looks and a blacker reputation.

✓ READING THE OPPONENTS

As we have seen, you're not entitled to take advantage of information you get from your partner's tone, manner, or hesitation. Should you use information of this sort that you get from the *opponents?*

You're fully entitled to do so.

For example, suppose you lead the jack of trumps from dummy, wondering whether to finesse for the queen or play for the drop. The opponent at your right thinks, hesitates, and fumbles with one card and then another. Finally he plays a small card.

Are you entitled to assume that this opponent has the queen of trumps?

You are.

What if it turns out that the opponent doesn't have the queen of trumps after all?

He has cheated you.

The only possible excuse for his action is that he is an inexperienced player and doesn't know that his action was an offense against bridge ethics.

Mind you, the same sort of deceptive action would

be perfectly legitimate—even praiseworthy—in poker and in some other games. But not in bridge.

It's largely a matter of the tradition. In bridge you're not supposed to try to deceive your opponents by your *manner*. If you go into a huddle, you should have something to think about. Nobody will believe you if you later say, "I was wondering where I parked the car."

It may seem illogical that your opponent is entitled to notice your hesitations and draw inferences from them while you are not allowed to throw him a fake hesitation now and then. However, this is part of the bridge code of ethics.

This need not concern you in a casual game of bridge. In a difficult match you should try to slow down your speedy plays and to speed up your slow plays so as to maintain an even tempo. If you can do this successfully, your opponents will not be able to read anything from your manner.

✓ BRIDGE LAWS

Nobody likes a clubhouse lawyer. In a casual session of bridge, pay very little attention to the laws of the game. They are meant for serious games and tournaments.

The trouble with adopting this easygoing attitude is that you may wonder what to do when an opponent's irregularity injures you severely. If you dismiss the matter, you have been hurt; if you try to enforce the rule, your opponents may feel that they are being singled out for punishment.

There is no sure solution to this problem. Everybody expects strict enforcement of the laws in a tournament or a serious match. Nobody expects it in a friendly game, even in a club.

As a member of the National Laws and Rules Commission, I should write a serious lecture to persuade everybody to enforce the rules at all times no matter how casual the game is. I won't do it, because it just isn't practical.

Just for the record, however, we should go into the meaning of the laws that are most frequently looked up in the rulebook.

✓ SIMPLIFIED DIGEST OF NEW OFFICIAL BRIDGE LAWS REVISED 1963

The material that follows is a digest of the Official Laws of Contract Bridge, authorized by the National Laws Commission (of which the author is a member). Each law is explained by simple examples.

There is no need to read this through. Just glance at a few of the laws from time to time to familiarize yourself with their nature so that you can find them in time of need. The laws are arranged in the order of the normal bridge game: preliminaries to the rubber, bidding, play, and scoring.

When an irregularity occurs in your bridge game, look up the laws by title until you come to one that seems to fit. Then apply that law.

One law is cited so frequently that we state it first and will refer to it in the text of the laws:

Lead Penalty: When declarer may impose a lead penalty (as a result of certain irregularities cited in the laws that follow) he may specify a suit and either require the lead of that suit or forbid the lead of that suit for as long as the opponent retains the lead.

Example: South is declarer at four hearts, and East leads the queen of spades out of turn. South may require West to lead a spade; or he may forbid a spade lead. In the latter case, if West wins the first trick, he may not shift to spades; and if West wins both the first and second tricks he still may not lead a spade. The spade lead is forbidden until West loses the lead and regains it. If East gains the lead in the meantime, however, he is quite free to lead a spade. The prohibition is in effect only against West.

1. New Shuffle and Cut: Before the first card is dealt, any player may demand a new shuffle and cut. There must be a new shuffle and cut if a card is faced in shuffling or cutting.

2. Deal Out of Turn: The correct dealer may reclaim the deal before the last card is dealt. Thereafter the deal stands as if it had been in turn and the correct dealer loses his right to deal in that round.

3. Redeal: There must be a redeal if:

- the cards are not dealt correctly
- the pack is incorrect
- a card is faced in the pack or elsewhere
- a player picks up the wrong hand and looks at it
- at any time during the play one hand is found to have too many cards and another too few (provided the discrepancy is not caused by errors in play).

When there is a redeal the same dealer deals (unless the deal was out of turn) and with the same pack, after a new shuffle and cut.

4. **Incorrect Hand:** If a player has too few cards and the missing card is found (except in a previous trick), it is considered to have been in the short hand throughout. If it cannot be found, there is a redeal. If it is found in a previous trick, see *Defective Trick,* Law 28.

Example: South bids his hand and plays it down to the tenth trick, whereupon he discovers that he has one card fewer than any other player. Somebody sees a card on the floor, and it is discovered that this is the missing card, The card is put in South's hand, and it is presumed to have been in South's hand during the entire auction and play. If he has bid badly or revoked because of the absence of the card, he may ask for a crying towel—but he must pay the penalty.

5. **Enforcing a Penalty:** Either opponent (but not dummy) may select or enforce a penalty. If partners consult as to selection or enforcement, the right to penalize is canceled.

6. **Card Exposed During the Auction:** There is no penalty for exposing a single card lower than a ten. If the exposed card is an honor card, or any card prematurely led, or more than one card, each exposed card must be left face up on the table; the partner of the offender must pass at his next turn; and each exposed card becomes a penalty card if the other side plays the hand.

7. **Change of Call:** A player may change a call without penalty if he does so without pause. Any other attempted change of call is canceled. If the first call was an illegal call, it is subject to the applicable law; if it was a legal call, the offender may either

   (a) allow his first call to stand, whereupon his partner must pass at his next turn; or (*b*) substitute any legal call (including a pass, double, or redouble) whereupon his partner must pass at every subsequent turn.

8. Insufficient Bid: If a player makes an insufficient bid, he must substitute either a sufficient bid or a pass (not a double or a redouble.) If he substitutes

(*a*) the lowest sufficient bid in the same denomination, there is no penalty;

(*b*) any other bid, his partner must pass at every subsequent turn;

(*c*) a pass, his partner must pass at every turn and declarer (if an opponent) may impose a lead penalty (page 448). A double or redouble illegally substituted is considered a pass and is penalized in the same way.

The offender need not select his final call until the law has been stated; previous attempts at correction are canceled. (But Law 9 may apply.)

Example: East deals and bids one spade; South then bids one diamond.

If South corrects his bid to two diamonds there is no penalty.

If South changes his bid to three or more diamonds, or to any other sufficient bid, such as three notrump or four hearts or the like, North must pass for the rest of that auction. (*South* may bid again if he has further turns to bid.) If South bids anything but diamonds in the process of correcting his insufficient bid, Law 9 applies.

If South passes, North must pass for the rest of that auction (but South may bid again if he gets further turns to bid). Moreover, if West becomes declarer, he may call a lead penalty (page 448) against North (the offender's partner).

If South tries to correct his insufficient bid by doubling one spade, the double is canceled and is treated as a pass. North must pass for the rest of that auction, and if West becomes declarer, he may call a lead penalty (page 448) against North.

9. **Information Given in Changing Call:** A denomination named, then canceled, in making or correcting an illegal call is subject to penalty if an opponent becomes declarer: if a suit was named, declarer may impose a lead penalty (page 448); if notrump was named, declarer may call a suit if the offender's partner has the opening lead; if a double or redouble was canceled, the penalties are the same as when a pass is substituted for an insufficient bid.

Example 1: West deals and bids one notrump. South bids two hearts out of turn. The bid is canceled, and West eventually becomes declarer at three notrump. West may require North to lead a heart; or West may, instead, forbid North to lead a heart for as long as he holds the lead. That is, if North wins the first trick, he may not then switch to a heart; and if North wins the first two tricks he may not lead a heart at the third trick; and so on.

Example 2: East deals and bids one spade; South bids one diamond. The opponents require South to correct the insufficient bid, whereupon South bids two clubs before the law has been fully cited. Upon hearing the law, South decides to bid two diamonds. There is no penalty for the insufficient bid; the bidding proceeds as if there had been no irregularity. However, if West becomes declarer, he may prohibit North (the offender's partner) from leading a club for as long as he holds the lead; or West may require North to lead a club. The theory is that North knows something about his partner's clubs by way of an irregularity, and South is entitled to protection against this improper information.

10. Call Out of Rotation (or "out of turn"): Any call out of rotation is canceled when attention is drawn to it. The bidding goes back to the player whose turn it was. Correct procedure then depends on whether the out-of-turn call was a bid, pass, double, or redouble. (Laws 11, 12, and 13.)

A call is not out of rotation if made without waiting for the right-hand opponent to pass, if that opponent is legally obliged to pass, or if it would have been in rotation had not the left-hand opponent called out of rotation. A call made simultaneously with another player's call in rotation is deemed to be subsequent to it.

11. Pass Out of Turn: If it occurs

(*a*) before any player has bid, or when it was the turn of the offender's right-hand opponent, the offender must pass when his regular turn comes;

(*b*) after there has been a bid and when it was the turn of the offender's partner, the offender is barred throughout; the offender's partner may not double or redouble at that turn; and if the offender's partner passes and the opponents play the hand, declarer may impose a lead penalty (page 448).

12. Bid Out of Turn: If it occurs

(*a*) before any player has called, the offender's partner is barred throughout;

(*b*) after any player has called and when it was the turn of the offender's partner, the offender's partner is barred throughout and is subject to a lead penalty (page 448) if he has the opening lead;

(*c*) after any player has called and when it was the turn of the offender's right-hand opponent, the offender must repeat his bid without penalty if that opponent passes, but if that opponent bids, doubles, or redoubles, the offender may make any call and his partner is barred for one turn.

Example 1: South deals, but West bids one spade before South (or anybody else) has spoken. The bid of one spade is canceled, and South has his proper turn to speak. West may bid, pass, double, or redouble whenever his turn comes, but East must pass for the rest of that auction.

Example 2: South deals and passes, whereupon East bids one spade out of turn. The bid is canceled, and West has his turn to speak—but West must pass for the rest of that auction. If South becomes declarer, in which case West is due to make the opening lead, South may require the lead of a spade or may prohibit a spade lead for as long as West holds the lead. If North becomes the declarer, however, there is no lead penalty against East. The theory is that East has not given himself any information by his illegal bid.

Example 3: North bids four notrump after strong North-South bidding, and South bids five hearts (showing two aces according to the Blackwood Convention) without waiting for East to pass. If East does pass,

South simply repeats his bid of five hearts and everything proceeds as though there had been no irregularity. If East wants to double four notrump, however, South may bid, pass, or redouble as he pleases. North must pass at his next turn but may get back into the auction if he has any further turns.

13. **Double or Redouble Out of Turn**: If it occurs

  (*a*) when it was the turn of the offender's partner, the offender's partner is barred throughout and is subject to a lead penalty (page 448) if he has the opening lead, and the offender may not in turn double or redouble the same bid;

  (*b*) when it was the turn of the offender's right-hand opponent, the offender must repeat his double or redouble without penalty if that opponent passes but may make any legal call if that opponent bids, in which case the offender's partner is barred once.

Example 1: North-South bid hearts, and East-West bid spades in a competitive auction. West bids four spades, and South doubles (at North's turn). The double is canceled; North must pass for the rest of that auction; and South may not double four spades when his turn comes.

If East bids on, South may double any other bid if he pleases; or South may bid or pass. If West becomes declarer, he may name a suit and require North to lead that suit, or he may name a suit and forbid North to lead that suit for as long as he holds the lead. If *East* becomes declarer there is no lead penalty.

Example 2: After the sort of competitive auction just described, West bids four spades and North passes. South doubles without waiting for East to speak. If East passes, South must repeat the double and the bidding proceeds as if there had been no irregularity. If East bids four notrump (or any other legal bid), South may bid, double, or pass; but North must pass at his next turn.

14. Impossible Doubles and Redoubles: If a player doubles or redoubles a bid that his side has already doubled or redoubled, his call is canceled; he must substitute

(*a*) any legal bid, in which case his partner is barred throughout, and if the partner becomes the opening leader, declarer may prohibit the lead of the doubled suit; or

(*b*) a pass, in which case either opponent may cancel all previous doubles or redoubles; the offender's partner is barred throughout; and if he becomes the opening leader, he is subject to a lead penalty (page 448).

If a player doubles his partner's bid, redoubles an undoubled bid, or doubles or redoubles when there has been no bid, he must substitute any proper call and his partner is barred once.

15. Other Inadmissible Calls: If a player bids more than seven, or makes another call when legally required to pass, he is deemed to have passed and the offending side must pass at every subsequent turn; if they become the defenders, declarer may impose a lead penalty (page 448) on the opening leader.

16. Call After the Auction Is Closed: A call made after the auction is closed is canceled. If it is a pass by a defender, or any call by declarer or dummy, there is no penalty. If it is a bid, double, or redouble by a defender, declarer may impose a lead penalty at the offender's partner's first turn to lead.

17. Dummy's Rights: Dummy may give or obtain information regarding fact or law, ask if a play constitutes a revoke, draw attention to an irregularity, and warn any player against infringing a law. Dummy forfeits these rights if he looks at a card in another player's hand.

If dummy has forfeited his rights, and thereafter

(*a*) is the first to draw attention to a defender's irregularity, declarer may not enforce any penalty for the offense;

(*b*) warns declarer not to lead from the wrong hand, either defender may choose the hand from which declarer shall lead;

(*c*) is the first to ask declarer if a play from the declarer's hand is a revoke, declarer must correct a revoke if able but the revoke penalty still applies.

18. Exposed Cards: Declarer is never subject to penalty for exposure of a card, but intentional exposure of declarer's hand is treated as a claim or concession of tricks.

A defender's card is exposed if it is faced on the table or held so that the other defender may see its face before he is entitled to do so. Such a card must be left face up on the table until played and becomes a penalty card.

19. Penalty Cards: A penalty card must be played at the first legal opportunity, subject to the obligation to follow suit or to comply with another penalty.

If a defender has two or more penalty cards that he can legally play, declarer may designate which one is to be played.

Declarer may require or forbid a defender to lead a suit in which his partner has a penalty card, but if declarer does so, the penalty card may be picked up and ceases to be a penalty card.

Failure to play a penalty card is not subject to penalty, but declarer may require the penalty card to be played and any defender's card exposed in the process becomes a penalty card.

Example 1: East, a defender, drops the ace of hearts face up on the table. He must play it as soon as he legally can: when hearts are first played, at his first chance to discard, or at his first turn to lead—whichever is first. If West gains the lead while the ace of hearts is face up on the table, declarer has a choice of penalties and the defenders should wait until South states his choice. Declarer may let West lead as he pleases, continuing to treat the ace of hearts as a penalty card. Or, instead, declarer may require West to lead a heart or forbid West to lead a heart for as long as he holds the lead; and in either of these cases, East may pick up the ace of hearts and play it at his own discretion.

Example 2: While East has the ace of hearts exposed, a heart is led from the North hand and East plays a *low* heart from his hand instead of the exposed ace of hearts. Declarer may accept the play or may reject it and compel East to play the ace; and in the latter case, East's low heart must stay face up on the table as a penalty card.

20. **Lead Out of Turn**: If declarer is required by a defender * to retract a lead from the wrong hand, he must

---

* A defender's drawing attention to declarer's lead from the wrong hand is equivalent to requiring its retraction.

lead from the correct hand (if he can) a card of the same suit; if it was a defender's turn to lead, or if there is no card of that suit in the correct hand, there is no penalty.

If a defender is required to retract a lead out of turn, declarer may either treat the card so led as a penalty card, or impose a lead penalty on the offender's partner when next he is to lead after the offense.

Example 1: South, declarer, leads from the dummy after winning the previous trick in his own hand. If East plays to dummy's lead, the irregularity is regularized. If either opponent calls attention to the irregularity before East plays, the card led from dummy must be retracted and South must lead a card of the same suit from his hand (if he can). If South has a card of the same suit but fails to lead it, he is liable to the revoke penalty (Law 26).

Example 2: East leads the king of hearts after South has won the previous trick. The king stays on the table as a penalty card, subject to play at East's first legal opportunity. If the king is still unplayed when West gets his first chance to lead, South must state his choice. He may let West lead as he pleases, in which case the king of hearts remains a penalty card; or he may require or forbid a heart lead, in which case East may pick up the king of hearts. If South forbids a heart lead, the prohibition continues for as long as West holds the lead.

Example 3: East opens the king of hearts against South's contract. South may inadvertently spread his hand as the dummy, thereby accepting the out-of-turn opening lead without penalty, but the laws say he is not supposed to do so on purpose. If South recognizes the irregularity he has a choice of action:

(*a*) South may treat the king of hearts as a penalty card, allowing West to lead as he pleases;

(*b*) South may require or forbid a heart lead from West, allowing East to pick up the king; the prohibition continues for as long as West holds the lead;

(*c*) South may accept the lead, in which case the dummy is put down; South then plays from his hand and plays last from the dummy on this trick.

21. Premature Play: If a defender leads to the next trick before his partner has played to the current trick, or plays out of rotation before his partner has played, declarer may require the offender's partner to play his highest card of the suit led, his lowest card of the suit led, or a card of another specified suit. Declarer must select one of these options, and if the defender cannot comply, he may play any card. When declarer has played from both his hand and dummy, a defender is not subject to penalty for playing before his partner.

22. Inability to Play as Required: If a player is unable to lead or play as required to comply with a penalty (for lack of a card of a required suit, or because of the prior obligation to follow suit), he may play any card. The penalty is deemed satisfied, except in the case of a penalty card.

23. Revoke: A revoke is the act of playing a card of another suit when able to follow suit to a lead. Any player, including dummy, may ask whether a play constitutes a revoke and may demand that an opponent correct a revoke. A claim of revoke does not warrant inspection of turned tricks, prior to the end of the play, except by consent of both sides.

Example 1: South, declarer, leads the ace of spades from dummy, discarding a diamond. West then also discards a diamond. Dummy may ask, "No spades?" addressing his question to South or West or both. Likewise East may address the same kind of question to South, West, or both. If it is clear that one of them must hold the missing spade, any player may halt play and insist that the revoke be corrected.

Example 2: At the ninth trick, South says to West, "You revoked three tricks ago, when spades were last led." West denies the statement. The correct procedure is to finish the play, *then* turn back the tricks to discover whether or not a revoke took place. If a player were entitled to inspect the turned tricks at once, anybody who couldn't remember a previous trick could get a look at the trick by accusing an opponent of revoking on that trick. (Nice people wouldn't do such things, but the laws should remove temptation from nice people.)

24. Correcting a Revoke: A player must correct his revoke if aware of it before it becomes established. A revoke card withdrawn by a defender becomes a penalty card. The nonoffending side may withdraw any cards played after the revoke but before attention was drawn to it.

Example 1: East leads a heart, defending against a notrump contract played by South. West discards the deuce of spades, and East immediately asks, "No hearts?" Meanwhile, declarer has won the trick with dummy's queen of hearts. West looks at his hand and discovers the king of hearts. He must play the king, leaving the deuce of spades on the table as a penalty card. Declarer may put the queen of hearts back in the dummy and play another heart from dummy if he wishes to do so.

Example 2: East leads a heart, as before, in the course of defending against South's notrump contract. South discards a spade; West plays a low heart; and dummy (holding A-Q) wins with the queen. The dummy asks, "No hearts?" and South discovers a small heart in his hand. South must play the heart but may pick up the spade he has played in error. West may change his play and may actually win the trick with the king of hearts even though dummy has the A-Q right behind West. Declarer may not change the play from dummy; only the *nonoffending* side may change the play after a revoke has been corrected. (This actually happened in the 1957 World Championship.)

25. Established Revoke: A revoke becomes established when a member of the offending side leads or plays to a subsequent trick (or terminates play by a claim or concession). When a revoke becomes established, the revoke trick stands as played (unless it is the twelfth trick; see Law 27).

Example 1: South, declarer, trumps the opening heart lead and immediately leads a heart. The ruff is a revoke, and South's lead to the next trick establishes the revoke.

Example 2: South, declarer, wins the ninth trick by ruffing a heart even though he has a heart in his hand. South then says, "I have the rest," and shows his hand. The claim establishes the revoke.

26. Revoke Penalty: The penalty for an established revoke is two tricks (if available), transferred at the end of play from the revoking side to the opponents. This penalty can be paid only from tricks won by the revoking side after its first revoke, including the revoke trick. If only one trick is available, the penalty is satisfied by transferring one trick; if no trick is available, there is no penalty.

There is no penalty for a subsequent established revoke in the same suit by the same player.

A transferred trick ranks for all scoring purposes as a trick won in play by the side receiving it. It never affects the contract.

Example 1: West, a defender, revokes on the fourth trick. The revoke is discovered a few tricks later, the defenders winning the fourth and fifth tricks against a small slam in clubs. The defenders must hand over these two tricks, and South scores as if he had won all thirteen tricks in play—his small slam plus a 20-point overtrick.

Example 2: West wins the first two tricks against South's small-slam contract. East revokes on the fifth trick, winning the trick. The revoke becomes established, and declarer takes the rest of the tricks. The revoke trick is transferred to declarer, but the first two tricks are not affected since they were played before the revoke took place. South is down one at his slam contract.

Example 3: South is declarer at two hearts. He wins eight tricks by normal play and two additional tricks because of a defender's revoke. He scores as if he had won ten tricks in normal play—60 points below the line and 60 points above.

27. Revokes Not Subject to Penalty: A revoke made in the twelfth trick must be corrected, without penalty, if discovered before the cards have been mixed together. The nonoffending side may require the offender's partner to play either of two cards he could legally have played. A revoke not discovered until the cards have been mixed is not subject to penalty, nor is a revoke by any faced hand (dummy, or a defender's hand when faced in consequence of a claim by declarer). A revoke by failure to play a penalty card is not subject to the penalty for an established revoke.

28. Defective Trick: A defective trick may not be corrected after a player of each side has played to the next trick. If a player has failed to play to a trick, he must correct his error when it is discovered by adding a card to the trick (if possible, one he could legally have played to it). If a player has played more than one card to a trick, he does not play to the last trick or tricks and if he wins a trick with his last card, the turn to lead passes to the player at his left.

Example 1: West has the ace of spades, defending against South's contract of seven spades. Declarer leads a trump, and somehow West fails to play to the trick. The play continues, and soon West notices that he has one card more than anybody else. The tricks are examined, and it is discovered that West failed to play to the first round of trumps. He must now supply a card to this trick—a trump if he has one, since trumps were led. If West's only trump is the ace, he must add it to South's trick—*and the ownership of that trick is not changed!* This is a situation in which the ace of trumps does not win a trick!

Example 2: South bids a grand slam in notrump, holding four aces, four kings, four queens, and the jack of spades. He plays the hand out somewhat unskillfully, since he manages to play two spades on the same trick. After playing to the twelfth trick, South has no cards left, and the turn to lead passes to West, at South's left. West, who started life with ♠ 5 4 3 2 ♡ 4 3 2 ◇ 4 3 2 ♣ 4 3 2, finds himself leading and winning a trick with the five of spades!

29. Declarer Claiming or Conceding Tricks: If declarer claims or concedes one or more of the remaining tricks (verbally or by spreading his hand), he must leave his hand face up on the table and immediately state his intended line of play.

If a defender disputes declarer's claim, declarer must play on, adhering to any statement he has made, and in the absence of a specific statement he may not "exercise freedom of choice in making any play the success of which depends on finding either opponent with or without a particular unplayed card."

Following curtailment of play by declarer, it is permissible for a defender to expose his hand and to suggest a play to his partner.

Example 1: South wins the first trick, draws trumps,

and spreads his hand, announcing, "I'll give you one heart." South has two small hearts in dummy and K-J in his own hand. Actually, South must guess the winning play in hearts unless East has both the ace and the queen. If it is possible for South to guess wrong, he must do so after making this kind of claim. Otherwise he could make a claim and rely on his opponents to give themselves away in disputing his claim.

Example 2: East wins the tenth trick, and South, declarer, faces his cards and claims the rest. West faces his own hand and suggests to East, "Lead a heart." This play produces another trick for the defenders. West is completely within his rights in doing so.

30. Defender Claiming or Conceding Tricks: A defender may show any or all of his cards to declarer to establish a claim or concession. He may not expose his hand to his partner, and if he does, declarer may treat his partner's cards as penalty cards.

31. Correcting the Score: A proved or admitted error in any score may be corrected at any time before the rubber score is agreed, except as follows. An error made in entering or failing to enter a part score, or in omitting a game or in awarding one, may not be corrected after the last card of the second succeeding deal has been dealt—unless a majority of the players consent.

Example 1: South fails to claim 100 honors held in the first hand of the rubber. He remembers just as the rubber ends and as the rubber score is being added. The other players remember his honors, and South gets credit for them on the rubber score. (If nobody else remembers the honors, South is probably out of luck.)

Example 2: South bids two spades and wins nine tricks on the first hand of the rubber. The scorekeeper writes 90 (instead of the correct 60) below the line. In the second deal of the rubber, South bids one spade and makes eight tricks, scoring 30 points below the line. He is credited with game for 90 and 30, and the cards are dealt for the third hand of the rubber. When the last card of that hand has been dealt, it is too late to correct the score of 90 points below the line for the first hand. South is entitled to his game and may well argue that he would have bid *two* spades on the second hand if he had known he needed more than 30 points.

32. Effect of Incorrect Pack: Scores made as a result of hands played with an incorrect pack of cards are not affected by the discovery of the imperfection after the cards have been mixed together.

/ LOSING AND WINNING

In every game there must be losers and winners. Part of the art of playing a game well is to be a "good" loser or a gracious winner.

Let the other fellow be the good loser. As for you, just accept your victory casually and naturally, as befits a player who has finished reading this entire book.

FINAL REVIEW

BY THIS TIME you are undoubtedly eager to put your knowledge to work in actual play. But before leaving this book, one last brush-up is in order.

We suggest you take the entire quiz again—from question 1 just below straight through to question 199. (If you have previously jotted your answers next to the questions, cover them up or erase them so that you have no clues.)

If you score 185 correct answers (answers begin on page 468), you can consider yourself an honor graduate from this bridge course and you are ready—not just to play—but to *win* at bridge.

NOTE: This book has been organized for easy reference —from the descriptive table of contents to the topical listing at the beginning of each chapter plus the bonus sections at the end of the book. Keep this book handy to look up or review particular subjects as they arise.

REVIEW QUESTIONS

As dealer, you hold each of the following hands. What do you say?

(1)	♠ A J 10 8 4	♡ K 9 3	◇ A Q 6	♣ 6 3
(2)	♠ 10 8 6 4 3	♡ A K J	◇ A Q 6	♣ 6 3
(3)	♠ K Q J 10 9 4	♡ K 9 3	◇ 5 4	♣ 6 3
(4)	♠ K 10 9 4	♡ A K J	◇ 8 5	♣ K 10 9 4
(5)	♠ K 10 9 4	♡ A K J	◇ 8 5 2	♣ K 10 9

(6)	♠ K 10 9 4	♡ A K J	◇ Q 5 2	♣ K 10 9
(7)	♠ K 10 9 4 2	♡ A K J	◇ 8 5	♣ K 10 9
(8)	♠ J 9 6 4 2	♡ A K Q 8 5	◇ A 5	♣ 3
(9)	♠ K J 6 4 2	♡ A 5	◇ 3	♣ A Q 7 3 2
(10)	♠ K Q J 6 4	♡ A 5	◇ 3	♣ A Q 7 3 2
(11)	♠ Q 6 4	♡ A 5 2	◇ A Q 5	♣ K J 3 2
(12)	♠ 6 4	♡ A Q J 2	◇ A Q 5	♣ K J 3 2
(13)	♠ A Q	♡ A Q J 2	◇ A Q 5	♣ K J 3 2
(14)	♠ A Q J	♡ A Q J 2	◇ A Q 5	♣ K Q 3
(15)	♠ A Q J	♡ A K J 2	◇ A K 5	♣ K Q J
(16)	♠ A K 5	♡ A K J 9 2	◇ A K Q 5	♣ 2
(17)	♠ A K Q	♡ 10 7 6 5 2	◇ A K Q J	♣ A
(18)	♠ A K J 10 8 7 6	♡ A 7 6 2	◇ K 2	♣ —
(19)	♠ A K J 10 7 6	♡ A K 7 6 2	◇ K 2	♣ —
(20)	♠ A J 4	♡ 9 6 3 2	◇ A K 10	♣ A Q J

The bidding has been:

SOUTH	WEST	NORTH	EAST
1 ♡	Pass	?	

You are North. What do you say?

(21)	♠ 6 3	♡ Q 7 4	◇ A Q 5 2	♣ 8 5 4 2
(22)	♠ 6 3	♡ Q 7 4 2	◇ A J 5 2	♣ K Q 2
(23)	♠ 3	♡ Q 7 4 3 2	◇ 5 2	♣ K Q 8 4 2
(24)	♠ K J 7 4	♡ 3	◇ J 5 2	♣ Q 8 5 4 2
(25)	♠ K J 7 4	♡ 3	◇ J 5 2	♣ A Q J 4 2
(26)	♠ 3	♡ K J 7 4	◇ A 5 2	♣ A K J 4 2
(27)	♠ K J 7	♡ 4 3	◇ A J 5 2	♣ K J 9 5
(28)	♠ J 7 3	♡ 4 3	◇ A J 5 2	♣ Q 9 5 2
(29)	♠ 7 3	♡ 4 3	◇ A J 5 2	♣ Q J 9 5 2
(30)	♠ 7 3	♡ 4 3	◇ J 6 5 2	♣ Q J 9 5 2

The bidding has been:

SOUTH	WEST	NORTH	EAST
1 NT	Pass	?	

You are North. What do you say?

(31)	♠ 9 2	♡ Q J 8 7 5	◇ 4 3	♣ K 9 6 3
(32)	♠ 9 2	♡ A Q J 7 5	◇ 4 3	♣ K 9 6 3
(33)	♠ 2	♡ A Q J 7 5	◇ K 3	♣ K Q 9 6 3
(34)	♠ 9 2	♡ A 7 5	◇ K Q J 9 6 4	♣ 8 2
(35)	♠ 8 3 2	♡ A 7 5	◇ K Q 3 2	♣ 8 6 2
(36)	♠ 8 3	♡ A 7 5	◇ K Q 9 3 2	♣ 8 6 2
(37)	♠ K 9 6 4	♡ 7 5	◇ K Q 8 2	♣ 8 6 2
(38)	♠ K 9 6 4	♡ 7 5	◇ K Q 8 2	♣ K 6 2
(39)	♠ K 9 6 4	♡ K Q 8 2	◇ 7 5	♣ K 6 2
(40)	♠ K J 9 6 4	♡ 9 5	◇ A 7 5	♣ 8 6 2

The bidding has been:

SOUTH	WEST	NORTH	EAST
1 ♡	Pass	1 ♠	Pass
?			

You are South. What do you say?

(41)	♠ A 7 4	♡ K Q J 9 2	◇ K J 4	♣ 6 3
(42)	♠ A J 7 4	♡ K Q J 9 2	◇ K J 4	♣ 3
(43)	♠ A K 7 4	♡ A Q J 9 2	◇ K 4	♣ 6 3
(44)	♠ 7 4	♡ A Q J 9 2	◇ K J 4	♣ A 6 3
(45)	♠ 7 4	♡ A Q J 10 6 2	◇ K 4	♣ A K 3
(46)	♠ 4	♡ A Q J 10 7 6 2	◇ K 4	♣ A K 3
(47)	♠ 7 4	♡ K Q J 9 2	◇ K Q 7 5	♣ A 3
(48)	♠ 7 4	♡ A K J 9 2	◇ A K J 7 5	♣ A
(49)	♠ 7 4	♡ A J 9 3 2	◇ K J 7	♣ K Q 6
(50)	♠ 7 4	♡ A J 9 3 2	◇ A K J	♣ K Q 6

The bidding has been:

SOUTH	WEST	NORTH	EAST
1 ♡	Pass	2 ♣	Pass
?			

You are South. What do you say?

(51)	♠ 5	♡ A J 8 5 3	◇ K Q 8	♣ A 9 6 2
(52)	♠ 5	♡ A Q J 5 3	◇ K Q 8	♣ A J 6 2
(53)	♠ 9 5 4	♡ A Q J 5 3	◇ K Q 8	♣ 6 2
(54)	♠ 4	♡ A K J 9 3 2	◇ K Q 8	♣ Q 3 2
(55)	♠ 4	♡ A K J 9 5 3 2	◇ K Q 8	♣ Q 3
(56)	♠ K Q 5	♡ A J 8 5 3	◇ K Q 8	♣ 6 2
(57)	♠ K Q 5	♡ A J 8 5 3	◇ K Q 8	♣ K 2
(58)	♠ 5 4	♡ A J 8 5 3	◇ K Q 8 4	♣ A 2
(59)	♠ 5	♡ A J 8 5 3	◇ A K Q 8 4	♣ A 2
(60)	♠ A Q J 5	♡ A K 8 5 3	◇ 4	♣ A 6 2

The bidding has been:

SOUTH	WEST	NORTH	EAST
1 ♡	Pass	2 ◇	Pass
2 ♡	Pass	?	

You are North. What do you say?

(61)	♠ 8 4	♡ Q 8 3	◇ A K J 6 2	♣ 9 7 3
(62)	♠ 8 4	♡ Q 8 3	◇ A K J 6 2	♣ K 7 3
(63)	♠ 8 4 2	♡ 3	◇ A K J 1 0 7 6	♣ 9 7 3
(64)	♠ 8 4	♡ 8 3	◇ A K J 1 0 7 6	♣ 9 7 3
(65)	♠ K 8 4	♡ 8 3	◇ K Q J 7 6	♣ K 7 3
(66)	♠ K J 4	♡ 8 3	◇ K Q J 7 6	♣ A J 3
(67)	♠ K 4	♡ 8 3	◇ A K Q 1 0 7 6	♣ Q 7 3

(68) ♠ K Q 8 4   ♡ 8 3   ◇ A K J 7 6   ♣ 7 3
(69) ♠ 8 4   ♡ 3   ◇ A K J 7 6   ♣ K Q 9 7 3
(70) ♠ 4   ♡ Q 8 3 2   ◇ A K J 7 6   ♣ A 10 3

The bidding has been:

SOUTH	WEST	NORTH	EAST
1 ♡	Pass	1 ♠	Pass
2 ◇	Pass	?	

You are North. What do you say?

(71) ♠ K Q 8 5 3   ♡ 9 6 2   ◇ 4 2   ♣ A 8 7
(72) ♠ K Q 8 5 3   ♡ Q 9 6   ◇ 4   ♣ A 8 7 2
(73) ♠ A Q 8 5 3   ♡ K J 9 6 2   ◇ 4   ♣ 7 2
(74) ♠ K Q 8 5 3   ♡ Q 2   ◇ K Q 4   ♣ 8 7 2
(75) ♠ K Q 8 5 3   ♡ Q 2   ◇ K Q 7 4 2   ♣ 7
(76) ♠ K Q J 5 3 2   ♡ Q 2   ◇ 4 2   ♣ 8 7 2
(77) ♠ K Q J 5 3 2   ♡ Q 2   ◇ 4 2   ♣ A 7 2
(78) ♠ K Q J 10 5 3 2   ♡ Q 2   ◇ 4   ♣ A 7 2
(79) ♠ K Q 8 5 3   ♡ Q 2   ◇ 7 4 2   ♣ A 7 2
(80) ♠ K Q 8 5 3   ♡ Q 2   ◇ 7 4 2   ♣ A K J

The bidding has been:

SOUTH	WEST	NORTH	EAST
1 ♡	Pass	3 ♡	Pass
?			

You are South. What do you say?

(81) ♠ 6 3   ♡ A K J 9 4   ◇ A 7 5   ♣ 8 5 2
(82) ♠ 6 3   ♡ A K J 9   ◇ A Q 7 5   ♣ 8 5 2

(83) ♠ 6 3   ♡ A K J 9 4   ◇ K Q 5   ♣ A 5 2
(84) ♠ 6 3   ♡ A K J 9 4   ◇ A J 5   ♣ A K 2
(85) ♠ K Q 4   ♡ K Q 9 8 4   ◇ A K 5   ♣ 6 3
(86) ♠ A K 4   ♡ A K J 9 4   ◇ 6 3   ♣ Q J 6
(87) ♠ K 8 6 3   ♡ A K J 9 4   ◇ ———   ♣ A J 6 3
(88) ♠ A 5   ♡ A K J 9 4   ◇ 3   ♣ K Q J 6 3
(89) ♠ A 5   ♡ A K J 9 4   ◇ K 3   ♣ K Q 6 3
(90) ♠ A 5   ♡ A Q J 9 4   ◇ A 3   ♣ A Q 6 3

The bidding has been:

SOUTH	WEST	NORTH	EAST
1 ♡	1 ♠	?	

You are North. What do you say?

(91) ♠ 8 5   ♡ Q 6 3 2   ◇ K Q 9 3   ♣ 7 5 4
(92) ♠ 8   ♡ Q 6 3 2   ◇ K Q 9 3   ♣ K 7 5 4
(93) ♠ 8   ♡ Q 8 6 3 2   ◇ Q 9 8 6 3 2 ♣ 5
(94) ♠ K J 5   ♡ 8 6 3   ◇ A 6 3 2   ♣ Q 5 4
(95) ♠ K J 5   ♡ 8 6 3   ◇ A J 3 2   ♣ K Q 5
(96) ♠ 5   ♡ J 6 3   ◇ A 8 6 3   ♣ K Q 9 5 4
(97) ♠ 5   ♡ K 6 3   ◇ A 8 6   ♣ A K Q J 5 4
(98) ♠ ———   ♡ K J 6 3   ◇ A 8 6   ♣ A K J 7 5 4
(99) ♠ K J 8 3   ♡ 4   ◇ A Q 6 2   ♣ Q J 7 4
(100) ♠ K Q J 9 2 ♡ 4   ◇ 9 6 2   ♣ J 7 6 4

With neither side vulnerable, the bidding has been:

SOUTH	WEST	NORTH	EAST
1 ♡	?		

You are West. What do you say?

(101)	♠ A K J 7 4	♡ 5 2	◇ Q 9 3	♣ 8 5 2
(102)	♠ 8 5 2	♡ 5 2	◇ A K J 7 4	♣ Q 9 3
(103)	♠ 8 5 2	♡ 5 2	◇ K Q J 10 4	♣ A 9 3
(104)	♠ 8 5 2	♡ 2	◇ A Q J 7 4 2	♣ A 9 3
(105)	♠ K Q J 7 4 2	♡ 5 2	◇ 8 3	♣ 8 5 2
(106)	♠ 8 3	♡ 5	◇ K Q J 7 4 2	♣ J 8 5 2
(107)	♠ K 3 2	♡ 5	◇ Q 10 7 4 2	♣ K J 8 2
(108)	♠ K 3 2	♡ K J 5	◇ A Q 10 7	♣ K J 8
(109)	♠ K 9 3 2	♡ 5	◇ A Q 10 7	♣ K J 8 2
(110)	♠ A K Q 9 3 2	♡ 5	◇ A Q 10 7	♣ K 2

With neither side vulnerable, the bidding has been:

SOUTH	WEST	NORTH	EAST
1 ♡	1 ♠	Pass	?

You are East. What do you say?

(111)	♠ Q 9 3	♡ 5 4	◇ K Q 7 6 2	♣ K 8 4
(112)	♠ Q 9 3	♡ 4	◇ K Q 7 6 2	♣ A J 8 4
(113)	♠ Q 9 3 2	♡ 4	◇ A K Q 7 6 2	♣ 8 4
(114)	♠ 9 3	♡ 5 4	◇ K Q 7 6 2	♣ K 8 4 3
(115)	♠ 3	♡ 5 4	◇ K Q J 7 6 2	♣ K 8 4 3
(116)	♠ 9 3 2	♡ 5	◇ A K J 7 6 2	♣ A J 8
(117)	♠ Q 9 3 2	♡ 5	◇ A K J 6 2	♣ K 8 4
(118)	♠ 9 3	♡ K J 5 4	◇ K Q 6 2	♣ Q 8 4
(119)	♠ 9 3	♡ K J 5	◇ K Q 6 2	♣ K Q 8 4
(120)	♠ Q 3	♡ K J 5	◇ A Q 6 2	♣ K Q 8 4

With both sides vulnerable, the bidding has been:

SOUTH	WEST	NORTH	EAST
1 ♡	Double	Pass	?

You are East. What do you say?

(121)	♠ J 9 5 2	♡ 8 4	◇ 10 9 4 2	♣ 8 5 3
(122)	♠ J 9 5 2	♡ 8 4	◇ K Q 4 2	♣ 8 5 3
(123)	♠ 9 5 2	♡ 8 4	◇ K Q 4 2	♣ 8 5 3 2
(124)	♠ 5 2	♡ 8 4	◇ K Q 4 2	♣ Q 8 5 3 2
(125)	♠ Q J 5 2	♡ 8 4	◇ A Q 4 2	♣ 8 5 3
(126)	♠ A K J 5 2	♡ 8 4	◇ 6 4 2	♣ 8 5 3
(127)	♠ A J 5 2	♡ 8 4	◇ A K 4 2	♣ 8 5 3
(128)	♠ 5 2	♡ Q J 8 4	◇ K 6 4 2	♣ Q 5 3
(129)	♠ 5 2	♡ J 8 5 4 2	◇ K 4 2	♣ Q 5 3
(130)	♠ 5 2	♡ Q J 10 8 5	◇ K 4 2	♣ Q 5 3

The bidding has been:

SOUTH	WEST	NORTH	EAST
1 ♡	Double	?	

You are North. What do you say?

(131)	♠ 8 4 2	♡ 9 6	◇ K J 7 6 3	♣ Q 10 4
(132)	♠ 8 4 2	♡ 9 6	◇ A K J 7 6 3	♣ Q 4
(133)	♠ 8 4 2	♡ 10 9 6 2	◇ K 8 7 6 3	♣ 4
(134)	♠ 8 4 2	♡ Q 9 6 2	◇ K 8 7 6 3	♣ 4
(135)	♠ 8 4 2	♡ Q 9 6 2	◇ K Q 7 6 3	♣ 4
(136)	♠ 8 4 2	♡ Q 9 6 2	◇ A K 7 6 3	♣ 4
(137)	♠ K 4 2	♡ Q 9 6 2	◇ A K 7 6 3	♣ 4
(138)	♠ K J 9 2	♡ 6 2	◇ K Q 7 6	♣ A J 5

(139) ♠ Q 9 2   ♡ 6 2   ◇ Q J 7 6   ♣ A J 5 2
(140) ♠ 4   ♡ 6 2   ◇ K Q J 9 7 6 3   ♣ J 10 4

The bidding has been:

SOUTH	WEST	NORTH	EAST
1 ♡	Double	Pass	1 ♠
Pass	?		

You are West. What do you say?

(141) ♠ K Q 8 6   ♡ 5   ◇ A K 9 4   ♣ J 9 6 3
(142) ♠ K Q 8 6   ♡ 5   ◇ A K 9 4   ♣ K 9 6 3
(143) ♠ K Q 8 6   ♡ 5   ◇ A K 9 4   ♣ A J 10 3
(144) ♠ K Q 8 6   ♡ 5   ◇ A K Q 9 4   ♣ A J 10
(145) ♠ K 8 6   ♡ 5   ◇ A K Q 9 4 3 ♣ A J 10

You are the dealer, non-vulnerable against vulnerable opponents. What do you say?

(146) ♠ K J 10 8 7 6 5   ♡ 6 2   ◇ 5 4   ♣ 7 5
(147) ♠ 6 2   ♡ K Q J 10 8 7 6 5 ◇ 4   ♣ 7 5
(148) ♠ 2   ♡ 5 3   ◇ K J 10 8 7 6 5 4 ♣ 7 5
(149) ♠ 2   ♡ ———   ◇ K Q J 10 8 7 6 5 ♣ Q J 7 5
(150) ♠ K 6   ♡ K 3   ◇ K J 10 8 7 6 5 4 ♣ 5

The bidding has been:

SOUTH	WEST	NORTH	EAST
1 ♠	3 ♡	4 ♠	5 ♡
?			

You are South, vulnerable against non-vulnerable opponents. What do you say?

(151)	♠ A Q J 7 4	♡ 5	◇ K Q 6 2	♣ J 10 4
(152)	♠ A Q J 7 4	♡ 5 2	◇ K Q 2	♣ J 10 4
(153)	♠ A Q J 7 4 2	♡ 5	◇ K Q 2	♣ Q J 4
(154)	♠ A Q J 7 4 3 2	♡ ——	◇ K Q 2	♣ Q J 4
(155)	♠ A Q J 7 4 3 2	♡ ——	◇ K Q 2	♣ A J 4

The bidding has been:

SOUTH	WEST	NORTH	EAST
1 ♡	Pass	2 ♣	Pass
2 ♡	Pass	3 ♡	Pass
4 ♡	Pass	Pass	Pass

You are West. What do you lead?

(156)	♠ A K J 8	♡ 5 2	◇ 9 7 4 2	♣ 8 3 2
(157)	♠ K Q J 8	♡ 5 2	◇ Q 9 7 4	♣ 8 3 2
(158)	♠ Q J 10 8	♡ 5 2	◇ Q 9 7 4	♣ 8 3 2
(159)	♠ J 10 9 6	♡ 5 2	◇ K J 7 4	♣ 8 3 2
(160)	♠ A 9 6 2	♡ 5 4	◇ Q 10 7 4	♣ 8 3 2
(161)	♠ K 9 6	♡ 5 4	◇ A 7 4	♣ Q J 8 3 2
(162)	♠ K 9 6 3 2	♡ A J 7 4	◇ 7 4	♣ 3 2
(163)	♠ Q 9 6 3	♡ A 5 4	◇ 7	♣ J 10 8 3 2
(164)	♠ Q 9 6	♡ A 5 4	◇ 7 4	♣ J 10 8 3 2
(165)	♠ K J 6	♡ Q 5 4	◇ J 10 8	♣ Q J 8 3

The bidding has been:

SOUTH	WEST	NORTH	EAST
1 ♣	Pass	1 ♡	Pass
1 NT	Pass	3 NT	Pass
Pass	Pass		

You are West. What do you lead?

(166)	♠ 9 6 3	♡ 5 4	◇ K Q J 7 4	♣ 9 6 2
(167)	♠ 9 6 3	♡ 5 4	◇ A K J 7 4	♣ 9 6 2
(168)	♠ K 6 3	♡ 5 4	◇ Q J 10 6 3	♣ 9 6 2
(169)	♠ K 6 3	♡ 5 4	◇ K J 10 6 3	♣ 9 6 2
(170)	♠ A J 3	♡ 5 4	◇ Q 10 9 7 3	♣ 9 6 2
(171)	♠ A J 3	♡ 5 4	◇ K J 7 3 2	♣ 9 6 2
(172)	♠ K J 3	♡ 5 4	◇ J 9 7 3	♣ Q 10 6 2
(173)	♠ K J 3	♡ J 5 4	◇ J 10 3	♣ Q 10 6 2
(174)	♠ J 8 2	♡ J 5 4	◇ 10 3	♣ Q 9 6 3 2
(175)	♠ A 8 2	♡ 5 4	◇ J 10 3	♣ K Q J 9 2

176. NORTH (dummy)
- ♠ 5 3
- ♡ K 8 6
- ◇ A Q 8 3 2
- ♣ 6 4 3

SOUTH
- ♠ A 4 2
- ♡ A Q 7
- ◇ J 10 9 4
- ♣ A Q 5 2

You are declarer at a contract of 3 NT. West leads the ♠ K. What is your plan?

177. NORTH (dummy)
- ♠ 6 5 3
- ♡ K Q J
- ◇ K 4 3
- ♣ K 10 5 2

SOUTH
- ♠ A K 2
- ♡ A 8 6
- ◇ Q J 10 2
- ♣ Q J 4

You are declarer at a contract of 3 NT. West leads the ♠ Q. What is your plan?

178. NORTH (dummy)
   ♠ A 10 9
   ♡ 9 8 7 3
   ◇ 8 7 3
   ♣ 9 5 4

   SOUTH
   ♠ K Q J
   ♡ A 4
   ◇ A Q J 6
   ♣ A Q 3 2

You are declarer at a contract of 3 NT. West leads the ♡ 2, and East wins the first trick with ♡ J. East leads the ♡ Q. What is your plan?

179. NORTH (dummy)
   ♠ A Q J
   ♡ 9 6 4
   ◇ 5 3 2
   ♣ K Q 10 5

   SOUTH
   ♠ K 10 4
   ♡ Q J 10 7
   ◇ A Q 4
   ♣ A J 6

You are declarer at a contract of 3 NT. West leads the ♠ 9, which you win in dummy. You lead a low heart from dummy, and East steps up with ♡ A and leads ◇ J. What is your plan?

180. NORTH (dummy)
   ♠ 8 6 3 2
   ♡ J 9 8 4
   ◇ Q 6
   ♣ K 7 4

   SOUTH
   ♠ K Q
   ♡ A Q 10 6 3
   ◇ A 5 2
   ♣ A 8 2

The contract is 4 ♡; West leads ♣ Q. What is your plan?

181. NORTH (dummy)
   ♠ A 10 9 3
   ♡ K 8
   ◇ 7 3 2
   ♣ A K J 7

   SOUTH
   ♠ K J 8 7 6
   ♡ A J
   ◇ K 5 4
   ♣ Q 5 3

The contract is 4 ♠; West leads ♣ 10. What is your plan?

182. NORTH (dummy)
- ♠ 7 6
- ♡ Q J 10 6
- ◇ A Q 5 3
- ♣ 9 8 4

SOUTH
- ♠ A K
- ♡ K 7
- ◇ K J 8 4
- ♣ Q J 10 6 2

The contract is 3 NT; West leads ♠ 5. What is your plan?

183. NORTH (dummy)
- ♠ Q 4
- ♡ A J 10 9 8
- ◇ 6 4
- ♣ A 6 4 2

SOUTH
- ♠ A 9 8 5
- ♡ K
- ◇ A K 5 2
- ♣ K 9 8 3

The contract is 3 NT; West leads ♠ 3. Dummy's queen is covered by king and ace. What is your plan?

184. NORTH (dummy)
- ♠ K 6 4
- ♡ 4 3
- ◇ 7 4 3
- ♣ K Q J 9 2

SOUTH
- ♠ 7 2
- ♡ A K 9 8 6 5
- ◇ A Q 6
- ♣ A 3

The contract is 4 ♡; West leads ♠ J. Spades are continued, and you ruff the third round. What is your plan?

185. NORTH (dummy)
- ♠ Q 9 8 3
- ♡ J 7
- ◇ A Q 5 4
- ♣ A 4 2

SOUTH
- ♠ A J 10 7 2
- ♡ A 9 5
- ◇ K 6
- ♣ 6 5 3

The contract is 4 ♠; West leads ♣ Q. What is your plan?

186. NORTH (dummy)
♠ K J 8 4
♡ A 5 4 2
◊ 9 8 4 3
♣ 6

SOUTH
♠ A Q 10 2
♡ 6
◊ A 6 5 2
♣ A 9 8 4

The contract is 4 ♠; West leads ♡ K. What is your plan?

187. NORTH (dummy)
♠ A Q
♡ 10 9 5
◊ A Q J 10 8
♣ K 6 2

SOUTH
♠ K J 10 9 7 3
♡ A K J 8 3
◊ 9 3
♣ ———

The contract is 6 ♠; West leads ♣ 3. What is your plan?

188. NORTH (dummy)
♠ Q J 9
♡ A J 9 6
◊ Q
♣ A K J 5 2

SOUTH
♠ A 7 3
♡ 5 4 3
◊ K J 10 9 8
♣ 6 3

The contract is 3 NT; West leads ♠ 2. Dummy's queen is covered by East's king. What is your plan?

189. NORTH (dummy)
♠ Q J 10 8 5
♡ A 6 3
◊ 7 4
♣ 7 5 2

SOUTH
♠ K 7
♡ K Q J 10 5 2
◊ A 6
♣ K Q 3

The contract is 4 ♡; West leads ◊ J. What is your plan?

190. NORTH (dummy)
   ♠ Q 8 5 3
   ♡ K J 9 4
   ◇ A 8
   ♣ J 6 4

   SOUTH
   ♠ A K J 10 9 7
   ♡ 10
   ◇ Q J 10 5
   ♣ A K

The contract is 6 ♠; West leads ♣ 10. What is your plan?

191. NORTH (dummy)
   ♠ 7 4
   ♡ 8 5 4 2
   ◇ Q 6 3
   ♣ 6 4 3 2

   SOUTH
   ♠ A K 10 9 6 3
   ♡ 5
   ◇ A K 2
   ♣ A K 5

The contract is 4 ♠; West leads ♡ K and continues with ♡ J. You ruff and lead out ♠ A, drawing two low trumps. What is your plan?

192. NORTH (dummy)
   ♠ K 10 9 6
   ♡ J 5
   ◇ A Q J 8
   ♣ 10 6 5

WEST
   ♠ 7 3
   ♡ K 9 6 3
   ◇ 6 5 3
   ♣ A K 8 3

The contract is 4 ♠. You, West, lead ♣ K. East plays ♣ Q; South, ♣ 2. What is your plan?

193. NORTH (dummy)
   ♠ 7 6 3
   ♡ J 9 4
   ◇ K 3
   ♣ A K Q 8 3

WEST
   ♠ J 4
   ♡ A K Q 10 3 2
   ◇ A 10 2
   ♣ 9 5

The contract is 4 ♠. You, West, lead ♡ K, drawing ♡ 7 from East and ♡ 6 from South. What is your plan?

194. NORTH (dummy)
♠ K 10 2
♥ 9 5 3
♦ K Q 10 8 7
♣ J 3

WEST
♠ 7 5
♥ A Q 4 2
♦ J 9 6
♣ A K 9 4

The bidding:

SOUTH	WEST	NORTH	EAST
1 ♠	Dbl	Pass	2 ♣
2 ♠	Pass	3 ♠	Pass
4 ♠	Pass	Pass	Pass

You, West, lead ♣ K. East plays ♣ 8, and South plays ♣ 5. What is your plan?

195. NORTH (dummy)
♠ A 8 7
♥ K 9 8
♦ 9 8
♣ K Q 10 9 8

WEST
♠ 5 4 3
♥ 6 5 4
♦ K 10 7 5 4
♣ A 3

The bidding:

NORTH	EAST	SOUTH	WEST
1 ♣	Pass	2 NT	Pass
3 NT	Pass	Pass	Pass

You, West, lead ♦ 5. East wins with ♦ A and returns ♦ Q. South follows with ♦ 2 and ♦ 3. What is your plan?

196. NORTH (dummy)
♠ Q 8
♥ 8 7 5 4 3
♦ A Q 7
♣ A 10 4

SOUTH
♠ A J
♥ A 10 9 6 2
♦ K 4 3
♣ J 5 2

The contract is 4 ♥; West leads ♦ 5. You win and lead out ♥ A, both opponents following suit. What is your plan?

197. NORTH (dummy)
- ♠ J 9 5
- ♡ A K 9 6 3
- ◇ A J 10
- ♣ 9 7

SOUTH
- ♠ A K Q 10 6 4
- ♡ 5 4
- ◇ K Q 9
- ♣ A J

The contract is 7 ♠; West leads ♠ 2. You draw two rounds of trumps, exhausting all outstanding trumps, then cash the top hearts, discovering that they break 5-1. What is your plan?

198. NORTH (dummy)
- ♠ A 9 8
- ♡ A K 5
- ◇ A 10 9
- ♣ A K 8 6

SOUTH
- ♠ K Q J 10 7 5
- ♡ J 9 6
- ◇ K 5
- ♣ J 7

The contract is 7 ♠; West leads ♠ 2. What is your plan?

199. NORTH (dummy)
- ♠ 10 3
- ♡ K 7
- ◇ A J 8 7 5
- ♣ A J 3 2

SOUTH
- ♠ A K J 9 8 7
- ♡ 6 5 3
- ◇ K 4
- ♣ 10 5

The contract is 4 ♠; West leads ♡ 2. East wins two hearts and leads a third heart, forcing dummy to ruff. You lead the ♠ 10 for a finesse, and West shows out! What is your plan?

ANSWERS TO REVIEW QUESTIONS

1. *Bid one spade.* 14 points in high cards and 1 point for the doubleton. Who could ask for more?

2. *Bid one spade.* The suit is shabby, but the strength is the same as Hand 1. A compulsory bid.

3. *Pass.* (Bid two spades if you use *weak* two-bids.) Excellent playing strength but not enough high-card stuff for an opening bid.

4. *Bid one club.* With 14 points in high cards you have an opening bid. With four cards in each black suit, bid clubs.

5. *Bid one club.* You *must* bid with 14 points in high cards. This "prepared" bid simplifies your rebid.

6. *Bid one notrump.* No need to bid a 3-card minor suit when you have the 16 to 18 points needed for a bid of one notrump.

7. *Bid one spade.* No need to bid a 3-card minor suit when you have a 5-card suit.

8. *Bid one spade.* In general, bid the higher of two 5-card suits.

9. *Bid one club.* With a weak two-suiter in clubs and spades, bid clubs first. You will probably bid one spade next.

10. *Bid one spade.* With a strong two-suiter in clubs and spades, bid spades first. If partner raises, you will bid game; if he bids a red suit, you are willing to bid three clubs next.

11. *Bid one notrump.* This shows 16 to 18 points, with balanced distribution and at least three suits stopped.

12. *Bid one heart.* Do not open one notrump with a worthless doubleton. (No penalty for bidding one club.)

13. *Bid two notrump.* This shows 22 to 24 points, with balanced distribution and all suits stopped.

14. *Bid three notrump.* This shows 25 to 27 points, with balanced distribution and all suits stopped.

15. *Bid two hearts*. No notrump bid can show 28 points. Despite the poor distribution you must open with a forcing bid.

16. *Bid two hearts*. You don't quite have nine absolutely sure winners, but you have 6 Quick Tricks to make up for any slight shortage.

17. *Bid one heart*. Do not make a two-bid in such a shabby suit. If partner responds, you will make sure of reaching a game.

18. *Bid one spade*. You will force to game if partner responds, but you cannot begin with a two-bid because you have fewer than 9 winners and fewer than 4 Quick Tricks.

19. *Bid two spades*. Roughly 9 winners, and more than 4 Quick Tricks.

20. *Bid one club* (or one diamond). You intend to jump in notrump at your next turn.

21. *Bid two hearts*. You have good values for this bid: trump support, with 8 points in high cards and 1 point for the doubleton. (Add 1 for the queen of partner's suit, but subtract 1 for raising with only three trumps—a stand-off.)

22. *Bid three hearts*. This shows strong trump support of at least four cards, with 13 to 16 points. You have 12 points in normal high cards, 1 point extra for the queen of partner's suit, and 1 point for the doubleton.

23. *Bid four hearts*. Five trumps, a singleton, and less than 9 points in high cards.

24. *Bid one spade*. The one-over-one response promises no more than 6 points.

25. *Bid two clubs*. The two-over-one response promises at least 10 points. You intend to bid spades later in the hope that partner can then go to notrump.

26. *Bid three clubs*. The jump takeout, forcing to game, shows about 19 points or more and hints that slam may be possible opposite a minimum opening bid.

27. *Bid two notrump.* This promises 13 to 15 points, with balanced distribution and all unbid suits stopped.

28. *Bid one notrump.* The hand is worth a response, but you cannot raise or bid a suit of your own.

29. *Bid one notrump.* You still cannot afford to bid the long clubs. Change one of the small clubs to the king, and you would bid two clubs.

30. *Pass.* The simplest way to stay out of trouble with a horrible hand is to pass.

31. *Bid two hearts.* You would pass with 5-3-3-2 distribution, but prefer the suit contract with two doubletons. This is a weak bid, and partner will probably pass.

32. *Bid three hearts.* Partner should raise hearts with K-x-x or any four hearts. Otherwise he should bid three notrump. You will be satisfied with either contract.

33. *Bid three hearts.* You expect to bid clubs next, trying for a slam in one of your long suits.

34. *Bid three notrump.* Slam is out of the question, and even game in diamonds is unlikely. Bid the game in notrump and give the opponents no information at all.

35. *Bid two notrump.* This shows 9 points and invites partner to go on to game with anything but the barest minimum.

36. *Bid three notrump.* A good 5-card suit may be counted as an extra point, and this hand therefore is worth a raise to game.

37. *Bid two clubs.* This is the Stayman Convention, asking partner if he has a biddable major suit. If he shows spades, you intend to raise to three spades. Otherwise you will bid two notrump.

38. *Bid two clubs.* The Stayman Convention again. This time you plan to raise spades to game, or to bid *three* notrump if partner's rebid is anything but two spades.

39. *Bid two clubs.* Once more the Stayman Convention. This time you are ready to raise *either* major suit to

game. If partner's rebid is two diamonds, you bid three notrump.

40. *Bid two clubs.* Another use of the Stayman Convention. If partner bids two diamonds or two hearts, you bid two spades. This promises a 5-card suit and at least 8 points in high cards.

41. *Bid two spades.* You have about 15 points in support of spades, slightly more than required for a minimum opening bid. (Take half credit for bidding two hearts.)

42. *Bid three spades.* You have 18 points in support of spades (15 points in high cards, and 3 points for the singleton).

43. *Bid four spades.* This shows about 19 or 20 points in support of spades and tends to deny slam controls in the unbid suits.

44. *Bid two hearts.* Just slightly more encouraging than a rebid of one notrump. (Take half credit for bidding one notrump.)

45. *Bid three hearts.* This invites but does not force partner to go on. It shows a very strong heart suit with about eight playing tricks.

46. *Bid four hearts.* This shows about nine playing tricks and an independent heart suit. Your failure to make a jump bid in a new suit (forcing to game) limits the strength of your hand.

47. *Bid two diamonds.* A bid in a new suit indicates more than a bare minimum opening bid, even if only in distribution.

48. *Bid three diamonds.* The jump in a new suit is forcing to game.

49. *Bid one notrump.* Balanced distribution and a minimum opening bid. Beware of rebidding the mangy heart suit when you have a comfortable rebid that describes your hand more accurately.

50. *Bid two notrump.* This bid usually promises 19

points, but your fifth heart may be counted as an additional point.

51. *Bid three clubs.* The raise to the level of three promises well above minimum opening-bid strength.

52. *Bid four clubs.* The raise to four of a minor promises a side singleton or void, with a total strength (including the short suit) of about 20 points. Slam must be considered.

53. *Bid two hearts.* Promises only a minimum opening bid with a rebiddable suit.

54. *Bid three hearts.* This promises a strong heart suit of six cards or more, with at least 15 points in high cards. The partnership should go to game—perhaps to slam.

55. *Bid four hearts.* This shows a good hand with an independent heart suit. If partner has a good hand, with two or more aces, he may try for a slam. If he has only one ace, he should be warned by the fact that you made no move of your own toward slam.

56. *Bid two notrump.* This shows 15 to 17 points, with balanced distribution and stoppers in the unbid suits.

57. *Bid three notrump.* This promises 18 or 19 points (or a mangy 20 points), with balanced distribution and stoppers in the unbid suits.

58. *Bid two diamonds.* As usual, show the side suit.

59. *Bid three diamonds.* Forcing to game.

60. *Bid two spades.* The "reverse" bid is forcing for one round since partner has made a strength-showing response.

61. *Bid three hearts.* This shows about 11 to 13 points in support of hearts. You bid a suit of your own and then raise. Partner is invited to go on but may pass.

62. *Bid four hearts.* Don't be content with an invitation when you are sure that you want to reach game.

63. *Bid three diamonds.* This sequence—two and then three of your suit—shows a good suit but a weak hand. Partner is expected to pass.

64. *Pass.* No need to insist on your own suit when partner's suit is rebiddable. Avoid this auction like the plague, however. In general, a response at the level of two indicates that you are prepared to bid at least once more.

65. *Bid two notrump.* This shows balanced distribution, with about 11 to 13 points in high cards.

66. *Bid three notrump.* This shows balanced distribution, with about 14 to 16 points in high cards.

67. *Bid three notrump.* The stopper in clubs is sketchy, but the solid diamonds more than make up for this weakness.

68. *Bid two spades.* The reverse by responder is treated by experts as forcing to game. You are trying for notrump. If partner can stop the clubs, he will bid notrump.

69. *Bid three clubs.* You hate to bid a new suit at the level of three with no sign of a fit, but you must take strong action with your 13 points in high cards.

70. *Bid three clubs.* You intend to raise hearts at your next turn. This is the best way to show a hand too strong for a double raise (13 to 16 points) but not strong enough for a jump bid in a new suit (19 points or more).

71. *Bid two hearts.* This should promise slightly better than 10 points in support of hearts. With less, you would raise to two hearts at your first turn.

72. *Bid three hearts.* A simple preference bid of two hearts would not do justice to this hand. Your bid promises about 13 or 14 points in support of hearts.

73. *Bid four hearts.* This sequence promises strong heart support and a long side suit, almost surely ten cards in the two suits. If partner has a control or two in the unbid suits, he should try for a slam.

74. *Bid three diamonds.* This encouraging bid shows the location of your strength and may help partner bid three notrump if he can stop the unbid suit.

75. *Bid four diamonds.* The jump past the level of

three notrump shows, as always, a singleton or void suit. Your strength is limited by the fact that you bid only four, not five, diamonds.

76. *Bid two spades.* This promises a good 6-card (or longer) suit and denies three cards in either of partner's suits.

77. *Bid three spades.* Not only a good 6-card suit but also enough strength to force to game—about 13 points or more.

78. *Bid four spades.* An independent spade suit and about 13 points in high cards (don't forget to upgrade the queen of partner's suit). Partner should think of a slam if he has a singleton or the king of clubs and controls in the red suits.

79. *Bid two notrump.* This promises balanced distribution, a stopper in the unbid suit, and about 11 to 13 points.

80. *Bid three notrump.* This promises balanced distribution, at least two stoppers in the unbid suit, and about 14 to 16 points.

81. *Bid four hearts.* Do not make a slam try with a minimum opening bid opposite a hand of only 13 to 16 points.

82. *Bid three notrump.* With a 4-card suit, suggest game at notrump.

83. *Bid four clubs.* You can afford to make one try for slam. Bid your side ace.

84. *Bid four clubs.* Even if partner signs off, try again by bidding the diamonds. You can afford to commit the hand to the level of five.

85. *Bid four diamonds.* You can afford one try for slam, and your failure to bid clubs should be very significant to partner.

86. *Bid three spades.* This is a cue bid, like the three previous cases. Do not use Blackwood with a worthless doubleton in an unbid suit.

87. *Bid four clubs.* Avoid Blackwood because you have a void suit.

88. *Bid four notrump.* With controls in each of the unbid suits (an ace, a king, and a singleton), you can afford to use the Blackwood Convention. If partner shows two aces, you expect to try for a grand slam by bidding *five* notrump.

89. *Bid four notrump.* The Blackwood Convention again. If partner shows two aces, you bid five notrump to ask for kings. A grand slam is far from unlikely.

90. *Bid four notrump.* You know that partner has no aces, but you intend to bid five notrump to ask for kings. This will tell partner that *you* have all four aces, which may enable him to jump to a grand slam.

91. *Bid two hearts.* A free raise of partner's major suit promises only 7 points or so. You have 7 points in high cards, 1 point extra for the queen of partner's suit, and 1 point for the doubleton.

92. *Bid three hearts.* Just as though no overcall had been made.

93. *Bid four hearts.* Ignore the overcall.

94. *Bid one notrump.* This promises at least one stopper in the opponent's suit, with about 10 to 12 points and balanced distribution. (The weakness notrump response is not needed after an overcall.)

95. *Bid two notrump.* Much the same as though the overcall had not been made, except that you promise *two* stoppers in the opponent's suit.

96. *Bid two clubs.* You intend to raise hearts later, just as though no overcall had been made.

97. *Bid three clubs.* The forcing takeout, hinting at a slam.

98. *Bid two spades.* This cue bid shows ace or void in the opponent's suit together with strong support for partner's suit and a very powerful hand. With lesser support

for partner's suit, you would make a jump bid in your own suit first (as in Number 97).

99. *Double.* The "light" penalty double.

100. *Pass.* You are unprepared for any other suit. The double of a low contract should promise at least 1½ Quick Tricks outside of the doubled suit.

101. *Bid one spade.* A minimum overcall.

102. *Pass.* Not enough playing tricks for an overcall at the level of two.

103. *Bid two diamonds.* This hand should take five tricks even against very bad breaks. It is just barely worth a non-vulnerable overcall at the level of two.

104. *Bid two diamonds.* A comfortable overcall. You would make the same bid even if vulnerable.

105. *Bid two spades* if you use weak jump overcalls. Otherwise you must bid *one* spade.

106. *Bid three diamonds* if you use weak jump overcalls. Otherwise, pass.

107. *Pass.* Do not overcall without a good suit.

108. *Bid one notrump.* This is the same as an opening bid of one notrump, except that it guarantees at least one (usually two) stoppers in the opponent's suit.

109. *Double.* A takeout double, asking partner to bid.

110. *Double.* You expect to bid vigorously at your next turn.

111. *Bid two spades.* If partner has a very strong overcall, he will go to game.

112. *Bid three spades.* Partner is expected to go to game unless he is ashamed of his overcall.

113. *Bid four spades.* You want to be in game even if partner is ashamed of his overcall. (Take full credit, also, for three diamonds.)

114. *Pass.* You have no reason to suppose you will be better off in any other contract.

115. *Bid two diamonds.* This shows a good diamond suit and denies spade support.

116. *Bid three diamonds.* You expect to raise spades next, forcing to game and hinting at a slam.

117. *Bid four spades.* Not enough for a slam try, but you certainly want to be in game.

118. *Bid one notrump.* This bid, as usual, shows balanced distribution and stoppers in the opponent's suit. The strength should be about 9 to 12 points.

119. *Bid two notrump.* Highly invitational but not completely forcing. The bid shows balanced distribution, stoppers in the opponent's suit, and about 13 or 14 points.

120. *Bid three notrump.* You are willing to be in game even if partner is ashamed of his overcall.

121. *Bid one spade.* Yours not to reason why.

122. *Bid one spade.* No need to hold your breath this time.

123. *Bid two diamonds.* Bid the better of two 4-card suits.

124. *Bid two clubs.* Bid the longer suit.

125. *Bid two spades.* Prefer a response in a major suit even if your minor suit is stronger. The jump is strength-showing but only invitational, not forcing.

126. *Bid two spades.* Much the same as the previous case.

127. *Bid two hearts.* The cue bid in the opponent's suit is the strongest response you can make to a takeout double. You expect to get to game in spades, but if partner insists on notrump, you accept game in notrump.

128. *Bid one notrump.* This strength-showing response denies a good major-suit holding but shows at least one stopper in the opponent's suit.

129. *Bid two clubs.* When your only long suit has been bid by the opponent, respond in your *lowest* 3-card suit.

130. *Pass.* The penalty pass shows solid strength and length in the opponent's suit. In effect, *you* are going to become declarer and you intend to draw trumps.

131. *Pass.* No need to intervene.

132. *Bid two diamonds.* In a good partnership this bid is treated as a force for one round.

133. *Bid two hearts.* Heart support and a *very* weak hand.

134. *Bid three hearts.* Heart support and the strength of a normal single raise.

135. *Bid four hearts.* The usual shutout bid.

136. *Redouble.* You intend to raise hearts one level at your next turn.

137. *Redouble.* You intend to jump-raise hearts at your next turn.

138. *Redouble.* You hope to double the opponents at any contract. (Take full credit for a pass.)

139. *Bid one notrump.* This shows scattered strength of about 8 to 10 points.

140. *Bid four diamonds.* An attempt to make life difficult for the opponents.

141. *Pass.* You have 16 points in support of spades, but your partner may have 0 points.

142. *Bid two spades.* You have 18 points in support of spades. There is little danger even if partner has a bust.

143. *Bid three spades.* You have 20 points in support of spades. This raise begs partner to go on if he has any strength at all.

144. *Bid four spades.* You have 22 points in support of spades and should have a reasonable play for game even if partner has as little as J-x-x-x of spades and no side strength. Don't be content to *invite* a game when you can bid it by yourself.

145. *Bid two diamonds.* This sequence shows a very powerful hand. If you had only modest strength, you would bid two diamonds at your first turn instead of doubling and then bidding your suit.

146. *Bid three spades.* This should show a strong but topless 7-card suit with no side strength.

147. *Bid four hearts.* The 8-card suit without side strength.

148. *Bid four diamonds.* Risky but worth a shot. Don't bid three of a minor when you can stretch to four. Bid your maximum or pass.

149. *Bid five diamonds.* Another case of bidding the maximum at once. You are not likely to make five diamonds, but you cannot be badly hurt and you have no defense against a slam.

150. *Pass.* Shutout bids and defensive strength do not mix.

151. *Pass.* You are unwilling to go on since you have a minimum opening bid, and unwilling to double since you have a singleton heart. Let partner make the decision.

152. *Double.* A pass would encourage partner to go on, and you have a minimum bid with mediocre distribution.

153. *Bid five spades.* You have enough strength to act by yourself. Don't ask partner to do what you can do yourself.

154. *Bid six spades.* The bidding indicates that partner's strength is not in hearts. It is hard to imagine what sort of hand North can have that will not provide a fine play for slam.

155. *Bid six clubs.* This commits the partnership to a slam and hints at a grand slam. If North can bid six diamonds, you intend to bid seven spades. (Take full credit, however, for six hearts or six spades.)

156. *Lead the king of spades.* This is a good attacking lead in an unbid suit.

157. *Lead the king of spades.* Much the same as the previous case.

158. *Lead the queen of spades.* Again, an attacking lead from a sequence of honors in an unbid suit.

159. *Lead the jack of spades.* You must lead one of

the unbid suits. The sequence in spades is safer than the broken strength in diamonds.

160. *Lead the four of diamonds.* It is better to lead away from a queen than from an ace.

161. *Lead the five of hearts.* The unbid suits furnish undesirable leads. Dummy's clubs are no threat. Lead a trump and let declarer develop the hand for himself.

162. *Lead the three of spades.* Try to develop a long side suit when you have four or more trumps. You want to force declarer to ruff your long suit.

163. *Lead the seven of diamonds.* The ideal time to lead a singleton is when you have reason to believe you can get the lead to your partner (if you can't in this case, the hand is hopeless) and when you can stop declarer from drawing all of your trumps in a hurry.

164. *Lead the seven of diamonds.* You may develop a ruffing trick, and in any case this is a good passive lead.

165. *Lead the jack of diamonds.* With strength in each of the other suits, you make the lead that is least likely to cost a trick.

166. *Lead the king of diamonds.* A good attacking lead in an unbid suit.

167. *Lead the seven of diamonds.* You are willing to give up the first diamond trick in the hope of developing the rest of the suit. (Take half credit for leading the king of diamonds.)

168. *Lead the queen of diamonds.* A good attacking lead in an unbid suit.

169. *Lead the jack of diamonds.* The conventional lead from this combination.

170. *Lead the ten of diamonds.* Once again, the conventional lead from a suit with an interior sequence.

171. *Lead the three of diamonds.* Fourth best from your longest and strongest.

172. *Lead the three of diamonds.* Not much of a suit,

but nothing else looks much better. (Take full credit likewise for leading the five of hearts.)

173. *Lead the jack of diamonds.* No lead looks very good, but this is least likely to cost a trick.

174. *Lead the deuce of spades.* Since you have nothing of your own to set up, you might as well try to set up something for your partner. When in doubt about a suit, lead the unbid *major* suit.

175. *Lead the king of clubs.* Declarer's suit may be short or weak. Even if he has a "real" club suit, you can probably set up enough tricks to worry him badly.

176. *Refuse the first two spade tricks and win the third.* Then take the diamond finesse. If this loses, East may be unable to lead a spade. If East returns a club, do *not* finesse. Take your nine tricks.

177. *Refuse the first spade and take the second.* You must tackle both minor suits to develop nine tricks. Unless West has both aces (and takes them promptly), the hold-up play will help you fulfill your contract.

178. *Win the heart, lead the ace of diamonds, and then lead the queen of diamonds.* When you eventually get to dummy with the ace of spades, you will return a club for the finesse. Since you can finesse only once, you try the finesse in clubs. A single finesse in diamonds is unlikely to help, but a single finesse in clubs will probably make a full trick's difference.

179. *Take the ace of diamonds and continue hearts.* If West has to win, your queen of diamonds is safe. If East has the king of hearts and leads another diamond, you can put up the queen or play low (in the hope of blocking the suit), as you judge best. There is no need to risk the finesse on the first round of the suit.

180. *Win with the ace of clubs and lead a low diamond.* If West puts up the king and leads another club, take the king of clubs, cash the queen of diamonds, and return a trump to the ace (refusing the finesse) in order

to cash the ace of diamonds and discard dummy's last club. If East has the king of diamonds, you must later try the heart finesse.

181. *Win the club, take the ace of spades, and then lead the ten of spades and let it ride for a finesse* (unless the queen shows up). If the finesse loses, you still make ten tricks; if it wins, you make eleven. You cannot afford to let *East* win a trump trick, since he will lead diamonds through your king.

182. *Win the spade and lead the king of hearts.* You have time to set up three heart tricks, but you don't have time to develop the longer club suit.

183. *Overtake the king of hearts with dummy's ace.* Then lead the jack of hearts to force out the queen. You can surely develop four heart tricks, assuring the contract.

184. *Cash the top hearts and give up a heart trick.* You want to run dummy's clubs without interruption.

185. *Take the ace of clubs and run three rounds of diamonds at once to get rid of a club.* If this all works, try the spade finesse next. (Take full credit for leading out the ace of spades before running the diamonds.)

186. Take all the side aces and then cross-ruff. That is, ruff clubs in the dummy and hearts in your own hand.

187. *Ruff the first club (unless dummy's king wins by some weird chance), draw trumps, and finesse the nine of diamonds.* If this loses, dummy's diamonds will afford discards for the losing hearts. If the nine of diamonds wins, lead the other diamond to dummy's ace! Then lead the ten of hearts for a finesse. (A repeated diamond finesse might lose to a crafty opponent, and then you would go down.) Take no credit for trying the heart finesse first: if it loses, you still need the diamond finesse.

188. *Refuse the first spade trick, and win the second in dummy.* Overtake the queen of diamonds with your king and continue the suit until the ace is played. Now

the ace of spades is your entry to the long diamonds.

189. *Win the diamond, draw trumps with the king and queen of hearts, then lead the king of spades and continue spades until the ace is played.* The ace of hearts is the entry to the rest of the spades. If one opponent has three hearts you must let the third heart stay undrawn until you have developed the spades.

190. *Win the club and lead the ten of hearts.* If West plays low, put up dummy's king. If you can "steal" this heart trick, you can survive the loss of the diamond finesse. However, if you try the diamonds first and lose the finesse, there is no chance of stealing a heart trick later on, for West will surely take his ace as the setting trick. Don't draw trumps first because you don't want East to have the chance to signal with a high diamond.

191. *Lead a diamond to dummy's queen and return a trump.* If East plays low, finesse the ten as a safety play. You don't mind losing the finesse, since the last trump will surely drop on your king. This protects you against Q-J-x-x in the East hand.

192. *Lead the three of clubs.* East will win (since the queen shows the jack or a singleton) and will return a heart up to dummy's weakness.

193. *Continue with the queen of hearts.* If both of the missing hearts appear (as you suspect when the five fails to drop), cash the ace of diamonds and lead a *low* heart. The idea is to make partner ruff as high as possible. If he can ruff with the queen, he will set up your jack as the setting trick. You will defeat the contract even if partner has Q-x or singleton king of trumps.

194. *Lead the four of clubs to partner's probable queen.* (His eight of clubs is an encouraging signal, almost surely based on possession of the queen.) He will then lead a heart up to dummy's weakness, and you can take two heart tricks to defeat the contract. If this defense doesn't work, nothing else will.

195. *Overtake the queen of diamonds with your king, and return the seven of diamonds to knock out the jack.* This establishes your suit, and the ace of clubs allows you to cash the rest of the diamonds in time to set the contract. If you fail to overtake, partner may have to shift. You get only three diamonds and the ace of clubs.

196. *Cash the rest of the diamonds.* If nobody ruffs, take the ace of spades and give up a spade! If East has the king of spades, he must now lead a club (or give you a ruff-sluff), limiting your loss to one club trick. Even if West has the king of spades and leads a club, you duck in dummy and let East win if he can. Now East is caught in the end-play. It would be wrong to take the spade finesse, for West might win and return a club. Now East could win and get out safely with a spade.

197. *Run the rest of the trumps, discarding a club and two hearts from dummy.* Then take three diamonds, ending in dummy. If the player with the hearts also has the king and queen of clubs, he will be caught in a squeeze.

198. *Draw trumps, cash the top clubs and top hearts, and ruff a club.* Then lead the rest of the trumps, playing for a double squeeze. If West has length in clubs and East has the queen of hearts, the double squeeze operates. A single squeeze works if West has the only diamond stopper and either length in clubs or the queen of hearts; or if East has the only diamond stopper and the queen of hearts. The squeeze does not work if East has the only diamond stopper and also length in clubs; he just discards whatever dummy does.

199. *Cash the top diamonds and ruff a diamond.* Lead a club to the ace and ruff another diamond. Exit with your low club and wait for the lead to come up to your A K J in spades.

V | DUPLICATE BRIDGE- WINNING TECHNIQUES

DUPLICATE BRIDGE-WINNING TECHNIQUES

THE BASIC IDEA of tournament bridge is that each hand is played by many different foursomes. When some players get better results than others with the very same cards, the difference is clearly due to skill.

Your score in a tournament does not depend on the cards you hold, but on what you do with them.

There are many advantages to tournament play:

- It enlarges your circle of bridge acquaintances.
- There's no need to telephone a dozen friends to arrange a good game.
- You can compete against famous experts without risking a cent more than the modest entry fee.
- There's always something to learn whenever your result is not as good as somebody else's.

Fundamentally, however, the thrill of tournament bridge is in the spirited competition. A good bridge player is a born competitor.

✓ MECHANICS OF TOURNAMENT PLAY

The best way to learn the procedure is to go to a tournament or a club duplicate game and watch the players. In a few minutes you'll feel like a veteran.

The first time a hand is played, the cards are shuffled and dealt just as in rubber bridge. But during the course of each trick the players, instead of throwing their cards into the middle of the table, merely show them face up. Thus, you have to look in four places to see the whole trick, but this becomes automatic after a few minutes.

When all four cards of a trick have been noted, each player places his card face down in front of himself—pointing it toward the side that won the trick. At the end of the hand, each player has his original thirteen cards arranged in front of himself—separate from any other player's cards.

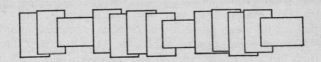

When the hand has been played each player picks up his cards and puts them into the correct pocket of a special tray.

The tray, called a *duplicate board,* is then passed on to another table—where four different players will withdraw the cards to bid and play the very same hand. Similarly, some of the players move to different tables, where they will encounter new opponents and different hands.

The board indicates which player is dealer and which side (if either) is vulnerable. Each deal is treated as a unit by itself. Part scores are not carried forward to the next hand; bidding and making a game does not make a player vulnerable on the next board.

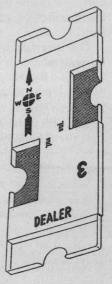

The penalties and bonuses are the same as in rubber bridge with these exceptions:

- Honors are not counted.
- Bonus for nonvulnerable game is 300 points.
- Bonus for a vulnerable game is always 500 points.
- Bonus for a part score is 50 points.

Your total score on each hand is treated as a single figure. For example, if you are nonvulnerable, bid six spades, and make all thirteen tricks, you get 1010 points —500 for the slam bonus, 300 for the game bonus, 180 for tricks bid and made, and 30 for the overtrick.

✓ PAIR CONTESTS

Bridge is primarily a partnership game, and tournament bridge is primarily a game of pairs competing against other pairs. You go to the club ready to play with your own partner.

In a club duplicate, one end of the room is labeled North (purely for convenience; it may actually be south-

southeast). The arrow on each duplicate board points to the North sign, establishing which pair at the table is North-South and which is East-West.

The North-South pairs remain at the same table throughout the session. The East-West pairs move to a new table for each round of play. Each table is numbered, and each pair takes the number of the original table as its pair number.

In a club duplicate, the score is kept on a folded slip of paper tucked into a pocket of the duplicate board and passed along with the board and cards. After a hand has been played, the North player unfolds the scoreslip, enters the result, and puts the slip back into the pocket.

Suppose North has doubled the opponents at four hearts and has set them three tricks on Board 25. He and his partner are North-South Pair 4, and their opponents are East-West Pair 8. North writes the score on the fourth line as shown in the diagram on the following page.

North does not carry forward the 800 points from this hand; he does not add it to what he has won on other hands. This form of scoring, used many years ago, was abandoned because it permitted a few "big" hands to decide the outcome of the tournament. There was no need to play carefully on most hands if you were either skillful or lucky on the big hands.

/ MATCH-POINT SCORING

In the method now used, you are awarded 1 match point for each pair whose score you beat and ½ match point for each pair whose score you tie. If you are North-South your score is compared only with that of other North-South pairs; if you are East-West, only with that of other East-West pairs.

OFFICIAL (Mitchell or Howell) TRAVELING SCORE

Bid, Play & Score this board without comment and Proceed immediately to the next.

NORTH PLAYER only keeps score

ENTER PAIR NO OF EW PAIR   Board No. __25__

N.S. Pair	EW Pair	CON-TRACT	BY	MADE	DOWN	NORTH SOUTH Net Plus	NORTH SOUTH Net Minus	EW Match Points	NS Match Points
1	2	3S	N	4		170			7
2	4	3S	N	3		140			4½
3	6	4S	N	4		420			9
4	8	4H^x	W		3	800			12
5	10	4S	N		1		50		1
6	12	3S	N	4		170			7
7	1	1NT	N	1		90			2
8	3	2S	N	3		140			4½
9	5	4H^x	W		2	500			10½
10	7	3NT	N		2		100		0
11	9	3S	N	4		170			7
12	11	4H^x	W		2	500			10½
13	13	1NT	S	2		120			3
14									
15									
16									
17									
18								1	10
19								2	5
20								3	7½
21								4	7½
22								5	1½

508

The top award for any hand is 1 point less than the number of foursomes that played the hand. In most tournaments conducted by the American Contract Bridge League, each hand is played 13 times so that the top score on each hand is 12 match points.

The bottom award for any hand is 0 match points.

Thus, all hands are equally important. It counts just as much to do well on a part score as on a slam.

Take the score of North-South Pair 1 in our diagram: They beat the score of six pairs (2, 5, 7, 8, 10, and 13) and tied the score of two pairs (6 and 11), so they receive 7 match points.

North-South Pair 4 get the top award of 12 match points for beating the score of all twelve other pairs. Pair 10 gets a bottom, 0 match points, because their score neither beat nor tied any other pair's score.

East-West are scored in the same way. East-West Pair 2 gets 5 points for being minus 170. They beat the score of four East-West pairs by *losing less* than those pairs, and they tied the score of two other East-West pairs.

As this example shows, you may receive several match points for a minus score. In theory, you may be top on a board even though your score is minus more than 1000 points.

At the end of the session all the scoreslips are matchpointed, and the results are added to obtain the total for each pair. The top-scoring North-South and East-West pairs are declared winners.

There are special movements to determine a single pair as the winner for both directions in one session, or in two or more sessions. Tournament direction and scoring require special study and experience. But, even though you may never be asked to help score a tournament, you should nonetheless know how it is done.

✓ SMALL DIFFERENCES

In rubber bridge you can afford to get the worst of the skirmishes if you win the big battles. Therefore you concentrate on bidding and making slams, on collecting large penalties, and on staying out of trouble on dangerous hands. You relax during the play of part-score hands, especially if the contract is in no danger. Similarly, you ease up during the bidding of part-score hands; it is no great tragedy if your opponents occasionally steal such a hand from you.

All this is different in tournament bridge. You don't need huge scores. You get just as many match points for an extra trick that nobody else managed to win as for collecting a penalty of 2600 points. A part-score hand counts for just as many match points as a slam hand.

In rubber bridge, you are satisfied with good results on four big hands and mediocre results on twenty others. In a tournament, the same result would put you hopelessly out of the running.

The search for a small extra score forces the tournament player to take big risks in both the bidding and the play:

WEST	EAST
♠ A K Q 9 4 2	♠ 10 3
♡ A 6	♡ K 7 3 2
♢ 7 3	♢ A 9 8 5
♣ 8 6 4	♣ A K 7

The bidding in rubber bridge:

WEST	EAST
1 ♠	2 NT
4 ♠	Pass

West wins eleven tricks if the spades break normally, and ten tricks even if the spades break badly. No problem, no risk.

Tournament experts might bid it differently:

WEST	EAST
1 ♠	2 NT
3 NT	Pass

If the spades break normally, East wins, at notrump, the same eleven tricks that can be made at spades. Even if the spades break badly, a heart or club opening lead permits East to win, at notrump, the same ten tricks that can be made at spades.

Still, there is a greater risk at notrump. Diamonds may be led, and the spades may fail to break normally. East may even go down at three notrump.

✔ NOTRUMP PAYS OFF

Why does the tournament player take this risk? Because he wants the 10 extra points for playing the hand at notrump. Vulnerable, the score for making five spades is 650 points; for making five notrump, 660 points. (The non-vulnerable scores: 450 and 460 points.) This trifling 10-point edge may bring in as many match points as bidding and making a slam on another hand.

The idea of trying for this extra 10 points does not occur to the rubber-bridge player. For him it's a poor gamble, since the game in notrump will be beaten two or three times in a hundred attempts, and this more than offsets the 10-point gain per success.

The experienced tournament player bids notrump instead of a major suit when the suit is solid and his distribution is balanced. But when the distribution is unbalanced even the ambitious tournament player will stick to the major suit.

WEST	EAST
♠ A K Q 9 4 2	♠ 10 3
♡ A 6	♡ K 7 3 2
◇ 7	◇ A 9 8 5
♣ 8 6 4 3	♣ A K 7

As before, West opens with one spade, and East bids two notrump. West should bid four spades whether the game is rubber bridge or tournament bridge.

At notrump, East could probably win only eleven tricks. At spades, West has a good play for a twelfth trick—and no tournament player wants to score 660 points when the rest of the field is scoring 680 points with the same cards.

In fact, a tournament player would aim for twelve tricks in the play of the cards—even at some slight risk of going down. Let's compare the play at rubber and the play at duplicate.

Assume a diamond lead, taken by dummy's ace. The rubber-bridge player draws trumps at once and then starts the clubs. If the clubs break 3-3, his last club is good; if not, he is content to give up a second club trick.

The tournament player does not draw trumps. Instead, he cashes the top clubs at once. If all goes well, he leads dummy's third club.

There is no need to draw trumps if the clubs break 3-3, and it costs nothing to test the suit before drawing trumps. If the clubs break 4-2, declarer's best chance for twelve tricks is to ruff his fourth club with dummy's ten of spades. This will work if the jack of spades is in the hand that has four clubs.

If the clubs are 5-1 or 6-0, declarer is in trouble. He may even go down. But the experienced tournament player faces this sort of risk several times a session. You cannot afford to be the only player in the room who fails to win a twelfth trick.

✓ MINOR SUITS—LAST RESORT

The time to play a hand at a minor-suit contract is when a major suit or notrump is out of the question. It's also acceptable when you expect to be defeated, since the penalties for minor suits are no worse than those for any other type of contract.

But if you expect to make your contract, stay out of a minor suit. You can usually score more points at notrump or a major suit, even though such contracts may be riskier.

WEST	EAST
♠ K 6 2	♠ A 5
♡ 8 4	♡ 7 6 3
◇ A Q J 9 5	◇ K 10 8 7
♣ A 7 5	♣ K Q 4 2

West opens with one diamond, and East raises to three diamonds. Where do they go from here?

In rubber bridge, West may bid three spades to show a stopper. East may shy away from notrump because he lacks a heart stopper. Good bidders would get to five diamonds, the safe and sane game contract.

In tournament bridge, West would probably bid three notrump at his second turn. If, instead, West bid three spades, East would bid three notrump.

West can score only 400 or 600 points at diamonds, depending on vulnerability. But at notrump, if hearts are not led, he has a fine chance to score 30 or 60 additional points. And even if hearts *are* led, the suit may block, or may divide 4-4. Notrump is riskier, but the chance for extra tricks is critically important in a tournament.

Unless you hold an unusually unbalanced hand, you don't want to play at five clubs or five diamonds. Once you get past three notrump, you usually keep going until you reach slam. Making game in a minor suit gets you next to nothing, so you might just as well bid the slam and try for something worthwhile.

WEST	EAST
♠ K 6 2	♠ A 5
♡ 8	♡ K 6 3
◇ A K J 9 5 4	◇ Q 10 8 7
♣ A 7 5	♣ K 9 4 2

West opens with one diamond. East should respond two notrump. If, instead, East makes the less informative response of three diamonds, the partnership may wander past three notrump.

WEST	EAST
1 ◇	3 ◇
3 ♠	3 NT
4 ♣	4 ♠
5 ◇	6 ◇
Pass	

West bids three spades to show a stopper, or to try for a slam—he isn't sure which. East bids three notrump, the best match-point contract.

West, wanting to do some more exploring, may bid four clubs, and East can afford to show the ace of spades.

By this time it is too late to get back to notrump. Four notrump would probably sound like Blackwood. West must bid five diamonds, and East should go on to six on the theory that a dead lion is no worse off than a dead mouse.

West will make the slam if the ace of hearts is in favorable position. A little ambitious, but which of us has never been in a worse slam?

At most tables, East will play this hand at three no-trump, making ten or eleven tricks. Any pair that plays the hand at five diamonds will score 30 or 40 points less and, therefore, will lose several match points.

The same principle applies to part-score contracts.

WEST	EAST
♠ K Q 2	♠ J 9 7 6
♡ 9 4	♡ 6 3 2
◇ A J 10 8 7	◇ K Q 9 6
♣ K Q 3	♣ J 5

West opens with one diamond. In rubber bridge, East may ignore his weak spade suit and simply raise to two diamonds. West can make three diamonds, losing one spade, two hearts, and one club.

In duplicate, East cannot afford to keep quiet about the spades. He responds one spade, and West raises to two spades. With a little luck, East will make the same nine tricks and will score 140 points (90 points for tricks and 50 points for bidding and making a part score). This is 30 total points and several match points better than the 110 points that West would get for making three diamonds.

You do play the hand at a minor suit when no better contract is available:

WEST	EAST
♠ K 6 2	♠ J 9 7
♡ 9	♡ 6 3 2
◇ A J 10 8 7	◇ K Q 9 6
♣ K Q 4 3	♣ J 5 2

WEST	EAST
1 ◇	2 ◇
3 ◇	Pass

East, having neither a major suit nor the side strength needed for notrump, raises to two diamonds. West immediately sees that the hand belongs to the opponents: since East cannot have either a good hand or four cards in a major suit, the opponents must have a fine fit in hearts and about half of the high-card strength in the deck.

If West pusillanimously passes at two diamonds, North will surely reopen the bidding. Then West will have to bid four or five diamonds as a sacrifice against a heart contract. Instead, West should go on to three diamonds at once. The opponents may know that West is trying to shut them out, but he has nevertheless made it harder for them to enter the auction.

✓ SACRIFICE BIDDING

It's hard to judge a sacrifice accurately in rubber bridge. Should you sacrifice 300 points to stop the opponents from making a nonvulnerable game? Is 500 points too much? What about giving up 700 points to stop a vulnerable game?

In rubber bridge you seldom know the exact value of a game. Sometimes you're not sure the opponents would bid the game if left to their own devices, or would make the game if allowed to play the hand.

In duplicate you know the exact value of a game. You know with certainty when a sacrifice is sound and when it is unsound.

Against a part score you can afford to sacrifice 50 or 100 points. The opponents can score more than this by making a small part score. Once in a blue moon you can afford to give up 150 points, but usually this is a fatal number. The enemy's part score is usually worth only

110 to 140 points. You cannot afford 200 points (down one, doubled, vulnerable). That number is death, because it is more than any part score the opponents normally make.

Against a nonvulnerable game you can afford to sacrifice 200 or 300 points. If the penalty gets up to 500 points, you are headed for a goose egg when the hand is matchpointed.

Against a vulnerable game you can afford to sacrifice 500 points. Not 700. Not 800.

∤ YOUR TRUE OPPONENTS

When you take a sacrifice at duplicate, you don't worry too much about what your opponents at the table would have done if you hadn't sacrificed. You're more concerned about your *true* opponents.

Your true opponents are not at the table. You never play against them. They are the players who hold *your* cards during the course of the session.

If you are sitting North-South, your true opponents are the other North-South players. If you are sitting East-West, your true opponents are the other East-West players.

Your objective is to score a bigger plus than your true opponents on the good cards, and a smaller minus on the bad cards.

Suppose you double your table opponents at an insane contract and have the chance to collect a penalty of 1700 points. You don't cry your eyes out when you drop two tickets and collect a measly 1100. That is still enough to defeat all your true opponents and earn you a top score on the board. You couldn't get more than top even if you boosted the penalty up to 2300 points.

If you get to a reasonable contract and are set one trick, you don't bewail your minus score. You may still have a finer score—even a top. Perhaps all your true opponents have bigger minus scores.

After gaining experience in tournament play, you often resolve a bidding problem by considering what the rest of the field will do. If you bid and play every hand exactly like the others, you wind up with an average score. The slavish conformist never wins a cup or a master point. Still, you do tend to go along with the field unless you have a special reason for doing something different.

/ GOING AGAINST THE FIELD

Unfortunately, your opponents may be unreliable enough to play well against you. Worse yet, your partner may make a few mistakes (we won't talk about *you*). And there you are, headed for the bottom of the ranking.

After a few such debacles, you may decide to go against the field in borderline cases. If you think the field will stop at part score, you bid game; and vice versa. You bid notrump when the field will be in a suit; you double the opponents instead of bidding on; you pass a hand out instead of opening in fourth position.

You can go against the field in the play as well as in the bidding. Suppose you have K-J-10-x-x of trumps in your own hand, with A-x-x in the dummy. The field will surely take dummy's ace and then lead another trump for a finesse (see Diagram 11 page 366). Instead, you take the king and then lead the jack for a finesse. You will have a top if you are right, a bottom if you are wrong.

Sometimes you have a particular reason for going against the field. You may have a special bidding wrinkle that tells you something the field doesn't know. It is certainly sound to go against the field if you are right and they are wrong.

When you are tempted to go against the field, check your reasoning. You cannot afford to be wrong very often. Nobody will blame you for making an unsuccessful bid or play that was attempted at all the other tables, but your partner will start to brood if you collect several bottoms for hunches that go sour. Part of the art of winning tournaments consists in keeping your partner happy enough to play well.

✓ OVERCALLS IN DUPLICATE

There are many reasons for getting into the auction at tournament bridge. Your overcall may:

- Get you to a good contract
- Steal the hand from the enemy
- Indicate the best opening lead
- Lead to a paying sacrifice
- Interfere with the enemy's bidding

Conversely, there are clear disadvantages. Your overcall may:

- Result in a disastrous penalty
- Keep the opponents out of trouble
- Tell the opponents where the cards are

On balance, the arguments favor bidding. You are less worried about penalties than in rubber bridge. A severe penalty gives you only one bad score; you may get it all back by stealing one overtrick on the very next hand. In rubber bridge, however, you must sometimes struggle for hours to recover from one disastrous penalty.

You can afford to overcall with a light hand in duplicate if your suit will stand a lead. But beware of bidding on a suit such as J-10-x-x-x. It may cost your partner a trick to lead the ace or king, and overtricks are usually worth several match points.

✓ COMPETITIVE BIDDING

Part scores are fiercely contested in tournament bridge. If each side can make a part score, it is a disaster to sell out and let the opponents get the plus score.

Even if the hand belongs to the opponents, you may still wish to put up a fight. Perhaps you can push them too high. Or maybe you can play the hand and get away with a loss of only 50 or 100 points.

A typical match-point struggle for the part score:

```
                    NORTH
                    ♠ K J 7 4
                    ♡ 5
                    ◇ Q J 10 7
                    ♣ J 8 5 4

    WEST                              EAST
    ♠ 5                               ♠ 10 9 8
    ♡ 10 9 8 4                        ♡ A K J 3 2
    ◇ A K 5 3                         ◇ 8 6
    ♣ 10 9 7 6                        ♣ A 3 2

                    SOUTH
                    ♠ A Q 6 3 2
                    ♡ Q 7 6
                    ◇ 9 4 2
                    ♣ K Q
```

EAST	SOUTH	WEST	NORTH
1 ♡	1 ♠	2 ♡	2 ♠
Pass	Pass	3 ♡	Pass
Pass	3 ♠	Pass	Pass
?			

In rubber bridge East would pass or bid four hearts without worrying very much about the hand. In duplicate East should consider doubling three spades.

Consider the jockeying that has already taken place. East could make just three hearts, since he would lose a spade, a trump, and two clubs. South could make only two spades, since he would lose one heart, one club, two top diamonds, and a diamond ruff. If North-South are not vulnerable, they would give up only 50 or 100 points for stealing the hand from East.

At the end of the session, the scoresheet will show a few East-West pairs tied for top with 140 points for playing the hand at two or three hearts; one or two Easts will have 100 points for doubling three spades; and the rest of the East-West pairs will be tied for bottom for getting only 50 points.

If North-South are not vulnerable, a penalty double is worth only two or three match points to East. If he fails to double, he gets ½ match point from each of the other East-West pairs that similarly collected only 50 points. If he doubles, he gets a full match point from all such pairs. The double is worth *something*, but not a great deal.

But if South is vulnerable, the double is worth a fortune. Then East collects 200 points, more than he could get for bidding and making a part score. He should have a top for his 200 points; he will be tied for bottom if he fails to double and so collect only 100 points.

This hand illustrates the power of the spade suit as well as the value of a close double. If the strength is fairly evenly divided, the side that holds spades can usually outbid the opponents. Among experienced tournament players, failure to get into the auction when you have spade length is considered almost on a par with revoking.

✓ PLAYING FOR AN OVERTRICK

The play of the cards in tournament bridge is full of special match-point considerations. A dozen times an evening you may make a play that would shock a rubber-bridge player. Jeopardizing the contract in an attempt to make an overtrick is commonplace.

WEST	EAST
♠ A Q J 7 2	♠ K 10 6 3
♡ A K 3	♡ 7 4 2
◇ 5 2	◇ A J 10 4
♣ A 6 2	♣ 8 5

WEST	EAST
1 ♠	2 ♠
4 ♠	Pass

The opening lead is a small heart, and you win with the king. You draw trumps, which takes three rounds, and then take a diamond finesse, losing to the king. Back comes a heart to your ace.

In rubber bridge, you would lead a diamond to the ace, just in case the queen happens to drop. If it doesn't, you give up a heart and a club and score your cold game contract.

In tournament bridge, you must take a second diamond finesse. If it succeeds, you are the proud possessor of one overtrick, worth 30 points. If it fails, you are down at four spades.

Isn't it insane to jeopardize your game for the chance at one overtrick? Not at all. Unless you make plays like this at match points, you will never win an important tournament.

What will happen when this hand is played at other tables? If a club is opened instead of a heart, West takes the ace of clubs, draws trumps, and tries a diamond finesse. The opponents cash a club and then lead a heart to the king.

West can afford a second diamond finesse without risk. If it loses, he can get to dummy by ruffing a club, and then discard a heart on the ace of diamonds. The contact is never in jeopardy, and West will make the extra trick if the second diamond finesse succeeds.

The same thing is true if the opening lead is a trump or a diamond. Only the heart opening lead puts you under any strain.

Then, too, think of what will happen toward the end of the session. The hand may be played by two or three East-West pairs who are desperate for match points to recover lost ground. They will take the second diamond finesse without batting an eye. You'd be surprised at how few eyes are batted toward the end of a tournament.

For one reason or another, therefore, at least half the field will take two diamond finesses and will make five-odd if the second finesse works. You can expect a poor score if you make only four-odd. Moreover, all experienced declarers are acquainted with this phenomenon and will, therefore, attempt the second diamond finesse, even if the defense makes this play risky. So if you play it safe, you may be the only declarer in the tournament to make just ten tricks. Nobody will congratulate you.

✓ ABNORMAL CONTRACTS

Almost any risk is justifiable when you are in an abnormal contract. If your gamble loses, you will merely get a square zero instead of a round one.

WEST	EAST
♠ A K Q 10 9 6	♠ J 8 7
♡ K J	♡ A 8 3
◇ 7 6 4 2	◇ A 10 9 3
♣ 5	♣ A 10 7

WEST	EAST
1 ♠	2 NT
3 NT	Pass

Clubs are opened, and you win the first trick with the ace. Clearly the contract is abnormal. All the sane East-West pairs will play the hand at spades, where they will win eleven tricks, provided diamonds break 3-2.

If you play your abnormal contract normally, you will win ten tricks at notrump. This will get you no match points at all.

Your only hope is to produce an eleventh trick at no-trump. The best chance is to finesse the jack of hearts immediately. If it loses, you will be down at three no-trump, but what of it? As Gertrude Stein might have observed, a bottom is a bottom is a bottom.

But if the heart finesse wins, you take eleven tricks at notrump and congratulate your partner on his brilliant bid!

✓ WHAT OTHERS ARE DOING

In some hands your play is determined by what you think will happen at other tables:

NORTH
♠ 7
♡ 6 5
◇ Q J 9 8 7 4
♣ 10 9 8 3

WEST	EAST
♠ 10 9 8 4 3	♠ K Q 5 2
♡ Q J 8 7 2	♡ A K 4 3
◇ K 6	◇ A 5
♣ 6	♣ Q 7 4

SOUTH
♠ A J 6
♡ 10 9
◇ 10 3 2
♣ A K J 5 2

EAST	SOUTH	WEST	NORTH
1 ♠	2 ♣	4 ♠	5 ♣
Double	Pass	Pass	Pass

West leads the ten of spades, East puts up the queen, and you win with the ace. You cash the ace of clubs, but the queen doesn't drop.

You ruff a spade in dummy and return a club. East plays low. Which is the better play—finessing the jack or banging down the king?

You are going to lose two hearts, two diamonds, and possibly a trump. You will go down either two or three tricks. Even if you are not vulnerable, the least you can lose is 300 points. This will be a good sacrifice only if enough East-West pairs bid and *make* four hearts or four spades at other tables. So your next step is to figure out what is likely to happen at these other tables when East-West plays the hand.

The South hand will take two spade tricks against East in defense. If your hand will also take two club tricks, then even minus 300 points is a phantom sacrifice and sorrow will be your portion.

Your only hope is that the clubs break 3-1, so that at other tables East will lose only one club trick. Therefore you must take the club finesse.

✓ SAFETY PLAYS

In general, the safety play is despised and rejected in tournaments. You cannot afford to concede the opponents a trick if all other declarers are playing the hand wide open and making one trick more than you.

The safety play is used when you are in a very good spot, such as a doubled contract that you are going to make, or a slam that will probably not be bid at most tables. You sometimes use a safety play to protect you against the loss of a trick that you can't afford to give up.

Both sides vulnerable:

```
                    NORTH
                    ♠ K 5 4
                    ♡ 6 5
                    ◇ 7 6 3
                    ♣ A 10 9 8 2

    WEST                            EAST
    ♠ J                             ♠ Q 9 8 3
    ♡ Q J 10 7                      ♡ A K 9 8 2
    ◇ A Q 9 8 4                     ◇ K J 10
    ♣ 7 6 3                         ♣ 5

                    SOUTH
                    ♠ A 10 7 6 2
                    ♡ 4 3
                    ◇ 5 2
                    ♣ K Q J 4
```

EAST	SOUTH	WEST	NORTH
1 ♡	1 ♠	3 ♡	3 ♠
4 ♡	4 ♠	Pass	Pass
Double	Pass	Pass	Pass

The defenders take two hearts and then lead three rounds of diamonds. You ruff the third diamond, lead a trump to the king, and then return a trump from dummy.

When East plays the eight of spades, you are tempted to climb up with the ace in the hope of dropping the queen. You must resist this temptation.

If you finesse the ten of spades and lose to the queen, you will be down two. You can afford to lose 500 points, for it is less than the 620 or 650 points most East-West pairs will get for making a heart game. You would be little better off if you held the loss to 200 points, so there is no real advantage in playing the ace.

As it happens, the finesse of the ten limits the loss in trumps to one trick. You cash the ace of spades next and then run the clubs.

If you played the ace of spades, you would lose two trump tricks. Then the sacrifice would cost you 800 points and would turn a very fine score into a cold bottom.

✓ DEFENDING AGAINST OVERTRICKS

In rubber bridge, you usually lead your long suit against a notrump contract. Although it occasionally gives declarer an unimportant overtrick, it offers the best chance to defeat the contract.

In duplicate, you avoid leading from a 4-card suit headed by the ace or king, because with this lead the chance of losing a trick is greater than the chance of defeating the contract. You prefer a sequence lead, even from a shorter suit, such as the jack from J-10-x or the ten from 10-9-x.

When the opponents have bid strongly enough, you even avoid leading from a 5-card suit headed by the ace or king. Strong bidding by your opponents usually indicates that you're not going to defeat the contract, so you should concentrate on limiting the overtricks.

To take a simple example, suppose the opening bid is two notrump and that dummy raises to four notrump. This is passed, and it is up to you to lead from this hand:

♠ Q 6 5 2   ♡ K 7 4 3   ♢ 9 8 4   ♣ 8 6

Lead the nine of diamonds. The bidding indicates that the opponents are trembling on the verge of a slam. Your partner has about 3 points in high cards. A spade or heart lead might give declarer a trick he couldn't get for himself, or it might relieve him of a guess. A diamond lead will probably give him nothing.

When the opponents do reach a slam, you will lead an ace far more often in tournament play than in rubber bridge. You are not trying to defeat the contract, although an ace lead sometimes works well for this purpose. Your chief purpose is to stop the overtrick.

✓ CASHING OUT

A good rubber-bridge player doesn't give up while there is still a chance to defeat the contract. A good duplicate player must often take what he can while the taking is good.

NORTH
♠ A
♡ J 10 5 2
◇ Q 8 4
♣ A K Q 10 3

WEST
♠ K Q J 10 4
♡ K 6
◇ A J 9
♣ 9 7 2

EAST
♠ 9 8 6 2
♡ 9 3
◇ 7 6 3 2
♣ 8 5 4

SOUTH
♠ 7 5 3
♡ A Q 8 7 4
◇ K 10 5
♣ J 6

NORTH	EAST	SOUTH	WEST
1 ♣	Pass	1 ♡	1 ♠
3 ♡	Pass	4 ♡	Pass
Pass	Pass		

West leads the king of spades, and dummy wins with the ace. The jack of hearts rides around to the king, and West must make an important decision.

In rubber bridge, West should lead the jack of diamonds. This will defeat the contract if East has the king of diamonds even if South has 10-x-x. Any other method of playing the diamonds will let South get away with losing only two diamond tricks.

In duplicate, West must cash the ace of diamonds or run the risk of not winning a diamond trick. It may go against the grain to let South make a contract that can be beaten, but in the long run West will win more match points by cashing out than by fighting on to the end.

✓ TAKING DESPERATE CHANCES

Don't get the feeling that defense at match points is a matter of sitting tight and playing like a good little boy. You take desperate chances to win the tricks that you need.

NORTH.
- ♠ J 2
- ♡ K J 10
- ◇ K 8 7 2
- ♣ K J 8 4

WEST
- ♠ A K 7
- ♡ Q 8 7 6 2
- ◇ 10
- ♣ A 7 5 2

EAST
- ♠ 6 5
- ♡ A 9 4 3
- ◇ Q 6 5 3
- ♣ Q 10 9

SOUTH
- ♠ Q 10 9 8 4 3
- ♡ 5
- ◇ A J 9 4
- ♣ 6 3

WEST	NORTH	EAST	SOUTH
1 ♡	Pass	2 ♡	2 ♠
Pass	Pass	3 ♡	Pass
Pass	3 ♠	Pass	Pass
Double	Pass	Pass	Pass

West opens the singleton diamond, and South wins with the jack. South leads a trump, and West steps up with the king.

If South is vulnerable, West will get 200 points for defeating the contract. West should lead a heart, since

East surely has the ace. East will return a diamond, and West will get three trump tricks and a club to add to East's heart trick.

West does not try for two clubs tricks because a low-club lead might backfire if South has a singleton club. West will get very close to a top score for his 200 points, so there is no reason to make a desperate try for 500 points.

If South is not vulnerable, West must try for a two-trick set. At other tables West will probably be allowed to play the hand at hearts, making 140 points. At this table West cannot be satisfied with a mere 100 points.

Upon winning the first trump, West must lead a low club. South may play the jack from dummy instead of the king. If so, the defenders will get two club tricks instead of only one. The penalty will be 300 points, and West will have a top instead of a bottom.

West cannot afford to lead the heart first and the club later. Once East has shown up with the ace of hearts, no expert declarer will play him to have the ace of clubs as well.

This leads to another important observation about bidding and play at duplicate. You meet all sorts of players, and they aren't all experts. If your only chance for a good score is to assume that your opponent is a bad player, make the assumption and take your chances. (But don't bother to tell the opponent about it. Let him work it out for himself.)

✓ TOTAL-POINT TEAM PLAY

The simplest form of duplicate play is the team contest. All you need is eight players, four on each team, and a set of duplicate boards. For this reason, team matches are very popular in the home as well as in clubs and tournaments.

At one time team matches were scored in the simplest possible manner. You simply wrote down your result for each hand and added them all up at the end of the match. You even counted honors. (This is the only form of duplicate bridge in which honors are counted.)

In a total-point team match, the emphasis is on slams and big penalties. You can afford to relax in the play of part-score hands, and you don't have to try very hard for overtricks.

The game is very much like rubber bridge. The part score is slightly less important than in rubber bridge, and vulnerable games are somewhat more important.

✓ I.M.P. TEAM PLAY

Total-point scoring has been replaced almost completely in recent years by International Match Points. They were devised to reduce the importance of big hands, just as match points do in pair contests.

To get your I.M.P. score for any hand you compare the results obtained at the two tables. A net gain of 10 points is disregarded. A net gain of 20 to 40 points is scored as 1 I.M.P., a gain of 50 to 80 points, as 2 I.M.P., and so on. The scale is changed from time to time by agreement among the various national bridge leagues. For an up-to-date table, write the American Contract Bridge League, 33 West 60th Street, New York 23, New York.

Your style in I.M.P. team play borrows both from rubber-bridge and match-point bridge. You don't jeopardize a contract to play for extra tricks, but you try for every trick that can be won without risk. Part-score bidding is fiercely competitive, much as in pair contests.

✓ BOARD-A-MATCH TEAM PLAY

When many teams are competing in a single session or in a small number of sessions, scoring is usually on a board-a-match basis. For each hand you play against another team you get 1 match point for a gain (whether it's 10 points or more than 1,000), ½ match point for a tie, and 0 for a loss.

The best board-a-match style is somewhat stodgy. You never step out of line, although you follow your judgment to make delicate or slightly unusual bids or plays. You wait for the opponents to make a mistake. If they do, you pounce, and the board is won at your table.

If the opponents do not make a mistake, you sit tight. Perhaps their team mates will make a mistake when they play the hand against *your* team mates. If so, your team will win the board at the other table.

If the opponents do not make a mistake at either table, you are satisfied with ½ point. As a rule, you can win most board-a-match contests if you can avoid zeroes. The opponents will lose enough boards to give you a very fine total score—but you must not give any of it back.

✓ TOURNAMENT ETIQUETTE

Serious tournament players try so hard to win that they are under considerable strain. This sometimes makes it hard for them to be amiable during the game, although many of them are normally the soul of geniality.

As a newcomer to the game you can avoid adding to the strain—your own or the other players'—if you follow a few simple principles.

Don't take forever over a bid or a play. The players must keep up with a schedule (e.g., two hands in 15 minutes or three hands in 20 minutes) or the tournament will just fall apart. If you cannot come up with the perfect bid or play within fifteen seconds, just plunge in and do whatever seems best. You can discuss the hand after the game, and some of the experienced players will probably be glad to give you their views.

Avoid discussing the bidding or play until you have finished the entire round. If you debate over the first hand, you may have to rush through the second.

Argue, if you must, with your partner. But never comment on the opponents' play or bidding, and don't enter into their disputes.

Move to the next table (if you are East-West) as promptly as possible after the signal to change. If the pair ahead of you is slow to move on, hang back at some distance from the table. Be careful not to arrive at a table while the cards or scoreslips are still exposed to view.

VI

FOR YOUR REFERENCE

MEANING OF BIDS

IN MANY bidding situations a player may wonder whether a bid is forcing or non-forcing, strong or weak. A number of such sequences are presented here, together with an explanation of the last bid.

1.

OPENER	RESPONDER
1 ♡	1 NT

Weak bid

2.

OPENER	RESPONDER
1 ♡	2 ♡

Weak bid

3.

OPENER	RESPONDER
1 ♡	1 ♠

One-round force

4.

OPENER	RESPONDER
1 ♡	2 ♣

One-round force

5.

OPENER	RESPONDER
1 ♡	2 NT

Game force

6.

OPENER	RESPONDER
1 ♡	2 ♠

Game force

7.

OPENER	RESPONDER
1 ♡	3 ♡

Game force

8.

OPENER	RESPONDER
1 ♡	4 ♡

Not encouraging

9.

OPENER	RESPONDER
Pass	1 ♡
1 ♠	

Not forcing

10.

OPENER	RESPONDER
Pass	1 ♡
2 ♣	

Not forcing

11.

OPENER	RESPONDER
Pass	1 ♡
2 ♠	

Almost forcing

12.

OPENER	RESPONDER
Pass	1 ♡
2 NT	

Invitational

13.

OPENER	RESPONDER
Pass	1 ♡
3 ♡	

Invitational

14.

OPENER	RESPONDER
1 ◇	1 ♡
1 ♠	

Not forcing

15.

OPENER	RESPONDER
1 ◇	1 ♡
1 NT	

Weak bid

16.

OPENER	RESPONDER
1 ♡	1 ♠
2 ◇	

Not forcing

17.

OPENER	RESPONDER
1 ♡	2 ◇
3 ♣	

Very strong

18.

OPENER	RESPONDER
1 ♡	1 NT
2 ♠	

Very strong

19.

OPENER	RESPONDER
1 ♡	1 ♠
2 NT	

Strong invitation

20.

OPENER	RESPONDER
1 ♡	1 NT
2 NT	

Strong invitation

21.

OPENER	RESPONDER
1 ♡	1 ♠
3 ♡	

Strong invitation

22.

OPENER	RESPONDER
1 ♡	1 ♠
3 ♡	3 ♠

Game force

23.

OPENER	RESPONDER
1 ♡	1 ♠
4 ♡	

Very strong

24.

OPENER	RESPONDER
1 ♡	1 ♠
2 ♠	

Not forcing

25.

OPENER	RESPONDER
1 ♡	2 ♣
3 ♣	

Invitational

26.

OPENER	RESPONDER
1 ♡	1 ♠
3 ♠	

Strong invitation

27.

OPENER	RESPONDER
1 ♡	1 ♠
4 ♠	

Very strong

28.

OPENER	RESPONDER
1 ♡	1 ♠
3 ◇	

Game force

29.

OPENER	RESPONDER
1 ♡	2 ♡
3 ◇	

One-round force

30.

OPENER	RESPONDER
1 ♡	2 ♡
3 ◇	3 ♡

Sign-off

31.

OPENER	RESPONDER
1 ♡	1 ♠
2 ♠	3 ◇

One-round force

32.

OPENER	RESPONDER
1 ♡	2 ◇
2 ♡	3 ◇

Sign-off

33.

OPENER	RESPONDER
1 ♡	2 ♡
2 NT	3 ♡

Sign-off

34.

OPENER	RESPONDER
1 ♡	2 ♣
2 NT	

Not forcing

35.

OPENER	RESPONDER
1 ♡	2 ◇
2 ♡	3 ♡

Invitational

36.

OPENER	RESPONDER
1 ♡	2 ◇
2 NT	3 ♡

Game force

37.

OPENER	RESPONDER
1 ♡	1 ♠
1 NT	2 ◇

Not forcing

38.

OPENER	RESPONDER
1 ◇	1 ♡
1 NT	2 ♠

Forcing ("reverse")

39.

OPENER	RESPONDER
1 NT	2 ♣

Asks for major suit

40.

OPENER	RESPONDER
1 NT	2 ♡

Not encouraging

41.

OPENER	RESPONDER
1 NT	3 ♡

Game force

42.

OPENER	RESPONDER
2 NT	3 ♡

Game force

43.

OPENER	RESPONDER
2 ♡	2 NT

Weak bid

44.

OPENER	RESPONDER
2 ♡	2 NT
3 ♡	

Game force

45.

OPENER	RESPONDER
2 ♡	2 ♠

Probable slam

46.

OPENER	RESPONDER
1 ♡	3 ♡
4 ♣	

Slam try

HOME AND PARTY BRIDGE

Let's face it: people are unreliable. You get on the phone and try to organize a simple bridge game for four people, but that night you'll have three or five players instead of four. What can you do with the wrong number of people?

BRIDGE FOR THREE

First Method: Take turns at dealing. The dealer distributes four hands as usual, turning six cards of the dummy face up. The highest bidder becomes declarer and wins the dummy as his partner. The dummy is shifted, if necessary, to the customary position between the two defenders.

In the original game, called Towie, there are complicated rules for play and scoring, but they aren't essential. Just follow the regular rules and score as usual. Give a player 300 points above the line when he scores his first game, 500 points more if he wins the rubber.

Second Method: A different, and very amusing, way for three people to play bridge is to scrap the bidding altogether. The dealer is always the declarer at a contract of two notrump doubled! The results are often funny, sometimes embarrassing —but it all tends to even out.

In both games the scores tend to run much higher than in ordinary bridge. People who are wicked enough to play for a stake should cut it in half for three-handed bridge.

At the end of the game, total each of the three columns to the nearest hundred. The winner collects from each of the others; the middle man collects from bottom man. For example: Scores are 3700, 2400, and 900. The top man (3700) collects 1300 and 2800; the middle man pays out 1300 and collects 1500; the bottom man pays out 2800 and 1500.

BRIDGE FOR FIVE

Each player draws a card. List the players' names on the

back of the score pad in the order of the cards drawn, highest card first and so on down to the lowest card.

The two highest cards play as partners against the players who drew the third and fourth highest cards. The player who drew the lowest card sits out and complains about the slowness of the game. (To keep him from brooding, the other players should impress the odd man into service—fixing drinks, preparing coffee, dehydrating the children, etc.)

At the end of each rubber, the out man comes in, taking the seat of the man who is scheduled to go out. (The fourth-highest man goes out first; then the third-highest; and so on. Look at the back of the score pad to settle the inevitable argument about whose turn it is to go out.) The player at the right of the incoming man changes seats so as to sit opposite him, thus altering the partnership for the new rubber. The new man deals to start the new rubber.

BRIDGE FOR SIX

Cut cards to see who plays and who stays out, as in bridge for five. Write the names of the players on the back of the score pad in the order in which they play—highest card first, and so on down to the lowest card.

The two highest play as partners against the players who drew the third- and fourth-highest cards. The two lowest sit out and play gin rummy or the like. For the next rubber, the third and fourth players go out; the two top players go out for the third rubber.

At the end of each rubber, the two out men come in, taking the place of the pair scheduled to go out. The two incoming men cut cards; the high man deals, but first the player at his right changes seats so as to be his partner for the new rubber.

BRIDGE FOR SEVEN

Set up two tables, four at one, three at the other. Send the dummy over to the other table as soon as the bidding ends.

Score each hand as a separate unit, and keep a score with seven columns (one for each player).

CHICAGO

Chicago is the best game to play when you have one or two players on the side lines, screaming to get into the game. Instead of playing a full rubber, which may take an hour or more, play just four hands.

In the first deal, neither side is vulnerable; for the second and third, dealer's side is vulnerable; for the fourth, both sides. If a hand is passed out, the same dealer redeals.

In this form of the game, it is winning tactics for the last man to open almost any hand when not vulnerable against vulnerable opponents. Otherwise the hand is redealt, and his opponents may get a vulnerable game or slam. To prevent this, the Cavendish Club of New York, America's high temple of topflight bridge, has changed the vulnerability rules: In the second and third deals the *non*dealer's side is vulnerable. If there are three passes the last man is vulnerable against nonvulnerable opponents; it is risky for him to open the bidding on junk. Moreover, first and third hands are nonvulnerable and may try a strategic or psychic bid against their vulnerable opponents. It's a better game, but very few players know about this change in the rules.

Score 300 points for game, not vulnerable; 500 points, vulnerable. There is no bonus for a part score earned in the first, second, or third deal; it is carried forward as in rubber bridge. A bonus of 100 points is awarded for a part score bid and made on the fourth deal.

BRIDGE FOR EIGHT

The simplest method is to set up two tables, never the twain to meet. It's better, but slightly more complicated, to switch the players from one table to another from time to time.

Fixed Partnerships: If you have four fixed partnerships, draw cards to see which pairs are opposed for the first rubber. Number the pairs according to the height of the card drawn: 1 for the highest card, down to 4 for the lowest. In the first rubber, Pair 4 plays against Pair 1; in the second, 4 against 2; in the third, 4 against 3. Then start over.

Changing Partnerships: Draw cards and give each player a number from 1 to 8. The setup for the first rubber is:

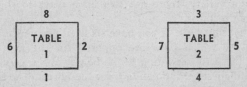

Thereafter, Player 8 sits still and each of the other players takes the seat previously occupied by the next lower number. The easiest way to do this is for each player to note who has the next lower number and where he is sitting. (Player 7 follows Player 1.)

To straighten out mix-ups, use this schedule:

	Table 1				Table 2		
1st Rubber	8-1	vs.	2-6		3-4	vs.	5-7
2nd Rubber	8-2	"	3-7		4-5	"	6-1
3rd Rubber	8-3	"	4-1		5-6	"	7-2
4th Rubber	8-4	"	5-2		6-7	"	1-3
5th Rubber	8-5	"	6-3		7-1	"	2-4
6th Rubber	8-6	"	7-4		1-2	"	3-5
7th Rubber	8-7	"	1-5		2-3	"	4-6

To keep the players in your game from getting mixed up, you might prepare individual guide slips for them. The slip for Player 1 would be:

1st Rubber:	Table 1, Partner No. 8
2nd Rubber:	Table 2, Partner No. 6

and so on

If the full schedule of seven rubbers takes too long, stop after the end of any rubber and call it a night. Better still, play Chicago (four deals) instead of rubbers.

BRIDGE FOR TWELVE

The simplest method is to set up three tables and let them simmer in their own juice for about three hours. If the players want more variety, there are two main ways to shift them from table to table.

Fixed Partnerships: If you have six fixed partnerships, draw cards to see which pairs are opposed for the first rubber. Number the pairs according to the height of the card drawn: 1 for the highest card, down to 6 for the lowest. The schedule is:

	Table 1	Table 2	Table 3
1st Rubber	6 vs. 1	2 vs. 5	3 vs. 4
2nd Rubber	6 " 2	3 " 1	4 " 5
3rd Rubber	6 " 3	4 " 2	5 " 1
4th Rubber	6 " 4	5 " 3	1 " 2
5th Rubber	6 " 5	1 " 4	2 " 3

Changing Partnerships: Draw cards and give each player a number from 1 to 12. The setup for the first round is:

Thereafter, Player 12 sits still, and each of the other players takes the seat previously occupied by the next lower number. The easiest way to do this is for each player to note who has the next lower number and where he is sitting. (Player 1 follows Player 11.)

The full schedule:

	Table 1		Table 2		Table 3	
1st Round	12-1	vs. 2-9	3-4	vs. 6-8	5-11 vs.	7-10
2nd Round	12-2	" 3-10	4-5	" 7-9	6-1 "	8-11
3rd Round	12-3	" 4-11	5-6	" 8-10	7-2 "	9-1
4th Round	12-4	" 5-1	6-7	" 9-11	8-3 "	10-2
5th Round	12-5	" 6-2	7-8	" 10-1	9-4 "	11-3
6th Round	12-6	" 7-3	8-9	" 11-2	10-5 "	1-4
7th Round	12-7	" 8-4	9-10	" 1-3	11-6 "	2-5
8th Round	12-8	" 9-5	10-11	" 2-4	1-7 "	3-6
9th Round	12-9	" 10-6	11-1	" 3-5	2-8 "	4-7
10th Round	12-10	" 11-7	1-2	" 4-6	3-9 "	5-8
11th Round	12-11	" 1-8	2-3	" 5-7	4-10 "	6-9

As in the case of the 8-player movement, it is possible to make up guide slips for the individual players. The slip for Player 1 would be:

1st Round: Table 1, Partner No. 12
2nd Round: Table 3, Partner No. 6
            and so on

Eleven rounds of four hands each would be a marathon, and eleven rubbers would take even longer. The best bet is to play only two hands per round. Score as in rubber bridge, starting a rubber for each round.

PROGRESSIVE BRIDGE

Progressive bridge simply means that the winning pairs *progress* toward the head table, while the losers stay put. It is great fun for sixteen or more players, but it takes a bit of planning. Make sure, to begin with, that you have enough tables, chairs, score pads, ash trays, pencils, and refreshments. Buy or prepare an individual score card or tally for each player. Ideally, get the tallies in one color for men and in a different color for women.

As the guests arrive give each a tally of the appropriate color. You may either assign seats for the first round or let them choose their own starting positions.

The host or game director should signal the beginning of play. If the players are inexperienced, the host should announce the rules briefly.

First Round: At each table there should be a man and a woman as partners against another mixed pair. The players cut, and the high player deals the first hand. There are three other hands, one dealt by each of the other players. The hands are scored as in Chicago (see page 542). The total score for *each* side is then entered on each player's tally.

First Change: The winners at Table 1 remain; the losers move to the highest-numbered table. At each of the other tables the *losers* remain, and the winners move one table up in the direction of Table 1. At each table the visiting woman becomes the partner of the man who has remained. Later changes follow the example of the first change. Each round should take about twenty minutes, and six or seven rounds make a satisfactory session.

Final Scoring: At the end of play, each player adds up all scores made by his side and all scores made by his opponents. The difference between the two totals is his net score for the session—either plus or minus. The winner is the player with the highest plus.

GHOULIES

The first dealer shuffles the cards, but they are *never* shuffled thereafter. The cards are cut once before each deal and then dealt out five at a time, five at a time again, and finally three at a time.

If a hand is passed out or is not played, the same dealer redeals. When a hand is not played, each player arranges his hand by suits, red and black suits alternating.

Any undoubled part-score hand is conceded and thrown in, except that the declarer scores only 30 points.

SCORING TABLE

TRICK SCORE (below the line)

Spades or Hearts	30 per trick	If doubled:
Diamonds or Clubs	20 " "	multiply by 2
Notrump	40 for first trick,	If redoubled:
	30 for each additional trick	multiply by 4

Game—100 points or more below the line

BONUSES (above the line)

Rubber Bonus: 500 if you win two games out of three
700 if you win the only two games

		NOT VULNERABLE	VULNERABLE
Slam Bonus:	Small slam	500	750
	Grand slam	1000	1500

Honors: 4 trump honors in one hand	 100
5 " " " " "	 150
4 aces in one hand at notrump	 150

Making Doubled Contract: 50 points (only the same 50 points if the contract is redoubled)

	NOT VULNERABLE	VULNERABLE
Overtricks: Undoubled	trick value	trick value
Doubled	100 per trick	200 per trick
Redoubled	200 " "	400 " "

PENALTIES (above the line)

	UNDOUBLED		DOUBLED	
	NOT VUL.	VUL.	NOT VUL.	VUL.
Down 1	50	100	100	200
" 2	100	200	300	500
" 3	150	300	500	800
" 4	200	400	700	1100
" 5	250	500	900	1400
" 6	300	600	1100	1700

If redoubled: multiply the doubled penalty by two

BIDDING GUIDE

POINT COUNT
Ace ......4 points
King ....3 "
Queen ..2 "
Jack ....1 "

KEY NUMBERS
26 points: game in notrump or major suit
29 " : game in minor suit
33 " : small slam
37 " : grand slam

HOW TO COUNT

FOR NOTRUMP: Count only high cards.

FOR OPENING SUIT BID: Count high cards and add 3 points for a void suit, 2 points for singleton, 1 point for doubleton.

FOR RAISING PARTNER'S SUIT: Count high cards and add 5 points for void, 3 points for singleton, 1 point for doubleton. You must have good trump support.

OPENING BIDS

POINTS IN YOUR HAND	BID
12 or 13, with a strong suit	1 of suit
14, with any suit	1 of suit
25 or more, with very strong suit	2 of suit
(may be reduced with longer suit or two-suiter)	
16 to 18, with stoppers and balanced distribution	1 NT
22 to 24, with stoppers and balanced distribution	2 NT
25 to 27, with stoppers and balanced distribution	3 NT

RESPONSES TO 1 OF SUIT

6 to 18	1 of new suit
10 to 18	2 of lower suit
19 or more	Jump bid in new suit
6 to 10, with trump support	Raise partner to 2
13 to 16, with strong trump support	Raise partner to 3
6 to 10, if unable to raise or bid new suit	1 NT
13 to 15, stoppers in all unbid suits	2 NT

REBIDS

BY OPENER		BY RESPONDER	
13 to 16	Minimum, or pass	6 to 10	Minimum, or pass
17 to 19	Invite game, but do not force	11 or 12	Invite game
20 or more	Force to game	13 or more	Force to game
		19 or more	Try for a slam